The Lure of Images

This fascinating history of the relationship between mass-produced visual media and religion in America takes the reader on a journey from the 1780s to the present: from early evangelical tracts to teenage witches and televangelists, and from illustrated books to contemporary cinema.

David Morgan explores the cultural marketplace of public representation, showing how American religionists have made special use of visual media to instruct the public, to practice devotion and ritual, and to form children and converts. Along the way, he views Jesus as an American idol, Jewish kitchens and Christian parlors, Billy Sunday and *Buffy the Vampire Slayer*, and *Uncle Tom's Cabin* and the anti-slavery movement. This unique perspective reveals the importance of visual media to the construction and practice of sectarian and national community in a nation of immigrants old and new, and the tensions between the assimilation and the preservation of ethnic and racial identities. As well as the contribution of visual media to the religious life of Christians and Jews, Morgan shows how images have informed the perceptions and practices of other religions in America, including New Age, Buddhist and Hindu spirituality, and Mormonism, Native American religions and the Occult.

David Morgan is Professor of Humanities and Art History at Valparaiso University. He is the author of several books including *Visual Piety* (1998) and *The Sacred Gaze* (2005), and the co-founder and editor of *Material Religion*.

Religion, Media and Culture series
Edited by Stewart M. Hoover, Jolyon Mitchell and David Morgan

Religion, Media and Culture is an exciting series which analyzes the role of media in the history of contemporary practice of religious belief. Books in this series explore the importance of a variety of media in religious practice and highlight the significance of the culture, social and religious setting of such media.

Religion in the Media Age
Stewart M. Hoover

The Lure of Images
A history of religion and visual media in America
David Morgan

The Lure of Images

A history of religion and visual media in America

David Morgan

Routledge
Taylor & Francis Group

LONDON AND NEW YORK

First published 2007
by Routledge
270 Madison Avenue, New York, NY 10016

Simultaneously published in the UK
by Routledge
2 Park Square, Milton Park, Abingdon, Oxon OX14 4RN

Routledge is an imprint of the Taylor & Francis Group, an informa
business

Typeset in Sabon by
RefineCatch Limited, Bungay, Suffolk
Printed and bound in Great Britain by
MPG Books Ltd, Bodmin

British Library Cataloguing in Publication Data
A catalogue record for this book is available from the British Library

Library of Congress Cataloging in Publication Data
Morgan, David.
    A history of religion and visual media in the United States :
the lure of images / David Morgan.
        p. cm—(Religion, media and culture series)
    Includes bibliographical references and index.
    1. Mass media in religion—United States—History.   2. Mass
media—Religious aspects—Christianity—History.   3. Mass
media—United States—History.   4. United States—Church
history.   I. Title.
    BV652.97.U6M67   2007
    201'.7—dc22

ISBN10: 0–415–40914–4 (hbk)
ISBN10: 0–415–40915–2 (pbk)

ISBN13: 978–0–415–40914–8 (hbk)
ISBN13: 978–0–415–40915–5 (pbk)

Contents

List of illustrations   vi
Series editors' preface   x
Acknowledgments   xi

Introduction   1

PART I
Print media in antebellum America   **5**

1   The aura of print   7

2   Religious visual media and cultural conflict   37

PART II
New visual media and the marketplace   **71**

3   Consumption and religious images   73

4   Parlors and kitchens: domestic visual practice and religion   103

5   Pictorial entertainment and instruction   135

6   Seeing in public: America as imagined community   165

PART III
The power and menace of images   **197**

7   Facing the sacred: image and charisma   199

8   Back to nature   230

Notes   263
Select bibliography   294
Index   301

Illustrations

1 Engraving after Peter Frederick Rothermel, *Patrick Henry delivering his celebrated speech in the House of Burgesses, Virginia, AD 1765, for presentation to subscribers to the Art Union of Philadelphia for 1852*, 1853 — 10

2 Alexander Anderson, engraver, Missionary preaching, *Christian Almanac for 1836* — 12

3 Printing press, American Tract Society Membership Certificate, 1840s — 13

4 Title page, *The Illuminated Bible*, 1846 — 22

5 Alexander Anderson, engraver, "Address," no. 1, 1825 — 25

6 Alexander Anderson, engraver, Women and children, cover of "Female Influence and Obligations," no. 226, 1842 — 27

7 Robert Roberts, engraver, cover illustration for "We Must Live," no. 474, 1845 — 35

8 "The Jew," from *Pictures and Lessons for Little Readers*, ca. 1863 — 40

9 Augustus Kollner, lithographer, *The Happy Family*, hand-tinted lithograph, for the American Sunday School Union, ca. 1850 — 41

10 "Sabbath School" and "Sabbath-School Graduates", *The Well-Spring* 19, no. 48 (November 28, 1862) — 43

11 "Statues of the Blessed Virgin," *Benziger Brothers Catalogue of Church Ornaments, Vestments, Material for Vestments, Regalia*, 1881 — 49

12 Father Paul Matthias Dobberstein, Nativity scene, Grotto of the Redemption, West Bend, Iowa — 51

13 Ambrose Serle, Esq., "The Happy Negro," no. 7, 1825 — 53

14 Thomas S. Sinclair, *Christian Union*, 1845 — 54

15 "Whipping a slave," *The Child's Antislavery Book*, 1859 — 56

16 Bishops of the African Methodist Episcopal Church, commemorative print, 1876 — 60

17 Frontispiece, *Proceedings of the Quarto-Centennial Conference of the African M. E. Church, of South Carolina*, at Charleston, SC, 1889 — 61

18 "An Anxious or Enquiring Meeting," *Orthodox Bubbles, or A Review of the First Annual Report of the Executive Committee of the New York Magdalen Society*, 1831   63

19 Thomas Nast, "Romish Politics–Any Thing to Beat Grant," *Harper's Weekly* (August 17, 1872), 637   66

20 Ex-voto retablo dedicated to Our Lady of Talpa by Silveria Camarena for a great wonder on the day of March 19, 1924, painting on tin   69

21 Currier & Ives, *Our Lady of Knock*, hand-colored lithograph, 1879   78

22 Currier & Ives, *Ira D. Sankey: The Evangelist of Song*, hand-colored lithograph, 1874   79

23 Nathaniel Currier, Memorial image, hand-colored lithograph, 1845   80

24 Unidentified artist, Memorial for Werter, pendant, ca. 1810   82

25 Angel at prayer, gravestone of Sarah J. Winston, 1859, Richmond, Virginia   86

26 *Masonic Chart*, chromolithograph, 1866   88

27 Millerite chart, lithograph and stencil on fabric, 1842   90

28 *The Great Commission*, for Sunday, May 12, 1901   98

29 Fred Carter, *Christ in Gethsemane*, ink on paper, 1984   102

30 "Devotion," *The Parlor Annual and Christian Family Casket for 1846*, engraving, 1845   107

31 Nathaniel Currier, *Reading the Bible*, hand-tinted lithograph, 1848   114

32 Nathaniel Currier, *Reading the Scriptures*, hand-tinted lithograph, date unknown   115

33 Nathaniel Currier, *Reading the Scriptures*, hand-tinted lithograph, ca. 1838–56   116

34 Nathaniel Currier, *The Way to Happiness*, hand-tinted lithograph, ca. 1850   118

35 Unknown engraver, cover illustration, "Family Worship," no. 18, 1824   120

36 Advertisement for Fischer Russian Caravan Tea, New York, ca. 1920   122

37 Title page from Esther J. Ruskay, *Hearth and Home Essays*, 1902   124

38 Jacob Ken, Girl playing upright piano, Jewish New Year postcard, postmarked September 17, 1910, Winooski, Vermont   130

39 Family at seder table, frontispiece, *Passover Services*, 1921   133

40 *Her Guardian Angel*, one half of stereographic image, 1897   139

41 Postmortem daguerreotype of unidentified child in bed with flowers, a cross, and lit candles, Anson's Studio, New York City, ca. 1840–50s   143

42 James VanDerZee, photographer, child with angels and Mary, New York, ca. 1935   144

43 Walter Satterlee, diagram of tableau vivant, frontispiece in
    Josephine Pollard, *Artistic Tableaux with Picturesque
    Diagrams and Descriptions of Costumes*, 1884   147
44 Two stereographic views of the Passion, Ingersoll View
    Company, of St. Paul, Minnesota, date unknown   149
45 William Rau, street scene in Nazareth, lantern slide, 1882   157
46 Menorah, souvenir purchased in Jerusalem, 2005   158
47 Rolling panorama device, Rev. Edwin M. Long, *Illustrated
    History of Hymns and their Authors*, 1875   162
48 Whore of Babylon and dragon, section from panorama of the
    Book of Revelation by Arthur Butt, painting on canvas, 1880   163
49 "Joseph Sold into Slavery," Oberammergau Passion play,
    lantern slide from Charles and Katherine Bowden illustrated
    lecture, "A Trip to Oberammergau and the Passion Play,"
    1900   166
50 *Passion Play*, brochure produced by Charles Bowden, 1899   169
51 "The Last Supper," Oberammergau Passion play, lantern slide
    from Charles and Katherine Bowden illustrated lecture, "A
    Trip to Oberammergau and the Passion play," 1900   170
52 Mihaly Munkácsy, *Christ before Pilate*, oil on canvas, 1881   171
53 Film still, "The Messiah's Entry into Jerusalem," from *The
    Passion Play of Oberammergau*, produced by Eden Musee
    Films, New York, 1898   176
54 Barbara Marks, *This Is the Enemy*, 1943. Second World War
    poster issued by the United States Office of War Information   186
55 "The Living Flag," Soldiers' Monument Dedication, May 30,
    1911, location unknown   191
56 Jacob Riis, photographer, Working-class children observe flag
    ritual in New York City school, ca. 1890   194
57 "Divines," in Samuel R. Wells, *New Physiognomy: Or, Signs of
    Character*, 1871   200
58 Darius Cobb, *The Master*, frontispiece in Bruce Barton, *A
    Young Man's Jesus*, 1914   203
59 C. V. Williams, photographer, Billy Sunday preaching, *I'll Fight
    till Hell Freezes over*, postcard, 1908   205
60 Heinrich Hofmann, *Boy Christ Teaching in the Temple*,
    Riverside Church, New York   208
61 Warner Sallman, *The Head of Christ*, oil on canvas, 1940   210
62 *The Ten Commandments*, Japanese film poster, after 1956   211
63 Tom Lovell, *Moroni Burying the Gold Plates*, oil on panel, 1968   214
64 Publicity photograph of Aimee Semple McPherson, ca. 1920s   215
65 Camilo José Vergara, photographer, hand-painted sign by John
    B. Downey at Emmanuel Baptist Rescue Mission, Fifth Street,
    Los Angeles, CA, 2003   221

66   Camilo José Vergara, photographer, Mural of Christ inviting
     passersby to come to him for rest, First Bethel Missionary
     Baptist Church, 19th Avenue, Newark, NJ, 2003   223
67   Ansel Adams, *Monolith, Face of Half Dome*, Yosemite
     National Park, 1927   231
68   James Smillie, *Manhood*, from *Voyage of Life*, 1853–56,
     engraving after Thomas Cole, *Voyage of Life*, 1839–40   233
69   Canopy enclosing sculpture of Swami Vivekananda, Hindu
     Temple of Greater Chicago, 1998   235
70   Zen rock garden designed by Onyumishi Kanjuro Shibata,
     Crossroad Gardens office court, Boulder, CO, 2006   237
71   *Hiawatha's Departure*, from promotional booklet, Katherine
     Bowden, illustrated lecture, "Pictorial Story of Hiawatha," 1904   240
72   Souvenir version of Navajo sand painting of yei, purchased in
     Sedona, Arizona, 1984; souvenir version of Hopi badger
     kachina, purchased at Grand Canyon in 1984   246
73   Camilo José Vergara, photographer, Elizabeth Valentin's
     bedroom with Santeria objects, Longwood Avenue, Bronx,
     NY, 1991   251
74   Minerva K. Teichert, *Loading the Ship*, oil on panel, 1935   257
75   Minerva K. Teichert, *Last Battle between Nephites and
     Lamanites*, oil on panel, 1935   258

Series editors' preface

Media, Religion and Culture is a series of interdisciplinary volumes which analyze the role of media in the history and contemporary practice of religious belief. Books in this series scrutinize the importance of a variety of media in religious practice: from lithographs and film to television and the internet. Studies from all over the world highlight the significance of the cultural, social and religious setting of such media.

Rather than thinking of media purely as instruments for information delivery, volumes in this series contribute in various ways to a new paradigm of understanding media as an integral part of lived religion. Employing a variety of methods, authors investigate how practices of belief take shape in the production, distribution, and reception of mediated communication.

Stewart M. Hoover, University of Colorado
Jolyon Mitchell, University of Edinburgh
David Morgan, Valparaiso University

Acknowledgments

Writing history depends on the good will of many people. This book relies fundamentally on the steady encouragement of Lesley Riddle at Routledge, and my fellow series editors Stewart Hoover and Jolyon Mitchell. Stewart and Jolyon have been good friends and partners in travel and world-wide imagination for many years. I'd also like to mention the members of the International Study Commission on Media, Religion, and Culture, funded by Stichting Porticus in Amsterdam, as a special group of colleagues whose conversations and travel together has done a great deal to shape my thinking and inform my writing over the years. Special assistance in the preparation of this book came in the support of a Franklin Research Grant from the American Philosophical Society, which allowed me to travel to several archives. A number of libraries and institutions remain vital for my work on American cultural history, most importantly the Library Company of Philadelphia and the American Antiquarian Society, the richness of whose collections are surpassed only by the generosity and knowledge of their exceptional staffs. Jim Green and Connie King of the Library Company of Philadelphia and Gigi Barnhill of the American Antiquarian Society have repeatedly proven themselves to be archival national treasures. I'd like also to thank Arthur Kiron, curator of Judaica Collections at the University of Pennsylvania Library and Menahem Blondheim of Hebrew University for gracious assistance. Karen Eberhart at the Rhode Island Historical Society was very helpful in showing me the records of the Providence Lithograph Company. Other archivists and staff members were very helpful: Sarah Weatherwax and Erika Piola at the Library Company; Leslie Kesler at the North Carolina Museum of History; Nancy Finlay of the Connecticut Historical Society Museum; and Judy Miller of the Christopher Center Library, Valparaiso University. And for various kinds of assistance, feedback, images, and bibliography thanks to: Jeffrey Shandler, Kristin Schwain, Johanna Sumiala-Seppänen, Erika Doss, Al Roberts, Tom Tweed, Birgit Meyer, Diane Winston, Susannah Koerber, Michael Clapper, Todd Early, Mel Piehl, Sandy Brewer, Charles Musser, Louis Nelson, Juan Carlos Henriquez, Lynn Schofield Clark, Camilo Vergara, Matt Hedstrom, Adán Medrano, Paul Gutjahr, Marcia Kupfer, Phillip Morgan, and Gretchen Buggeln. My thanks to Gregg Hertzlieb and the

Brauer Museum of Art for constant generosity and the use of its helpful collection. To Valparaiso University, Provost Roy Austensen, and the Ziegler Fund I remain indebted for key support in bringing this book to completion.

Brief portions of Chapters 5 and 6 appeared in Kate Cooper and Jeremy Gregory, eds., *Elite and Popular Religion*, vol. 42, Studies in Church History (Woodbridge, Suffolk: Boydell Press for the Ecclesiastical History Society, 2006). And part of Chapter 7 appeared in John M. Giggie and Diane Winston, eds., *Faith in the Market: Religion and the Rise of Urban Commercial Culture* (New Brunswick, NJ: Rutgers University Press, 2002). My thanks to each publisher for permission to reproduce parts of my essays here.

Introduction

This is a book about the history of mass-produced, popular images from tract illustrations to feature films, and how American believers of one sort and another have seen and used them. The interest that drives it aims at popular visual media rather than fine art. *Popular* means what large numbers of people have spent their time looking at for the purpose of uplift, instruction, amusement, devotion, or propaganda; *media* refers not only to mass-produced imagery such as lithographs, postcards, lantern slides, or videos, but also to hand-made media like panoramas and performative imagery such as tableaux vivants, which travel to large audiences.

But for all the talk of visual media and imagery, the space in front of the image, occupied by viewers, is as important as the object itself. That is because images are social phenomena. They are never viewed in a vacuum. Rather than presenting information to a passive audience they are better understood as cultural dynamos that configure social relations in what may be called visual fields or gazes. If we wish to understand the cultural work of images, religious or otherwise, we need to scrutinize how they enable vision, which is at least as much a cultural and social process as it is a biological one. The aim of this book from beginning to end is to explore how religious imagery operates as part of different ways of seeing.

In regard to religious belief it is important to say at the outset that this study does not approach images as ancillary illustrations to the "real" nature of religion as theology, creed, sermon, or clergy. Instead, images and the manner in which they are used are primary forms of evidence – visual evidence; they are, materially speaking, religion at work. The purpose of the book, then, is to examine major themes in American cultural history and religion in tandem with the ways that images and visual practices have constituted the medium of belief. The operative question, which I consider the informing principle of the study of religious visual culture, is: How does religion happen visually?

The book is entitled *The Lure of Images* in order to signal this substantive approach to the study of image and visual practice. The lure of images lies in the promises they make. By definition, they begin their work at a distance when viewers first see them. Vision is a sense that oscillates between scanning and concentrated focus. To see means skimming the surfaces of things in a broad range in search of what one wishes to hone in on and inspect more closely. When an image arrests our attention, we move closer. Another way of saying this is that we look in order to behold, and behold with the prospect of holding. Vision leads inexorably to touch, and taste, even when it does not actually end in tactile experience. Seeing also runs in the opposite direction – rushing toward us rather than only streaming from our eyes. The image on the cover of this book is a striking example. A store owner (who is also a street preacher) had the image of a large eye painted on the metal shutter he lowered each night over the window of his Laundromat along Martin Luther King Jr. Drive in Jersey City. The gaze of this eye of God fixes itself on passersby in a steadiness that the proprietor felt would be daunting, arresting any impulse to vandalize or rob the establishment. The lure of images includes their power over us, the bodily impact of a piercing gaze that refuses us invisibility, placing us under surveillance and thereby evincing certain forms of behavior. Bearing the embodied nature of seeing in mind helps to register the spatial reality of seeing, that it takes place within a physical setting and always under the power of desire. That is where the promise of images comes in. They offer us something we seek – happiness, nourishment, desirability, glamour, security, power, love, fellowship, social status, health, divine presence, refuge from the muddle of daily life, a lost past, a better future.

Such promises make images all but irresistible, empowering them to shape human experience in ways that are often almost invisible. If the power of images is to be understood, their construction of visibility must be made visible. This book is organized under three broad headings in order to explore the power of images and ways of seeing in the history of American religions. I have structured the book more or less in chronological order from the early republic to the present day, but chapters overlap, backtrack, and wander where certain historical issues and themes may take them. A straightforward chronological march through two hundred years of national history in a metered search for narrative continuity and uniform coverage quickly becomes dull. I have tried, therefore, to let the themes drive the discussion. Their selection is keyed to what I understand to be the social life of images: the circulation of imagery, the cultural politics of visual representation, and the many practices that put images to use. In all of this, religion is not something hermetically sealed off, the singular domain of clergy, bound up within sacred edifices. Nor are images merely self-contained bearers of artistic intent. It is the social career of images that receives attention here. Commerce, entertainment, the public sphere, and the private home are the circumstances in which the social life of religious images and ways of seeing take place.

In the first part of the book, "Print media in antebellum America," the lure of images consists of their ability in the case of illustrated books and tracts to corroborate and build upon text and utterance in order to make their claims more fetching, authoritative, or trustworthy. In the book's second part, "New visual media and the marketplace," the lure of images is their promise to consumers of an ethos that accompanies the acquisition of a commodity, which is often an image itself such as a lithograph. The lure also resides in providing the occasion for many people to see the same thing together and in doing so to experience a sense of community. Finally, under the rubric of "The power and menace of images," discussion fixes on how images have exerted a fascination and appeal by conveying the charisma of a leader, on the one hand, and by envisioning the promise of the American landscape, on the other.

This brief sketch offers only a few of the ways in which images command attention. Rather than summarize any further, I'll let the chapters speak for themselves. It may be worth pointing out, however, that this is a history of religion *and* visual media, which means that it is not simply a history of images per se. There is as much religion here as there is imagery. As I wrote the book, it occurred to me that one might go about combining images and the history of religion in several ways. One is the "illustrated history" – a densely visual text in which images trump words, reducing them to brief paragraphs or long captions. Another model is the more common academic style of "history with illustrations," which reverses the coffee table style of the illustrated history by featuring a long text with a few images added as an afterthought, gathered in a clump or scattered in the text without comment. A third option is the conventional art historical approach, which selects a certain set of images and their makers to investigate, treating religion only where it casts light on understanding them better. Each of these has its place, but none is able to demonstrate how images may serve as visual evidence in the study of religion; and none takes a robustly interdisciplinary approach.

In this book I have tried to write a visually driven study of the history of many religions in the United States. The intention is to show how visual media and ways of seeing are a fundamental part of that history. I hope that the book's success will be determined by the case it makes for integrating the study of American visual culture and the history of religion since the late eighteenth century. I could spend another paragraph apologizing for everything I have left out, but I'd rather end by inviting others to regard such absences as the opportunity to make their own contributions to a large and emerging field that will continue to welcome new work for some time to come.

Part I

Print media in antebellum America

Chapter 1

The aura of print

As the American Revolutionary War drew to a close with the Battle of Yorktown in the autumn of 1781, the young Noah Webster was teaching school in Sharon, Connecticut. The recent Yale graduate was appalled at the gross variations in spoken English among his pupils and had become convinced that the success of the emerging nation depended on fixing the proper rules of spelling and speaking *American* English. Much would depend, he insisted, on securing the practice of what he called a "federal language," which meant teaching children to read, write, and spell a version of English that was both purged of regional differences and distinct from its British origin. And so he set about producing an "American Speller," which first appeared in 1783.[1] Language would serve as the savior, not *saviour*, of the national soul.[2] The genius of a people was invested in its language and bequeathed to the future through the proper education of the young. This held with particular force, according to Webster and his contemporaries, for the new republic, a polity whose power to cohere depended on good will, on a shared national vision, on electoral good sense, and therefore on a degree of public literacy that could not be left to cultivate itself.

Common or public schools were an indispensable institution for promoting public good through the acquisition of cultural no less than academic literacy. And Webster, whose livelihood was producing school books and dictionaries, never ceased insisting that Americans needed to speak, read, and write as Americans, which they were to learn by reading his books in school. A print culture that would educate and inform students and the broader public to that end was essential. Certainly this was the view of another early vendor of popular print, the Rev. Mason Locke Weems, an Episcopal clergyman best remembered for his biography and apocrypha of George Washington. But Weems spent much of his time hawking books as the agent for Philadelphia publisher Mathew Carey. In 1811, Weems shared with his employer and investor a publication project, which, like many of his ventures, was never realized. But the project registers the Republican ideology of Federalists and later Whigs as they regarded the nation and devised ways to bind it up in a unity, which they faulted the vices of aristocratic luxury and the teeming mob alike for resisting. For Weems, as for others, the term "Christian" was synonymous with

"Republican."[3] After spending years planning many bible editions with Carey, and then selling them throughout the North and South, Weems urged upon him a tract that might be inserted in the bibles that Weems sold for Carey:

> I contemplate a noble addition to the Bible. Kingly governments you know are the curse of the Human Race. The Bible, you also know, is point blank against Kingly governments. The People of America enjoy a REPUBLIC, which, next to a Theocracy, must be the most perfect form that can be. But they don't know its value. And therefore like Esau they may sell it for a song. To set their own form of Government before them in all its Amplitude & brightness of Blessings must in my opinion at least be one of the most patriotic services that any man can do to this Country. Now what book so proper as a vehicle (to print it in) as the book which in consequence of the universal veneration attached to it, finds a ready admission into every house?[4]

The significance of literacy and print had been recognized and celebrated by Protestants in colonial America since the early seventeenth century. Puritans and Pilgrims both stressed the reading of the bible and provided for the education of the young no less than the preparation of young men for teaching and the pulpit. The size and number of personal libraries in colonial America is striking. Literacy rates in colonial America generally exceeded contemporary rates in England and Europe. Yet book production was considerably less, long yoked to London. The first bible published in America did not appear until 1777.[5] The largest-selling books published after the founding of the new nation were not, however, religious in the institutional sense. Webster and his competitors in the textbook trade issued spellers and readers that went through multiple editions and sold hundreds of thousands of copies. But if they were not religious in a narrowly sectarian sense, books such as Webster's *American Speller* and Caleb Bingham's *American Preceptor* (1794) and *Columbian Orator* (1797) did promote a piety of the republic, a civil religion that was unmistakably Christian. Bingham stocked the *Columbian Orator*, a collection of passages for learning eloquence, with texts that promoted the importance of religion for the success of republicanism, including poetic passages that were explicitly Christian. Although a Jeffersonian rather than a Federalist like Webster, Bingham nevertheless believed that the American republic required the Christian practice of virtue in order to resist the corruptions of luxury and wealth that led to tyranny. Webster and Bingham made sure they included texts promoting the value of religion in American society because they believed it was the most powerful avenue for the inculcation of virtue. And the religion was Protestant Christianity. The unity of religion and republic was considered fundamental. Religion and eloquence each kept vice in check – the one by instilling the practice of virtue, the other by championing liberty in the public life of government, press, and law.

Bingham's *Columbian Orator* was dedicated to teaching American students the art of oratory. "Eloquence," to quote the opening oration of the book's selections, "can flourish only on the soil of liberty."[6] The book serves to remind us that the practice of public speaking not only remained a fundamental feature of political life during the early republic, but also was regarded as a cornerstone of education and an indispensable component of making American citizens. In fact, the character of print that Protestants developed in tracts and printed sermons was deeply shaped by the oral culture of early national life. The concept of the American republic in the early national period drew importantly from what might be called the oratorical imagination, that is, the power of eloquence to evoke an ideal communicative situation in which a republican speaker moved citizen-listeners with the sublimity of speech, persuading them to endorse the speaker's point of view. The result was a public sphere in which republican justice prevailed. Print was the actual substitute for the forensic practice of oratory – print in the form of newspapers, books, and pamphlets, which constituted what Bingham, echoing an eighteenth-century tradition, proudly called the "republic of letters."[7]

As the official oral culture of the day, oratory as Bingham presented it helped usher in a momentous shift toward imagery in print culture. In the introduction to his volume, Bingham framed his definition of eloquence with a theory of the passions, which understood language as their vehicle of expression. He asserted that the ancient orators of Greece and Rome "did not think language of itself sufficient to express the height of their passions, unless enforced by uncommon motions and gestures."[8] Bingham noted that authorities of eloquence were conflicted on the rank of speech and gesture, but for his part he believed gesture to work more directly on the mind of listeners since it operated by sight, which was "the quickest of all our senses."[9] The sublime style, which operated by sweeping listeners away with emotional gestures and powerful diction, relied less on abstraction and more on the appeal to feeling. As a result, its use of visual signifiers of feeling – gesture and facial expression – magnified the effect of words and fostered greater sympathy for the visuality of speech. This interdependence of word and image in oratory was paralleled in print by the growing use of illustrations. Oratorical practice argued that seeing and saying were importantly linked. It did not take textbook publishers long to agree.

The capacity of oratorical gesture to paint the passions had long been a vital interest among history painters in the European academic tradition, which provided the visual template for American painters who described the patriotic heroism of the Revolutionary War. In 1851, the Pennsylvania-born Peter Frederick Rothermel, who studied painting in Paris, produced his large canvas *Patrick Henry in the House of Burgesses*, delivering the famous speech against the Stamp Act of 1765, in which he warned King George III of the republican lesson of an autocrat's demise. Two years later an engraving offered a more widely available reproduction of Rothermel's painting to Americans (Figure 1). Rothermel observed the physiognomy of the grand style, showing

Figure 1 Engraving after Peter Frederick Rothermel, *Patrick Henry delivering his celebrated speech in the House of Burgesses, Virginia, AD 1765, for presentation to subscribers to the Art Union of Philadelphia for 1852,* 1853. Courtesy American Antiquarian Society.

the animated speaker gesturing dramatically, which is echoed in a forceful diagonal that moves upward through the audience, visualizing the effect of his
speech. In the balcony above, women seem to flee the thrust of his diction;
below them a British officer rises to unsheathe his sword, as if to defend England against the orator's treasonous attack. Tories and Loyalists in the audience
grimace at the effect of Henry's words. As an early moment in the sacred
narrative of American nationhood, the scene seems to ground the genesis of
national consciousness in the daring act of speech. The power of the speaker is
registered everywhere in this iconic moment of incipient democratic spirit.[10]

The cooperation of word and image was a lesson not lost on Evangelical
publishers. The need to develop persuasive oratory during the early republic
was intensified for Evangelical Christians by the new political culture of democracy, particularly democracy in which state religion was eliminated. Tract
societies conceived of an ideal homiletic situation that bore close resemblance
to the practice of eloquence. An illustration by Alexander Anderson on the
cover of the American Tract Society's *Christian Almanac* from 1836 (Figure 2)
models the ultimate form of evangelism: a preacher commanding the rapt
attention of the world's populace as he announced the Word of God. In the
same way that Rothermel would use gesture to demonstrate the homology of
seeing and saying, Anderson uses the body to deliver the message of the
preacher's words. The gesture of his hand visualizes the spoken word and deftly
converts the printed word of scripture into spoken as well as visual language.
An image like this – and there were many in Evangelical tracts, almanacs,
and magazines – visualized the transparency of scripture and the authority
of the text it adorned, fashioning it as the printed version of what the preacher
proclaimed. Such images helped craft a transition from the oratorical tradition
of preaching to the illustrated print culture of the nineteenth century, tutoring
Americans to regard print as a faithful conveyance of scriptural truth and
illustrations as an affirmation of the authority and reliability of print. Illustrations endorsed the iconicity of texts by showing the object of the preacher's
speech, authorizing tracts and other print as equal to preaching or an even more
effective means of disseminating scripture. Illustrations like Figure 2 assured
Protestants that printed texts worked like spoken discourse, encouraging them
to imagine everyone in the nation as an extended gathering waiting to "hear"
the message of Christianity.

If a republican understanding of oratory stressed the importance of public
speaking and the cooperation of seeing and speech in the creation of an ideal
form of discourse, the disestablishment of religion created a new condition for
the relevance of imagery, particularly illustrations that accompanied texts.
Protestants had made use of print imagery from the very beginning of the
Reformation. Even the most stringently iconophobic Puritans in England
found certain kinds of illustrative imagery acceptable. American Protestants
illustrated versions of Bunyan's *Pilgrim's Progress*, broadsides, New England
primers, and almanacs among other standard texts. Bibles even appeared in the

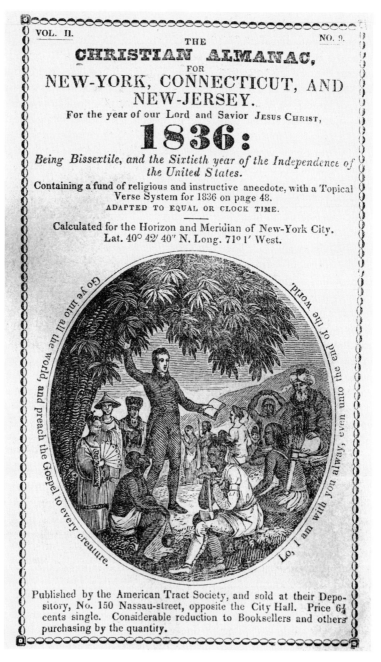

Figure 2 Alexander Anderson, engraver, Missionary preaching, *Christian Almanac for 1836.* New York: American Tract Society, 1835. Photo author.

later part of the eighteenth century with a scattering of engraved plates. But the new nation consisted of many audiences for whose attention zealous Protestants competed: unchurched immigrants, growing urban neighborhoods of laborers, passengers aboard steam ships and railroads, passersby in the street, and most especially, the children of frontier towns and eastern cities. Conservative Protestants found it necessary to enhance the appearance of their religion and to teach its precepts to consumers whose loyalties were increasingly drawn toward secular print and its sometimes lurid forms of entertainment. Accordingly, the purveyors of Protestant print had remarkably little difficulty recognizing the desirability of illustrated publications and often spared little expense investing in them. Evangelical publishing associations often engaged in hard-hitting rivalry with secular printers and book sellers for the patronage of the American consumer. Illustrating books and tracts made very good commercial sense. The lure of images was unmistakable.

There was another reason for Protestants to use images in the publications of tract and mission societies. The image of the printing press reproduced here (Figure 3) is a good example. Placed on a certificate of contribution to the American Tract Society (ATS) that was presented to those who offered a financial gift to the Society, the image visualizes the ideology of Evangelical print.

THIS IS TO CERTIFY

that *Elihu Loomis*

Figure 3 Printing press, American Tract Society Membership Certificate, 1840s. Courtesy of Billy Graham Center Museum.

Appearing on a mound, a printing press radiates light over a dense crowd of people whose costume indicates they come from far reaches of the globe. Dressed in full-length drapery that recalls allegorical personifications populating emblematic imagery as well as neoclassical art of the late eighteenth and early nineteenth centuries, two female figures distribute the produce of the press to the people about the mound. One of the figures looks heavenward, as if responding to a divine commission to disseminate the pamphlets and books. Beneath her left arm appears a conspicuously labeled "Holy Bible." The central arrangement of the press on the mound surrounded by a quiet gathering recalls contemporary portrayals of Jesus' Sermon on the Mount or the discursive situation pictured in Figure 2.[11] If the association is correct, the mechanism of the printing press replaces the preaching Christ and missionary, substituting printed text for oral discourse, and directing the printed word to all peoples, who gather about the radiant epiphany of print as a kind of millennial assembly whose many languages no longer separate them, as if the spread of the printed Gospel reverses the effect of Babel in a latter-day Pentecost of pages and ink. The shift from oral discourse to print as the primary medium of evangelism did not mean the loss of orality or oratory eloquence, but the switch to a visual register that sought to incorporate orality into print. As we shall see, the tendency was to animate print. Images helped endow print with an aura that rooted the visual in the spoken, serving to authorize imagery as well as to enliven print.

In the left foreground of the image sit a mother and two children, who share a book passed to them from the Evangelical press. About the group appear a shepherd, two soldiers, a kneeling old woman, a fisherman holding his net, businessmen, a mounted figure in a turban, and an old man on crutches. Behind the press stand a Native American in a headdress and a black figure with prayerfully clasped hands. Most figures in the crowd are engaged in reading newspapers, books, tracts, or broadsides. It is striking that no missionary or preacher appears in this image of global evangelism. Two bald and enrobed men in the left foreground stand beside an Indian brave who holds a tomahawk. The two figures in robes do not preach to the Indian; one of them appears to be engrossed in reading a book. Judging from their dress, they may represent judges or academics; or they may be Catholic clergy or monastics humbly consuming sacred print.

The absence of preachers in the image suggests their redundancy. Print triumphantly and universally replaces the spoken word. The message of the Good News proceeds in print that is generated with divine blessing and finds its way into the world under the imprimatur of the bible itself. The message of the image was that the flurry of print put into circulation by the Tract Society issued as the purity of biblical truth. The tracts were, as an annual report of the Religious Tract Society of Baltimore put it, "silent witnesses for Jesus." Tracts were reliable "epitomes" of scripture: "Any one of them, falling into the hands of a person who had never heard of the gospel before, and might never hear of it again, would teach him truths by which his soul might be saved."[12] Although some Evangelical Protestants of the antebellum era were anxious about or even adamantly opposed to images of Christ or his saints, they were not at all against using images to underscore the iconicity of their texts, the Evangelical tracts which they were convinced were "the most efficient instruments of extending the Redeemer's Kingdom," to cite the Baltimore report again. Tract advocates needed to assure their fellow Christians that tracts were authorized and reliable bearers of biblical truth. Images like Figure 3 helped make this case for them by showing the tract as a material version of the Word, sacred information to be strewn in the manner of the biblical parable of the sower of seed. Accordingly, one of the figures atop the mound casts the printed sheets widely as the other holds scripture in one hand and printed folios in the other.

Voluntarism and the system of Evangelical print

Most colonies throughout the British territories in America operated after the British model of state-sanctioned religion. This arrangement was widely accepted as a necessary condition for the public good. Morality needed to be enforced by the governing power in order to maintain order and decorum, and organized religion was generally accepted as the best way to do that: not only organized, but also Christian and sponsored by the state, even written into the charters of the colonies and the constitutions of most of the states of the new nation. Thomas Jefferson and James Madison offered an alternative model in their state constitution for Virginia. Eventually, this won the day at the federal level in the Bill of Rights, but not without bitter disagreement. Jefferson was forever criticized by many of his opponents as the impious product of the secularizing, free-thinking, atheistic French Revolution and Enlightenment. For many American Protestants of Calvinist persuasion, human nature was far too grim to be entrusted to the sunny disposition of democracy. Virtue would inevitably give way to vice, the true nature of the human soul in its state of innate depravity. Consequently, strong moral authority was required to instill in children and adults the proper respect for law and deity. State-sanctioned Christianity was considered by conservative Whigs as the best means for securing the commonweal.[13]

Calvinists expected little good from human nature. When disestablishment finally emerged as the law of the land, they lamented it as a dark day indeed. But not for long. Already underway in the United States was a new system of Evangelical activism that had been imported from Calvinist Protestants in Britain. In 1799, the Religious Tract Society (RTS) was founded in London. Chief among its promoters was the Rev. David Bogue, a Congregationalist minister, author, and mission seminary founder. On May 18, 1800, the occasion of the first anniversary of the Tract Society, he addressed the company assembled in London on the topic of "The Diffusion of Divine Truth." Bogue began by acknowledging that the oldest method of disseminating truth was the act of preaching. "But there is another method of diffusing truth," he insisted, one

> which can plead in its favour divine example and command. Man has a hand to write, as well as a tongue to speak; and God has employed the pen of the ready writer, as well as the tongue of the learned, to convey a word in season to him that is weary.[14]

Bogue went on to list a host of biblical writers from Moses to the Apostles, naming them all composers of "Religious Tracts for the benefit of mankind." If that were not persuasive enough, even "God himself becomes the author of a short Religious Tract: with his own hands he wrote the Ten Commandments of the law."[15]

Bogue also authored the RTS's first tract, issued in 1799, which argued for the timely, compelling, efficacious resource of tracts as an Evangelical method. The tract was a primer in tract production, distribution, and use. Its clarity and systematic counsel were apparently so fetching that the tract was republished in the United States as early as 1802.[16] In 1813, the recently formed Virginia Religious Tract Society issued the Address again, bound in its first volume of tracts. Seventeen of the volume's eighteen tracts were lifted directly from the publications of the RTS in London.[17] Writing, Bogue proclaimed, "is God's chief way of making himself known to the human race from age to age."[18] Many of those in heaven today, he said, were doubtless there by virtue of having read God's word. "What is a religious tract, but a select portion of divine truth designed and adapted to make the reader wise unto salvation?"[19] As a small reproduction of Scripture, a tract was launched into the world bearing the full authority of its original. Print, the implication seems clear, ensured no loss of the truth of the prototype. Mechanical reproduction suffered no fading of aura.

The context of Evangelical print culture in the United States

How was Bogue's rationale received in the United States? What social and theological matrix did it enter, which in turn shaped its application to the American scene? The first annual report of the Virginia Religious Tract Society carried a brief preface and a sermon preached by the organization's new president, Andrew Davidson, before the assembly of members in the autumn of 1812, even as British forces were sacking Washington in a brief renewal of armed conflict between Britain and the United States. The preface and Davidson's sermon make only slight references to the British campaign. It may have been a bit embarrassing for the Tract Society to inaugurate its effort on the model of the London RTS in the midst of British attacks. Or perhaps not. British Dissenters were generally pro-American. Moreover, British and

American Evangelicals shared a millennial sensibility that regarded wars less in geopolitical than in theological terms.

Not surprisingly, therefore, a distinct apocalyptic mood surcharges the preface as well as Davidson's sermon as the framework for the new society's print enterprise. The preface opens the volume with a gloomy notice of the troubled condition of the modern age: "The present state of the world presents to the pious, and reflecting mind, a picture truly alarming. Confusion, disorder, and bloodshed seem universally to prevail. Kingdoms and Empires have become cankered with iniquity, and are tumbling into ruins."[20] Davidson sounded the same note in his sermon, but with more direct allusion to present circumstances: "The whole world is in arms . . . and even our own once happy land has not escaped the general conflict."[21] But if the reader expected the Tract Society to train its scorn on the British, the preface confounded the expectation by doing something remarkably familiar: if this country is in travail, it has got no one to blame but itself. The opening address slipped quickly into the standard Evangelical device of the jeremiad: "in our own country," the speaker lamented, the "morbid affection" for corruption "daily increases." A list of national offenses followed:

> Vice stalks abroad unmasked. The tongue of Infidelity, which for some years past has been palsied by the powerful attacks of the friends of Christianity, begins again to lift up its voice in a thousand mutilated forms. False Prophets and Teachers, vain and filthy Dreamers, are labouring to unsettle the faith of many, and to lead them astray.[22]

What did all this mean? The signs were clear to the Evangelical leadership as well as the membership of Tract societies from Virginia to New York – as the preface put it: "we are drawing near to the last days . . . Antichrist is now in the full vigour of his strength." Rev. Davidson contended that

> it is not at all improbable but that we are now entering upon those dark and dismal days spoken of by the Prophet Daniel, when "there shall be a time of trouble, such as never was since there was a nation."[23]

But as the forces of Satan and the age of cosmic battle and millennium drew nigh, there was no time for despair or flagging zeal. True, the preface conceded, there was an insufficient number of clergy to circulate among the nation's peoples and preach the redeeming Word of God. But there was a remedy for that inadequacy: "a Society for distributing religious Tracts." The advantage was that

> at a very cheap rate, saving instruction can be disseminated through every part of our country: and will afford an opportunity to superannuated and disabled Preachers, as well as Lay-members of both sexes, to render

essential service to the cause of Christ, by carrying the precious truths of the Gospel, to the houses of their ignorant neighbours.[24]

Tract distribution could activate a dormant labor pool of retired clergy and lay men and women to counteract the paucity of clergy.

But the expediency of print addressed more than the shortage of clergy. It promised to tackle the "corruption of manners" that afflicted the day's youth, who lacked "proper instruction and restraint."[25] Evangelicals like Davidson and the membership of the Tract Society looked to print as an effective means of waging war in the new nation's most important public institution: the public school. They urged the use of the bible as a text book in the schools and resented its withdrawal from the curriculum: "The Bible, the fountain of all light and knowledge, is cautiously kept out of their hands, in schools, while they are learning the first rudiments of knowledge." But it wasn't only that the bible was increasingly absent, it was the substitution of secular print that alarmed Evangelicals:

> In the place of this book of God, are substituted fabulous stories of heathen deities, novels, plays and romances. Thus the youthful mind is filled with mere trash, or what is worse, poisoned with the principles of infidelity, which are interwoven with the stories of most novels.

To this end, the American Tract Society in Boston, celebrating its tenth anniversary in the summer of 1824, announced in the inaugural issue of its *American Tract Magazine* that it had improved the quality of paper used for its tracts, was beginning to trim the edges of its publications, had begun to use stereotype plates, and had "ornamented about fifty of [its] Tracts with cuts," or illustrations.[26] These were all significant improvements in the material form of the Society's product. Rag had been used for paper hitherto, which created a rough surface for printing and varying coloration. Pulp paper became available in the mid-1820s, providing a smoother, more easily trimmed, brighter, and more uniform printing surface. With the opening of the Erie Canal, pulp supply was also much more consistent than rag. By trimming the edges of the published pages, the Society enhanced the visual appearance of its publications, especially the bound volumes of books that were major sellers. Stereotyping lowered printing costs dramatically by freeing up letter press and keeping plates on hand for subsequent reprinting on demand, allowing the Society much greater flexibility in responding to consumer desire.[27] The effect of the Tract Society's initiative to beautify its publications was beneficial. A decade later, Robert Baird, a Presbyterian minister, supporter of the ATS, and general agent for the American Sunday School Union (ASSU), complained to Frederick Packard, editor and corresponding secretary of the ASSU, that the bindings of our books should be more attractive. Our books are as ugly in their appearance as old German books. Why do the Committee keep to the yellow edges? It may be cheap, but it is abominable. Our hymn book is too bad. I would rather have none, than retain it. It is not well selected, arranged, or any thing else, in my opinion.[28]

Baird obviously had marketing in mind. The look of literary products mattered if they were to be competitive.

Publishers and vendors of religious print had found this to be true since the late eighteenth century in the United States. Weems had not spared Carey comparable complaints regarding the paper, engravings, and bindings of his bibles. "I am not unhappy," he wrote in his typically florid style, "lest you ponder not sufficiently the importance of giving Plates to Public Admiration. The Engravings are the wings of that very Costly Work. Elegantly woven and webbed they will bear it up."[29] Weems based his confidence of the appeal of engravings on his experience in the street. In order to encourage subscriptions for a quarto illustrated edition of the bible planned by Carey, Weems had created a prospectus including specimen prints of the bible, which included an engraving. "My Bible business," he wrote Carey in the fall of 1800 from his native Dumfries, Virginia,

goes on as favorably, perhaps, more so, than I could have expected. Immense numbers of the Cuts [used to illustrate the forthcoming edition] may be sold separately. At what can you let the whole set go? I mean the 17 cuts? The question is often put to me, and at what could you put them in plain neat frames? . . . I have good reason to believe that elegant engravings will sell admirably here. One Gentleman in this town, Lawyer Harrison, who has seen the Bible proposals, not only takes a bible but wants a full set of the engravings neatly framed.[30]

Several years later, Weems summarized in another letter to the publisher the appeal of illustrations for children in justification for another, far more extensively illustrated bible, which would retail for $15.00 and carry seventy engravings.

Historical Engravings are excellently calculated for the Good of Children. They excite a vehement desire to read the passage illustrated by the picture. And by doing this from picture to picture, and with that lively interest which accompanies Juvenile curiosity, young People are apt to acquire both a knowledge & a veneration for the Holy Scriptures that may do Immortal Service.[31]

Children, Weems knew very well, were becoming an engine powering the consumption of print.

The Tract Society's use of "cuts" or illustrations, typically wood engravings, followed the same logic that Weems had advised. Images adorned its publications for the purpose of appealing to adults, but were especially present in its items aimed at children. Tract Society members and supporters cared about the appeal of Christian publications to children. In 1825 a mother from Connecticut wrote to the ATS publishing committee to declare her belief in the benefit of religious books for children, and offered the following recommendation, which seconded the claim of a contemporary moralist and educator:

> Will you allow me to make a suggestion as to the character of the Engravings which may be employed? Miss Edgeworth says, and my observation abundantly confirms her remark, "Prints will be entertaining to children at a very early age. They should be chosen with great care, should represent objects which are familiar, and the resemblances should be accurate. Perhaps the first ideas of grace, beauty, and propriety are considerably influenced by the first pictures which please children."[32]

The correspondent acknowledged that an improvement of the quality of engravings would likely increase the cost of children's books, but urged the Tract Society to consider that "the subject of education is constantly increasing in importance in the estimation of parents in our country, and such a consideration as this ought not, I presume would not, diminish sales." A shrewd argument based on demographics supported her claim: the number of white children under the age of 16 in the 1820s was greater than the number of white adults over the age of 20. The national population was growing not only because of immigration, but also by virtue of increased births. Moreover, a new understanding of children and child-rearing was beginning to regard the development of children, including their religious formation, as not only beginning early in life, but also as disproportionately important during early years. Parents and educators found that pictures were a sure means of engaging children in study and edifying conversation.

The largest number of illustrated publications during the 1820s and 1830s by the Tract Society were children's books, though many tracts aimed at adults were also illustrated. The ASSU, under the leadership of Frederick Packard, encouraged the use of illustrations in its literature, most of which was directed at children of varying ages, either to be used in Sunday schools or as domestic reading. Many of its volumes were installed in Sunday school libraries, from which children borrowed. Illustrated volumes and tracts were also given as gifts and rewards for attendance, exemplary performance in class such as the recitation of memory work, or as allurements to attend Sunday school. Packard's correspondence includes many exchanges with authors concerning illustrations. One of these, the Rev. James Alexander, who taught rhetoric at the College of New Jersey at Princeton and the Theological Seminary, was author of many articles in the *Princeton Review* as well as over thirty tracts and books for the ASSU, and served as a member of the Executive Committee of the ATS in the mid-1840s.[33] Alexander often wrote pieces for the *Sunday School Journal*, published by the ASSU, which were inspired by and built around woodcuts that Packard sent him. Many of his letters to Packard include his praise or criticism of the cuts he received. In every case, whether his reaction to an image was dislike or approval, it is evident that Alexander greatly appreciated the power of images to engage the attention of children and to generate his ideas as a writer.[34] In a letter of 1840, Alexander even enthusiastically proposed a pictorial edition of the bible to his colleague:

> I have so high a value of pictures in teaching, and in teaching what Dr. Bache [of the American Philosophical Society], after the Germans, calls real-knowledge, that I am sure there is a great deal yet to be done in this way, especially in our Religious Juvenal Literature. I wish to see a grand *picture-Bible* published and I should like to join you in helping it on. There is, I know, a "Pictorial Bible," but this is for the wealthy. My notion regards a book for the people. The German *Bilder-Bibel* comes nearest . . . and might serve as a model in several particulars, as (1) the intertexture of the cuts in the letter press, (2) the great number of them, (3) the reduced copies or sketches of *master-pieces* (for such is the case with some of these), (4) the cheapness of the book.[35]

A pictorial bible published on the model of the German *Bilder-Bibel* was a novel idea in American bible publishing because, if it closely followed the German prototype as Alexander's letter suggests it would have, the bible would have departed markedly from the inexpensive, mass-produced bibles issued by the American Bible Society (ABS), which inserted no imagery or commentary of any kind in its bibles. Alexander recognized the market for an inexpensive pictorial bible apparently within the price range of the Bible Society's mammoth niche. The visual apparatus of the bible Alexander had in mind would have reduced the number of "master-pieces," by which Alexander meant separate plates, usually copperplate engravings after the works of such artists as Raphael, Leonardo, Titian, and Rembrandt. Long the standard, used especially in upscale, large-format bibles that were acquired for display and collected for their production value, such engravings were separately printed and stitched in as the text was bound. Alexander appears to have intended wood engravings that could be set within blocks of letter press, allowing for simultaneous printing, which meant considerably less expense and the seamless integration of word and image. Judging from the contemporary *Bilder-Bibel*, Alexander entertained something progressive in the amount of page accorded to imagery. Indeed, he was willing to reduce the amount of text to a bare minimum in order to augment the size and frequency of illustrations. He was convinced such a venture would succeed: "if the prints, or blocks, could be cut somehow cheap, as for instance in Germany . . . the work might defy competition." That the

ASSU never issued such a bible was no doubt due to the great success of the *Illuminated and New Pictorial Bible* published by Harper's between 1844 and 1846, a mammoth single volume with over 1,600 illustrations.[36] Though the *Illuminated Bible* was not cheap, costing $13.50 per copy, an illustration from that bible (Figure 4) demonstrates that it accomplished the other three

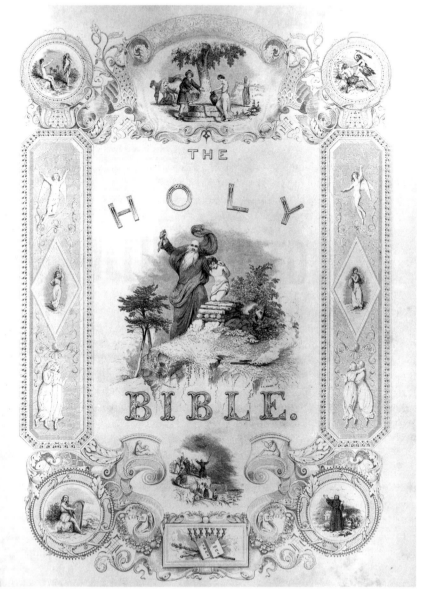

Figure 4 Title page, *The Illuminated Bible*. New York: Harper & Bros., 1846. Courtesy American Antiquarian Society.

objectives presciently identified by Alexander several years before its appearance.[37]

The ATS and the ASSU were mindful of the allure of imagery in the way they deployed Evangelical print. Tracts and books represented a primary weapon in the Evangelical arsenal to wage the "print wars" of the early republic. The stakes could not be more compelling, according to Davidson. The soul of the nation was in question since vice took root with poor parenting. Children who were raised without the care of learning the "principles of true religion" succumbed to vice. The result was the decay of virtue, "which is the main pillar of a republican government; and it is this, which is now pulling down the vengeance of Heaven upon our guilty land."[38] Tracts had the power to take "saving instruction" to the young and their families, which could transform them from vice to virtue. "Let religion be revived in any neighbourhood," Davidson proclaimed, "and what a happy change immediately ensues." Christianity exerted the power to change "the character of mere devils to good and virtuous citizens."[39] He cited recently formed tract societies in New York and Philadelphia, and the older organizations in England as encouragement to undertake the experiment in Virginia. In order to avoid the negative association of partisan print, the preface to the volume assured Americans that the tracts contained therein were in no way to be confused with the political tracts that had flooded the postal system and print seller's trade during American presidential elections, most contentiously the bitter paper wars that surrounded Jefferson's two elections. "This is no Party-contest; no Electioneering dispute; no Self-interested object."[40]

Yet Protestants regarded Christian benevolence as a form of philanthropy. Davidson and his counterparts throughout the land called "for all friends of Zion to 'be up and doing.' "[41] Print became the means of a new activism, which would extend from the street to the school and the docks, from the neighborhoods of the poor to the new settlements spreading west in the Ohio River valley and into the South. But while the rhetoric was charged with millennial expectation, the imagery that illustrated tracts and books produced by mainstream Presbyterians, Congregationalists, and Baptists generally avoided visions of Armageddon. The prophetic arithmetic and hermetic imagery of Adventist charts (see Figure 27, p. 90), broadsides, and illustrated books and newspapers abounded in visual portrayals and references to the second coming of Jesus and the end of the world. But mainstream Evangelical culture generally sidestepped such matters, keeping to vague millennial proclamations – in part because setting the time of the end was risky, and in part because mainstream Protestants did not wish to be associated with Millerite, Mormon, or Seventh-Day Adventist sects. But perhaps even more importantly, post-millennialism had no use for the catastrophic visions of the end because the real significance of the millennium was national ascendancy through spiritual renewal. The purpose of the American nation was the focus. The task was to clarify public recognition of the nation as God's own, to promote virtue, and to contain vice.

The iconography of the Evangelical mainstream reflects this aim without exception. Consider the illustration used by the ATS on the cover of its first tract (Figure 5), which was its own version of David Bogue's "Address to Christians." Tract societies assumed that sharing the good word was inseparable from curtailing vice. An annual report of the Religious Tract Society of Baltimore regarded each tract it distributed as "a messenger from the Lord to admonish its perishing recipient of things that concern the life to come, and another restraint to hold in check the lusts that distract and defile the life that now is."[42] The image that inaugurated the ATS's long series of tracts portrays a well-dressed family handing out tracts to a working-class counterpart, which willingly receives and reads them. It is not only a personalized version of the mechanized print production of Figure 3, but also one that explicitly structures tract distribution as a means of class formation. A middle-class family practicing the voluntaristic religion of Christian benevolence distributes tracts and books for free. The poor receive the literary alms of the well-to-do. The philanthropic act confirms the respective social locations of giver and receiver. The accompanying address to the Christian public from the executive committee of the ATS was directed to those of means, not to those in need. Middle- and upper-class Christians were encouraged to engage in Christian benevolence by providing tracts to the poor, the aged, children, the infidel, and the laboring classes. Nationhood was an imagined community of Protestant believers wrought by the volunteer work of Christian citizens among those who remained outside of the community, separated by vice, unbelief, or poverty.

The national print network of Evangelical Protestantism: "A thousand streams of information"

The earliest tract societies appeared in Philadelphia and New York metropolitan organizations. City tract societies found the dire circumstances of the urban poor and laboring classes cause for their efforts, and so dedicated themselves to providing inexpensive, readable tracts keyed to laborers and children. Women's membership in tract auxiliaries steadily grew over the first several decades of the nineteenth century, even outnumbering male counterparts in many cases, though leadership at national levels remained almost exclusively male, and dominated by clergymen. Yet tract societies, like other benevolent organizations in Victorian America, allowed women, including women of color, a public presence, fellowship with one another, and an organizational control that was denied them in other respects. In the African Female Auxiliary Tract Association of New York City, for example, which was formed in the fall of 1826, all "members and officers, with the exception of the Directress, consist entirely of coloured females."[43]

Membership in women's tract auxiliaries varied by region early on. The Female Branch of the New York Religious Tract Society, formed in 1822, began

THE   **NO. 1.**

ADDRESS

OF THE

EXECUTIVE COMMITTEE

OF THE

AMERICAN TRACT SOCIETY,

TO THE

CHRISTIAN PUBLIC.

PUBLISHED BY THE

AMERICAN TRACT SOCIETY,

AND SOLD AT THEIR DEPOSITORY, NO. 144 NASSAU-STREET, NEAR

THE CITY-HALL, NEW-YORK; AND BY AGENTS OF THE

SOCIETY, ITS BRANCHES, AND AUXILIARIES, IN

THE PRINCIPAL CITIES AND TOWNS

IN THE UNITED STATES

Figure 5 Alexander Anderson, engraver, "Address," no. 1. New York: American Tract Society, 1825. Courtesy American Antiquarian Society.

with the financial support of 175 women subscribers. Their treasurer was Mrs. Arthur Tappan, wife of the dry goods magnate and underwriter of the American Tract Society.[44] In the South, however, female membership began on more modest terms, though it quickly grew. Some degree of the dramatic growth of women's presence in tract societies becomes evident when the small number of four women is compared to the total of eighty-seven subscribers listed in the Second Annual Report of the Religious Tract Society of the City of Washington for the year of 1820. But the list of subscribers named in the Fifteenth Annual Report of the Religious Tract Society of Baltimore (for the year 1829) included sixty-two who are identifiably female out of a total of 120. The same report lists the names of the officers of auxiliary tract societies in ten Maryland counties. Forty-eight are the names of women; only thirty-eight of men.[45]

In addition to performing much of the work of local distribution, women were a primary financial engine powering tract societies. Within a year of its national formation, the ATS was making special appeals to women members for financial support. *The American Tract Magazine* carried a special plea to "Female Friends of the American Tract Society" for urgent financial aid, asking "ladies in different parts of the country" to raise five thousand dollars since the publishing committee of the ATS had exhausted its funds.[46] Women were fund-raisers, organizers, and the executors of Christian benevolence. Their activation as agents of good was clearly signaled in the cover of a tract on the influence of women, published by the ATS in 1829 (Figure 6). The image shows women in the public setting of a town, appropriately bonneted, gathering children and leading them to Sabbath school. One Christian woman shakes the hand of a mother, whose three children gather around, presumably to listen to the female evangelist offer to escort the children to receive sacred instruction. But if the women are shown out of doors, intervening in the lives of others to bring them to Christ, the text of the tract is unambiguous about the proper sphere of women: "her dominion is the fireside and family circle."[47] The only respect-able exception was the activities provided by the volunteer work of Christian benevolence. Women in the United States and colonial America had long established the pattern of primary responsibility for activities in the church. They attended in much greater number than men and had assumed principal responsibility for the daily spiritual formation of children.[48]

In addition to the need to organize regional and national efforts, and to economize on production, it was the migration westward and the increase of immigration to the United States beginning in the 1830s that motivated the national organization and proliferation of the ATS. Drawing from the New York Religious Tract Society, founded in 1812, and the Boston-based New England Tract Society, founded in 1814 (renamed the American Tract Society in 1823), the national ATS assumed an ambitious leadership role. Consisting largely of Presbyterians and Congregationalists, the ATS quickly assembled the diverse energies of tract societies across the northeast into a highly organized

NO. 226.

FEMALE

INFLUENCE AND OBLIGATIONS,

You are the very persons to collect the little wanderers—*Page 6.*

Figure 6 Alexander Anderson, engraver, Women and children, cover of "Female Influence and Obligations," no. 226, *Publications of the American Tract Society.* New York: American Tract Society, [1842], vol. 7, 389. Photo author.

enterprise that integrated local initiatives into an ever expanding national network, and relentlessly looked for ways to streamline and to augment the production and dissemination of tracts.

The ranks of the organization were more or less united in the cause of blanketing the United States with Evangelical tracts. In 1821, the New England Tract Society (the predecessor of the ATS in Boston) announced that every family in the country should possess a set of tracts. More practically, the Baltimore Religious Tract Society set itself the goal in 1829 of distributing one new tract each month to every family in the city of Baltimore, but was forced to report the following year that it had been unable to meet the goal.[49] The way in which tract societies proceeded toward the goal of universal distribution, even though they never succeeded in it, established a long-enduring pattern and set of ideas. Fundamental to this systematic plan was the belief that text was an efficient means of dispersing the message of Christianity, and that the tract did so in a way that both avoided sectarianism and conveyed the unadulterated truth of the bible. The plan constitutes what may be considered an Evangelical ideology of print that has remained a part of religious media production and use to the present. Its features consist of: (1) the systematic networking of small and large organizations across the country, (2) the integration of production, distribution, and reception, (3) a robust embrace of the commercial market-place, and (4) the imbrication of textuality on orality. Together, these features demonstrate how modern Protestantism, especially Evangelicalism, is a highly *mediated* religion. Understanding this is crucial to understanding Protestant visual culture and its operation.

Systematic networking

Tract societies spread like a kind of Evangelical fever. They began in major cities like Boston, New York, and Philadelphia, and quickly took root in places like Baltimore and Harrisonburg (Virginia), but spread at the same time in small towns and congregations. Individuals within Presbyterian, Congregationalist, Baptist, and Methodist congregations often started them, soliciting the support of clergy and prominent business leaders, physicians, and lawyers. Tract reposi-tories were established in cities whose locations would help assure access and constant supply. Communication among the national and local organizations and between leadership in New York and members across the country was regular and detailed in the Society's many house organs such as the *American Tract Magazine*, a bi-monthly and then monthly illustrated periodical, which included letters, narratives, minutes, editorials, and notices and prompts from the national leadership. Anecdotes of the "utility" or "usefulness" of tracts were often included in annual reports, and were commonly lifted from the reports and publications of tract societies across the United States, from Scotland and England, and from the mission fields of Asia.[50]

The idea was always to stimulate growth. The reports delighted in calculat-ing burgeoning production of print, the expansion of titles, and the growing audiences among which they distributed their publications. Tract societies, according to one speaker at the third annual meeting of the Religious Tract Society of Baltimore, were part of "the vast moral machinery" that God had deployed "to secure the accomplishment of his own Prophecies."[51] Therefore, entering into and publishing the correspondence with far-flung auxiliary soci-eties incorporated the local association into a grand and ultimately divine plan for the universal proclamation of the Gospel, which would usher in the dawn of the millennium.

Integration of operations

The print system of Evangelical organizations like the ATS, ASSU, and the ABS operated by integrating production, distribution, and reception; by linking producers with readers; and by creating print products that were designed for the occasions that they helped bring into being such as Sunday schools, common schools, religious revivals, efforts at moral reform that involved manual distribution, and private devotional reading. There were also other publications aimed at parents, children, Sunday school teachers, and colporteurs (hawkers and traveling agents). The ATS provided an ever-expanding list of tracts, which it published in bundles and in bound volumes. The tracts were organized by theme in order to assist in their deliberate distribution as Bogue had encouraged in his rationale. This articulation of Evangelical print enhanced the fit between product and consumer. In addition to the tracts, it issued classic texts such as *The Pilgrim's Progress*, devotional and theological texts by Richard Baxter, Philip Doddridge, Jonathan Edwards, and David Brainerd. It provided entire libraries of sacred literature to Sunday schools at affordable prices and catered to children, offering illustrated tracts and books for various ages. One of the most interesting features of the ATS and the ASSU is the effective way in which they integrated production and reception.

The ATS made writers of its readers by conducting competitions for tract writing and by coaching potential writers among their readership in how to write a good tract. They accomplished this by regularly printing letters from readers of tracts, which recounted the salutary effects of certain publications on those to whom tracts had been given. The reception of tracts was circulated in order to prompt the further circulation of tracts among readers. The *American Tract Magazine* regularly ran prompts for new tracts, informing readers of themes and offering cash awards of $50–80 as remuneration for the winning submission, which the ATS then published.[52] Dozens of submissions were received and several tracts published. Another important form of feedback was information garnered by colporteurs or itinerant salesmen, who began working for the ATS in 1841, when the Society had determined that a system of salesmen would work better than the broad and often unreliable scatter of auxiliary societies.[53] Colporteurs kept daily journals from which they extracted annual reports that were submitted to the New York office and excerpted in turn for publication in the Society's annual reports.

Commercial marketplace

Evangelical print was designed to enter the marketplace and compete successfully with the commercially driven secular market in print. Staffed by volunteers, auxiliary tract societies could operate with no profit margin since proceeds came as acts of Christian philanthropy and since the local groups relied for their supply of tracts on the national organization, which produced at low

prices since it operated on a large economy of scale. The tract societies deliberately targeted Sunday schools and common schools, developing curricular
materials such as primers and catechisms for use in organized instruction. The
American Tract Magazine reprinted an address in 1825 in which a clergyman
urged the use of tracts in Sunday schools since

> in these schools thousands and hundreds of thousands are learning to read.
> If we can fill their hands with small and interesting religious publications,
> to exert upon them a moral influence, we may hope that their attainments,
> with the blessing of God, will be of service to their souls; but if we neglect
> this means of usefulness, they will be naturally inclined to peruse perni-
> cious books, and their education, instead of being a blessing, will prove
> awfully injurious.

The clergyman warned his audience of the move afoot "to give currency to
pamphlets and books of an improper character. Every peddler's basket is filled
with them. Dying confessions of criminals, impure ballads, and fictitious biographies, are widely diffused, and they must be supplanted by Religious
Tracts."[54] The first tract issued by the Tract Society of the Methodist Episcopal
Church in New York City, published in 1826, called for tract societies, individuals, book sellers, and printers to "unite in the generous design" of tract
distribution since "each will have peculiar channels of circulation" such that "a
thousand streams of information will be united in one flood, till 'the knowledge
of the Lord shall cover the earth as the waters do the sea.' "[55] In case one of
these "streams of information" did not find its way into the very heartland of
vice, the New York City Tract Society struck an agreement with the city's
bar-keepers, "according to which, the Tracts would be offered for sale at their
respective bars."[56]

Textuality and orality

Print was patterned very carefully on oral culture, and often designed to facilitate face-to-face encounter when it did not seek to replace it. The *Tract
Magazine* published instructions on the distribution of tracts, encouraging
people "not so much to scatter indiscriminately a large number, but to do it
judiciously and effectually," taking care to follow up with personal visits and
prayer.[57] The ATS also suggested procedures in its first tract publication, derived
from Bogue's "Address to Christians." Moreover, the many anecdotes published from letters of tract users offered a steady supply of hints about the use
of tracts in a variety of daily circumstances. While the deployment of tracts
clearly relied on face-to-face encounters in the street or school, or at the front
door, tract societies also stressed the power of print to operate in the place of
the spoken word. This idea strongly appealed to tract society proponents who
yearned to address the masses of unchurched and non-believers in America and

far beyond. An annual report of the New England Tract Society hypothesized that someone who provided a gift of $100 to the Society would furnish 30,000 tracts of four pages in length:

> Thus with $100 he may speak to 30,000 persons. Suppose each of these Tracts goes into a family, and is read by 5 persons. He then speaks to 150,000 persons, and as effectually perhaps as he would were he personally to address them.

Indeed, tracts could even perform better than living preachers: "How many persons have been more benefited by reading the Swearer's Prayer, a Tract of 4 pages, than they probably would be, by hearing the best sermon which any missionary could preach upon that subject."[58] Not only could tracts exceed the preached word, but they also allowed the modern world of Evangelical print to surpass Pentecost's gift of tongues. In 1824, a speaker before the annual meeting of the New York Religious Tract Society proclaimed that

> the primitive church . . . possessed astonishing facilities for the diffusion of Christianity, in her gift of tongues. But do we not possess more than an equivalent of this advantage? Those inspired men died, and all that remains of them are a few Tracts bound up in a small volume, forming the New Testament. These Tracts, in the time of the Apostles, could be multiplied only by the slow and tedious process of transcription – a process so slow, and so expensive, that a copy of the Scriptures could be purchased by a labouring man only with the earnings of forty years. . . . The evangelist may now transfer his feelings to the printed page, and with the aid of the typographic art, that page may be indefinitely multiplied and sent abroad upon every wind. Give me this art, and you may have the gift of tongues. Give me these Tracts, charged with God's message, and able to repeat it again and again, and you may spare the labour of ten thousand lungs. A Tract goes where the living preacher may not go.[59]

Print, authority, and aura

Print offered the additional advantage among Calvinists of providing a bulwark against heterodoxy. Since the Reformation, print and its distribution of systematic theology had been deployed to resist the inroads of "enthusiasm." Both Luther and Calvin had relied on pamphlets and printed sermons and theological treatises in the early sixteenth century to oppose the challenge of contemporary "prophets" like Thomas Münzer, who supplanted scriptural authority with the spiritual revelations that came to them. Lutherans and Calvinists continued to oppose this and other heterodoxies over following centuries, arguing that revelations beyond those recorded in and sanctioned by scripture were an unauthorized departure that constituted a threat to the order of the Christian community. The written text of the bible and the authorized interpretation of it were regarded as necessary stays against "enthusiastic" interpretation and revelation. Enthusiasm referred to any supposed in-breathing of Spirit that might trump established ecclesiastical authority. Print offered a stabilizing device. In a sermon of 1816 before the Prayer-Book and Religious Tract Association in Boston, Presbyterian clergyman and divine John S. J. Gardiner commended the adoption of a prayer book by Presbyterians as a way of opposing the influence of enthusiasm that he found at work in the Church of Scotland in the use of extemporary prayer among "the indecent freaks and senseless rant of the itinerant and unlettered enthusiast." Furthermore, he contended, an official prayer book would bar the advance of the heterodoxy that had decimated the Scottish and English Calvinists in the later eighteenth century. A prayer book would check the influence of Unitarianism and Deism by providing "the choicest portions of the holy scriptures, which its prayers, and articles interpret in the true and orthodox sense – in that sense, in which they have uniformly been understood by the greatest and best men that ever lived."[60] A prayer book would operate, in effect, as a lay person's bible commentary, guiding the orthodox reading of scripture in accord with recognized authorities. Print was believed to be able to stabilize orality among Evangelicals in a way that paralleled Noah Webster's national campaign to stabilize American English as the storehouse of national identity and well-being.

As the presence of the bible in Figure 3 suggests, tracts were paired with the bible in Tract Society literature as its indispensable companion. The Rev. Dr. John Scudder, a celebrated American medical missionary in India and Sri Lanka, boldly stated in 1838, "I think no portion of the Scriptures should be given [to Indians] without being accompanied with a Tract explaining the outline of the plan of salvation with a refutation of heathenism, if possible."[61] For Scudder, tracts were to operate as instruction guides in reading the bible. The *Tract Magazine* published the remarks of a speaker who told his audience at an annual meeting of the ATS that "religious tracts are pioneers of the bible; they prepare the way for its circulation." Another clergyman commenting on the use of tracts to promote religious revival challenged those who claimed that reliance on tracts came at the expense of the bible. To the contrary, the clergyman replied, tracts "bring the Bible into constant use. The more Tracts are read, the more the Bible is read."[62] Yet another clergyman reported finding a woman on her deathbed with her bible resting on a tract. The tract, she told him, "is, next to the Scriptures, my comfort in my affliction: through it I was first led to read the sacred volume, and it shall remain my companion till my soul is parted from my body."[63] Such accounts endorsed the tract's reliability and authority, extending the aura of biblical print to the tract. ATS literature is full of references to tracts that infuse it with a charisma that suggests print enjoyed a substance or presence among conservative Protestants that could be expressed only in terms of its aura. Producers may broadcast an Evangelical message in what appears to be a strictly instrumental form of information such as a humble tract.

But if we are to believe what nineteenth-century tract producers and readers reported, the flimsy, inexpensive paper covered with dense print was a medium that did not bear an indifferent relation to its message and the meaning that readers discovered in it. For example, a clergyman from Ohio related how much he relied on his single copy of a favorite tract, which he often read from the pulpit, in schools, to those he visited, and while riding his horse. Though offered money for it, he refused to part with his tract:

> I felt that its value as an assistant in my labours was too great for me to be induced to part with it; and though I have since procured and distributed a great many copies of the same, I still carefully preserve my old copy. And although it is much sullied, and leaves broken by frequent folding, yet I think I can read the story better from it, than from the new ones.[64]

A collection of anecdotes published by the American Tract Society in the 1820s states that "divinely inspired" truths were "stamped in bold relief on the face of religious Tracts, and extended to every city, and town, and village, and family, and soul." Tracts were not simply messages conveniently recorded in an inexpensive format, but objects

> blazing with the effulgence of the truths which God has revealed, in the aspect and connection in which he has revealed them, and attended, in answer to the prayers of God's people, by the Holy Ghost sent down from heaven.[65]

Far from diminishing the religious aura of sacred artifacts, as Walter Benjamin asserted of modern technologies of reproduction, mechanically produced texts such as tracts enhanced the production and distribution of sacredness attached to printed objects in mass culture.[66]

When many discussed the power of tracts as rivaling or even surpassing the preacher's spoken discourse for effectiveness, they would ascribe to the tracts the power of speech, animating print with sound, action, or luminosity. A Sabbath school teacher from Pennsylvania who had distributed "an unknown amount" of tracts among students said that he considered tracts "as little heralds of the cross, who sometimes proclaim the truths of the Gospel more effectually than some good ministers who have long laboured in the vineyard."[67] A clergyman from Worcester, Massachusetts, called the religious tract "a little herald of truth and righteousness" that makes no pretensions.

> It comes forth meek and unobtrusive. It is a little fold of paper; and, as may be, you may read it in a moment. But . . . how right its contents. It carries precept and doctrine pure as from the word of God, and presents example in all but actual life before you. It goes in a thousand places where a preacher cannot go, and always with plainness and fidelity.[68]

Rev. Samuel Eastman, agent for the ATS, hailed tracts as "little Gospel peace-makers" that would effectively negotiate the challenges facing the Tract Society.

> Look at maps of Kentucky, Tennessee, Mississippi, Louisiana, and other States and Territories in the valley of the Mother of Rivers, occupied by four millions of inhabitants, multiplying every year by a constant tide of emigration . . . more in need of Religious Tracts than any other part of our population.

Unable to supply these regions with preachers, the Society could, however,

> say to these Religious Tracts, "Go beyond the Allegany Mountains, and tell those that sit in darkness . . . that God so loved the world as to give his only begotten Son . . . Yes, Sir, we can give these little printed messengers what commission we please. We can send them, rapid as the wings of the wind . . . we can rest assured that they will always tell the truth, and never apostatize."[69]

Eastman was in the employment of the ATS, which sought to convince Protestants of the power of tracts. It is not surprising, therefore, that he and the publications of the ATS would hyperbolize about the efficacy of tracts. But that they did so in order to move Protestant evangelism from its traditional orality and to exert the influence of their project to the far ends of the expanding nation shaped the Evangelical ideology of print media in an enduring way. The celebration of the tract as a cherished object, as a print artifact, may also have contributed to a growing recognition of the power of images by Evangelicals. An ATS annual report from mid-century included an account gathered by a traveling salesman who took tracts and books door to door. A woman in Pennsylvania related to the salesman that one of her neighbors "had become a confirmed inebriate."

> Calling at his house one day, she read him the tract, "We must live" [which addressed the issue of selling liquor]. After reading it, she showed him the picture [illustrating the tract (Figure 7)], and told him of the wretched condition of his family, who were really in want; after which he promised that he would drink no more. This promise he has been able to keep several years, maintaining his family, and living respectably.[70]

Showing the man the tract's image bolstered the impact of its message. The illustration referred to (Figure 7) appears to have intensified the effect of the tract's text by turning its printed message into a concrete talisman that compelled the drunkard to repent. The image portrays a tavern interior in which three idle men smoke. Through the window appear a line of people filing into a church. The inebriate in question may have recognized himself in this slothful

No. 474.

" "WE MUST LIVE.""

PUBLISHED BY THE

AMERICAN TRACT SOCIETY,

150 NASSAU-STREET, NEW YORK.

Figure 7 Robert Roberts, engraver, cover illustration for "We Must Live," no. 474, in *Tracts of the American Tract Society*, vol. 12. New York: American Tract Society, 1845. Courtesy The Library Company of Philadelphia.

fellowship, violating Sabbath and wasting away in the grip of many vices (note the spittoon on the floor and the poster advertising horse races). The title of the tract, "We Must Live," was the proprietor's reply to an Evangelical who objected to sales on Sabbath. But by visualizing the dissipating life of the tavern in contrast to the life of the devout, the image helped bestow an auratic quality on the tract, augmenting its consequence, making the reader into a viewer, that is, making the experience of being told the truth into the experience of seeing it. The effect of this act of visual piety was to transform the Evangelical message of repentance and contrition into a personal encounter that demanded a heartfelt response.

Mass-produced religious imagery is grounded in the print culture of early national Protestantism, which gave images a new place in American religious culture. The Protestant ideology of print used images to signal the power of the printed text. The history of religious visual media begins in print, whose capacity for waging public debate gave images a broad circulation and cultural mission, as the next chapter will show.

Chapter 2

Religious visual media and cultural conflict

The social arrangements of American life changed dramatically during the course of the nineteenth century as factories and mills began to attract a pool of labor that had traditionally been centered in agriculture, working on the farm. In addition to the rise of industry and the shipping of raw materials and manufactured goods, the nation's major cities expanded with the arrival of European immigrants beginning in the middle decades of the century. Living in cities involved a wide range of activities and experiences unparalleled in rural life: encountering racial and ethnic groups other than one's own; living outside of the surveillance of elders, the extended family, and the network of the entire community; facing the temptations of amusements and diversions offered by the city; and living within a new regime of structured time. One of the biggest problems that religious authorities found with city life was the new importance of leisure, time which boys and young men were drawn to spend in the streets, where they were lured into games of chance and the bawdy entertainments of urban night life. Tracts and stories warned against the dangers of such allurements.[1] Although most Americans would continue to live on farms and in villages and small towns well into the second half of the century, the city became a symbol of the changing nation much earlier. Protestants, Catholics, Jews, Blacks, and Whites all considered and occasionally even undertook various schemes of colonizing rural regions of the nation in order to remove people from the difficulties of city life and to pursue a cherished republican ideal of the yeoman-farmer.

The promise and threat of urban America

Moralists trained their sights on boys and young men itching to move to cities and towns. A flood of tracts and periodicals issued from the religious press imploring youthful readers to resist the influence of a profane lifestyle. *Frank Harper; or, The Country-Boy in Town* was a short novel written by James Alexander in 1847 that told the story of a boy who came to New York City from a country village to live in a boarding house and work in a store. Urban life instantly made young Frank a consumer in a competitive religious marketplace.

Bewildered by the size and complexity of the city, he spent his first Sabbath wandering from church to church in search of a congregation that felt right. First, he entered a crowded church that "was full of the fumes of incense; he saw pictures and crosses, and heard prayers in a strange tongue; he did not remain long."[2] He tried another, whose "pews were filled with rich-looking people" and whose young clergyman "was preaching about the evils of enthusiasm." But Frank became bored and soon left. In these descriptions Alexander, a conservative Presbyterian clergyman, it will be remembered, took aim at the unsuitable setting of both immigrant Catholicism and the fashionable scene of liberal urban Protestantism (with its dismissal of the revivalism of Evangelical Protestantism as "enthusiasm"). Frank did not find a church that engaged him until he came upon "an old-fashioned building" where the minister's message of self-examination pierced the young man's heart with conviction and moved him to soul-searching.

Entertainments were a chief source of temptation facing Frank and other boys in the city. Not content to linger in fictional narrative, Alexander repeatedly directed the narrator's voice directly to his readers:

> The circus, the theater, the low concert draw multitudes night after night. These persons afterwards become ripe for crimes. Boys in town, who have no one to look after them, are early tempted to such places. But if they love their own souls, they would resolve to avoid them, lest they be drawn into greater depths of iniquity.[3]

The city required special effort since it subverted the traditional patterns of village and farm life by pulling young people away from their families, elders, and the moral influence of church attendance. In an essay published a few years later, Alexander urged young men to undertake a program of reading and study and to begin creating a personal library.[4]

Cities were places where farm boys saw things they never knew existed. The sites of leisure were one menace; another for Anglo Protestants was the growing presence of immigrants, whose languages and religions were exotic and alien. One day Frank Harper wandered up the East Side of Manhattan and encountered European immigrants he had never seen before:

> [Chatham Street is] a region of pawnbrokers and old clothes-sellers. Many of these are Jews. The national physiognomy struck him at once: they were almost like brothers. He observed that they stayed as little as possible in their dark shops, and spent most of the time pacing up and down the space before their doors: it is a custom which they have brought with them from abroad. Thus it is that they may be observed in Frankfort, in Amsterdam, and in Posen. Most of them were smoking and speaking German. . . . He called to mind that they are the seed of Abraham, and resolved to read over the tenth and eleventh chapters of Romans, on his return.[5]

The text is a kind of Evangelical travelogue that describes the city's Jewish population in picturesque terms that underscore their foreign origins and persistent difference in the American metropolis. The reference to Paul's Letter to the Romans frames Frank's perception and Alexander's message: Jews mean the chosen nation that rejected the messiah, but whose stumbling, according to Paul, redounded to the eternal benefit of non-Jews. Romans 11: 11, "But through their trespass salvation has come to the Gentiles, so as to make Israel jealous." Alexander had Frank tour the Jewish neighborhood in order to conjure up both the strangeness of the city and its promise as a field of Evangelical proselytism. An illustration from the Boston American Tract Society's *Pictures and Lessons for Little Readers* (ca. 1863) takes a much harsher view of the urban encounter of Christian and Jew (Figure 8). The image shows a young Jewish boy who converted to Christianity being ejected from his home by his angry parents. The father and mother express scorn and anger that would have troubled young Christian readers. The text accompanying the picture indicates that the boy had converted.

> But his father is a Jew ["The Jew" of the story's title], and he has just told his boy that he will not have him in the house any longer; that he must find another home for himself. So the little boy takes his bag of clothing from his father, and goes away, he knows not whither.[6]

"The Jew" was the commonplace rubric of the latter-day Israelite who stubbornly resisted assimilation (as their forebears had refused to recognize Jesus as messiah) by living in ethnic urban enclaves, speaking a foreign language, and practicing a strange religion. The otherness of the Jewish father in Figure 8 is clearly registered in the abundance of facial hair, the tip of the hat, and his malevolent gaze. The Christian convert, by contrast, appears quite Anglo, having accepted Christ and joined the mainstream of American culture. It is an icon of Protestant assimilation.

The city remained at mid-century a place best avoided, according to most Evangelical moralists. Frank quoted British poet William Cowper's oft-repeated line in a letter to his sister back home: "God made the country, and man made the town."[7] The fear of the man-made leviathan was stoked in an essay by Rev. W. W. Everts in 1851. Rev. Everts contrasted the city with the country as "a community without homes, made up of the fragments of families, and the association of strangers."[8] The social organization of a city, he contended, "is anti-domestic in leading tendencies," chief among which were "social entertainments and foreign alliances."[9] City life bombarded its inhabitants with an endless battery of sensations and distractions that resulted in a debilitated mental and spiritual state, which led Everts to conclude that "the race always deteriorates in cities."[10] Everts sounded a nineteenth-century commonplace about the danger of urban life: mental disturbance or enervation.[11] The overstimulation of city life stood in stark contrast to the ideal of quiet evoked in

54   PICTURES AND LESSONS.

THE JEW.

Figure 8 "The Jew," from *Pictures and Lessons for Little Readers*. Boston, MA: American Tract Society [ca. 1863], p. 54. Courtesy Billy Graham Center Museum.

religious depictions of prayer and domestic piety, where tranquility, silence, and solitude prevailed. Whether it was the "religion of the closet" or family bible reading, the tone was orderly, subdued, and shut off from the hubbub of the outer world, particularly the city. This was clearly the visual message circulated by tract illustrations and popular lithographs such as the common motif called *Reading the Scriptures* (see Figures 31–34), which was issued by several different lithographers in competition with one another.

Evangelical publishers issued many different depictions of domestic devotion in the decades before Nathaniel Currier and others offered their lithographic versions of the subject. Typically, the American Tract Society attached illustrations of the entire family gathered before the hearth or in a parlor, reading together or listening to the paterfamilias reading scripture. When piety was not set within the home, it was far more likely during the antebellum period to be portrayed as taking place in the countryside, as in the case of a lithograph called *The Happy Family*, which was issued by the American Sunday School Union around mid-century (Figure 9). A family is pictured on Sabbath morning, leaving home for the short trek to worship. The church looms in the distance. The male members of the family hold scripture beneath their arms while the mother and daughters tend to one another. The print taught that the happy family was the rural pious one. But the implication of the image, which the ASSU distributed among its Sabbath school teachers and members, was that piety also yielded happiness, whose principal indices were domestic unity, pastoral calm, neat attire, and clearly limned gender roles. City life meant aggressive commerce and the open indulgence of competitive instincts in the pursuit

THE HAPPY FAMILY.

The happy family are on their way to the place of public worship It is Sunday morning, and with neat attire and cheerful heart they go up to the courts of the Lord.

Figure 9 Augustus Kollner, lithographer, *The Happy Family*, hand-tinted lithograph, for the American Sunday School Union, ca. 1850. Courtesy The Library Company of Philadelphia.

of wealth for its own sake, which both weakened the constitution and propelled it toward the distractions of profane amusement.

In spite of the critique and deep suspicions of urban life, Protestants recognized the importance of the city as a site for mission work and revival and developed an iconography that coexisted with the home and country piety of religious prints. If "man made the city," he could remake it in the image of Christian manhood. A great deal of popular iconography portrays the ideal of this manhood, which should not be confused with a later machismo, but regarded as a mid-century Victorian conception of masculinity that identified young men as an untapped source of Christian spirit. "There is something lovely," Alexander sang of young men,

> in the manly beauty, the health, the robustness, the frankness, fire and heroism, which belong to this stage of life. Who, that is of a generous turn, does not feel his heart glow at the very pressure of a young man's hand?[12]

But it was not a model of hyper-masculinity that Alexander had in mind. When the young Frank Harper returns to the farm to celebrate Thanksgiving with his parents one autumn, he wanted to confide in his father about his spiritual searching, but was unable to muster the courage. Instead, he turned to the parent to whom he owed his principal spiritual formation.

> "I tried to tell father, but I could not; but I *can* tell you mother. I am in trouble about what will become of my soul." Mrs. Harper was overcome with her emotions. She wiped away Frank's tears while shedding many of her own. She advised him, she prayed with him, and before he went away she gave him two or three books and some tracts, and also procured a letter . . . to introduce him to a worthy clergyman.[13]

Appealing directly to his male readers, Alexander warned against a lifestyle of aggressive competitiveness: "There is indeed a vicious love of power, which is properly called ambition; but there is also a sound and virtuous influence which every man ought to desire."[14] Muscular Christianity, a term imported from contemporary Britain, advocated an ideal of Christian manhood that formed boys and young men in sport and Evangelical association, but without the antagonism and resentment for the influence of mothers that later generations of Christian masculinists would voice.

Muscular Christianity was a model for the formation of young men that was designed to secure the transition from country to city life. Its ideal trajectory was visualized in one of the favorite nineteenth-century devices, the before-and-after motif (Figure 10), in an illustration from *The Well-Spring*, a Sunday school newspaper published by the Massachusetts Sabbath School Society of Boston. The left image portrays three friends, named John Hunter, James Jones, and Peter Bird, on their way to Sabbath school in the country. On the right side,

SABBATH SCHOOL.   SABBATH-SCHOOL GRADUATES.

Figure 10 "Sabbath School" and "Sabbath-School Graduates", *The Well-Spring* 19, no. 48
(November 28, 1862). Courtesy Billy Graham Center Museum.

the same three are portrayed as adults, still friends, but now living in a city
and enjoying the stature of well-educated and professionally accomplished
Christian gentlemen as the Rev. John Hunter, Peter Bird, M.D., and James
Jones, Esq. The accompanying article argues that the three (apostolically
named) men owed their professional status as clergyman, doctor, and "wealthy
merchant" to the formation they received in Sabbath school. Led by John, who
went on to become a pastor, the three boys

> forsook the "street school," and, after a few months, became so steady at
> their homes that their parents wondered "what had got into them." The
> word of God had got into them, and was sowing the good seed of piety,
> industry, and virtue in their hearts.[15]

The picture on the left shows the boys as "lads," older than the other children,
but still faithfully attending Sabbath school. Taken together, the two images
present the ideal trajectory of Christian boys, shepherded from youth to manhood and from rural setting to city life by the formative influence of religious
instruction. In contrast to the image of rural piety (see Figure 9), this image
affirms the calling of the professions in the urban world of mid-century America.
The leafy spray of rural elms and the lone steeple of a country church secure the
character of American boys who migrate without trouble to the top hats and

tails of business life in the big city. The article addresses the young reader directly with the image:

> Look at those three Sabbath-school graduates. Don't you think it was a good thing for them that they went to the Sabbath school, stuck to it, and practiced what was taught them, and became Christian men? . . . every boy who sticks to the Sabbath school and practices its precious lessons will graduate into a happy manhood – he will become a good man.[16]

The image seems to illustrate an assertion, which Max Weber might have put to portentous use, by theologian and Hartford preacher Horace Bushnell: "True piety is itself a principle of industry and application to business."[17]

City and country: migration among Blacks and Roman Catholics

The picture of white, Protestant urban men of respectability, grounded in a bucolic image of rural piety, comported with neither the squalid reality of many Roman Catholic immigrants living in the city nor with the condition of African American slaves and poor free Blacks in the South and North. One strategy embraced by Blacks and by white Catholics was migration in the United States to rural regions where they might become landholders. At the National Convention of Colored People in 1847 the committee on agriculture happily reported that Gerrit Smith, a wealthy white lawyer of Petersboro, New York, and strong advocate of abolition, had donated 140,000 acres in the state of New York to 3,000 black citizens, including Frederick Douglass, in order to provide them with the status of landholders and therefore qualify them to vote.[18] The committee's report also presented the argument that since "the cultivation of the soil" was the pursuit in life best adapted to free people from "undue care and anxiety about the necessaries and comforts of life," African Americans should be encouraged to move from cities and take up farming.[19] Moreover, the committee's members contended, "an agricultural life offered independence as well as "moral, mental, and physical culture" and is "peculiarly adapted to, and promotive of scientific pursuits." In addition to intellectual value, life in the country encouraged spiritual refinement: the farmer "sees the order, variety, the beauty, and the wonders of nature, and must be led to look from nature up to nature's God."[20] Most important for the social welfare of Blacks, the agricultural life "tends to equality" since each member of an agricultural community exists on a common level.[21] Gerrit Smith's gift would enable its recipients to

> work for themselves a character and create an influence that shall command the respect for themselves and their brethren, of those who now very little respect us . . . and will exert an influence upon our brethren who have

not shared in those gifts, to turn their attention to and engage in the pursuit of Agricultural life.

The committee's report ended with a series of resolutions, including the following:

> That we recommend to our people, also throughout the country, to forsake the cities and their employments of dependency therein, and emigrate to those parts of the country where land is cheap, and become cultivators of the soil, as the surest road to respectability and influence.[22]

At a moment when debate among black leaders grew increasingly divisive with regard to black separatism and the idea of armed insurrection, on the one hand, and relocating to the black American colony of Liberia, on the other, colonizing rural American farmland must have seemed the most constructive option. If insurrection would have meant "a catastrophe," as Frederick Douglass warned a national conference of black leaders in 1843, colonization of West Africa would have drained free Blacks from America and played into the hands of American slave owners who would welcome the departure of black supporters of abolition.[23] Although African colonization had its advocates among African Americans, most agreed with David Walker when he proclaimed in his "Appeal to the Colored Citizens of the World" (1830): "This country is as much ours as it is the whites."[24] Farming was one way of making that an economic reality. The ideal persisted among African Americans. In 1870 Sojourner Truth delivered a speech on behalf of a project requesting Congress "to set apart for them ['the freed colored people in and about Washington'] a portion of the public land in the West, and erect buildings thereon for the aged and infirm."[25] In 1879 an exodus from the South took place and would continue over the next several decades, though the move for most southern Blacks was to large urban locations in the North such as Chicago and New York.

Although migration and colonization were forced on Native Americans throughout the nineteenth century, it was willingly pursued by some Blacks, Jews, and Catholics as a viable alternative to prejudice and discrimination and the threat of conversion for some in eastern cities. Fearing the rise of anti-Semitism in eastern metropolitan regions where many Jewish immigrants were settling in the final decades of the century, Jews established settlement places as far from New York as South Dakota, Oregon, and Louisiana, where tilling the soil became an ideal that Zionists were just beginning to raise as the focus for a return to the ancient homeland.[26] Much larger rural migration was undertaken by Catholic leaders. Arriving in growing numbers from the 1840s, Roman Catholics from Ireland tended strongly to gather in large cities like Boston, New York, and Chicago, or in industrial centers associated with shipping, coal mining, and manufacturing across the northeast and the Great Lakes region. Leaving behind deplorable poverty in Ireland, the Irish often found the poverty of urban America less difficult because of higher wages and greater availability of food and the diversions of city life. Moreover, prejudices against the Irish were so intense that living in urban enclaves where employment was possible tended to concentrate Irish immigrants in larger cities. In 1843, German Catholics in Philadelphia and Baltimore formed the German Catholic Brotherhood to plan emigrating west in order to escape Protestant opposition. The organization bought land in rural Pennsylvania, where over sixty families settled.[27]

Other plans at the time were discussed for Catholic settlements in Wisconsin, which were supported by Bishop John Hughes of New York. But when a number of laity, priests, and Western prelates gathered in Buffalo in 1856 to propose plans for sponsoring interior emigration of Irish from eastern cities to Iowa and Nebraska, where a colony named St. Patrick was to be formed, Hughes, now Archbishop of New York, opposed the idea and became a critic of Catholic colonization in general.[28] Hughes' public and private statements on colonization reveal a variety of reasons for his opposition. He asserted that emigration would remove people from their churches, creating spiritual danger, even though colonizers proposed the formation of churches and the placement of priests in settlements. Moreover, proponents of colonization insisted from the beginning of the movement that it was the cities that most endangered the Irish immigrant in America. Hughes disparaged the "search of the el dorado of independent agricultural life, where every man might repose under his own vine and fig-tree" and worried that colonization would lead to eastern, northeastern, and northwestern dioceses being emptied of parishioners, resulting in "hardly Catholics enough left to keep the grass from growing green in the vestibules of the churches."[29]

Many Western prelates disagreed with Archbishop Hughes. The most outspoken advocate of Irish colonization was John Lancaster Spalding, Bishop (later Archbishop) of Peoria, who issued a passionately and closely argued manifesto on behalf of colonization and the Irish in 1880.[30] Hughes worried about concentrating the Irish in settlements beyond firm clerical control and appears to have deeply resented lay Irish activists at work among the immigrant population in the United States. This probably explains Spalding's characterization of Hughes' opposition to colonization as "a disregard of his episcopal authority."[31] Spalding entertained no such fears. He regarded the Irish as God's Chosen, repeatedly portraying them as a new Israel. Persecuted and bitterly oppressed by an unfeeling English Parliament, the Irish had suffered enslavement but found exodus to the Promised Land of America. In the early Middle Ages, the Irish had served European Christendom as the ark that preserved the remnant amidst the flood of paganism, then rebirthed the church by an extensive mission campaign from the emerald island.[32] Likewise, the Irish were the ark carrying the Catholic Church to the New World in nineteenth-century America, where their special mission, according to Spalding, was to resist the secularizing effects of modern life. English Protestantism had destroyed the church in England, but the Irish had achieved a rebirth of Catholicism "amongst the English-speaking peoples" and were therefore "the providential instrument through which God has wrought this marvelous revival."[33] In a meeting in Chicago in 1879, the colonization movement among American Catholics succeeded in creating the Irish Catholic Colonization Association of the United States, which operated as a stockholding company that promptly purchased land in Nebraska and Minnesota for resale to Irish Catholics. Spalding became the founding president of the Association. The appraisal of country life over the city would persist among Catholic leaders for the next several decades.[34]

Not only did the move to rural America promote the moral superiority of country over city, and include Catholics in the settlement of the great continental interior, but it also conveyed a spiritual and aesthetic attitude shared by many Americans. The land was deliverance, a kind of redemption – the place where God reveals himself in beauty to bless the faithful with a share of the nation's bounty. In 1905 Spalding published a paean to religion and art, a long essay that praised the experience of beauty in the rural landscape in the spiritualizing tones of high Romanticism.[35] Spalding asserted that art and religion were allied in the mission to recognize "the infinite peering through the finite, the heavenly reposing in an earthly bosom."[36] Catholic churches were, therefore, not only "temples of the living God," but also "the sanctuaries of art, which points heavenward." He presented Roman Catholicism as the true Christian Church, the historical repository of the spirit and authority of God on earth, and regarded the arts and artists as ministers of the church. Catholicism performed the redemptive historical task of rescuing the arts from pagan antiquity and ushering them into the modern world. Although "the Hebraizing spirit of the Reformation weakened" the love of artistic perfection practiced by the Catholic tradition, it was not able to destroy it. The sense of beauty was alive and well in the church of the present day. Since Spalding believed that Protestantism in America was in the process of dying, beauty in the arts would serve the church there as yet another powerful means of bringing true Christianity to the nation and the English-speaking Protestant world.

If he was prepared to recognize the American separation of church and state that Pius IX had condemned in his *Syllabus of Errors* (1864), Spalding nevertheless endorsed the spirituality of Ultramontane piety by stressing the aesthetic ideal of Marian devotion. In addition to the pastoral beauty of the landscape from which he drew inspiration, Spalding praised painting as the art that bore the influence of the church more than any other. He singled out images of Christ and the Madonna as "the most exalted ideals" and he expatiated on Mary as the shrine of homely and maternal values that Protestants, as we shall see in Chapter 4, associated with mother and the hearth:

> We cannot think of Mary but religion melts into poetry; and the thousand heavenly thoughts and heavenly sentiments which in Christian lands and

Christian hearts center in the hallowed names of mother, sister, wife –
highest names of love, beauty, and truth – owe their sweetness and their
power to her influence.[37]

For Spalding the reinvigoration of traditional piety set within and inspired by
the beauty of life in the countryside was the aim of Catholic colonization. The
spiritual renewal that would issue from the realization of this aim was the mission of the Irish and the Catholic Church in America. His endorsement of the
rural ethos combined with his advocacy of Catholic higher education (he was a
main force behind the founding of the Catholic University of America in 1888),
and his aestheticization of Marian piety. As devotion to Mary swelled in the
popular response to Marian apparitions, Spalding advocated a highly refined,
artistic view of her. The Marian imagery that he singled out for praise was the
fine art of Giotto, Fra Angelico, Lippo Lippi, and Guido Reni – masters of Italian
painting from the fourteenth to the sixteenth centuries.[38] Popular purveyors of
artistic beauty such as the Benziger Brothers, a Swiss firm with several offices in
major American cities, specialized in church ornaments during this period. What
Spalding would have thought of such imagery is difficult to say, but in 1888
Benziger Brothers, which had already been official printers to the Apostolic See,
acquired the coveted imprimatur of "Pontifical Institute of Church Art," official
acknowledgment by the Vatican as a producer of sacred imagery. As a page
from the company's 1881 catalogue indicates (Figure 11), a range of Marian
imagery was available, including Our Lady of Lourdes.[39] The statuary shown
ranged in size from three to nearly seven feet in height and was cast in zinc,
which was suitable for exterior display on church grounds and in cemeteries.
    The Marian connection with the American Church had been formally
declared in 1846 when the Sixth Provincial Council of Baltimore had made the
Immaculate Conception the patronal feast of the United States. Irish Catholics
were fond of Our Lady of Knock, who appeared in 1879 (see Figure 21, p. 78).
But the image of Mary that attracted the most attention among lay Catholics
in Spalding's day was Our Lady of Lourdes, who appeared repeatedly to the
teenage girl named Bernadette Soubirous in 1858 at the village of Lourdes in
southwestern France. Visual responses to her devotion vary considerably – from
the fine art statuary produced by Benziger Brothers to a range of grottoes. The
latter were popular in the Midwest, where they corresponded strongly to the
rural ideal that also comported with the living tradition of Marian apparitions.
Pope Leo XIII had a Lourdes grotto built in the Vatican Gardens. Father Edwin
Sorin dedicated a copy of the grotto to Our Lady of Lourdes on the campus of
the University of Notre Dame, just outside of Southbend, Indiana, which he
founded in 1865. Numerous grottoes appeared throughout Midwestern states,
built by immigrant Catholic clergy such as Father Paul Matthias Dobberstein, a
Franciscan priest who emigrated from Germany in 1892 and produced grottoes
or shrines at seven sites in Iowa, Wisconsin, and South Dakota, dedicating those
in Riverside and Carroll, Iowa, to Our Lady of Lourdes and to the Immaculate

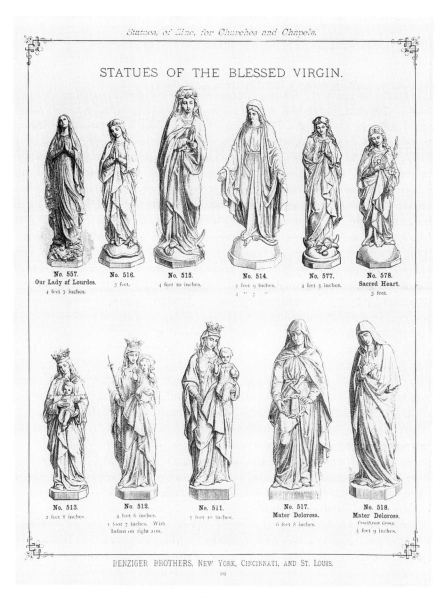

Figure 11 "Statues of the Blessed Virgin," *Benziger Brothers Catalogue of Church Ornaments, Vestments, Material for Vestments, Regalia*, 1881. Courtesy of The Winterthur Library: Printed Book and Periodical Collection.

Conception. Perhaps the most extensive was the Grotto of the Redemption in West Bend, Iowa (Figure 12), which Dobberstein began planning in 1901, began constructing in 1912, and left uncompleted when he died in 1954.[40]

Slavery, anti-slavery, and black activism

Faced with ever expanding groups of Catholic immigrants, most of whom voted with the Democratic Party, and, after the Civil War, with the prospect of American Blacks in the South doing likewise, northern Protestants who belonged to the Whig and then Republican parties considered growth key to the success of religious revival and the millennial future that defined the mission of the nation. In order to achieve the order of growth necessary, advocates of systematic benevolence like James Alexander believed that the church needed to adapt its means, which meant endorsing the non-sectarian ideal of Evangelical associations committed to influencing mass audiences through print. The emphasis placed on "union" by Evangelical benevolent societies such as the American Tract Society, Bible Society, and Sunday School Union during the nineteenth century was intended to negotiate the sectarian boundaries separating the large number of Protestant denominations. On the whole, it worked, in spite of the many, perhaps inevitable squabbles over doctrine that intermittently arose – or at least until the benevolent organizations ran into the obdurate issue of slavery, which tore the Tract Society asunder and pitched the ASSU into controversy. Only the American Bible Society, which had from its inception pledged itself to bible publication "without note or commentary," avoided the rending pressures of slavery and abolition. Although they differed dramatically in how they interpreted scripture, some starkly in favor of slavery, others staunchly against it, American Protestants uniformly agreed that the bible needed to be inexpensively published and universally distributed. The union achieved among white Evangelicals in the North and South enabled a system of print production and distribution that was an essential part of a national campaign dedicated to realizing the millennial mission of the nation as God's chosen Christian republic.

This Christian Republic was avowedly white, Protestant, and paternalistic. As far as African Americans were concerned, this meant supporting a Christian practice of slavery and pursuing a policy of the colonization of Africa. In his private letters, Alexander was forthright about matters of race and faith. Faced with the growing numbers of European immigrants in America, Alexander exulted in a letter of June 1840: "What a blessing it is to belong to the Teutonic race! The more I see of the black-eyed races of the South of Europe, the less I respect them. Next to Britain I would live in Prussia." A week later he wrote the same correspondent, John Hall, close friend and agent for the ASSU: "My mind has run very much lately on colonization (in general) as God's means of civilizing and Christianizing the world, and on the part which the Anglo-Saxon race is taking."[41]

Figure 12 Father Paul Matthias Dobberstein, Nativity scene, Grotto of the Redemption, West Bend, Iowa. Photo courtesy of Phillip Morgan.

Evangelical union was a network measured by growth that was keyed to the traffic or circulation of print, which was understood by many in America as an Anglo-Saxon means of influence. Print was the medium of a believer's aware-ness of the church's properly international body, which would consist of many races and ethnicities, though its spark and agency were white. James Alexander complained of black Methodists at Princeton who practiced exorcism, or what he called "orgies," resulting in a significant loss of numbers from the black congregation in which he was preacher.[42] The Protestantism of print was a religion promoting a mode of order that did not conform to the orality of popular black religion. The ideology of print, as already noted, relied on union to avoid or at least to ignore as long as possible the looming rift over slavery. Alexander, like many Presbyterians and Protestants in the North, believed that slavery would eventually fall away, but he expressed strong opposition to abolition and defended slaveholders when he visited Virginia in 1842:

> I am more and more convinced of the injustice we do the slaveholders. Of their feelings toward their negroes I can form a better notion than formerly, by examining my own towards the slaves who wait on my wife and mind my children. It is a feeling most like that we have to near relations.

And a few days later: "They are, under ordinary masters, a happy people."[43] This was certainly the picture that the ATS circulated in its few portrayals of slaves in tract literature. Figure 13 shows a docile, deferential slave on a tract cover published in 1825, who is paired with a genteel British visitor to an American plantation where he makes a point to inquire of the slave "whether his state of slavery was not disagreeable to him, and whether he would not gladly exchange it for his liberty." Anti-abolitionists must have been reassured to learn that the slave wanted nothing of the sort: "Massa," he addressed the gentleman, "I have a wife and children; my Massa take care of them, and I have no care to provide anything; I have a good Massa who teach me to read; and I read good book that makes me happy."[44] In fact, in some southern states it was illegal to teach slaves to read. But the idea of slaves reading the bible was for many northern Evangelicals the only balm they required in their Gilead.

It is no surprise, therefore, that, like many of his caste, Alexander came to accept the theological position advocated by many southern Presbyterian clergy in defense of slavery. In a reference to Onesimus, the slave mentioned by Paul in his epistle to Philemon, one of the hotly debated New Testament texts on slavery since it was often invoked in southern pulpits in the defense of slavery, Alexander wrote:

> I see no proof that Onesimus ever ran away, in the technical sense, at all. I can go a peg higher than you about slavery, and fail to see the scripturalness

NO. 7.

THE HAPPY NEGRO.

By the late Ambrose Serle, Esq. England.

Figure 13 Ambrose Serle, Esq., "The Happy Negro," no. 7. New York: American Tract Society, 1825. Photo author.

of much that is postulated nowadays, respecting the popular idol, liberty. As existing, slavery is fraught with moral evil; the want of marriage, and of the Bible, and the separation of families, etc., etc., are crying sins; but I am totally unable to see the relation to be necessarily unjust.

Though he regarded "slavery as a transition-state," Alexander considered that "immediate emancipation would be a crime."[45] Rather than pursue the emancipation of slaves, Alexander encouraged their conversion to Christianity. "I am more and more of opinion," he wrote in 1846,

that the great Missionary work of America should be among the two races which we have most injured, viz., the black and the red. I have misgivings whenever we send men to Northern India (British ground) and neglect the perfectly open field among our Indians.[46]

In view of the fact that Alexander had been elected to the Executive Committee of the American Tract Society a year before penning those lines, it seems clear that the ATS was installing clergy in leadership positions whose view of slavery would support the policy of the organization to avoid confrontation over the issue. The emphasis that the ATS had from its beginning placed on union became in the course of events an implicit statement on race. The gradualism regarding slavery and the ascendancy of Protestant union around the agency of print was proclaimed in a lithograph by Thomas Sinclair of 1845 entitled *Christian Union* (Figure 14), in which a number of Protestant clergy – Episcopalian, Congregationalist, Presbyterian, and Quaker – gather about an altar holding the bible. Irradiated by the descending dove of the Holy Spirit, the scene is blessed by the millennial peace of the lion and the lamb. The eschatological union of Evangelical Protestants is accompanied by a Native American who drops his weapons and an African man who hearkens to the heavenly epiphany. Union meant the assembly of right-thinking Protestants about the biblical text and the conversion of Indians and Blacks. The lithograph endorsed

Figure 14 Thomas S. Sinclair, *Christian Union*, 1845. T. Sinclair Lithography, Philadelphia. Courtesy Library of Congress.

religion as the instrument of real liberation rather than presenting religion as a spur toward a policy of emancipation. Viewing slavery as transitional allowed northern Evangelicals to support the practice of slavery while urging the evangelization of slaves. It was a policy of tacit accommodation that enraged the proponents of abolition among ATS membership and led in 1858 to the secession of a large number in New England, who founded the rival Boston American Tract Society. *Atlantic Monthly* commented on the split by excoriating the intransigence of the Society, claiming that the organization's founders would be appalled to know that their descendants

> would hold their peace about the body of Cuffee dancing to the music of the cart-whip, provided only they could save the soul of Sambo alive by presenting him a pamphlet, which he could not read, on the depravity of the double-shuffle.[47]

Advocates of abolition in the northeast, centered in Boston, scolded the ATS for failing to print tracts and to edit existing titles to address the injustice of slavery. The ATS refrained from doing so in order to avoid a breach with the many Protestants in the North and South who opposed abolition. The controversy heated up over the course of the 1840s and 1850s and finally erupted in a secession of abolitionists, who set immediately to publishing and distributing tracts that objected to slavery as sinful and unacceptable to Evangelical Christians. The Boston ATS included illustrations in its tracts against slavery, such as *Pictures and Lessons*, which was issued in the midst of the war when the New York ATS was still avoiding the topic of slavery in its publications. A series of pictures and brief descriptive texts aimed at young readers, the booklet clearly draws on the sentimental condescension of pious white children to black slaves made famous by the illustration of Eva reading the bible to Uncle Tom in Harriet Beecher Stowe's *Uncle Tom's Cabin*. "Many little girls can now read who would never have learned but for the war against the Rebels," the booklet assured its readers.[48]

Abolitionist publications had included illustrations as early as the mid-1830s, in which the portrayal of slaves was charged with cues of stark racial differentiation, contrasting corpulent white slave owners with desperate victims of enslavement.[49] Anti-slavery groups intended their publications to be incendiary and antagonistic, on the assumption that drawing brutal contrasts between inhuman slave owners and the slaves they mistreated would generate indignation among white viewers. The Boston ATS visualized its abolitionist cause by borrowing several illustrations from the 1853 edition of Harriet Beecher Stowe's *Uncle Tom's Cabin*, a book which had remained a national lightning rod for opposition to slavery from the time of its appearance in 1852.[50] An illustration from *The Child's Antislavery Book*, issued by the Boston ATS in 1859 (Figure 15), shows a slave lashed to a post and mercilessly beaten by two other black men under the cruel direction of an angry overseer. Although the book does not

WHIPPING A SLAVE.

Figure 15 "Whipping a slave," *The Child's Antislavery Book*. Boston, MA: American Tract Society, 1859. Courtesy The Library Company of Philadelphia.

identify the situation, most northern readers would probably have recognized it as the heart-rending scene from Chapter 40 of *Uncle Tom's Cabin*, when the sadistic Simon Legree directs the slaves Sambo and Quimbo to scourge Tom. An ethereal Christ figure appears before the beaten man, who looks in quiet agony to the white savior who had likewise suffered scourging at the column in his Passion. Stowe not only intermingled the suffering of Tom and Jesus in her narrative, but also paralleled those who stood by watching Jesus tortured and executed with those in her own day who likewise inertly witnessed the passion of slaves: "O my country! These things are done under the shadow of thy laws! O Christ! Thy church sees them, almost in silence!"[51] Stowe indicts viewers who look upon the scene and would remain impassive. The illustration underscores the martyr death of Tom while evoking pity and even shame. The luminous Jesus does not intervene, but seems to bless Tom's suffering with a gesture of benediction that meekly counters the clenched fist of Legree. This manner of addressing the scourged man recalls ancient portrayals of the death of martyrs at the hands of the Roman state. The *Martyrdom of Polycarp*, composed in the mid-second century, hailed the solemn end of martyrs in terms that recall Figure 15. These heroes of the faith

> displayed such nobility that none of them either grumbled or moaned, clearly showing us all that in that hour, while under torture, the martyrs of Christ had journeyed far away from the flesh, or rather, that the Lord was standing by, speaking to them.[52]

The message of Stowe's scene, displayed and circulated by the illustration, urged white Americans to regard indifference to slavery as synonymous with pagan Rome's persecution of Christians.

But black activists in the North did not welcome the portrayal of brethren in the South in terms that were calculated to encourage white pity or sympathy. In an early tract entitled "A Dialogue between a Virginian and an African Minister" (1810), the black minister Daniel Coker inverted the traditional relation of deferential Black and superior White.[53] A Virginian slaveholder presents himself respectfully before the minister to debate slavery on historical, legal, and theological grounds, but is defeated at every turn and repeatedly accedes to the superior arguments of the clergyman. The biblical interpretations in favor of slavery that Rev. James Alexander encountered and accepted during his visit to Virginia were successively refuted by Coker's persona who blithely demonstrates the Virginian's biblical illiteracy. When the slave owner argues that emancipation of slaves is imprudent because their vices preclude their being "useful members of civil society," Coker's spokesman subverts the assertion in Socratic manner, introducing what was to become a key point in black and abolitionist discourse. "You have very justly observed," he replies, "that holding these men in slavery is the cause of their plunging into such vicious habits as lying, pilfering, and stealing; then I say, remove the cause, that the effects may cease."[54]

Coker and other black activists argued that Blacks were not by nature inferior to Whites, but suffered moral degradation in the grip of enslavement. Nurture, not nature, was the cause of vice. The intellectual inferiority of the white Virginian slaveholder to the black clergyman in the dialogue only underscored the point. More than equal to the white man, the minister was his superior in reason. The message was a powerful one for African Americans. In an open address to the people of the United States, Frederick Douglass asserted in 1853 that the aim of black opponents of slavery "is not to excite pity for ourselves, but to command respect for our cause, and to obtain justice for our people."[55] In his autobiography, Douglass acknowledged the importance of another dialogue between a master and a slave, which he found in *The Columbian Orator*. In that dialogue, not unlike Coker's, the tables are turned when the slave is able to convince his master by skillful discourse and gain his freedom.[56] In each case, the strategy was not to concede intrinsic inferiority, but to assert that unjust oppression could be overcome by the exercise of the slave's inherent abilities activated by learning. In its report to the National Convention of Colored

People in 1847, the committee on a national press insisted that "we must command something manlier than sympathies. We must command the respect and admiration due men, who, against fearful odds, are struggling steadfastly for their rights. This can be done through a Press of our own."[57] The committee's report urged the establishment of a national press wholly owned and operated by Blacks "because a printing press is the vehicle of thought – is a ruler of opinions." The press would enable the cause of education, which was considered "the most powerful means of our advancement."[58] Control over the means of print production would remove Blacks from the unwelcome position in which they were placed by white philanthropy, that is, the object of condescending pity that reinforced their subaltern status. Black educator and missionary Mary Still urged women members of the African Methodist Episcopal Church to persist in "the cause of the moral and mental improvement of our race." In explaining how to accomplish that aim, Still echoed the conceit of the printing press as Christ delivering his sermon on the mount, which had been employed in the image of the Tract Society printing press (see Figure 3, p. 13): "by establishing our press on the hill of science and literature that thousands may yet see the rays of living light emanating from its influence and words of everlasting truth to those who sit in darkness."[59]

For Thomas Morris Chester the matter was best articulated as a matter of "Negro Self-Respect and Pride of Race," the title of an address he made at the Philadelphia Library Company in 1862. Chester was keenly aware of the influence of print and imagery as propaganda that influenced black self-consciousness. He advised African Americans to replace the plethora of white images in their homes with black counterparts. "Remove as far as practicable, from all observation and association, every influence which tends to weaken your self-respect," he told his audience and readers.[60]

> Take down from your walls the pictures of Washington, Jackson, and McClellan; and if you love to gaze upon military chieftains, let the gilded frames be graced with the immortal Toussaint. . . . Remove from the eyes of the rising generation the portraits of Clay, Webster, and Seward, and if superior intellects present any attractions, hang in the most conspicuous place the great Ward, the unrivalled Douglass, and the wise Roberts. . . . Tear down the large paintings in which only white faces are represented, and beautify your walls with scenes and landscapes connected with our history, which shall win our praise and inspire our admiration. . . . If you wish bishops to adorn your parlors, there are the practical Allen, the pathetic Payne, the logical Burns and the eloquent Clinton.[61]

Chester's strategy was to replace the visual presence of white heroes in every facet or department of life with black figures, a form of cultural intervention whose first step was iconoclasm, but only as a means of removing the negative influence of white paradigms that enforced the black community's sense of inferiority. Chester endorsed a censorship that would "commit to the flames all of your books which ignore our superiority" and he urged Blacks not to allow their children to read any literature before they were "deeply imbued with an unwavering confidence of self-respect and an exalted pride of race." His concern over the nefarious effects of print and imagery extended to Christianity's most prized instrument, the bible. "I am confident," he humorously chided the Whites among the audience,

> that God and his winged seraphs are black, while the Devil and his howling imps are white ... The Italians have very properly represented his satanic majesty as white. Now when you want a scene from the Bible, and this cloven-footed personage is painted black, say to the vendor, that your conscientious scruples will not permit you to support so gross a misrepresentation, and when the Creator and his angels are represented as white, tell him that you would be guilty of sacrilege, in encouraging the circulation of a libel upon the legions of Heaven.[62]

On the occasion of the nation's centennial, which occurred in the sixtieth year of the African Methodist Episcopal (AME) Church's existence, the church issued a commemorative print (Figure 16) that declaimed a visual rhetoric of venerability. The print hailed its first eleven bishops, two of whom Chester named and commended for visual display: the founding bishop Richard Allen (center) and Daniel Payne, sixth bishop (to the right of Allen). The other images in the print convey the priority placed by the church's leadership on education, literacy, and cultural institutions. Wilberforce University (upper left), founded by Payne in 1856, was the first black college in the United States. Each of the bishops is pictured in the manner of honorary portraiture, the esteemed personages of cultural and stately achievement. As black literati and men of ministerial stature, the bishops were the very icons of respectability that Chester enjoined American Blacks to display in their homes for the purpose of encouraging black self-respect and shaping youth. It is difficult to imagine portrayals of Blacks that contrasted more strongly to those intended to instill pity and sympathy such as Figure 15. Images of Bishop Allen from the early decades of the century had commonly stressed his intellectual stature by picturing him with a bible or other book. The author and clergy portrait contrasted strongly with the "darky" scenes issued by Currier & Ives, portraying racist stereotypes of African Americans.[63]

In his remarkable address, Chester identified a new (and visual) culture war that would continue to engage African Americans for some time to come. Two visual tactics tended to dominate the use of images among black activists and church leaders. Portraiture like the commemorative print of AME bishops was broadly used to herald and celebrate black respectability. In the published proceedings of a major AME conference in South Carolina in 1889, for example, there appeared seventy-two biographical sketches of elders, clergy, church officers, seminary faculty, judges, and legislators, most of which were

Figure 16 Bishops of the African Methodist Episcopal Church, commemorative print, 1876. Printed by J. H. Daniels, Boston, MA. Courtesy American Antiquarian Society.

accompanied by wood engravings taken from daguerreotypes.[64] The second visual tactic is evident in the frontispiece published in the volume (Figure 17). The frontispiece pictures an African-American preacher holding a bible and pointing to the celestial revelation of the Cross, which emits the words, "Lo! I am the way." The heavenly voice replies to the question inscribed on parchment held by a Chinese man: "Which way to GOD?" The preacher stands before a line of immigrant figures – Asians and an African man – and two seated figures: a Native American and notably a Caucasian figure, who is lowest and placed at the feet of the erect preacher, who towers above all. The African-American preacher replaces the white Protestant figure in antebellum evangelist imagery to undertake the Christianization and Americanization of Asian as well as African immigrants (see Figure 2, p. 12).[65] The image and its caption boldly assert that assimilation is now the instrument of American Blacks. The special mission of the AME Church "to the darker races," the caption proclaims, is literacy, love, and labor.

Issued in the year of the nation's centenary anniversary, Figure 16 represents the AME Church's aim to challenge racial formulations of American national identity. If the antebellum white portrayal of national mission was to identify a

The Special Mission of the A. M. E. Church to the Darker Races is to

" Teach the Mind to Think, the Heart to Love, the Hand to Work."

Figure 17 Frontispiece, *Proceedings of the Quarto-Centennial Conference of the African M. E. Church, of South Carolina*, at Charleston, SC, May 15, 16, and 17, 1889, ed. Bishop Benjamin W. Arnett, D.D., presiding bishop of the States of South Carolina and Florida. 1890. Courtesy The Library Company of Philadelphia.

union of Protestant churches committed to proselytism, the AME illustration endows African-American churches, preachers, and evangelists with the same task of assimilating racial others to a mainstream American Christianity in what appears an apocalyptic age ushered in by lightning and stormy clouds. Although the AME Church focused its efforts on African Americans, developing cultural institutions such as schools, colleges, and seminaries to promote literacy and advanced education, the image signals that clergy had transcended the prevailing white perception that Blacks were among those who needed to be evangelized in order to be properly Americanized.

Print and the polemical image

For its cultured despisers, Evangelical print did not emit an aura, but rather a cloud of fraud, vanity, and mystification. Some of the benevolent societies that

Protestants conceived and operated for the purpose of moral and social reform during the antebellum period attracted public criticism because of alleged political agendas. Presbyterian activist Arthur Tappan, the wealthy New York businessman who ruled over a dry goods empire before he lost everything in the economic crisis of 1837, was a strong promoter of Christian reform causes including the American Tract Society. In 1831 he served as the founding president of the New York Magdalen Society, a philanthropic organization dedicated to the Evangelical reform of the city's prostitutes. The Society's executive committee gathered many of New York's leading Whigs and conservative Protestants. Its first annual report drew the ire of an anonymously published pamphlet entitled *Orthodox Bubbles, or A Review of the First Annual Report of the Executive Committee of the New York Magdalen Society*. The author(s) of the *Review* took great offense at the Magdalen Society's methods as well as what was considered its underlying aim. The Society had established an "asylum" for women released from Bellevue, the female penitentiary of New York City, where it had established a Sabbath school to attract inmates to the study of Christianity. The Society also created a Sabbath school in the city's notorious neighborhood of impoverished residents, Five Points, where members of the Society visited brothels in order to distribute tracts and bibles to prostitutes.[66] The *Review* took exception to this method, asking if the aim was to reform morals and prevent prostitution,

> why not, instead of prayers, bibles, and tracts, afford them the means of an honest living by an honest employment? This would do more towards a real reformation than all the prayers, bibles and tracts, which they can bestow upon them.[67]

Neither pious print nor "all the hell-fire and brimstone that ever were preached, or ever will be" would ever enact lasting reform. The implication was that Tappan and his colleagues were interested not in the economic welfare of the women, but in converting them to "orthodoxy," by which the *Review* meant the conservative Calvinism of the Whig party, which was committed to overturning the civil liberties ensured by the separation of church and state. For the *Review*, it was "plain enough that this Institution is to be an auxiliary to the 'Church and State' party. To make the remedy worse than the disease."[68]

The *Review* provocatively summarized its bold assertions in a visual parody called "An Anxious or Enquiring Meeting" (Figure 18), which pictures Ezra Stiles Ely, Presbyterian clergyman and chaplain at New York City hospital. During his time as chaplain, Ely had kept a journal, which he later published in two volumes under the title *Visits of Mercy*, in which he had first called for the establishment of a "Magdalen Hospital," an asylum for the permanent placement of young women whom no foster family would receive.[69] Two others caricatured in the print are Arthur Tappan and George Strong, who was alderman of New York City's sixth ward, which contained Five Points.[70] The

Figure 18 "An Anxious or Enquiring Meeting," *Orthodox Bubbles, or A Review of the First Annual Report of the Executive Committee of the New York Magdalen Society.* Boston, MA: printed for the publishers, 1831. Courtesy The Library Company of Philadelphia.

Evangelical or "orthodox" party is lampooned in the compromising situation of seducing the prostitutes whom their society proclaimed to want to convert. Tappan appears as a smiling dolt carrying tracts (in 1829, Tappan had proposed the universal distribution of tracts in New York City). The entire scene is organized in a manner that recalls Dr. Benjamin Rush's "moral thermometer," which was designed to measure the increments of spiritual awakening and spiritual torpor.[71] But in Figure 18 the range, registered in gradations marked by letters spelling "orthodoxy," from "pious" to "passions" with the names of eminent

Evangelical Whigs appearing as intermediate grades. The image also recalls political cartoons of the day, which could be caustically partisan and dedicated to character assassination. The dialogue attending the cartoon of the Anxious Meeting (the Evangelical term for a gathering to provoke spiritual introspection) lampoons Tappan, his associates, and their Society, and also takes broad swipes at Sunday schools, Princeton Seminary, and the use of tracts in public schools as well as Sunday schools.[72]

As the critique of the Magdalen Society continues in the pages of the *Review*, it becomes clear that the attack had conservative Christianity in its sights. The text invoked Jefferson against the "hierophants of our particular superstition" and delivered the judgment that eighteen hundred years of Christianity had failed to rectify the wrongs of human society.[73] "Religion," the author(s) put it directly, "is insufficient to produce virtue; nay, even to save from the extreme of vice." Even Jefferson would not have made that claim, but it was directed at the raison d'être of the Evangelical benevolent societies, which understood philanthropy in terms of evangelization. Any attempt to install religion in public life, it would appear, is unwelcome and morally unwarranted. Tappan's party of "Orthodoxy," engaged in a bounding network of print and national initiatives, was targeted as preeminently menacing because it represented the national project of Evangelical benevolence. Most important, the *Review* argued, it was a project dedicated to erasing the Constitution's separation of church and state. The opposition of "orthodoxy" and free thinking suggests that the source of the *Review* may have been the editors of *The Free Enquirer*, a journal produced by Utopian reformers and freethinkers Fanny Wright and Robert Dale Owen. *The Free Enquirer* was a vocal opponent of city missions such as those conducted by Presbyterians, whom Wright and Owen considered their enemies in the battle for civil liberties.[74]

Freethinkers were not the only group that resisted the print efforts of proselytizing Protestants. In January of 1836 Rabbi Isaac Leeser responded with a courteous but decisive open letter to the American Tract Society the day after a tract distributor stood at the door of the synagogue of Philadelphia's congregation Mikveh Israel and handed out "copies of a tract, of a controversial nature, and contravening the tenets which we profess, to ladies, gentlemen and even children." In a rhetorical marvel of velvet-clad force, Rabbi Leeser stated that it was his "duty to warn you against a repetition of a similar kindness," observing that another such visit would likely "be received rather unkindly" and that he "could not answer for the forbearance of the zealous ones amongst us, who might perhaps be induced in their honest indignation, to eject an impertinent intermeddler, mildly if they can, forcibly if they must."[75]

Sparks between Evangelicals and freethinkers or Jews paled in comparison to Protestant–Catholic culture wars, which began in the 1830s and lasted into the twentieth century. For Nativist American Protestants there were two dangers facing the nation, both of which originated in Europe – the infidelity of revolutionary thinkers like Paine and Voltaire, on the one hand, and, on the other, the invading hordes of Catholics swearing allegiance to the Pope, a foreign ruler who opposed republicanism and democracy and regarded Protestantism as a renegade heresy that must be overcome. American Protestants who believed Catholicism represented a grave threat to the republic were encouraged by tracts, printed sermons, polemical treatises, putative exposés such as *The Awful Disclosures of Maria Monk* (1835), and by a variety of engravings and woodcuts that circulated in books, newspapers, and magazines.[76] At first many Catholic leaders counseled a response of silence for fear that engaging in full polemical challenges might make matters even worse. Violent riots did break out in Philadelphia in 1844, resulting in thirteen deaths and the burning of two Catholic churches. Among those responsible for the riots were members of the American Protestant Association, which had formed two years earlier when nearly one hundred Protestant clergy from a dozen denominations gathered in response to a petition of Francis Kendrick, the Bishop of Philadelphia, to the Philadelphia Board of Education. The bishop objected to Catholic students in the public schools being exposed to the reading of the King James Version of the bible and to their presence at devotional exercises such as hymn-singing and prayer in the schools.[77] It was during this period of conflict that Bishop John Hughes of New York emerged as an outspoken controversialist.

Conflict between Catholics and Protestants was most frequently keyed to Protestant fears about Catholic influence and to Catholic fears of the reverse. There were real ideological differences between American democracy and the political sensibilities of the Vatican. In 1832, the second year of his pontificate, Gregory XVI issued an encyclical that castigated political liberalism as it was grounded in liberty of conscience, freedom of speech, and a free press.[78] Gregory and his successor, Pius IX, sought to resist the steady and sometimes violently dramatic losses of the papacy in the face of republican revolutions in Italy and Europe. In 1864 Pius issued the encyclical *Quanta Cura*, which was accompanied by the *Syllabus of Errors*. He affirmed Gregory's position against liberalism's proclamation that the liberty of conscience and worship were the inalienable rights of everyone.[79] Protestantism, freedom of worship, and the need for the Roman pontiff to reconcile himself to such modern errors as "progress, liberalism, and modern civilization" were all condemned in *Quanta Cura*.[80] Even closer to the situation in the United States, the *Syllabus* denounced the view that the governance of public schools should be ascribed entirely to civil powers (Error 45) and the claim that church and state should be separated from one another (Error 55). But American Catholic priests never commanded the seditious influence or intent that Protestant Nativists feared they did. Indeed, many charted a much more accommodationist course. But the most important flashpoint was the conflict regarding religion and public education in the United States.[81] From the perspective of Protestant Nativists who felt under siege by Catholic petitions for state funding of Catholic schools or for the removal of the King James bible from classrooms and the proscription of devotional exercises in the public schools, the conflict represented a struggle for the Christian (Protestant) republic of America.

Harper's Weekly was a primary organ for voicing Protestant and Republican Party fears and provoking opposition to litigation on behalf of Catholic plaintiffs and school boards that supported the secularization of the public schools. Thomas Nast produced a number of memorable (and vicious) illustrations for the magazine that portrayed Catholic clergy and the Irish in very negative, even racist terms (Figure 19). Nast contributed incendiary images to *Harper's* during the widely watched court case in Cincinnati in 1870, when a group of parents

AUGUST 17, 1872.]   HARPER'S WEEKLY.   637

ROMISH POLITICS—ANY THING TO BEAT GRANT.

Figure 19 Thomas Nast, "Romish Politics – Any Thing to Beat Grant," *Harper's Weekly* (August 17, 1872), 637. Photo author.

objected to the decision of the city's school board to remove all religious texts from use in the classroom. Figure 19 accompanied an article that expressed rage over the decision of the superintendent of education for the state of New York to remove the bible from the public schools of Hunter's Point in 1872. *Harper's* and zealous Protestants felt strongly about this because it occurred in the wake of Ohio's appellate court decision to overturn the Cincinnati ruling against the school board two years earlier. In the illustration reproduced here, Nast portrays an ape-like Irishman, whom the caption styles an "Irish Roman Catholic Invader," accosting a compliant superintendent of education, whom the article identifies as a member of the Democratic Party "dependent upon the Romish vote." Eugene Lawrence, the author of the article, compounded the many claims of Protestant Nativists into a recent history of the Catholic–Democratic alliance: "No Democratic politician," he asserted,

> dares to oppose the Romish influence and the papal vote. Hating republican institutions because they have led the way to the downfall of the Romish power in Europe, the extreme papists joined the party of disunion, and when the slave-holders rose in rebellion they found their most constant allies in the Romish priests.[82]

The scene that Nast drew depicted an unholy alliance, "any thing," the caption states, "to beat Grant," that is, Ulysses S. Grant, the Republican candidate for the presidency in the election of 1872. A bible sits on a rostrum behind the two figures and beneath a presidential seal with the motto "The Bible in the Public School is an American Institution." Lest the image fail to deliver its message, Nast emblazoned the US shield on the binding of the bible. An enrobed priest slinks behind the Irishman and is countered by a bold youngster who rolls up his sleeve in preparation for a righteous battle with the Catholic invaders.

The range of views among American Catholics on the issue of public schools was considerable. It is encapsulated in the arc of positions taken by one man, Orestes Brownson, a convert from Protestantism to Catholicism who became an arch defender of the Roman Church in America. Although Brownson's ideas evolved over the course of his career as a Catholic writer, by 1874 he defended the Pope's insistence on the necessity of Catholic schools, condemned "purely secular schools," and urged the "necessity of Catholic education" in terms that were no longer sensitive to Protestant offense.[83] The public school system could not teach virtue because only the Catholic Church was able claim that right. "The [Protestant] sects," he announced,

> are all from the devil; they form no part of the Church of God. . . . None but the Catholic Church can train up the child in the way he should go. . . . Obviously then the Church is the only competent educator, and only a thorough Catholic education has or can have any value for men or nations.[84]

Brownson ended his essay with a claim that was sure to fire Protestant indignation:

> Nothing will save ["our daily deteriorating republic"] but the conversion of the people to Catholicity. . . . We believe that this country will yet be converted. Catholicity has the right to it, for it was first discovered by Catholics, and taken possession of in the name of the Cross.[85]

The ambitious final point sought to accent the Catholic history of early explorers in North America – Columbus, Amerigo Vespucci, and Ponce de Leon. He did not stop there. In an essay on "The Papacy and the Republic" (1873) Brownson asserted that

> the great conservative element in the American democracy, hitherto, has been the Common Law inherited from our Catholic ancestors . . . not, as so many foolishly imagine, in the superior virtue, wisdom, and intelligence of the American people, not in the democratic principle itself, nor in any self-adjusting power in the Constitution of the republic. The Common Law, which is of Catholic origin . . . has hitherto operated as a check on the political passions and vagaries of the people.[86]

America, he argued, was by origin and political ancestry, Roman Catholic.

Given the ethnic diversity of Catholic immigrants in the United States, it is not surprising to find a varied, but broadly central role of the Virgin in the Americanization of Catholic newcomers. Robert Orsi has argued that when the Madonna of 115th Street was crowned with papal blessing in 1904, Italian Americans of East Harlem felt their place in American history and its providential unfolding deeply affirmed.[87] Orsi's study of the festa dedicated each year to celebrating the Madonna's presence in the community showed how popular religion served an immigrant community that was often regarded as an embarrassment by non-Italian Catholics in the United States and even by members of the Catholic hierarchy. If Bishop Spalding and others wanted to relocate the Irish to the Midwest, Italians who arrived in New York tended largely to remain in inner-city neighborhoods and nearby boroughs in the orbit of the Madonna, who emerged from the church of Mount Carmel each July to process through the streets of Italian Harlem. Thousands returned each year to honor her and to reaffirm the chain of intergenerational linkages that defined family, community, and person. For these Catholics, Orsi shows, city life became a communal experience focused on the symbol of the Madonna, whose veneration enabled the faithful to cope with myriad difficulties.

Like Catholics everywhere, Latinos who migrated to or were born in the United States during the nineteenth or twentieth centuries engaged in a broad range of devotions – to many different saints whom they venerated in the formal rites of diocesan worship as well as in private devotion and in the informal corporate practices of local celebrations or pilgrimage. But the Virgin in various forms enjoyed perhaps the widest and most devoted following. Among Mexicans and Mexican Americans it has been devotion to Our Lady of Guadalupe. The image of Guadalupe is found in great variety among Chicanos, migrant workers, and Mexican Americans throughout the nation. Guadalupe appears as tattoos, graffiti, neighborhood murals, and devotional paintings in churches. She is invoked for blessing and protection and deployed as an icon of Latino Catholicism and as the emblem of Mexican transnationalism.[88] But devotion to the Madonna has always taken a variety of forms since she has always revealed herself within the guise of local, regional, and national traditions, tailoring her devotion to the needs and identities of ethnic and racial groups. Each manifestation of the Virgin acquires its own iconographical tradition, devotional practices, and, once officially sanctioned by the Church, her feast day. One of the distinctive devotions among Mexicans is to the Virgin of San Juan de los Lagos, who is sacred to Mexicans who sojourn in the United States as migrant workers.

Votive retablos (Figure 20) were produced by local painters and commissioned by those who rely on the Virgin for help. Among Mexicans who pass into the United States in search of work, the images are commonly dedicated with thanks for relief from problems with health, violence, employers, or the law encountered while working in the United States.[89] Upon returning to Mexico, devotees arrange for the production of the paintings, which tell their particular

Figure 20 Ex-voto retablo dedicated to Our Lady of Talpa by Silveria Camarena for a great wonder on the day of March 19, 1924, painting on tin. Courtesy Kristin Schwain.

stories of miraculous deliverance in word and image. The retablo paintings – images meant to be placed near an altar (retablo) in a pilgrimage church dedicated to the Virgin – often capture the traumatic experiences of migrant workers who pass from the peasant life of rural or small town Mexico to the bewildering urban domains of Los Angeles, Chicago, or El Paso.[90] Dedicated to the Virgin, the images are a material and public acknowledgment of the mercy the Virgin bestowed upon those who sought her aid. The term "ex-voto," Latin for "from a vow," refers to the formula of calling upon the Virgin for assistance and vowing to honor her with the retablo when the individual is delivered from his or her hardship. The images of thanks are placed on display in churches dedicated to Our Lady, one of the most important of which is the pilgrimage church of the Virgin of San Juan de los Lagos in the western highlands, in the state of Jalisco, and lake district of Mexico, which is a common source of migration to the United States.[91] Another center of pilgrimage devoted to the miracleworking Mary is Talpa de Allende, also in the state of Jalisco, where a shrine holds a statue of the "Rose of Allende," which performs miracles of healing. In 1924 a woman named Silveria Camarena had the image reproduced here (Figure 20) painted in order to thank the Virgin for the favor she was granted. Following the practice, the retablo painting bears the patron's inscription: "I dedicate this retablo to Our Lady of Talpa for having bestowed on me a great wonder for which I asked on March 19, 1924."[92] The image appearing in clouds before the kneeling Silveria is the Virgin of Talpa as she appears at the shrine of Talpa de Allende. The empty bed with a rosary on one post may indicate that Silveria was delivered from a bed-ridden illness.

The Latino experience in the United States is diverse because of the wide range of national traditions in Latin America, all of which are represented in the United States through extensive migration and transnational circulation. Although Latinos in North America are no longer only Catholic, many having converted to Pentecostalism or Evangelicalism before or after arriving, certain groups remain deeply committed to the Catholic tradition, especially in the form of devotion to Mary. Thomas Tweed has investigated the central significance of a shrine to the Madonna in Miami founded by Cuban Americans.[93] For the Cuban Americans whom Tweed studied, the shrine of Our Lady of Charity, the patroness of Cuba and the Cuban Diaspora centered in Miami, marks the ritual center of a displaced Cuban nationalism, a nationalism in waiting, nurturing a community in exile that anticipates a triumphant return to its homeland.[94] The Virgin's power to organize and bless the communities of her devotees, whether in rural provinces or large inner cities, has long been one of the central features of lived Catholic faith. She has been able to exert some symbolic power in mediating the sometimes sharp rivalries between the different ethnic groups devoted to her. The diversity of her images – from Guadalupe to Lourdes to Fatima – has served as one way of maintaining a balance of sameness and difference.[95]

Part II

New visual media and the marketplace

Chapter 3

Consumption and religious images

Consumption is a form of exchange in which consumers take little or no role in the production of the goods they acquire by money, credit, or barter. Commodities are things produced for the purpose of exchange in a marketplace by those who possess knowledge, skill, and locale that consumers generally do not have. The value of a commodity is determined entirely in terms of the marketplace, which operates with a history and competitive range of options. Value is determined in part by the use-value of a thing and certainly by consumer demand for a particular commodity. But the dominant basis of value is established by the degree to which producer, merchant, and consumer collectively determine desirability. Consumption consists of the practice of relying on the marketplace for the acquisition of commodities. Greater dependence on commodities means living life with increased expectation of the availability of goods. When consumption itself becomes a fundamental constituent of a consumer's social status or desired status, the economic culture that constructs identity through practices of consumption is called consumerism. Understanding commodities and consumption as part of world-making cultural practices has been the thrust of recent thinking, which is especially conducive to the study of objects as possessing a social life. Commodities exhibit biographies as they move through the cultural marketplace of values.[1]

Consumption involving money pivots on ready-made items acquired from sales catalogues, department stores, or specialty shops. According to the *Oxford English Dictionary*, "shopping" first appeared in print in the mid-eighteenth century (1764) to describe the practice of frequenting shops in order to purchase a range of commodities, items that consumers had formerly relied on the open marketplace to make available. As urban shops proliferated, shop windows emerged as the architectural structure conducive to the new transaction of purchasing commodities of meaning. Visual display and packaging were the inevitable result. Shop ownership became an anchor of the petite-bourgeoisie or lower middle class by becoming part of a systemic practice of prompting consumer notions and whims. Consumerism relies on the merchant's mediatory role, since it is the merchant who is able to stimulate demand by brokering the consumer's desires, displaying commodities that might direct the consumer's quest for identity. As a special form of consumption, consumerism inverts the conventional logic of supply and demand. Consumerism happens when commodities are used to create demand, when supply is not a response to need, but the stimulation of an impulse to own it since doing so will confer especially desirable and less tangible qualities on the owner. To understand this, it is necessary to consider the cultural context in which consumerism becomes a *meaningful* act, not principally, if at all, a sustentative one. Fashion, taste, and status competition are the attending forces that prompt and shape demand, and have been carefully studied by historians of early modern European and American consumption.[2] Consumerism therefore depends on a cultural setting in which these factors constitute a shifting system of significance that informs consumer demand.

What role did religion play in the history of American consumption and consumerism? Studies of the history of consumption in early modern Britain, colonial America, and the early national period of the United States indicate that Christianity was instrumental in contributing to a shift from the early consumption of luxuries among the British aristocracy with its attendant culture of gentility to the modern conception of respectability, in which consumption was guided by the practice of taste and forms of association that celebrated the practice of key virtues.[3] If aristocrats consumed luxury items in the seventeenth and early eighteenth centuries because they were aristocrats by birth and pedigree, one became a member of the respectable bourgeoisie in the eighteenth century by virtue of the things one chose to consume in accord with the taste and moral codes that defined respectability. Such a neat distinction may blur historical nuances and exceptions nearly as much as it clarifies the overarching change, but from the distance of the nineteenth century, the view is instructive.

Respectability as a middle-class value system was grounded in the home. The Protestant Christian home was the place where prayer and the study of scripture prevailed as the heart of domestic life. Comfort was properly sited in the home, and therefore it is not surprising that the Christian home became the centerpiece of Protestant ideals and practices of consumption. A great deal of scholarship has argued in recent years for a closer look at the relationship between American religions and commerce.[4] This has been a productive and very important development. Among Protestantism's principal locations in American culture – church, home, school, hospital, orphanage, philanthropic institutions – the home was the most important for Protestant consumption as far as the early development of Protestant iconography and visual practice is concerned. Within the home, the parlor was dedicated to consumer-friendly display, a place where consumption and morality intermingled to define respectability in a powerful way for nineteenth-century American Protestants as well as Catholics and Jews. The parlor was the place for devotions, for display of the bible, for a close association of family and friends and for such practices as eating, reading, singing, storytelling, and receiving visitors. It is no surprise therefore that the parlor served as the primary iconography of home life in popular prints (see Figures 31–36 and 38, pp. 114–22 and 130), in Sunday school illustrations, in engraved illustrations in books and tracts (see Figures 30 and 39, pp. 107 and 133). It was the place where daguerreotypes were displayed and other images such as photographs, stereographs, and cartes de visite. Photo albums were stored and viewed in the parlor. The visual commodities of Christian respectability also circulated beyond the home in many forms. But the source of piety was the home, and its principal influence flowed from the domestic throne of mother, whose proper sphere in the antebellum period came to be defined as the home and Sunday school. It follows that much domestic lithography and engraving deals with mothers and their children. Mothers were, after all, consumers and came to rely very much on the religious print commodities that publishers (secular as well as religious) made a point of offering to customers who managed the American household. If consumerism is supply-driven demand, increasingly oriented toward the visual allurement of advertisements that inform and evoke consumer preferences, the host of lithographs and engravings placed in circulation by religious and commercial publishers were aimed at infusing the religious imagination with visual prompts to pious consumption.

Visual piety and religious consumption: Currier & Ives lithography

The national system of Evangelical print had demonstrated its power to dominate the market in religious publications with illustrated tracts and books. Yet this was only the beginning of commercially successful religious imagery in antebellum America. During the 1830s, lithography became an enduring part of American print and visual culture, first appearing in print shops in major cities that presented their wares in large picture windows for street traffic. But lithographers soon took advantage of mail-order business, issuing catalogues and flyers to advertise product. Lithography was a versatile medium, allowing the same print shop to produce everything from office forms, trade cards, and certificates, to sheet music, devotional imagery, genre scenes, political cartoons, illustrations of late-breaking news events, and nature scenery.

Before photography was invented, let alone used in print publication, lithography emerged in antebellum America as the rival of wood engraving, the hitherto dominant form of mass-produced imagery. Copperplate engraving was the preferred method for creating images of high quality since the single, large metal plate avoided the necessity of splicing the many small wooden blocks of wood engraving. Both means, however, were expensive and time-consuming on a large format. Lithography was limited only by the size of the limestone bed on which images were created, which could be reused for many years of service. Should the printer wish to reissue a lithograph, the etched stone could be stored away. Lithography also boasted the attractive advantage of preserving the freshness of the crayon drawing, even to the degree of fooling the eye by making the lithograph appear as a charcoal sketch. Moreover, lithography produced larger editions of prints in a shorter time. This allowed for lower retail prices as well as a quick response to current events.

Because of the speed of producing a large lithographic edition, many lithographers used their medium to cover sensational news stories such as disasters, scandals, and battles. Few were as timely or as entrepreneurial as Nathaniel Currier. Born in 1813, by the age of 15 Currier was apprenticed to the first litho firm in America, operated by William and John Pendleton in Boston. After studying a year in Philadelphia with another lithographer, Currier settled in New York City in 1834, where he established a partnership with another man and opened a litho firm. It lasted no more than a year producing work to order. In 1835 Currier founded his own business.[5]

Woodcuts and engravings had long been used to exploit the news value of current political events or to appeal to public curiosity. From the beginning of his commercial career, Currier found that lithography could accommodate public interest in late-breaking news, and so cultivated a form of pictorial journalism.[6] His capital ventures in lithographic production took the form of several major tactics of commoditization. In every case, he sought to link product to demand, but in key respects he demonstrated the nature of consumerism by leveraging demand for the product he supplied. Currier and his competitors – such as Kellogg and Thayer in Hartford and Buffalo, Duval and Kollner in Philadelphia, Strobridge in Cincinnati, and Bufford, Pendleton, and later Prang in Boston – relied on a variety of means of distribution: mail order, sales over the counter, mass-distributed flyers and catalogues, wholesale supply to street vendors and agents around the country, and commission work with individuals, businesses, religious institutions and groups, and event organizers.[7] Evidence from other litho firms suggests that there was nothing unique about Currier's approach except his ambition, timeliness, and the size of his operation. The scale and zeal of his entrepreneurship make it easier, however, having left far more documentary information in its wake, to grasp how the commerce of lithography was able to pursue a systematic integration of production and distribution that recalls the ATS. In fact, according to one historical account, Currier even worked with the ATS to provide two prints that the Tract Society would use as premiums to reward contributors and members.[8]

Generally speaking, four different approaches to commodifying prints are discernible in Currier's production. The earliest economic mode for prints was the most traditional: *job printing*. This was the bulk production of standard items for which there was a constant need: handbills, letterhead, labels, ledger pages, or office forms. Lithography provided a quick means of issuing large print runs for these items. These were the work-horse of print firms, many or even most of which specialized in this reliable source of income. These items might be produced in bulk or they might be done on *commission*, which was the second aspect of production that occupied printers. Working with established firms, especially during his early years, Currier hired out his press and crayon as a subcontractor. Profits were lower and the opportunity to highlight his own firm was subordinated to the primary credit line given the publisher. But it meant income. Currier, like most lithographers, would continue to execute such jobs through the career of his firm, working on commission with Sunday school and mission societies to produce certificates of membership. Although documentation in most instances is lacking, it is likely that some of the commemorative portraits of religious leaders that Currier & Ives issued over the years were produced on commission with organizations that wished to celebrate the individuals by sponsoring their portraits. Thus, a portrait of Brigham Young or one of Richard Allen might have been underwritten by the Mormon Church or the African Methodist Episcopal Church.

If such portraits were not commissioned by religious patrons, they were the result of a third economic procedure: *speculation*. Currier as entrepreneur must have discerned an opportunity for selling such prints on the open market. This was the nature of his early efforts in pictorial journalism, sensing quite accurately as he did that the public would pay for dramatic visual portrayals of sensational disasters. Instances of religious portraiture that may represent this venture are portraits celebrating the election of new popes, in particular Pius IX (1846) and Leo XIII (1878), a commemorative image of Pope Pius IX lying in state (1878), or the three-hundredth anniversary of the death of John Calvin (1846). Other examples may include *Our Lady of Knock* (Figure 21), a lithograph showing the miraculous apparition of the Virgin on the side of an Irish church in 1879, a subject that was especially dear to Irish Catholics in major market centers like New York and Boston. In 1874–75 the Chicago revivalists Rev. Dwight Moody and his musical counterpart, Ira D. Sankey, conducted a series of highly publicized revivals in major cities, shortly after returning from a celebrated campaign in England and Scotland. Currier & Ives likely speculated on the successful reception of Moody and Sankey by issuing two commemorative portraits of the men (Figure 22). Editions of at least two mottoes consisting of lines from the widely familiar hymns sung at revival meetings, "Rock of Ages" and "Simply to the Cross I Cling," were printed in 1872, 1873, and 1874. Another popular hymn, "Heart of Jesus Reign Thou Ever in My Heart," appeared in 1876, and "Nearer My God to Thee," though undated, was published by Currier & Ives during the 1870s or 1880s, and may also have been directed at the Protestant audiences at various revivals. Yet another example was Currier & Ives' speculative efforts to match lithographs to new visual practices, such as Sunday school rewards given out to children to encourage attendance, or the emerging domestic piety that found an important place for devotional imagery and religious themes in the home (see Figures 31–34, pp. 114–18). Although Americans had displayed prints of one kind or another in their homes for many generations, a new popular aesthetic of home decoration and moral formation was taking shape at mid-century and Currier & Ives were quick to develop product to this use.

The final economic technique governing production for Currier & Ives, as well as other lithographers, was what might be called *translation* or

Figure 21 Currier & Ives, *Our Lady of Knock*, hand-colored lithograph, 1879. Courtesy Billy Graham Center Museum.

IRA D. SANKEY.
The Evangelist of Song.

NEW YORK,   PUBLISHED BY CURRIER & IVES, 125 NASSAU ST.

Figure 22 Currier & Ives, *Ira D. Sankey: The Evangelist of Song*, hand-colored lithograph, 1874. Courtesy Billy Graham Center Museum.

recapitulation, or, more plainly, product updating. This consisted of producing lithographic versions of established genres of imagery traditionally produced in other media such as engraving, woodcut, or painting, particularly current versions issued by one's competitors. Lithographers actively sought out images that they could replicate in the new medium and supply as more readily available and less expensive in order to supplant rival media. The aim was to tap into a ready-made market. In the realm of religious images this procedure is most evident in the massive issue of Catholic devotional imagery such as saints, the Stations of the Cross, or the many versions of the Virgin such as Our Lady of Knock (Figure 21), of Sorrows, of Lourdes, of the Rosary, of Guadalupe, and Mount Carmel.[9] The variety, ethnic preferences, liturgical seasons, and different purposes of Catholic devotional images made them ideal for commodification since they could be targeted to particular audiences and times of the year, and could be regularly replenished. And there were abundant examples of visual types available for lithographic translation. Moreover, the steadily growing numbers of Catholic immigrants arriving in New York City meant a burgeoning market of customers.

One of the most common forms of recapitulation undertaken by Currier was the widely reproduced motif of the memorial image (Figure 23). This image marked a key turn in nineteenth-century Protestant visual practice and iconography because it took the image of the gravestone and the practices of display

Figure 23 Nathaniel Currier, Memorial image, hand-colored lithograph, 1845. Courtesy Billy Graham Center Museum.

associated with mourning at graveside into the home. Linked to the rise of mourning clothes and the formation of the profession of the undertaker, this image helped American Protestants find a place for imagery. As we shall examine in Chapter 4, the parlor came to be understood as the site for display in middle- and working-class homes. The popularization of the new iconography of mourning as remembrance highlights the importance of recapitulation as a viable form of visual production and consumption.

The memorial pendant (Figure 24), brooch, miniature, or watercolor painting had appeared in the late eighteenth century as a device for mourning. These used the neoclassical style to picture urns atop a plinth in a pastoral setting, as seen in Currier's adaptation of the motif (Figure 23). Originally altars and receptacles for cremated remains in ancient Rome, the visual formula became widely used in Europe and England during the second half of the eighteenth century when neoclassicism dominated the decorative and fine arts. The neoclassical taste was championed in the United States by Thomas Jefferson and others and intermingled with Christian mourning practices in the transposition of the urn and plinth to the Christian graveyard. The appeal of the neoclassical style was complex. It struck Jefferson as especially suitable to the modern democratic ideal of civic virtue championed by advocates of republican government. Neoclassical elements entered the visual vocabulary of modern republicanism in the seventeenth century, but received a major boost when the archeological finds at Herculaneum and Pompeii in 1740 attracted attention. The most influential admirer of classical art was Johann Winckelmann, whose prolific career and dithyrambic prose as a critic and arbiter of the new taste helped establish neoclassicism from Rome to Monticello. According to Winckelmann, the classical style endorsed and inspired a solemnity and grandeur that elevated the soul, infusing the human figure with a sublime nobility that befitted the decorum of such occasions as funerals, public ritual commemorations, and the virtuous examples of dying heroes and tragic figures that were depicted in murals and paintings. The iconography of the noble death – whether it was monarch, civic hero, military commander, or pious father – dominated the public imagery of the eighteenth century. In the last quarter of the century, the visual language in which this subject was treated most frequently was neoclassicism.[10]

A variety of mass-produced commodities brought the neoclassical style into mainstream consumption – from wall paper to illustrated books, calendars, and almanacs to ceramic ware. Josiah Wedgwood's internationally successful Staffordshire business in neoclassical pottery (for which he imported tons of clay from South Carolina) popularized the cameo-style figuration and spare contours of imagery taken from ancient examples. By 1772 Wedgwood had determined that his aristocratic market was flagging due to saturation. Since he had acquired a stock of molds, material, and technical skill, he was able to mass-produce porcelain ware to be sold at lower prices. "The Great People have had their Vases in their Palaces long enough for them to be seen & admir'd by

Figure 24 Unidentified artist, Memorial for Werter, verso, pendant, glass with watercolour on ivory, ca. 1810. Yale University Art Gallery, promised bequest of Davida Tenenbaum Deutsch and Alvin Deutsch, L.L.B 1958, in honor of Kathleen Luhrs.

the Middling Class of People," he reasoned. The illustrious character of the vases "is established & the middling People would probably buy quantities of them at a reduced price."[11] Because the middle class consisted of those who longed to imitate the aristocracy in matters of style, Wedgwood offered consumers a way of doing so. Significantly, he espoused an aesthetic of the copy that championed the industry of mass production and the lucrative commerce it supplied. "Nothing can contribute more effectively," he wrote, "to diffuse good taste through the Arts, than the Power of multiplying Copies of the Things, by which Means the public Eye is instructed."[12] Copies did not demean the original, but celebrated it, according to Wedgwood. Currier & Ives would have heartily agreed, even if the exacting standards of Wedgwood far exceeded what was required for the even larger market to which the American printers catered.

Although the mourning picture used neoclassical vocabulary, it was infused with Romanticism's cult of sentiment. One early example of neoclassical mourning imagery carries the name "Werter" (see Figure 24), presumably the name of the otherwise unidentified man whose portrait appears on the opposite side of the pendant. Werter was also the name of the subject of Johann Wolfgang Goethe's enormously popular first novel, *Sorrows of the Young Werther* (1774). This tale of an excessively sensitive young man, given to self-effacing acts of empathy, the innocent joys of children, and long bouts of gloomy introspection, culminates tragically in suicide, and consists of letters to friends and a lover. More than any other product of the German Sturm und Drang, this short novel fueled the international romance with fine feeling, particularly melancholy, which suited the heightened emotional state of mourning. As a novel and a figure, Werther's theme is loss, especially a passionate expenditure of oneself in the face of inevitable loss. Though the name "Werter" on the brooch likely did not refer to Goethe's Werther, the Romantic mood of memorial art around 1800 sanctioned a turn inward, giving permission to restrained Protestants in America to indulge feelings that more traditional practice had thought best to suppress. Thomas Gray's "Elegy Written in a Country Church-Yard" (1751) cultivated the same turn within: the poem's opening stanza marks "the knell of parting day" that "leaves the world to darkness and to me." Immersed in twilight gloom, the poem's narrator is left to himself to contemplate how "the paths of glory lead but to the grave." The use of the neoclassical idiom in mourning art allowed Americans to display grief in a new way, to pin it to their bodies in the form of painted ivory brooches bearing miniature portraits of the deceased, and present it in works of art in their parlors. In particular, it was a practice of expression undertaken by women and understood to be one that conveyed their taste and breeding. While Protestant moralists commonly inveighed against the reading of novels for the surfeit of feeling that fiction encouraged (especially among young ladies and women), there was no corresponding critique of mourning art.

The cult of mourning was an aspect of Victorian culture dominated by women. Gender is perhaps the key element in the visual culture of mourning and the sentiment it cultivated as part of the broader culture of sentimentalism.

In a major study of middle-class society in nineteenth-century America, Karen Haltunen defined sentimentalism as a culture of attitudes and practices grounded in the notion that, as Haltunen put it, "private experience was morally superior to public life."[13] It was women who reigned in this private sphere – whether it was the parlor or the human heart. They were the engine of refinement, the register of finer sensations, the warmer soul, the source of home nurture. Naturally, this ideology tended to keep women within a bounded circumference, but it also placed them in charge of domestic consumption, tutored by a growing avalanche of advice books and fashion magazines – from *Godey's Lady's Book* (begun in 1830) to Catherine Beecher and Harriet Beecher Stowe's *The American Woman's Home* (1869). The greater evaluation of the private sphere emerged from eighteenth-century British and antebellum American estimation of rural and private life over the distractions and enervations of the city. Haltunen points out that sentimentalism was linked to the older idea of sensibility, which "meant the responsiveness of a delicate heart to the slightest emotional stimulus."[14] Sentiment represented a proper balance of the soul – neither too cold nor too hot, neither sullen nor reactive. Avoiding the latter excess, especially among women, was precisely why many Protestants deplored fiction: it indulged in the mesmerizing traffic of emotional delicacies, a kind of extravagance or luxury that ruined the moral structure of the heart. Moreover, shunning a dissipating excess of feeling is why many antebellum Protestants regarded the city as such a menace: its surfeit of sensations was overwhelming, swamping the Christian soul in stimuli that clouded moral judgment and compromised the sovereignty of good character. One of the corollaries of the cautionary censure of novels, gambling, drinking, night life, and public activities beyond the carefully limned zone of teaching and benevolence was the ideal of the parlor.

The memorial prints issued by Currier began as ivory brooches and took the form of watercolor paintings on paper that were displayed in the home's best room, the parlor. The genealogy is evident in Currier's print in the presence of the brooch, which the mourning woman fondly holds to her heart as she gazes upon the grave (see Figure 23). A man's bust is visible in the miniature. Appropriately, Figure 23 was used to remember a man, one Wilson Failor, whose name, birth, and death dates appear hand-written on the plinth. Whether as jewelry or framed paintings, the mourning imagery focused attention on the act of mourning, which was simultaneously an act of memory and an act of display. As the home's space dedicated to display, the parlor was the destination for most instances of the watercolors or their lithographic equivalents. The images typically envision a country scene of loss remembered – a rural graveyard in which mourners gather at the side of a tombstone or urn, often beneath a willow, with a church in the distance. The willow marked the grave site, a tree rooted in the abundance of water that flowed from the aggrieved. The willow encouraged the open and generous expression of grief, the manifest investment of the self in the act of mourning, which was not only a remembering, but also a displaying of memory. As such, the willow was a symbol that both expressed grief and endorsed its display. The graveyard scene is typically set far from city life, remote from noise and everyday traffic. When placed in the parlor, the images located commemoration in the home's most socially ritualized space. Display and memory were dominantly managed by women and became commoditized with the rise of the mass-produced lithographic mourning picture.

The mourning art crafted in ivory, silk, and watercolor, learned by girls at finishing schools, produced by well-heeled young women and older ladies for exchange among their upper-class peers, was gradually replaced during the 1840s by Currier and other lithographers, who made their versions of the mourning iconography available to a much broader American public.[15] Rather than commissioned for individual patrons, the lithographs were mass-produced and left to customers to personalize, as in Figure 23.[16] By adding the deceased person's name to the memorial print, the object ceased being a generic commodity and became a cherished memento for display. Inscriptions on the prints followed the pattern of miniatures, in which the initials of the deceased were commonly inscribed. But this was not the only association. In the second half of the eighteenth century, American gravestones began to replace the older formula of "Here lies the body of" with "In (or sacred to) the memory of."[17] By the second decade of the nineteenth century, the new formula appears to have completely replaced its predecessor. The shift is significant since it takes the focus of mourning from the state of the deceased to the sentiments of the aggrieved. Memory belonged to the experience of the mourner.

The rite of mourning came to take place in the quasi-public space of the new cemeteries built on the outskirts of mid-century cities. The rural cemetery movement exchanged the crowded and often decrepit colonial graveyard, "where heaves the turf in many a mouldering heap," to borrow another line from Gray, for the rolling and plangent grounds of Mount Auburn in Cambridge (1831), Laurel Hill in Philadelphia (1835), or Hollywood Cemetery in Richmond (1847). All were carefully planned to reveal pastoral vistas in which ornate funerary devices such as those in Currier's views of graves (see Figure 23) were nestled. These restful parks came to feature another version of mass-produced religious images: sculpted figures at graveside, embodying the act of mourning as a kind of melodramatic tableau vivant.[18] A familiar feature found in these cemeteries was an angel (Figure 25), at prayer or poised in grief, enacting memory in artful poses that raised commemoration of the departed to an aesthetic act of contemplation. The grounds of the new cemeteries offered quiet and broad pathways for calm, detached strolling that welcomed the practice of memory enjoined by tombstone inscription and the memorial art displayed in the home.

Lithography and religious subject matter

Religious subjects were a fundamental feature of nearly all major lithography firms in the mid-nineteenth century. In a *Catalogue of Colored Prints*, listing

Figure 25 Angel at prayer, gravestone of Sarah J. Winston, 1859, marble, Hollywood Cemetery, Richmond, Virginia. Photo author.

500 items issued by E. C. Kellogg (New York and Hartford) and Horace Thayer (Buffalo) in 1852 or 1853, seventy-one titles are identifiably religious.[19] Most were Roman Catholic – e.g. Stations of the Cross, Sacred Heart of Mary and Jesus, St. Patrick, Father Matthew, and Pius IX. Yet others were subjects that appealed to Protestant consumers: Wesley, Washington at Prayer, Camp Meeting, Temperance, Ten Commandments, Prodigal Son, Christ Blessing the Children, Reading the Scriptures, and Morning and Evening Prayer. Generally speaking, the list consists of three kinds of themes: biblical subjects, devotional subjects, and contemporary or historical portraiture. The first group is the largest, accounting for thirty of the seventy-one titles. Identifiably Catholic themes number twenty-seven, with the likely possibility that several of the biblical scenes were aimed at the Catholic market since Currier supplied Catholic immigrants with such scenes (Paradise, Noah's Ark, the Deluge, Guardian Angel, Flight to and Return from Egypt, the Transfiguration, and Christ at the Well) by placing captions in French, Spanish, or Italian.

One unmistakably Protestant subject for many lithograph producers during the second half of the century was the Masonic chart. Currier & Ives issued one in 1876 and an Odd Fellows Chart in 1887, but John Bufford in Boston had already produced a chromolithograph in 1866 (Figure 26). Masonic organizations did not stress religious beliefs with the same consistency, but Freemasonry was grounded on a theology that incorporated biblical motifs and lore regarding the ancient craft of mystical Masonry practiced by Solomon, builder of the first temple of Israel. Calling it "the greatest light of Masonry," the encyclopedic *Library of Freemasonry* (1911) asserted that "no Lodge exists without the acknowledged Bible, and would, without, be illegal and unwarrantable."[20] Theologically, Freemasonry affirmed belief in the "Supreme Being" or "Great Architect of the Universe," the deity of the Enlightenment which is symbolized by the eye of God at the top of the chart. Though it insisted on belief in God, Masonry left its members to their "peculiar opinion" and prohibited them from introducing their beliefs into the lodge.[21] Nevertheless, eminent American Masons were also eminent Evangelical Christians (such as John Wanamaker). Some American Masons writing about the craft did not hesitate to assure readers of its ultimately Christian nature.[22] But this was not enough to placate many Protestants who deeply resented secret societies and fraternal organizations and banned members who joined lodges. The Catholic Church had forbidden membership in the eighteenth century by papal order, which was reinforced during the nineteenth century. In 1882 the Knights of Columbus were formed as a Catholic fraternal organization in part to counter the Protestant character of Freemasonry.

Masonry cultivated a sense of mystery by couching its teachings in symbols, arguing that "nature is shrouded in mystery; and mystery has charms for all men."[23] The chart shown here assembles the three degrees of the Mason – apprentice, fellow, master – in the vertical arrangement of scenes. Each bears its appropriate set of symbols, conveying the virtues, teachings, and practices that

Figure 26 Masonic Chart, chromolithograph, J. H. Bufford's Lithography, Boston, MA, 1866. Courtesy American Antiquarian Society.

marked the discrete levels of attainment in Masonry. The allegorical and mysterious character of the symbols was a fond feature of the craft. "One of the most striking characteristics of our Institution is its system of mystical instruction," the *Library of Freemasonry* explained of a diagram of the master mason's level, the top scene in Figure 26. If outsiders did not understand it, that was part of the point: Freemasonry's "regalia and forms are not the puerile display or empty ceremonies which they might seem to an ignorant spectator. Each particular is alive with meaning and use."[24] Charts like the one reproduced here could be used by Masons to study the system of beliefs and prepare for advancement, but they also no doubt struck non-Masons with curiosity or suspicion, serving to visualize a provocative boundary separating outsider and insider.

The use of lithographed images to convey special knowledge was an important part of another antebellum Protestant group known as the Millerites. Among the many sects that emerged in the nineteenth century, this dramatically premillennialist group was named after its leader, William Miller (1782–1849), who became convinced that he had determined the date of the second coming of Jesus. Miller came to this conclusion after spending years contemplating the apocalyptic books of the bible – Daniel, Ezekiel, and the Book of Revelation. From these, and from centuries of speculative interpretation among British and American Protestant theologians, Miller constructed a set of symbolic readings of biblical symbols, figures, numbers, and dates, all of which he believed corresponded to historical periods of time that could be combined to measure the time from ancient Babylon to the day when Jesus would appear on the clouds and come to end the present age.

Miller preached and wrote his ideas during the 1830s and gradually gathered a following of evangelists and teachers committed to spreading his beliefs. One of the leaders of the group, Joshua Himes, was a publisher who undertook a tireless campaign of publishing newspapers and magazines as well as stationery and charts (Figure 27) that were illustrated with the prophetic symbols and arithmetic of Miller's biblical interpretations. Even though the group probably never numbered more than forty or fifty thousand brief adherents, it is remembered not only for its unusual belief that Jesus would appear in 1843, but perhaps most because of its aggressive use of visual media. At a meeting in Boston in 1842, a group of Adventists – Protestants convinced that the advent of the Lord was nigh – gathered to discuss the many doctrines they held in common. Among those present, two preachers allied with Miller displayed a chart painted on cloth to present the prophetic interpretations championed by him. Those who supported him at the meeting determined to produce several hundred lithographed charts after the prototype. The result was a hand-tinted lithograph on muslin fifty-four inches high. Himes published the chart using a lithography firm in Boston, though it is unknown which one. Millerite preachers and teachers used the image as an important aid in their itinerant ministries of spreading the word. The chart's integration of numerical calculation, biblical

Figure 27 Millerite chart, lithograph and stencil on fabric, 1842. Courtesy American Antiquarian Society.

text, and visual imagery allowed evangelists to make the arcane interpretations more concrete as the speakers worked their way across and down to the bottom to arrive at the imminent date of 1843. Although Jesus did not appear in 1843, or in October of 1844, following Miller's recalculation, the imagery of the chart did not vanish. A handful of Millerites regrouped and formed a new sect, the Seventh-Day Adventists, who recycled the scheme of the 1843 chart. Like the Millerites, the new Adventist group made ambitious use of graphic imagery to promote its cause and demonstrated a pattern among new religious sects in Victorian America: long before they laid a brick or founded a seminary or built a library, they invested in a printing press and secured the use of mass-produced imagery to assist in teaching and proselytism.[25] In the marketplace of culture, media were more important to fledgling groups than bricks and mortar.

Like most of Currier & Ives' antebellum lithographs, the Millerite chart was hand-colored after being printed in black-and-white. But color printing was not far off. Louis Prang began publishing chromolithographs in Boston in 1866. His aim with these, which achieved color effects not by hand-tinting mono-chromatic prints, but within the printing process itself, was to provide products marketed as facsimiles of works of art for the home. His chromos sold from $3.00 to $15.00 each depending on size (from 8 × 14 inches to 20 × 25 inches), which was two or three times the prices advertised by Currier & Ives. They were printed to achieve the airy quality of watercolor or the lustrous effect of oil, the paper was embossed to register the texture of canvas, and the finished print was varnished so as to yellow like oil paintings. One company catalogue stated confidently that "all our Chromos are fac-similes of oil or water-color paintings by the best artists, in most cases equal to the originals."[26] Once again, copies suffered no loss of the original's quality. Art critics rarely agreed with this claim, and criticism of the chromo aesthetic's putative "deception" or "fraud" mounted to acidic rejection by the 1870s and 1880s.[27] But for far more middle-class home makers and their husbands, Prang's chromos were regarded as an obligatory form of decoration that could enhance the beauty and moral influ-ence of the home. Because Prang aimed at making fine art affordable for the American home, his catalogues identified the artist after whom the print was taken. Subject matter followed the fine art market: landscapes, human figures, genre scenes, animals, portraits, and flower pieces.

Convinced that chromos would elevate American taste by placing high-quality reproductions of original works of art within the home and school, Prang focused his production on what he felt would be appealing subjects. That meant "sentimental" or endearing themes like children, animals, and flowers. It did not mean many religious subjects. In the catalogue for 1879–80, the entire list of chromos contains eleven religious themes.[28] In most instances, these were Madonnas or Magdalens after Old Masters (Murillo, Raphael, Correggio). But Prang produced hundreds of religious-themed images in the form of illumin-ated scripture texts for Sunday schools. No fewer than 67 items appear under this rubric; 111 of 149 mottoes were of a religious nature. All 39 floral mottoes were biblical or religious themes; 67 illuminated or floral crosses of various sizes are listed in a separate category in the catalogue. Additional items of a religious nature were book marks, Sunday school membership certificates, and patterns for (do-it-yourself) panel paintings. And in yet another separate category, the catalogue offered 44 rustic, stone, or floral crosses as gilt-edge panel pictures on heavy mounts for placement in an easel or on a parlor mantel. Prang distinguished fine art facsimiles in his production, which were only rarely religious in theme, from the items he offered for explicitly religious functions such as teaching and moral formation in the home, in which images were deployed with a message-laden presence of reminding family members of the piety they were expected to observe. But Prang couched these items in the same decorative aesthetic of a sentimental piety that dominated the floral motifs of no religious content. The piety his work endorsed was non-sectarian and com-mitted to the notion that beauty itself was morally uplifting. This is evident in the Christmas and Easter cards he produced from the 1870s to the 1880s. The holidays were not marketed as sectarian Christian rituals, but as seasons to be observed with taste and due regard for the morally tinged character of beauti-ful images. Leigh Schmidt has argued that Prang's Easter cards "effectively reimagined popular Christian piety" for a largely Protestant female clientele for whom a bleeding savior was no longer a current image.[29]

Matters were different with Nathaniel Currier's work. The bulk of religious imagery he issued in the 1840s when his business was finding its financial feet was unambiguously Roman Catholic and consisted of translations of devo-tional imagery from engravings and other media with no attempt to create facsimile reproductions of the original medium. Currier did not seek to appeal to a decorum or decorative taste, but to build the supply of religious lithographs on the traditional demand which he hoped the new medium would answer. There was much more reason to transpose images for a Catholic market than for a Protestant since the visual piety of Catholics was much more conducive to single-leaf images. Protestants had always made use of images set within texts – illustrated bibles, tracts, primers, almanacs, and devotional booklets – but they had comparatively little use for stand-alone images. The market for lithographs among American Protestants was only beginning to be developed in the memorial imagery that Currier was producing during the 1840s.

Precise numbers of the religious output of Currier & Ives are difficult to determine since not all of the prints are available for inspection and many prints of moral subjects would have counted as religious topics for Protestants and Catholics in the nineteenth century. We also lack detailed knowledge of the size of individual print runs. But there is enough information to be found in a carefully compiled catalogue raisonné of Currier & Ives prints and various sales lists produced by the firm itself to make some telling estimations. Between 1835 and 1893, Currier and (after 1856) Currier & Ives produced no less than 530 different editions of religious prints with approximately 340 different themes.[30] This compares substantially with non-religious subjects according to the index subject of the best catalogue: 583 horse racing themes, 341 rural scenes, 253 steamships, and 203 Civil War scenes.[31] Walton Rawls counted about 350 lithographs of "farm, village, and countryside scenes."[32] More than other areas, much of the firm's religious production consisted of variations of the same theme such as the baptism, crucifixion, or resurrection of Jesus. The greatest amount of religious material produced by the firm was aimed at the market among different American Catholics. A total of 333 different editions of prints may be reasonably assigned to Catholic consumers based on the subject matter (Sacred Heart of Jesus or Mary, Catholic saints, church leaders such as cardinals and popes, the Eucharist, the Stations of the Cross, and various images of the Virgin such as Guadalupe, Mater Dolorosa, or contemporary apparitions of Mary such as Our Lady of Lourdes and Our Lady of Knock) or the presence of Italian, Spanish, French, or German titles in the prints' captions, especially of saints beloved of immigrants from Catholic regions of Europe where these languages were spoken. Careful study of production lists also indicates that many subjects were printed in the 1840s for Catholic immigrants and therefore likely continued to be sold in subsequent editions to Catholics. These themes include the birth of Jesus, the flight to Egypt, the Holy Family, miracles performed by Jesus, the Transfiguration, the ascension of Jesus, and the creation and fall cycle from Genesis, even though there may be nothing about the prints themselves that singularly marks them as Catholic. Certainly many of these themes could appeal to Protestants, but not until later in the century, a topic we shall address shortly.

The production of Catholic themes by Currier & Ives is steady through the 1880s. From 1840 to 1856, at least 116 themes may be identified as Catholic, and 49 of these themes were repeated after Ives joined the firm; 32 were discontinued. From approximately 1860 to 1893, an additional 81 Catholic themes were introduced. The approximate total of Catholic themes over the life of the firm is 198. By decade, the most prolific periods of Catholic production were the 1840s and the 1870s, with the 1840s constituting by far the single greatest period for issuing Catholic themes. Currier produced no fewer than 63 dated print editions for Roman Catholics during that decade, with a total of 178 editions of Catholic images in the twenty-one years before Ives joined him as a partner in 1857, many of which were no doubt issued during the 1840s. The reason for this concentration is immigration and the election of Pius IX in 1846. When Pius IX died in 1878, Currier & Ives issued a print of him lying in state in the Vatican as well as a portrait of his successor, Leo XIII. But immigration patterns tell the larger story. In the 1820s, just over 150,000 immigrants arrived in the United States. Over the following decade four times as many came. Between 1841 and 1850, 1.7 million people immigrated to the United States. In each of the following three decades the numbers were even greater: between 2.3 and 2.8 million people. Most of these were from Ireland and Germany – between 1841 and 1870, nearly 4.5 million citizens immigrated to the United States from Ireland and Germany alone in virtually equal numbers. A majority of these immigrants were Catholic. Significant numbers of Spanish-speaking American citizens of Hispanic ethnicity had, of course, always lived in the southwest, from Texas to California. Italian immigration did not get underway in significant numbers until the 1880s.[33]

By comparison, Currier & Ives produced far fewer images for a strictly Protestant market. During the 1840s, only five dated prints may be clearly identified as aimed at an exclusively Protestant market and fifteen during the 1870s. This increase of an overall small amount reverses the earlier preponderance of Catholic production. But the total number of prints that may be reasonably identified as Protestant is much smaller. Just over fifty appear to be clearly Protestant. An additional 145 were likely created for Protestant and Catholic consumers or are incapable of being exclusively assigned to either market. Protestant images are identifiable by subject such as the Death of Calvin and commemorative portraits of celebrated Protestant clergymen and evangelists John and Charles Wesley, Richard Allen, Dwight Moody, and Ira D. Sankey; or themes familiar from Protestant literature such as *Pilgrim's Progress*; or favorite Protestant hymns like "Rock of Ages," "Nearer My God to Thee," and "Simply to the Cross I Cling." Other Protestant themes include "Reading the Scriptures," the bible, and family devotion, and emblems serving as Sunday school rewards. Currier & Ives produced birth and baptismal certificates for use among German and English-speaking Protestants, as well as marriage certificates and family registers that picture Protestant churches or indicate Protestant clergy as officiating. Two prints served as official receipts for membership in a Methodist mission society. Yet it was among the Protestant imagery that we see consumerism most at work since it is there that Currier & Ives needed to create a demand in order to meet it. By keying images to major personalities who were frequently mentioned in religious and secular media, Currier & Ives appealed to the interest in celebrities. Home decoration, particularly parlor décor, was another need that lithographers stoked by diversifying their stock. The lure of images in this instance consisted of the promise of a fashionable yet instructive and pious decorum.

Images and children: lithography and the Sunday school movement

With the countless bible scenes and Sunday school certificates they produced, Currier & Ives and their competition contributed to the iconography that Protestants eventually incorporated into the religious education of children in Sunday schools. As Protestants systematized religious pedagogy and expanded the network and outreach of Sunday schools, using them as missionary inroads to the foundation of congregations on the frontier and among immigrant populations, they formalized the Sunday school curriculum. Imagery came to play a role in religious instruction, especially in the publications of the Providence Lithograph Company, which became a leading publisher of mainstream

Protestant Sunday school lessons by the end of the century. Beginning in the late 1860s as a small litho shop in Providence, Rhode Island, catering to local industry's need for trade tickets, labels, print forms, and letterhead, Providence Lithography Company slowly expanded over the next decade to include calendars, trade cards, and maps. Business was brisk enough to warrant engaging in direct competition with Louis Prang in the production of greeting cards, which Louis Prang had undertaken in 1874. In 1878 the firm began publishing black board illustrations for use in Sunday schools, entering into further rivalry with Prang.[34]

During this time several Protestant denominations in the United States and Britain were cooperating to form the International Sunday School Association, whose first international convention took place in Baltimore in 1875. The practice of convening national meetings to promote Sunday school organization and curriculum had been undertaken as early as the 1830s by the ASSU, one of the early organizations to promote the alliance of Protestant denominations in the campaign of print evangelization of the nation. That effort, visualized in prints like *Christian Union*; (see Figure 14, p. 54) or the American Tract Society's familiar iconography of preachers and printing presses (Figures 2 and 3, pp. 12 and 13), encountered serious problems of fragmentation over slavery. After the Civil War, however, the project was renewed by Presbyterian, Congregationalist, Baptist, Methodist, and other mainstream Protestant leaders in the national and international organizations dedicated to producing a unified Sunday school curriculum. The principal energy of the group was invested in developing, publishing, and maintaining what was called the uniform lesson plan, a system of presenting the bible in Sunday school lessons that moved through scripture from Sunday to Sunday, teaching the same material to all age groups. The hope was to achieve a systematic and universal study of the bible that would maximize learning and, in concert with the ecumenical goals of the Evangelical alliance, avoid sectarian rivalries, which would allow for national unity and greatest possible effect.[35]

In 1880 the Providence Lithography Company began publishing very large images, measuring 34 × 44 inches, depicting biblical scenes that illustrated the lessons of the Sunday school curriculum of the uniform lesson plan. Within a few years these images became known as "Bible Lesson Pictures," which became the company's staple commodity. Although all the major denominational groups involved in the Sunday school lesson program had a publishing arm and editorial offices, the sheer scale of production involved exceeded their capacity. The leaders of the National Sunday School Association began meeting with publishers in the early 1870s in order to create a means of publication and circulation that would accommodate the broad scatter and annual consumption of curricular materials. Providence Litho competed with a number of firms for the Sunday school business and secured contracts with individual denominational organizations such as the Methodist Book Concern as early as 1882. John Vincent, Methodist leader, president of the International Lesson Committee, and founder of Chautauqua, a major consumer of religious educational materials, praised Providence Litho early on as a purveyor of Sunday school materials. With this endorsement and increasing inroads among Protestant denominations, the firm followed the lesson pictures with the Bible lesson cards in 1889. These were 3 × 4 inch color facsimiles of the large images, but became a major commodity since they were produced in enormous volume in order to be distributed to each Sunday school student to use in class and take home afterward. Sunday schools had long issued reward devices such as illustrated cards and tickets. But the lithographed images were in full color and replicated the large posters used in class by the instructors to present the lessons. The cards were presented to children as collectible and served to integrate the lesson into the lives of young people by crossing into home life.[36]

By 1894, Providence Lithography Company was supplying materials and lesson cards to Northern Baptists, Congregationalists, and the United Brethren. By 1902 the firm was also printing curricular materials for Presbyterians and the Dutch Reformed Church among others. The commercial advantage of the uniform lesson plan was that the same product was sold to a wide variety of groups, many of which preferred to have their denominational identity stamped on the material. The editorial offices of many of the denominational publishers worked closely with Providence Litho to ensure that nothing was included in the illustrations that would provoke sectarian offense. The lesson pictures and cards were an ideal mass-market commodity: generic products that were inexpensively appropriated by many different particular groups. Not only was the market national, but also Providence Litho shipped its Sunday school products to Britain, Australia, New Zealand, Canada, and British South Africa. Lessons were also translated into German for the European market.[37] To some degree the firm was even able to recapture the Evangelical North-South market of antebellum days. In 1901 the Presbyterian Board of Publication authorized arrangements with Providence Litho to provide approximately 142,000 sets of lesson cards for the Philadelphia-based organization of the Northern church and 26,000 sets for the Southern wing of the church headquartered in Richmond. The agreement stated that the cards were to be printed with the same lesson, but with "a separate imprint and name."[38] Although Northern and Southern Presbyterians (as well as the Baptists) had been unable to resolve their history of differences with one another and reunite as a single national body, all of them relied on Providence Litho for Sunday school materials.

How did the publisher achieve this commercial ideal? The key to the success of the lesson cards and pictures was their close relation to text. Like tract illustrations during the antebellum period, Providence Lithography produced images that were not intended to stand alone but were part of a textual regime. The images were keyed to biblical narratives and were used to tell the stories and teach the moral lessons that Protestant Sunday school was designed to impart. The full color and many details in geography, costume, and history that were commonly registered in the cards made teaching easier. Illustrators working for the firm made use of popular reference works in order to make their work appear (what they considered to be) historically authentic. One artist introduced himself to the art director in 1931 by stating "I have done a vast amount of Biblical and historical illustrations, and have built up a very good private research library of my own so as to insure accuracy of costume and detail."[39] But not all the imagery issued by the firm was biblical. The image of *The Great Commission* (Figure 28) portrayed the lesson from Matthew 28 for Sunday, May 12, 1901, by placing a Caucasian evangelist before a group of Native Americans seated outside of a teepee, set against the broad American plains. The intention was to bridge the biblical text and the contemporary world of Sunday school students. In order to do this, the artist borrowed the established motif of the preaching missionary, bible in hand, orating before a calm assembly of docile listeners (cf. Figures 2, 3, and 17, pp. 12, 13 and 61). Whether ancient or modern in subject, the picture cards aroused the attention of children and assisted in the task of teaching. In 1885, the president of the Indiana Sunday-School Union wrote Providence Litho that he was

> much pleased with "The Bible Lesson Pictures." They are pretty, attractive, and helpful; and a marvel of cheapness at the present price. To tens of thousands of Sunday-schools they would be as a cheerful visitor every Sabbath, and overcome the complaint of dullness, which is so common.[40]

Crisis began to loom, however, in the mid-1890s, when a growing number of teachers lobbied for a graded lesson plan. Spurred by contemporary educational psychology, which was identifying the phases of personal development among children and adolescents, Sunday school instructors desired to tailor learning to different age groups and wanted to use illustrated materials like the lesson cards to do so. Educators believed that young people responded differently to images depending on their age and sought to provide a rationale for the use of images of various kinds – from idealistic and nurturing for younger children to realistic and descriptive for older and heroic for yet older.[41] This represented a serious menace to Providence Litho since its mainstay was the uniform lesson material. In 1911, for example, the firm's annual sale of lesson cards alone numbered 6,512,000.[42] Providence Litho eventually responded to the challenge by proposing a graded curriculum of its own, though the use of the uniform plan remained in place for many denominations. But the need to vary imagery and the growing competition with other American firms issuing lesson cards as well as other illustrated religious items pushed Providence Litho into pursuing the use of images by widely recognized and admired religious artists in Britain and Europe.

The imagery most often stipulated from the 1890s through the first several decades of the twentieth century for use in instructional material was the highly narrative, easily legible, pageant-like tableaux of biblical scenes by painters Heinrich Hofmann (see Figure 60, p. 208) and Bernhard Plockhorst from Germany and Harold Copping, a British painter. Providence Litho

Figure 28 The *Great Commission*, for Sunday, May 12, 1901. Providence Lithography Company. Courtesy Sandy Brewer.

expended a great deal of energy in tracking down copyright holders and negotiating with them over fees for the use of images by these artists. Denominational editors preparing lesson material specifically asked for these artists' biblical works. When the images were unavailable or copyright fees were prohibitively expensive, the art director at Providence Litho sent reproductions of paintings by them to free-lance artists as guides in the preparation of curricular illustrations. Because Providence Litho was a supplier rather than a denominational publisher, it worked closely with these editors, several of whom, drawn from the leading denominational patrons, constituted a standing committee that had to approve every image that was used in the lesson cards and other materials. The art director communicated the desires of the editors to the artist hired for the job. After deciding the subject to be illustrated, the editorial committee focused intense effort on what artists provided them, commonly sending specific instructions before the artist began work. The art director often ran interference between artist and committee, attempting to anticipate editorial criticisms in order to expedite the production process. The editors, who were almost always women from one of several major denominations – Presbyterian, Baptist, Congregational, and Methodist – suggested examples from the corpus of existing images, such as those by Copping, Hofmann, or Plockhorst. But when one or another among them felt an image departed from scripture or introduced anything possibly offensive to their denomination's doctrine, they stipulated its correction. For example, a suite of letters exchanged in 1936 between the art director at Providence Litho and editorial committee member Ms. Robbie Trent, of the Sunday School Board of the Southern Baptist Convention, indicates finely tuned objections to the precise locale of a scene from the life of Jesus in a painting by Harold Copping. Having consulted with a Baptist theologian in Nashville, Trent pointed out to the hapless art director that

> the scene in Copping's picture could not be on the way to Gethsemane because there is no mountain effect on the road. You will also recall that Judas went out during the Last Supper and was not present with the group which went to Gethsemane. This picture shows twelve disciples present.[43]

Conservative Protestant groups like the Southern Baptists cared about minute details of scriptural accuracy, but so did children as they gazed upon pictures in Sunday school lessons and compared them to the biblical texts they were studying. So the editors did not hesitate to task the artists and Providence Litho with the closest attention to detail and to the expressive impact of the imagery. The correspondence between art director and artists abounds with instances of special requests for modifying illustrations in order to avoid infelicitous effects. In a letter of 1942, the art director Phillips Booth transmitted the comments of one editor to an artist regarding a sketch of Christ the artist had submitted. The editor objected to the formal character of Christ and in particular to his raised hand:

I would rather have him reaching out in a friendly way to one of the children [in the image], or tending solely to the business of driving the donkey. This [the raised hand] is too much the authoritative gesture the Catholics employ. Please ask the artist not to make Christ too introspective, but, if possible, showing some response either with an outstretched hand or a pleasant human expression.[44]

The art directors were careful to coach each new artist they engaged on the general nature of imagery they sought. For example, in 1932 an art director wrote a New York artist that the editors had "repeatedly pointed out to us" that "we must be very careful to have the story so completely and clearly told that for small children the picture can stand without explanatory text."[45] Another artist was introduced to the firm's line of imagery by being urged to "keep it in mind to lean over backwards in not offending any 'church-goers' and also [to] avoid causing nightmares among 6 to 8 year old children."[46]

Providence Litho art directors and the editorial committee warned artists to avoid contemporary visual sources that viewers might find profane. Booth instructed an artist to modify the image of Abel selecting a lamb for sacrifice:

the feeling seems to be that he looks too much like a girl. I realize what you are up against, being compelled to try to get a very gentle, kind expression to the face, but it does seem to be very much a resemblance to our "cinema star" Jean Arthur.

The likeness to secular print imagery was not less acceptable. "Don't forget," Booth reminded another artist, "that although we wish to have the women in this material [an image of Boaz and Ruth] look attractive, we must avoid any 'glamour girl' appearance."[47] Almost always Booth and his colleagues sent artists reprints of images by Hofmann, Copping, or Plockhorst to convey what they had in mind, urging them to observe the precedent in style and conception that the popular reception of these artists had long established. Not unlike Protestant publishers committed to the ecumenical marketplace since the antebellum period, Providence Litho identified and sought to maintain over the course of the first half of the twentieth century a look to its bible lesson imagery that avoided doctrinal or social controversy, that preserved a clear sense of gender distinction, and that avoided association with any visual media that connoted the secular culture against which conservative Protestants were inclined to define themselves. Providence Lithography Company discovered how to walk this line in a commercially viable manner.

Race sometimes received special attention in the production of imagery. For the purpose of a mission effort among African Americans in 1936, Providence Litho was instructed by the denominational editors to seek out a black artist who might contribute an illustration. In a memo to himself, the art director records having identified a black illustrator in Philadelphia, Samuel Brown, and inviting him to produce

> a painting for Thanksgiving illustrating something for which both races might be thankful. Told him we didn't think they [the editors] meant anything highly symbolic or treating on such hazardous subjects as Emancipation. Perhaps it might be well in one sketch to have a scene showing what we Northerners generally think of as a typical Southern Negro scene, the kind of thing we visualize after reading "Uncle Tom's Cabin," or seeing Porgy.[48]

That "Emancipation" should still have been considered "hazardous" in 1936 speaks loudly of the state of racial affairs in the nation. Falling back on "a typical Southern Negro scene," set before the Civil War, registers the deeply anachronistic imaginary of white American Protestants in the North and South. DuBose Heyward's novel *Porgy* (1924) tells the story of a poor crippled black man who lives on Catfish Row among a community of poor, illiterate Blacks on an island off the coast of South Carolina. Porgy falls in love with Bess and kills her murderous husband in self-defense, but loses his love when he returns from police examination to find that Bess has been taken to New York by a drug dealer to resume what appears to have been her life as a prostitute. There are strong elements of Christianity introduced by figures in George Gershwin's operatic version (1934), including a chorus, which may have appealed to the art director at Providence Litho. Whatever the case, the vision of black life was hardly flattering. The iconography of Stowe's illustrated novel (see Figure 15, p. 56) and the racial stereotypes deployed in Heyward's novel and Gershwin's opera (which premiered on Broadway in the fall of 1935 and traveled about the country in the following year) were the paradigms invoked for use among Protestant denominations in Providence Litho material. In both instances, the operative emotion was sympathy, an intense pathos that was intended to instill admiration for the longsuffering and patient fortitude of the humble Black beset by injustice.

Religious illustration for Sunday schools did not remain anachronistic, however. Following the turbulent years of the Civil Rights movement, publishers helped create new markets for instructional material aimed at African-American audiences. Inspired by African-centric theological inquiries, which argued that the principal figures of the bible were in fact of African or African-Asiatic descent rather than the Caucasians conventionally shown in Christian art and illustrations, publishers produced Sunday school material and illustrated bibles that developed suitable iconography. The work of Fred Carter is an example of this imagery. Carter, who also is a primary illustrator for Jack T. Chick's notorious tracts, has produced extensive programs of illustration for one major African-American publisher in Illinois. His imagery of Jesus from the 1970s and 1980s (Figure 29) often reflects both the attempt to reimagine his

Figure 29 Fred Carter, *Christ in Gethsemane*, ink on paper, 1984. Courtesy Urban Ministries, Inc.

race and his masculinity. The image diverges from both the traditional white Christ and the common treatment of him as ethereal, mystical, or tender. The suffering of Jesus in Gethsemane that Carter portrays is intended to register his manful, even superhuman struggle. The style of Carter's illustrations suits this reconception of the black Christ, distancing it considerably from the models circulated by Providence Litho and most other religious publishers in the nation before the 1960s. Conceived in the visual mode of a cartoon strip superhero, Carter reframes Christ's suffering in a dramatic way – changing him from the meek victim of abuse to the hyper-masculine hero figure who is sure to triumph in spite of his opposition.

Chapter 4

Parlors and kitchens
Domestic visual practice and religion

Images are consumed within the framework of a physical context – whether they are fine art within a museum or popular imagery used in the shrine or classroom. For the mass-produced religious imagery that American Christians and Jews used and displayed during the nineteenth century, the context was overwhelmingly the home. But even a home consists of several discrete spaces. Parlor, bedroom, study, and kitchen possessed different purposes and constituted very different places for the display of imagery. It is easy to overlook the fact that the home for most Christians and Jews was not only the center of daily life, but also the most important religious site in their lives. This is not to deny the importance of the church or synagogue. Each possessed its own significance – the Catholic parish church was the center for the ethnic neighborhood among Catholics in large cities; the Protestant building was the often picturesque symbol of worship, placed prominently to act as a kind of giant billboard; and only the Reform synagogue allowed mixed seating, bringing genders together. Yet these powerful public symbols did not overshadow the centrality of religious practice in the Catholic, Protestant, or Jewish home. This chapter examines domestic spaces as the setting for the use and display of different kinds of images, especially with regard to practices of consumption, which came increasingly to constitute behaviors that shaped the religious identities of different Americans.

The iconography of domestic practice: religion and the American parlor

Parlors were features in the homes of European gentry as early as the seventeenth century, serving as formal spaces reserved for hosting the salon life of fine society.[1] The practice of dedicating a room to the social rituals of reception, conversation, and polite amusement continued through the eighteenth century. Among middle-class home owners in American cities in the early nineteenth century, the parlor was often a front room, facing the street, and situated beside the hallway leading from the front door. Here the parlor was set off from the private spaces upstairs (where bedrooms were located) and at the back of the house on the ground floor (which was usually reserved for the kitchen, and sometimes included a less formal "back parlor"). Parlors were formal spaces that contained the home's finest furniture, which was produced specifically for the parlor space. As Kenneth Ames and others have noted in their studies of nineteenth-century parlors, parlor chairs commonly sacrificed comfort to stiff-backed seating and rectilinear arrangements that somatically enforced the rigid protocols of courtesy, the knowledge and performance of which demonstrated either the gentility of the gentry or the corresponding respectability of the bourgeoisie. Slouching and sprawling were for the back parlor, not for what was often called "the best room." The parlor served as the public face of the household and was the room where visitors were received and where social gatherings were conducted. In the nineteenth century parlors became features in middle-class and working-class homes – whether farm houses or immigrant flats. By the 1830s, an industry in home design, decoration, and furnishing had taken shape, making the parlor an American institution that would endure through the century and leave a telling legacy in twentieth-century home design. Though class distinctions continued to prevail in the size, number, and furnishing of Victorian parlors, the use of the space for the purpose of domestic display and socializing formed a "parlor culture" that historian Richard Bushman has claimed "was one of the great democratic movements of the nineteenth century."[2]

At the same time that Protestant clergy were voicing suspicion and alarm at the menace of urban life for religion, American cities were developing greater forms of refinement and beauty in parks, boulevards, shopping districts, and residences. The second half of the century witnessed the rise of important cultural institutions such as operatic and orchestral halls, theaters, and museums, and corresponding tastes and audiences. Certainly for some the "fashionable amusements" of theater-going and dancing constituted the threat of city life. But the far more pervasive response of Americans was to resolve the contradiction by engaging in forms of consumption that linked refinement to religious identity. Commodities such as lithographs, engravings, stereographs, and gift books and annuals commonly espoused Christian piety and were meant for display in the parlor. Here they were able to display religious themes in a way that cultivated the respectability and refinement of the household that wished to present a sense of the genteel.[3]

Because it was the principal domestic space for display, the parlor was regarded by visitors as the outward physiognomy of a family's soul. Parlors became those spaces where presenting the public face of identity welcomed the display of lithographs as well as family bibles, organs, periodicals, furniture, and wall paper. Decoration of the parlor became the consumer's forum to construct personal and family identity for public consumption. But as middle-class American Protestants engaged in the commoditized practices of home decoration and turned their attention to the demands of the parlor as the public face of the home and its ethos, a host of advice books appeared to tutor and guide consumption in order to avoid vulgar taste and the menace that many Americans considered excessive consumption to present to the integrity and mission of the home. One of the most prolific writers in the industry of advice books on home décor at mid-century, before the much more celebrated appearance of Catherine Beecher and Harriet Beecher Stowe's *The American Woman's Home* (1869), was Caroline Kirkland (1801–64). Author, school teacher, and editor (*Union Magazine of Literature and Art*), Kirkland published *The Evening Book, or, Fireside Talk on Morals and Manners* in 1852. She carefully stipulated the purpose and appearance of the parlor: it was to be a "radiating centre of light and love" where family members meet each day to share in the fellowship that is the heart of the home.[4] Kirkland was at pains to stress the function of the parlor and the home in general as the vessel in which the virtues of sociability were infused into Americans. The parlor was the domestic means by which the home was linked to the larger social world and formed children for membership in it.

> Social feeling is an element of home; pride is the enemy of both. A home pervaded by the true spirit is gladdened by the voice of a friend. A home in which the education of children is a sacred object, covets the conversation of intelligent and various guests. A home of whose harmony religion is the diapason [tuning fork], breathes a spirit of hospitality. In none of these will the alternation be between seclusion and display – two extremes equally inimical to joyous domesticity.[5]

Kirkland endorsed a parlor that avoided the formality of the parlor of gentility and the expensive appointments of upscale consumerist display. Comfort was the aim, but respectable, socially minded comfort dedicated to domestic happiness and practice of the social virtues that educated children in the arts of sociability. For Kirkland, the American home was charged with a powerful task in the American cultural politics of order and authority. "The decay of the household fire," she proclaimed, "is the cause of our social coldness." Americans, in her view, had lost the vital practice of social virtues. The home "is indeed a little world; and in each household we see in some sense a resemblance to the society of which it forms a part." Therefore, in order to improve the social world, "we must reform our domestic maxims."[6]

What was wrong with American society? In a word, the loss of humanity that the parlor was meant to reinscribe into the protocols of American life. Kirkland registered familiar Victorian complaints about the competitive ethos of the emerging capitalism and its preoccupation with wealth and display, which came at an unacceptable price:

> in the wild chase after wealth and social distinction, the old-fashioned, fundamental, patriarchal, God-given idea of the household is merged into a sort of domestic republic, in which all are free and equal, and the very

notion of natural headship is repudiated, the prominent object being not the family but the world; not the ark of shelter, but the struggling waves around it, and the floating, slippery treasures upon them. For these we venture all.[7]

Democracy threatened the respectability of republican virtue grounded in the paternalistic home, where the parlor acted like a brake on the ambitions for financial gain and social advancement that tended to undermine the vertical structure of respectable society. This represented a longing to which many image producers were keen to provide a visual reply, as many of the images reproduced in this chapter will show.

Antagonistic as Kirkland and others were toward the American penchant for acquisition, this did not mean, however, that the parlor was sealed off from consumption. To the contrary, it was the room that brought consumption into the home, though it was filtered according to taste and, in pious households, by a sense of sentimental Christian decorum. The Victorian parlor represents the influential force of a domestic ideology dedicated to securing and shaping character within the new matrix of American consumption, an economic behavior and culture applied to the refinement of taste, intended to elevate national as well as individual character. Among the most characteristic forms of heavily illustrated pious parlor print in antebellum America was the gift-book annual.[8] From the mid-1820s to the Civil War, publishers issued annual volumes under such titles as *The Christian Souvenir, The Religious Keepsake*, and *The Rose of Sharon*. The volumes were lavishly produced, stocked with poetry, music, short prose pieces, and a growing number of engravings (Figure 30). Printed on fine paper and bound in thick, embossed leather bindings, the books often sold at high prices. They were intended for display on the large round tables that Americans fondly placed in their parlors. The rite of exchanging annuals as gifts was likely practiced for the most part among female friends, who visited one another in their parlors where the gifts were placed for conversation as well as personal enjoyment.

Protestants had probably never enjoyed such visual excess as the antebellum women who took delight in the abundance of engravings in gift books. Reflecting on the course of American publishing at mid-century, Samuel Goodrich, himself an early publisher of a serially issued annual (*The Token*, 1828–42), not surprisingly remembered the heyday of gift book publication with appreciation. Nevertheless, his remarks offer some insight into the Victorian view of the genre and its readership. In his memoirs Goodrich listed a variety of characteristic titles (e.g. Diadems, Pearls, Gems, Amulets, Talismans) and then declared:

> Under these seductive titles, [the gift-book annuals] became messengers of love, tokens of friendship, signs and symbols of affection, and luxury and refinement; and thus they stole alike into the palace and the cottage, the library, the parlor, and the boudoir. The public taste grew by feeding on

Drawn by E.T. Farris.   Engraved by A.L. Dick.

Figure 30 "Devotion," *The Parlor Annual and Christian Family Casket for 1846,* engraving, 1845 following page 148. Courtesy The Library Company of Philadelphia.

those luscious gifts, and soon craved even more gorgeous works of the kind.[9]

Luxury and taste were not incompatible, which was perhaps necessary for a refinement of taste that stretched from the palace of an Astor to the cottage of a mechanic. It is the case that some annuals were sold for as little as 37 cents. But Goodrich reserved his praise for annuals that were beyond the means of the working class. He believed the

> effect of the circulation of such works as these, in creating and extending a taste for the arts, and in their most exquisite forms, can only be appreciated by those who have examined and reflected upon the subject. Even in the United States alone, four thousand volumes of one of these works, at the price of twelve dollars each, have been sold in a single season![10]

One is left to wonder if Goodrich was more impressed by the profitability to the publisher that was signaled by the volume of sales or by the democratic benefit from wide circulation. Perhaps both, but it was the dazzling effect of the annual's visual program that struck him as "having produced a certain revolution in the public taste." The very existence of the annuals, he claimed, owed no little debt to the technology of visual production: the steel engraving.

> This enabled the artist to produce works of more exquisite delicacy than had ever before been achieved; steel also gave the large number of impressions which the extensive sales of the Annuals demanded, and which could not have been obtained from copper.[11]

Goodrich was certainly correct to note that the annuals changed American publication for all time by demonstrating the appeal of well-reproduced works of art. Indeed, the trade in "coffee table" art books has not abated since his day. Moreover, the sentimentalist piety that infused annuals helped make the case for art as a refining or civilizing agent by linking image to religious subject. As Goodrich himself pointed out, many of the successors to the annuals after their decline in the 1850s were illustrated books with religious subjects, issued by such major publishers as Appletons and Harpers.[12]

"Devotion" (Figure 30), which appeared in *The Parlor Annual and Christian Family Casket for 1846*, is a richly engraved, full-page image that highlights the genteel practice of domestic piety. Engraved specifically for the annual, the image portrays a wealthy young woman named Juliet who, as an accompanying verse explains, has stolen away "from gorgeous halls and festive throng" in response to the sudden memory of home and childhood. In particular, Juliet heard the tones of her mother's voice intermixed with the chimes of a clock:

> O'er Juliet's heart that chime had power/ For that had been a holy hour,/ The hour when childhood's sport and glee/ Were hush'd, and at her mother's knee,/ In love and faith her heart had given/ Its first best offering to Heaven.[13]

The image gives viewers another clue to the sudden return of childhood piety, the power that compels her to kneel in prayer as she turns from the lavish lifestyle signaled by her clothing and jewelry and the sumptuous interior: her hands clasped in prayer rest on a bible. But it is no ordinary bible that comforts the troubled Juliet by helping her recall her mother's spiritual counsel. The thick bindings and ornate metal clasp indicate it is a bible commensurate in cost with the rest of the parlor décor. The extravagance of the religious artifact that offers Juliet refuge from the mirth of a worldly soirée argues visually that luxury and piety are not deeply antagonistic. Like other images of domestic piety we will examine in this chapter, childhood memory is intermingled with piety. The memory calls her away from the empty festivities, but *not* from the lifestyle of abundance. The engraving implies that Juliet does not repent of wealth, but of neglecting the sound of maternal devotion. If the music of the party rivals the sounds of memory, it does not succeed in blotting them out. Different as her station in life now may be from the early piety of her mother's lap, the call of piety does not threaten to turn Juliet to a life of sacred poverty or Yankee thrift. The riches and gentility of the refined life need only be sanctified by the domestic practice of prayer.

There were, in fact, many different ways of decorating parlors, each of which corresponded to class and ethnic identity. Images played a role in conveying these distinctions. As the American parlor became a central fixture in the middle-class American domestic experience in the early decades of the nine-teenth century, the concomitant industry of lithographs targeted the home, especially the parlor, to supply the rising interest in domestic display. Working-class as well as middle- and upper-class homes had commonly displayed broad-sheets or engravings, even before the modern era. But a new decorative aesthetic of accenting the middle-class domestic interior with prints, providing conver-sation pieces for a home's parlor, or decorating the home with imagery that might contribute to the formation of children all supported the market for lithographs that Currier & Ives and other firms sought to supply. Litho sales were so plentiful and inexpensive that by the 1860s lithographs rivaled the older medium of engraving without ever supplanting it.

As a form of display that conveyed the class, religion, and ethnicity of their owners, prints offered consumers the ethos they desired and acquired in some sense by purchasing prints for their homes. This becomes especially clear in nineteenth-century popular literature, which is an instructive source of infor-mation regarding visual display in Victorian parlors. Mid-century novels frequently mention and often describe individual engravings or lithographs within homes and apartments, typically as a way of locating the characters within the social world of contemporary America. In a light-hearted fictional account of the visit of Albert Edward, Prince of Wales, to Boston, the author Edward Everett Hale related the story of a waggish character named Hali-burton who, word had it, showed the royal visitor about town. Haliburton elected to take his guest to several Bostonian households of various means and ethnicity, ranging from a recently arrived Irish immigrant to the home of "a staid old Bostonian."[14] In each case, Hale registered the social status of the household by the manner of images on the wall or mantel. Haliburton began with a visit to the tenement-house apartment of Mrs. Rooney:

> On the mantel, a china image of St. Joseph with the infant Saviour; a canary-bird, in wax, fastened on some green leaves; a large shell from the West Indies; a kerosene lamp; three leather-covered books without titles on their backs; a paper of friction-matches; and a small flower-pot with a bit of ivy in it – placed in the order I name, going from right to left. On the wall behind, a colored lithograph of Our Mother of the Bleeding Heart, her bosom anatomically laid open that the heart might be seen, and the color represented accurately by the artist; another colored lithograph of Father Mathew.[15]

The next home to visit was "the pretty suites of a 'model lodging-house' " belonging to the "pretty Caroline Freeman," who received her guests "in her pretty parlor," which featured a brilliant view of many miles from her vine-clad windows. Hale continued by describing the parlor, which exhibited "a cheerful glow from the bright carpet; a good water-color by her brother – scene in the harbor of Shanghae, or Bussora, or somewhere outlandish, no matter; and a good chromolith[ograph]."[16] Albert and Haliburton then called on Lucy Coleman, who lived in Charles Street, near Boston Common, in a mansion whose "parlors were perfectly finished and hung" with painted portraits in oil by Copley and Allston.[17] The tour continued, but the point of detailing the images in each household is clear. Along with the objects on mantels and tables, the furniture, and the nature of the apartment, suite, or manse, the imagery belonged to an urban physiognomy that revealed the social location of its owner. People display the pictures that bespeak their status. This hierarchy begins with a hand-colored lithograph at the bottom, beneath a chromolithograph and a watercolor painted on international tour, and is topped by original oil paintings of a family's esteemed forebears by artists of international renown. Religion, particularly the Roman Catholicism of the Irish immigrant, Mrs. Rooney, assumes the form and content of the nadir of social rank, while landscape occupies the middle range and portraiture in oil marks the apex of distinction.

Other authors relied on the domestic display of Catholic iconography in lithographs and engravings to evoke the ethos of the room, its residents, and the social world to which they belonged. When she arrived at her cousin's rural home where she took up residence, in Catholic novelist Mary Hoffman's *Alice Murray*, the novel's central character entered the parlor:

> Over the table hung a small mirror, and on the walls were several cheap pictures in poor frames. A glance at them showed they were of a religious

character – the "Crucifixion," "Sacred Heart of Jesus," "The Virgin and Child," "Saint Patrick," and "Saint Liguori."[18]

As with the lithographs described in Mrs. Rooney's tenement apartment, those in Alice's new home were prints then available from Currier & Ives' large stock of Roman Catholic subjects. But other authors made use of the telling lithograph in the American parlor to communicate the Protestant ethos of its owner. In his stinging and often hilarious series of sketches of Gotham's housing establishments and their proprietors, *The Physiology of New York Boarding-Houses* (1857), Thomas Butler Gunn described "the 'serious' boarding-house" in terms of its austere décor and suitably "hard shell" Presbyterian mistress:

> On applying for board . . . expect to be inducted into a grim front parlor. There, you will . . . observe a book-case filled with volumes of sermons and such light literature (which is always kept locked, possibly from motives of humanity), half a dozen strait-backed and very unaccommodating looking chairs, a cheerful lithograph, representing a number of savages engaged in knocking a missionary's brains out with big clubs, and badly executed portraits, in oil, of the landlady and her husband.[19]

Whether they were comfortable or excruciatingly painful, parlors as portrayed by many mid-nineteenth-century American popular novelists were the visual signatures of the souls that lived in them. In a set of moralizing sketches of everyday American life, one author stressed the importance of pictures in the home in a way that registers the distinctions of class, but argues for an overarching sensibility of taste:

> We don't care whether pictures abound in a house from pride, fashion, or taste, so that they be there. . . . How cheerful the walls of a home look with them; and, by the rule of opposites, how cheerless without them! It is a garden without flowers, a family without children. Let an observing man enter a house, and ten times in ten he can decide the character of the proprietor. If he is a mean man, there will be no pictures; if rich and ostentatious, they will be garish and costly, brought from over the water, with expensive frames, and mated with mathematical exactness; if a man of taste, the quality is observable, and, whatever their number or arrangement, regard has evidently been had to the beauty of subject and fitness, with just attention to light and position. In humble homes, when this taste exists, it still reveals itself, though cheaply, but the quick eye detects it and respects it. We have seen it in a prison, where a judicious placing of a woodcut or a common lithograph has given almost cheerfulness to the stone walls on which it hung.[20]

Even the incarcerated felon can beautify the grim interior of his cell with the tasteful virtue of homeliness. Orah Howland, wife of Judge Howland in Mary

Wolcott Janvrin's *Peace, or, The Stolen Will!* (1857), was a tasteful, highly stationed, and proud woman whose home, "elegant, stately, and refined, was an index of her character. Is not *every* home," the narrator continues, "an exponent of the character and tastes of its inmates? The furnishing of an apartment betrays the mood and mind of its occupant."[21] The physiognomy of the parlor lithograph was revealing because it was within the reach of every American:

> All may not have elegant and luxurious homes – but, thank God, all can have *beautiful* ones! Flowers, birds, books, pictures – it does not need a fortune to procure *these* . . . pictures – the choice engraving, the exquisite lithograph, the cheap print, all embodying some artist's idea of the Beautiful – such are within the reach of all.[22]

For middle-class Americans bothered by the inequity of class in their society, lithographs offered an aesthetic means of concealing modesty behind the veil of good taste.

But taste was not understood to be dissimulation. The hope was that beautiful images would transform those who lived with them in the American home. In the story of Violet, a pious young girl, Maria McIntosh described the intentions of Violet's guardian, Captain Ross, who decorated her room with deliberate aims regarding the girl's formation:

> Over the mantel-piece hung a pretty engraving of Raphael's child-angels. It was the only thing in the room not intended for use. Perhaps it is wrong to say that even this was not designed for a useful purpose; for it was a belief of Capt. Ross that all, but especially children, were apt to grow into the likeness of those things which they most frequently contemplated.[23]

The notion that images in the home exerted this manner of influence extended the ideas of child nurture that were promoted most notably by Congregationalist theologian Horace Bushnell. In his book *Christian Nurture* (1861), Bushnell argued against a conception of the human being as an atomic or insular being whose practice of virtue is "the product of separate and absolutely independent choice." Human character was governed by what Bushnell characterized as "organic laws," by which he meant the "organic connection between parent and child."[24] Rather than autonomous beings, humans are intimately interlinked with one another. "We possess only a mixed individuality all our life long," Bushnell wrote. "A pure, separate, individual man, living wholly within, and from himself, is a mere fiction."[25] Children bear the imprint of their parents, their character is drawn from their parents, "the mold of their being."[26] At the core of his idea of nurture was a visual no less than a tactile metaphor: children are cast in the matrix of mother and father, whose responsibilities for the formation of their offspring continue intensively in the early years of a child's life when his or her being remains plastic and subject to the parent's shaping influence. The greatest portion of this formation occurs in the home: "Religion never thoroughly penetrates life, till it becomes domestic. Like that patriotic fire which makes a nation invincible, it never burns with inextinguishable devotion till it burns at the hearth."[27] As this passage implies, Bushnell claimed that human life ideally consists of three organically corresponding spheres, which he stipulated in his book as "a national life, a church life, [and] a family life."[28] These were the matrices into which children are born and mature. Without these corresponding spheres, human life was unable to generate the virtue that consists of a shared spirit, a state of being rather than a series of discrete actions based on choice. Grounded in the home, Christian nurture was the organic molding of the child's character that formed the basis for the Christian adult's relation to church and nation as larger forms of family.

If antebellum Protestant consumers of prints found little to display in the large selection of explicitly Catholic imagery issued by Currier & Ives, as noted in Chapter 3 the firm was able to provide a smaller but growing range of images that appealed directly to Protestant domestic practice. Chief among these was imagery of the home, particularly the parlor, as the domestic site for Christian devotion and the formation of children. The primary motif in this iconography of domestic religion for Protestant consumers of lithographs comprised images of individuals or groups reading the Scriptures, as found in the Currier & Ives corpus as well as among the output of the company's competitors. A Currier print dated 1848 (Figure 31), entitled *Reading the Bible*, shows a fashionably dressed young women before a tall bay window and abundant curtains, her feet posed primly on a low footstool and her bible resting on a round, marble-top table. She sits with the formal posture dictated by the refined parlor and its stiffly decorative furniture. As Karen Haltunen described the Victorian denizen of the parlor, she "rules as a kind of constitutional monarch whose responsibility was to enforce the hundreds of rules governing polite social intercourse."[29] This is certainly how she appears in Currier's litho (Figure 31) as well as in gift-book plates (see Figure 30, p. 107). But such images hardly evoked the comfortable place for family life urged by Kirkland. Currier's young queen sits in a parlor that is situated in a large home, as the faint indication of a manicured lawn and airy trees through the window suggests. Always pitching his goods to the variety of consumers he sought to engage, Currier was no doubt interested in the market consisting of middle- and upper-middle-class antebellum readers of gift books or *Godey's Lady's Book*. But he did not limit himself to that patronage, as the difference between Figure 31 and other images of parlor religion make clear (see Figure 32). The difference may consist of different generational cohorts. Figure 33 is an image of domestic piety for fashionably inclined younger consumers circa 1848.

Contrasting with the fine appointments of Figure 31, *Reading the Scriptures* (Figure 32) envisions the domestic piety of a husband and wife seated before a hearth in a parlor of considerable austerity, one that would have appealed to Evangelical Protestants possessed of a sensibility more restrained than Caroline

Figure 31 Nathaniel Currier, *Reading the Bible*, hand-tinted lithograph, 1848. Courtesy Billy Graham Center Museum.

Figure 32 Nathaniel Currier, *Reading the Scriptures*, hand-tinted lithograph, date unknown. Courtesy Billy Graham Center Museum.

Kirkland's. Although the origin of the image may have been a British painting or print, several versions of the subject were executed by American lithographers in the mid to late 1840s, many of which may have been copied from one or another American copy of the British original.[30] Currier's print delivers a simple tonal massing, stark symmetry, and a still solemnity in the figures. The wife gazes quietly at her husband, who reads from a large folio bible. The rendition of details falls short of other versions of the print issued by rival publishers. The bible in Currier's image appears larger and overlaps with the lamp. The perspective of the chairs is not carefully observed. The artist did not know what to do with the woman's hands, which seem to vanish abruptly just beneath the surface of the table. All of these infractions of anatomy and perspective and the blurring of sundry details indicate that Currier did not concern himself with fidelity to his prototype, whatever it may have been (likely the work of another American lithographer). His print focuses the viewer's attention on the pious act of the husband and wife who direct their gazes toward their respective object of authority: the husband to the scriptures, the wife to her husband's face, listening to his somber voice in the humble attempt to reclaim something of the "natural headship" that Kirkland missed in the American home and hoped the parlor would recover. Like some other versions of the print, but not all, Currier portrayed the woman's chair without arms.

Thomas Schlereth has pointed out in a discussion of Victorian parlor furniture that "ladies chairs lacked arms (in part to accommodate their full skirts) and were designed to reinforce the era's postural requirements for women – to sit upright, away from the chair back, with one's hands folded on one's lap."[31] Parlor seating could be gender-specific – men's chairs typically sported ponderous arms. Currier even enhanced the gendered distinction by posing the woman as leaning forward to attend raptly to the solemn lection of her husband, thereby breaking the protocol, which expected women to sit upright.

Not one to settle for a single commodity when variation should do better in an articulated market, Currier also issued a print of the same title and format (Figure 33) at approximately the same time, to judge from the date of the identical print as it appeared from a rival firm.[32] In this instance, Currier wanted to appeal to a more fashionable and younger clientele since the print's protagonists are younger, much better dressed, display more current hairstyles, and occupy an interior that, though skeletally identical to Figure 32, is decorated with ornate wall paper, thick drapes, embellished furniture (note the tassels and carved volutes), and a mantel of books accented with flowers. The composition still focuses one's attention on the relationship between the reader and listener, but their age, mode, and station signal the relevance of piety for a different set of Americans. Judging from the tastes of the authors of sentimental novels and advice books in mid-century America, it may be that middle- and upper-middle-

Figure 33 Nathaniel Currier, *Reading the Scriptures*, hand-tinted lithograph, ca. 1838–56. Courtesy Billy Graham Center Museum.

class American Protestants might have purchased lithographs like Figure 33 to hang in their parlors as a way of keeping parity with the older piety redressed in the more contemporary fashion of the present.

The many different images of bible reading in the parlor produced by litho firms and engravers in the middle decades of the century certainly reflect the variety of parlor spaces in American homes. Some parlors were highly formal; others, as Caroline Kirkland advocated, were less so. We don't know how people viewed particular images in every case, though there are some clues. When we regard Figure 32, for instance, it is helpful to examine it through the lens of another, contemporary print by Currier which may tell us something about how he crafted the image to be seen by his customers. *The Way to Happiness* (Figure 34) portrays a young woman in a very fashionable interior, that is, embellished by wall paper and drapery. Her hands are folded prayerfully over an open bible, supported by a velvet, tasseled pillow on a draped table. In reading and praying over scripture, which is opened at the book of Jeremiah, the young woman gazes piously at an ornately framed lithograph on the wall, which turns out to be Figure 32 (inverted in the printing process). In the ninth chapter of Jeremiah the prophet laments the plight of Judah as "the daughter of my people," wondering if there is "no balm in Gilead" (9: 21–2). This might suggest that the print addresses itself to daughters separated from the parental home. Jeremiah had written in the midst of Judah's foreign occupation, first by Egypt, then during its destruction by Babylon. The implication may be that life in a nicely appointed parlor and home was not the secret to happiness. "Devotion" (Figure 30) had taught that piety could reconcile itself with luxury if only Juliet recalled her mother's piety. By contrasting the bourgeois parlor with the austere parlor of mother and father, Currier's print may take a more sober view. The "balm" it offers is a quiet sermon teaching that the "way to happiness" is to practice in one's parlor what mother and father faithfully practiced before the hearth of their home of yesteryear. In a hand-colored version of Figure 34 at the Billy Graham Center, the young woman and her surroundings are tinted, but the litho within a golden frame on the wall is left in black-and-white, using the absence of coloration to locate the scene in the past, where it hovers as a visual memory to guide the latter-day piety of the young woman.[33] Placing one of Currier's own prints on the parlor wall also smartly endorsed the display of his own products in the pious home.

Yet the young woman's gaze was more than a clever way for the firm to promote its products. Memory was a central feature in the domestic piety of American Christians. The sentimental literature of mid-century redounds with the motif of recalling the steady presence of parents and grandparents in the home. Caroline Kirkland intermingled the parlor of yesteryear with the one she urged her contemporaries to create in their homes. She began her account with an evocation of "the old-fashioned parlor – what a nice place it was!"[34] "Grandmamma" sits quietly in the corner; next to the window is "mamma with her capacious work-basket" and the sundry accoutrements of needlework, "the

Figure 34 Nathaniel Currier, *The Way to Happiness*, hand-tinted lithograph, ca. 1850.
Courtesy Billy Graham Center Museum.

very emblem of seamstress-thrift in the good days of old." Then Kirkland seamlessly morphed her sentimental memory into a description of "our household parlor," which she then distinguished explicitly from "the morning room of fashionable houses."[35] In her *Memories of a Grandmother* (1854), Mrs. A. M. Richards remembered her "early home" and saw her grandmother "as of yore" and her grandfather poring "over his favorite volume," the bible.[36] Her grandfather's link to the bible was manifold in her memory. She recalled that his beautiful face resembled "a fine engraving I have of Moses," which came from an illustrated bible. He even treated the sacred tome with the tenderness of a doting mother: "His affection for the Bible was singular. I have seen him open it caressingly, as a mother would fondly and gently unclose the folds concealing the worshipped features of a sleeping infant's face."[37] Nathaniel Currier published an image of such fond memory in the 1850s, "Search the Scriptures."[38] A young woman embraces her aged, bespectacled grandfather, who reads from a large edition of the bible as the two sit on a plushly upholstered sofa, enshrouded by a brocaded curtain above them, two standard features of the contemporary American parlor. Sentimental memory of family piety served as the stabilizing force that kept the home intact. Without the pious gaze of memory, the family was deprived of the past and the home was exposed to the ravages of modern vanity and a consumerism driven by self-interest.

Memory was increasingly managed and evoked by visual means. The subject of family worship was the subject of a chapter entitled "Home Religion" in Harriet Beecher Stowe's *House and Home Papers* (1865). Stowe gathered the family of her novel, the Crowfields, about a hearth one Sunday evening for a colloquy on the domestic observance of Sabbath. The narrative is delivered in the first person of the father, but the greatest force in the conversation is the mother, whom the father describes as "a Bible-believing, Sabbath-keeping woman, cherishing the memory of her fathers, and loving to do as they did."[39] Their son-in-law Bob Stephens, by contrast, a spirited fellow who considers Sabbath-keeping "the iron rod of bigots," suspects that family worship amounts to nothing more than "mere forms."[40] Mr. Crowfield defends domestic practices, arguing that "Forms are, so to speak, a daguerreotype of a past good feeling, meant to take and keep the impression of it when it is gone."[41] Stowe used the term "daguerreotype" in a familiar mid-century sense of an exact copy or memory. It was the evocation of fond memories that family religion brought to Mrs. Crowfield:

> I remember the great old Family Bible, the hymn-book, the chair where father used to sit. I see him as he looked bending over that Bible more than in any other way; and expressions and sentences in his prayers which fell unheeded on my ears in those days have often come back to me like comforting angels. We are not aware of the influence things are having on us till we have left them far behind in years.[42]

Father Crowfield adds his admiration of another old scene: "the stateliness and regularity of family worship in good old families in England – the servants, guests, and children all assembled – the reading of the scriptures, and the daily prayers by the master or mistress of the family."[43] This was just the mental image prompted by a tract illustration issued by the Boston-based American Tract Society in its 1824 edition of a text by the eighteenth-century British preacher Philip Doddridge, called "Family Worship," which shows family members in the foreground and servants in the back of the room participating in the devotions prescribed by the eighteenth-century British preacher (Figure 35). Images of family worship like Doddridge's text and the wood engraving that adorned its cover operated as a form of memory, an evocation of the past that transmitted piety by actively remembering it. Lithographs and engravings nurtured a visual piety of memory and domestic practice by seeding memory with visual prompts.

But it was more than nostalgia for an idealized past, a fanciful concoction of memory that Stowe's account promoted. The assertive Bob Stephens is happy to point out the difference separating the English and Puritan past from the American present: "No such assemblage is possible in our country. . . . Our servants are for the most part Roman Catholics, and forbidden by their religion to join with us in acts of worship." His father-in-law concedes the difference, allowing that American democracy does not operate with a state religion.

Figure 35 Unknown engraver, cover illustration, "Family Worship," no. 18. Boston, MA: American Tract Society, 1824. Photo author.

But then he registers the underlying concern, something which had occupied Sabbatarians since the first decades of the century:

> If the Sabbath of America is simply to be a universal loafing, picnicking, dining-out day, as it is now with all our foreign population, we shall need what they have in Europe, the gendarmes at every turn, to protect the fruit on our trees and the melons in our fields.[44]

Wishing for neither state religion nor a police state, Mr. Crowfield urges the practice of family religion envisioned in memory and popular imagery. Keeping Sabbath in the home was the private exertion of Christian influence in American democracy, Christian nurture's way of making good citizens to secure the public order and commonweal against the threat posed by immigrants.

From the Christian parlor to the Jewish kitchen

Christians were not, of course, the only group in the United States that concerned itself with investing its cultural identity in the protocols, organization, and decoration of the home. American Jews were deeply concerned with domestic religion, particularly in view of the fact that the synagogue did not perform the same purpose in congregational life as the church did among Protestants or Catholics. Among Conservative and Orthodox Jews, men and women sat separately, with women in a gallery.[45] Women stayed at home to prepare for the family's Sabbath observance. Major religious holidays such as Passover and Rosh Hashanah (New Year) and lesser festivals such as Hanukkah were conducted in the home and structured around a meal. The imagery that circulated among Jewish consumers presented a vision of plenty – plenty of food, comfort, family, and material forms for celebration. For example, an advertisement for Fischer Russian Caravan Tea, a New York firm, portrays a family enjoying a richly set holiday table (Figure 36), celebrating an ideal that many recently arrived Jewish families had not enjoyed before immigration. If religion was not always of primary importance to immigrants in America, it became so in one way or another for many, as a rediscovery of their Jewish identity in a new world. This was especially true for the early-twentieth-century Conservative movement among American Jews. Another energetic force behind domestic initiatives devoted to enhancing Jewish identity was represented by the women's groups that dedicated themselves to elevating the domestic ideal among Jewish immigrants as a way of assimilating them to life in America in a manner that would also affirm Judaism as a religion.

The role of domestic religion took on critical importance among middle-class American Jews, especially Jews of German extraction during the late nineteenth and early twentieth centuries for two prevailing reasons. In the first instance, established American Jews, especially members of Conservative Judaism, sought to resist the allure of assimilation to American Christian

Figure 36 Advertisement for Fischer Russian Caravan Tea, New York, ca. 1920. The Jewish Museum, gift of Dr. Harry G. Friedman, F 4983. Courtesy The Jewish Museum/Art Resource, New York.

and capitalist culture as well as the secularizing strand of Jews attracted to Adler's Ethical Culture in New York City. Conservative Jews, inspired by the intellectual and spiritual leadership of Solomon Schechter and the Jewish Theological Seminary, wished to affirm Jewish tradition as a developmental history replete with wisdom and religious authority, yet they wanted to avoid the religious fundamentalism of Orthodoxy, on the one hand, and the loss of tradition undertaken by Reform Judaism, on the other. Domestic life was vital for the appropriate balance of tradition and modern life.[46] The home is where books were read, children raised, Jewish artifacts displayed, and religious holidays celebrated. Conservative women promoted a kind of Jewish revivalism that targeted intermarriage and ceremonial laxity as equal threats to Jewish identity. In the second instance, as Eastern European (largely Russian) Jewish immigration mounted in the 1880s, American Jews of German heritage, who were already in place from New York to Philadelphia to Cincinnati, undertook a campaign of integration that made keen use of domestic material culture. Various congresses and associations formed, many of them organized by women, dedicated to gathering the resources and energies of American Jews and Jewish newcomers to address the task of making and maintaining the Jewish home.[47]

A flood of advice literature began to appear in the late nineteenth century and never ceased. The manner, tone, even the terminology of this literature just before and after the turn of the century recall the moralistic and revivalist campaign of antebellum Christian print. Esther Ruskay's advice book, *Hearth and Home Essays* (Figure 37), was issued in 1902 by the Jewish Publication Society of America (JPS), which was the Jewish counterpart to Evangelical publishers like the ATS. In fact, the first version of the JPS was founded in Philadelphia in 1845 to counteract the influence of Christian missionary efforts among American Jews.[48] Reconstituted in 1888, the mission of the JPS became to provide books from the Jewish heritage translated into English for the children of Jewish immigrants. Mirroring this mission, Ruskay's essays repeatedly referred to "Israel as a missionary people" and even matched something of the millennial sensibility of Evangelical Christians by hailing what she and fellow Conservative Jews considered "the general revival . . . in matters Jewish, which seems to be the distinguishing mark of these latter days." (The title page of her book even carried an emblem that portrayed a child seated peacefully with a lion and lamb above the motto "Israel's Mission is Peace" and before a distant Jerusalem on the horizon – see Figure 37.)[49] Writing in furniture designer Gustav Stickley's journal, *Craftsman*, in 1905, Jewish reformer Bertha Smith stressed the aesthetic value of austerity and cleanliness in an essay entitled "Gospel of Simplicity as Applied to Tenement Homes."[50] The theme of domestic hygiene pervaded the literature on reform and charity produced by Jewish women during the period.[51] This certainly reflected Progressive era discourse regarding immigrants and the urban poor, but it had a special tenor among Jewish female reformers who sought to purge Eastern European Jews (they had Russians and Poles in mind) of their old world habits of dress, diet, and domestic organization. Smith and her countrywomen felt such changes were essential in order to achieve the integration necessary to "convert" the immigrant to American life.

Some Jewish reformers insisted that the elimination of the Three Ds – Dirt, Discomfort, and Disease – would not come about by efforts at instilling cleanliness alone. A spiritual element was necessary. In her presentation at the Jewish Women's Congress at the Columbian Exposition in Chicago in 1893, New York reformer and Settlement house operator Minnie Louis spoke of "mission work among the unenlightened," by which she meant inculcating the religious values of Judaism. Louis lamented the loss of Jewish identity as a religious community.

> We do not want so much to Americanize them [newly arrived and poor Jews] as to Judaize them, or rather to help them to know their Judaism. But who amongst us are the enlightened ones to go down to teach them? Are the unenlightened only amongst the poor? And are all the poor unenlightened? . . . In what of real worth are we wiser or better than they? We glorify the Jew while we almost abandon Judaism.[52]

Louis explicitly regretted the way in which Jews in the United States had taken to imitating "others," that is, the lifestyle of American wealth and greed:

SPECIAL SERIES No. 6

HEARTH AND HOME ESSAYS

BY

ESTHER J. RUSKAY

PHILADELPHIA

THE JEWISH PUBLICATION SOCIETY OF AMERICA

1902

Figure 37 Title page from Esther J. Ruskay, *Hearth and Home Essays*. Philadelphia, PA: Jewish Publication Society of America, 1902. Photo author.

But before we can lead other peoples to the pure hill of the Lord, we must ourselves be pure; before we go down to purge the infected quarters, we must first cleanse ourselves. We must put away the stranger's gods – pomp and luxury – that have defiled our sanctuary.[53]

She cited a Jewish scholar who had asserted that the disarray of the Jewish community during the early years of the Christian Church had resulted in the loss of Jewish peasants to the new religion. "And when we see to-day," Louis continued, "Christian missions springing up among our neglected Jews, we have no right to condemn them; it is we who deserve the condemnation for unfaithfulness to our duty." When Rebekah Kohut rose to reply to Louis' paper, she underscored the need for a dual mission: first, to the refined Jew who "has neglected his great and foremost duty, the salvation of his own soul," and easily indulges in what she called "semitic anti-semitism" by regarding the Russian Jew as a pariah. Second, Kohut continued, Jewish women reformers must set to work in "the great Ghetto of America" among Jewish immigrants in New York, "the dumping ground of the Russian exile."[54] She sounded the charge of Americanization regarding the role of charity among the Russian Jews on the lower East Side. They should not be allowed to enclose themselves in their ethnicities, but should be encouraged to integrate into American society as deliberate Jews. "Act in every sense of the word as *American Jews*," Kohut counseled.

> This is the great lesson we must teach. It is a glorious privilege to be a Jew, but it is also glorious to be an American, and we must appreciate those privileges by acting up to them in the fullest sense of the word. Refined, chaste, quiet in our manners and dress, we must adopt the vernacular of this blessed free country, and perfect ourselves in it. No foreign tongue, no jargon! We are Israelites, but we are Americans as well.[55]

It was a tenuous balance, easier said than done. Life in American consumerism is rather like dancing with the devil. Still, many shared Kohut's passion to abandon the provinciality and ethnocentrism of old world Jewish life and find in the abundance and liberties of American society a new grounding for being Jewish. If the reforming zeal of many Jewish men and women echoed the Evangelical activist rhetoric of Christian moral reformers, it was a formal not a substantive influence. What Jewish advocates learned from Evangelical discourse and moral reform efforts was a sense of urgency, the importance of advocacy as a strategy for maintaining cultural identity, and the bourgeois arbiter's taste for a commanding perch in the messy society of immigrant America. As several scholars of Jewish culture in America have shown, visual display, advertisement, and consumption played a key role among Jewish immigrants and the Jewish establishment.[56] The role of visual and material artifacts and practices in this process of integration or Americanization becomes especially clear in regard to the importance of domestic culture and the role of women.

In her *Hearth and Home Essays* Esther Ruskay wrote with a special consciousness of time, assuming, as she did, that Judaism in America occupied a unique or "missionary" moment, lodged between what secular Jews considered a "bemuddled" or "old-fashioned" past and what Ruskay feared was a future threatening the complete abandonment of "the ideals and traditions cherished with such love and loyalty by their forefathers."[57] Arguing for the need to remember and revive, Ruskay presented to what she considered her ill-informed readers, a kind of primer of Jewish life centered in the home and dominated by women. Sidestepping the contemporary debate over patriarchalism and women's suffrage, Ruskay asserted that Jewish scripture recognized the right of women to participate in public councils and to reign over the home. She further distanced Conservative Judaism from the moralistic extremism of temperance and vegetarianism by arguing that scripture countenanced the consumption of wine and meat.[58] In this manner, Ruskay tried to segregate middle-class Jewish women in America from their progressive Protestant contemporaries, who were, like Jewish women, engaged in public aid and benevolence societies. Frances Willard, Elizabeth Cady Stanton, and Carry Nation did not represent the ideal Jewish homemaker, in Ruskay's view. Throughout her book, she situates the Jewish woman at home, rearing children, preparing meals, presiding over domestic ritual observances, remembering the Jewish domestic liturgy of feasts and holidays. Indeed, she organized her book around the rhythm of Jewish festivals observed with meals and domestic gatherings.

Women were the living memory of domestic religion, according to Ruskay. The home brought extended relations into a singular fellowship on holidays and Sabbath and was the matrix from which the Jewish race was generated and kept pure. Ruskay was adamant that synagogue and Sunday school instruction were inadequate to secure the faithful. The Jewish home was indispensable. Violation of this domestic sanctuary was the gravest threat facing American Jews. Ruskay saved her harshest words for castigating assimilation and intermarriage. She insisted in the first instance that Jews who shed their Jewish identity stood to gain nothing:

> Men and women who aspire to assimilation with their [non-Jewish] neighbors, and start out with disloyalty to their own religion, become justly a mark of opprobrium to their own race, and receive scant courtesy at the hands of those whose favor they would curry.

Indeed, Ruskay regarded such Jews as guilty of betraying their own people. Jews who took no pleasure in family reunions, domestic ritual, or the Jewish holidays "do not deserve to be called Jews," but were "a portion of our race forever to be discountenanced, condemned, and despised."[59] Of intermarriage, she had little better to say. Jews who intermarried did so from ignorance of "the idea of race purity, which includes that of Israel's Divine mission to humanity," and without realizing that "no good, earthly or spiritual, ever results from these ill-assorted unions."[60]

For activists like Ruskay, religion was key to the survival of Jewish identity and Judaism as a non-geographical nation. Religion was as fundamental to Ruskay as a Conservative Jew as it was to Protestant and Catholic mothers in defining the home as the basis of family, ethnic, and national community. Jewish and Protestant ideologies both charged their adherents with a divine mission as a chosen people. Each focused on the home and the importance of women in conducting its culture, particularly as regards the formation of children. And both Protestants and Jews looked to consumption as a tool for domestically practicing and maintaining the faith. To be sure, Ruskay urged the need to curb consumption, especially where it undermined Jewish ritual, and in a way that instantly recalls Protestant anxieties:

> Man's cupidity, his love of amassing wealth, is a factor that must be taken into consideration, and so long as it remains potent in his life, Sabbath-breaking must be reckoned among the sins and misdemeanors of mankind . . . There are those who rate worldly advantages higher than the advantages that accrue to them from sources not perceptible to the eye of man.[61]

But she was most critical of consumption among Jews where it blurred the all-important distinction from Christian practices. Ruskay pilloried those lavishing time on a Christmas "shopping-list": "A crescent and star bracelet for Hannah, an oyster set for Aunt Sarah, a card-table for papa, a gold-headed cane for Uncle Simon, a cheap dress-pattern for the cook." Jews who displayed a Christmas tree and exchanged presents, especially with their Christian acquaintances, had all but extinguished their Jewishness, and Ruskay imagined that Christians thought the same:

> "What kind of people are those?" questions a Christian neighbor, referring to just such a family. "They look like Jews, and I do not see them go to any church, but at Christmas they sent us just the loveliest presents – and such a tree as they had!"

"They are not Jews, whatever they look!" was the reply. Ruskay agreed.[62] The observant Jewish home that she described as the model for reviving Judaism among American Jews was replete with the material culture of Jewish rites. In a chapter entitled "Preparations for Passover," the author detailed the features of the domestic shrine and connected it to the Jewish version of a Victorian aesthetic of homely beauty whose effect on the family was nothing less than enchanting:

The week just preceding Passover is a busy one for Jewish housekeepers. . . . [T]ake a peep on the day before Passover into the pantries and closets, the cupboards and larders of those who have infused their soul and spirit into all this preparation, into every detail of the House Beautiful. Row upon row – on lace-edged shelves or newly oil-clothed ones – stands ranged the special Passover service of china, polished till it gives back the sun's rays, and near by the burnished coppers and shining tins view with the quaint old silver on the dining-room sideboard, tankards, bowls, loving-cups of gold and silver taken out in honor of the occasion. The linen-closet, too, upstairs, which is to yield up its finest patterned table-cloths, doilies, and napkins to the decking of the table for the Seder nights, is quite in keeping with the rich smell and spicy fragrance that ascends and penetrates from the well-stocked larder below. . . . If there is not something stimulating and rejuvenating to our sated adult senses in all this array of beauty and usefulness, watch its effects on the children.[63]

The House Beautiful was a new Jewish domestic ideal, a version of a movement of the same name across America, which, in a zealous spirit of reform, stressed sanitary, efficient, simple, and flexible forms of design and furnishing, which were perhaps best conveyed by the California bungalow and the Mission style of furniture, which were endorsed by Bertha Smith and other Settlement workers and advocates of reform among working Jewish immigrants.[64]

Ruskay's dense list of items sounds expensive and suited to conspicuous display. Though many of them were handed down, many were increasingly being purchased by American Jews in a market that catered to Jewish consumers, especially home makers who were influenced by the body of literature to which Ruskay contributed. Whether Orthodox, Reform, or Conservative, American Jews looked to one form of consumption or another as a tool for practicing the faith, especially at home. While the Jewish Home Beautiful could easily fall into the venerable American practice of conspicuous consumption,[65] much of the Jewish advice literature urged against this, especially the literature directed toward lower economic classes such as those living in Lower East Side tenements. Smith's "Gospel of Simplicity" endorsed the Model Flat, a Nurses' Settlement project dedicated, as she put it, to "the regeneration of New York's East Side." Smith lamented "the dread tyranny of things" that gripped new American home makers, immigrant housewives who buy whatever they are shown by salesmen "thinking, and quite truly, be it confessed, that she is becoming Americanized" by doing so. Driven by the concern to properly Americanize Russian and Polish Jews arriving in New York and settling on the Lower East Side, Smith shared the view of other Jewish women that some form of philanthropic intervention was necessary to shape immigrant domestic consumption. Smith cited Mabel Hyde Kittredge, of the Association of Practical Housekeeping Centers of New York and supervisor of the Model Flat in New York:

The foreigners who come to this country want to adopt our civilization. They want to do things as we do them. But they have no way of knowing what to choose and what not to choose. They have not been educated to choose between that which is in good taste and the tawdry ... in their anxiety to be like us we find them adopting our barbarities instead of our better things.[66]

Although they addressed themselves to all tenement housing in New York, Kittredge referred explicitly to "the Russian immigrants" and Smith to the "Jewish homes" of East Siders. In all cases, however, simplicity and cleanliness were the core message of the Model Flat. Home makers should not buy ornate, fancy furniture, shouldn't cover the floors with carpet or the walls with wall paper. "The chairs are all of wood," Smith wrote, "with good, honest, straight lines."[67]

Most noteworthy for Jewish domestic culture, perhaps, at least according to the activists doling out advice to lower-class immigrants, was the repudiation of the parlor as the scene for conspicuous display of stuff, and the emphasis placed on the kitchen. "We have been taught respect for our mothers and grandmothers," Bertha Smith averred, "but the way they meekly submitted to the tyranny of tidies and throws, of whatnots full of impossible junk known as bric-a-brac, of dust-catching, insect-breeding, microbe-sheltering plush furniture and hangings" was enough to make her wonder why women today submitted to the faulty and unhealthy aesthetic.[68] An uncluttered living room, regularly scrubbed clean, was the modern answer to the Victorian parlor. By contrast, "the kitchen is the hub of the home, and the woman who pinches in the kitchen to spend in the parlor makes a mistake."[69] Kittredge certainly agreed, claiming that "the most important possession of the home is the stove." In case her readers wondered why, she bluntly explained herself: "Without it we should freeze and starve."[70]

Reformers urged working-class home makers to articulate the use of a tenement flat's discrete rooms, making the parlor an uncluttered space for socializing and the kitchen a hygienic and practical space for food preparation. But as Lizabeth Cohen showed in an important study, this logic did not appeal to many immigrant workers.[71] Becoming American was something they sought to do on their own terms rather than those prescribed by the reformers. Jewish vendors were happy to accommodate the newly arrived consumers. Deutsch Brothers Furniture advertised its parlor and dining room furniture in the *Jewish Daily Forward* in Hebrew in 1910, showing lines of the overstuffed, ornate seating, carpet, tables, cabinets, and sideboards that enraged reformers like Smith and Kittredge.[72] Considerably out of fashion by then among bungalow dwellers, the furniture promoted in the newspaper ad was eyed by Jewish and other Eastern European immigrants as the imprimatur of comfort and home ownership. This was the immigrant parlor visualized in a postcard, postmarked in the same year, and used to convey wishes for a Happy New Year (Figure 38).

Figure 38 Jacob Ken, Girl playing upright piano, Jewish New Year postcard, postmarked September 17, 1910, Winooski, Vermont. New York: Hebrew Publishing Company. Courtesy American Jewish Historical Society, Newton Centre, MA and New York.

A young girl sits at the parlor piano (another item avidly sought out by Jewish immigrants), playing a piece as a well-dressed couple quietly listen, seated formally on a parlor settee, before a round Victorian table. If the woman is the girl's mother, and the gentleman her grandfather, the card communicates the parlor ideal of American Jewish life: the generations joined in the pious home, observing Rosh Hashanah as a family that safeguards tradition in the unifying aesthetic of the nineteenth-century parlor, where abundance has not compromised the family, but helped enable its coherence and secure its well-being.[73]

Just as one must distinguish production and reception in the life of tracts or lithographs, it is necessary to differentiate what reformers preached and what home makers actually did. Cohen pointed out that working-class immigrants readily ignored the message of the reformers by regarding the plush appointments, carpet, and wall paper of the parlor as well as the use of ornate furniture and cluttered displays as a comfort often denied them in the Old World, but now attainable in the New. And the kitchen was not simply a cooking space, but the primary gathering spot for the immigrant family. While Smith and Kittredge allowed for the sparing use of pictures in the Model Flat, Cohen showed by examining photographs of working-class homes that the walls were commonly and abundantly occupied by all manner of mass-produced images, "if only cheap prints, torn-out magazine illustrations and free merchant calendars."[74] The aesthetic of the densely cluttered Victorian parlor of yesteryear, which always seemed to include lithos or engravings, appealed to immigrants around the turn of the century, Cohen argues, because it "suited workers' rural based material values, while satisfying their desire to adapt to mass produced goods, just as it had for the middle class several generations earlier."[75] Recognizing this dimension of domestic life among immigrants is crucial for recovering a sense of their agency as consumers. Reform literature, as noted, tended to regard recent Jewish immigrants as especially destitute, ill-equipped to adapt to the new world of American ways. But Andrew Heinze has argued that "immigrants could refashion those aspects of the American environment which their traditional culture had prepared them to understand."[76]

As Bertha Smith indicated and bemoaned, the principal problem of the tenement household was that due to rent rates among impoverished tenants, it was necessary to sublet beds each night. These were spread throughout the flat, filling all rooms with sleeping space for boarders. This meant that for family members, the parlor or living room could not be reserved for family gathering in the evening. Smith insisted that the kitchen not be let out for bed space. As the hub of the home, the center of the home maker's activity, it had to be preserved for family purposes. Irving Howe recalled from his childhood growing up in an East Side tenement that the kitchen was "the heart of the family." While the rest of the apartment was crammed with boarders, "only in the kitchen could the family come together in an approximation of community." Howe's description of Sabbath in the tenement flat conveys how the home was a special refuge with an aesthetic order all its own:

> On most days everyone ate helter-skelter, whenever he could, but on Friday nights, in the mild glow of the Sabbath, the whole family would eat together. Decorum reigned again, the pleasure of doing things as everyone knew they should be done.[77]

Andrew Heinze has observed that the practice of taking in boarders was a primary form of revenue raised by Jewish women, especially recent immigrant women who felt it inappropriate to work beyond the home.[78] It was in part this revenue that enabled the purchase of the items that decorated the home and facilitated the nurturing experience that Irving fondly recalled.

Whether it was the Sabbath table or the seder on the high holy day of Passover, the image of the family meal remained the stable icon of Jewish identity in images of commerce and ritual practice. The advertisement for Fischer Russian Caravan Tea, in circulation around 1920 (see Figure 36, p. 122), shows an unmistakably ethnic family at the Passover table. The men hold copies of what appears to be the Haggadah as a boy poses the key questions about the meal's significance. Plates of matza, flasks of water and wine, and a vacant chair left for Elijah register the iconography of the seder. It is an image of continuity, dressed in old world costume, practicing the ancient rite of remembering Israel's exodus from bondage. But even this quaintly picturesque and nostalgic glimpse of the old ways is consumer-friendly. As the menfolk conduct the textual performance of the rite, and mother and two sisters listen raptly, a third woman on the far left prepares the Fischer Russian Caravan tea. The walls of the cluttered parlor evince clear evidence that the old world, like the new, was not bereft of visual materials.

The robust publication history of the Haggadah proves the same. Indeed, illustrated copies of the order of the Passover meal appeared at least as early as the late fifteenth century in Europe.[79] American publishers of the book were able to connect with their customers in important ways. From the early years of the century to the middle, several included stanzas of the "Star-spangled Banner" and "My Country 'tis of Thee" among songs at the back of the book as expressions of Jewish patriotism.[80] The back cover of a mid-century edition noted that the Exodus, as "the beginning of mankind's concept of FREEDOM[,] was started when the Israelites fled slavery in Egypt – over 3,000 years ago!" The constitutions of the United States and modern Israel and the charter of the United Nations, the note pointed out, were likewise descendants of that original act of liberation.[81] A Haggadah published in 1951 featured a cover showing a paschal lamb surrounded by the historical foes of Judaism – a Roman soldier, an Assyrian or Babylonian king, an Egyptian figure, a Crusader, a crucifix-wielding monk, a Russian officer, and a Nazi brownshirt.[82]

As Jewish parents and elders struggled to maintain their religious identity in America in the twentieth century they made use of the inexpensive and annually repackaged editions of the Haggadah each Passover. The illustrated features of American Haggadot changed markedly in the attempt to balance currency and constancy. Figure 39 shows the familiar table scene in a 1921 edition: a modern-day family surrounds the table, at whose head is the patriarch, the only one dressed anachronistically. His hand rests prayerfully on what may be a covered plate of matza before him. Like nearly all Haggadot, Figure 39 does not show the traditional four sons – the wise, wicked, simple, and the unspeaking – who participate in the text, though the first three may appear in the 1921 illustration, set apart by age and fashion, each asking in his way about the meaning of the meal.[83] Alternatively, the 1921 edition may represent an effort by the Hebrew Publishing Company to appeal to a broad market among assimilated American Jews. The candelabra hanging above the table in Figure 36 has become a gas lamp (with four lights rather than seven candles) in Figure 39. The very fashionably dressed man in the center does not appear to be the traditional wicked son who disowns the ritual meal and sacred history, but simply a modern-day, assimilated young man who respectfully joins his family for the ceremony. The shadowy photographs on the back wall assure viewers that the ritual meal unfolds in harmony with the ancestors, who are visually present as the modern family keeps parity with the old through the living prayer of the patriarch. His Mosaic profile contrasts with the dress of his sons, but their careful attention to the father's prayer suggests ritual continuity despite the evident change. The derisive or daft expressions registered on the faces of

Figure 39 Family at seder table, frontispiece, *Passover Services*. New York: Hebrew Publishing Company, 1921. Courtesy Center for Advanced Judaic Studies Library, University of Pennsylvania.

the wicked and simple sons in the tradition do not appear here. Drawn in the loose pen-and-ink style of contemporary magazine illustration, the image seeks to appeal to young and old, assimilated and traditional, in order to keep the rite alive over the generations.

In his study of the role of consumption in the adaptation of Jewish immigrants to American life, Andrew Heinze asserts that the loss of the traditional calendar or annual liturgy of holidays as they structured time in the old world was replaced by "work as the organizing principle of time."[84] The resulting hike in income transformed the observance of holidays, which became, as Heinze says, "a pretext for shopping."[85] In order not to vanish into the economic and cultural maelstrom of Christmas, which came to dominate American holiday commerce by the 1880s, American Jews elevated the importance of Hanukkah, formerly a minor festival. "Through the ritual of gift giving," Heinze claims, "newcomers demonstrated their devotion to the belief in monetary generosity that reflected the American perspective of material abundance."[86] By 1911, an image of Santa Claus, the commercial American version of St. Nicholas who was popularly revered by Christians in Eastern Europe, could be used in an ad for Schubert Piano Company in Manhattan to sell pianos to Jews on the occasion of Hanukkah. "In the European setting," Heinze comments, "it would have been inconceivable that a Christian saint enter the psychic world of Jews."[87] It was not the Christian gospel that Santa brought to the Jewish home, but the American way of life, which understood religion to work happily with commerce as the occasion for consumption. The age-old practice of the gift was transposed to the economic relations of capitalism, where abundance meant the capacity to spend. Holidays, for American Jews and Christians alike, became the occasion for acquisition. God and mammon were working things out.

Chapter 5

Pictorial entertainment and instruction

The parlor remained the center of home life and religion for many Americans into the twentieth century when it was gradually replaced by the living room and den, rooms which came to house the electronic hearth – first the radio, then the television and eventually the computer. The nineteenth-century parlor by mid-century had acquired its key features – formal seating, sideboards, curtains, carpeting, wall paper, mantel, round center table, bookcases, organ, and étagère. The last several items were crucial for the display of visual materials such as prints, paintings, and illustrated publications. The parlor was also the site of the greatest visual invention of the century, the daguerreotype, the photograph, and a host of related commodities consumed as visual entertainment and instruction such as the stereograph and the carte de visite.

Daguerreotypes

The first form of photography to claim broad American attention was the daguerreotype immediately upon its invention in France in 1839. The first press accounts in the United States appeared in the spring of 1839 and by early fall the first successful daguerreotype was produced in New York. Louis Jacques Daguerre's process printed a single reversed image on a silver-coated copper plate, which was polished to mirror-like reflectivity. After rinsing the exposed plate, the daguerreotypist or "operator" could show it to the sitter, as quickly as two or three minutes after having taken the image. The rapid result only enhanced the enchantment of the image. The registration of light was so precise that details captured on the plate far exceeded the naked eye's ability to discern them. Contemporaries raved at the minute and meticulous detail that required a magnifying glass to be seen. The tonal range of the imagery was especially rich and seemed to inhere beneath the polished metal surface of the plates, which were commonly very small – the majority of commercial portraits were 2¾ × 3¼ inches (see Figure 41, p. 143).[1]

Daguerreotypists came from various walks of life as the new medium became known in the United States during the 1840s. Some lithographers, for example Napoleon Sarony and Matthew Brady, saw the new technique as rivaling their craft and so left one novel medium for another to open daguerreotype studios in major cities, relying on portraiture and landscape as the principal means of attracting customers. (Brady went on to great fame as proprietor of the firm that documented the Civil War.) Following the practice of lithographers, daguerreotypists opened studios where they displayed their work. Their primary fare by far was the portrait, so they presented themselves as a manner of artist, arraying the walls of the shop like an art gallery and eventually installing parlor-like décor where customers could sit leisurely as they waited or looked over product. While some daguerreotypists pursued their craft as a fine art and submitted highly finished and carefully themed work to art exhibitions, most are better described as artisans who pitched their services to all classes and were successful at conducting a business with a great range of customers.

In a short story published in *The Amaranth*, a gift book for 1855, Sarah Roberts placed herself within a "daguerrian gallery" to watch the panoply of patrons one day. She began her story by noting the economic and cultural democratization that daguerreotypes had promoted:

> In years gone by, to procure the precious likeness of a friend was only in the power of those who had great wealth at command; but now, in the twinkling of an eye, for a single dollar, the humblest citizen can possess the treasure. Wonderful discovery! Kind, blessed power![2]

Roberts proceeded to describe in a physiognomy of contemporary types the steady flow of customers, to provide in fact the literary version of their daguerreotype portraits. By the 1850s, the term was used in popular fiction as a synonym of a precise copy – both a noun and a verb. Harriet Beecher Stowe introduced Uncle Tom to readers accordingly: "as he is to be the hero of our story, we must daguerreotype [him] for our readers. He was a large, broad-chested, powerfully-made man."[3] Roberts began her daguerreotyping with a young sailor and his blind mother. "Though she cannot see," the dutiful son explained to the operator, "she says she can hold it [the daguerreotype] in her hand and kiss it, and know that it is me. I am her only child, sir – all she has left out of a husband and ten children."[4] Daguerreotypes were commonly associated with memory, particularly memory necessitated by death.

By conceiving her story as literary sketches of what the daguerreotypist saw and recorded, Sarah Roberts may have been asserting parity in the gift book genre between text and image. That was a losing battle for writers, who were forfeiting share to illustrations in gift books. Whatever the case, her impressions bear more resemblance to caricature than to actual life. Perhaps the most picturesque patrons in Roberts' story were John and Susey, a young couple from the countryside who come to the city to have their picture taken. When the operator completes the exposure of the plate in less than a minute and tells the couple he is done, the yokel John is incredulous: "Done! That you can't make me believe. 'Stonishing how these city folks thinks we country folks are all fools."[5] But when the daguerreotypist returns in a few moments with the completed image, the couple are ecstatic: "I looks like a gentleman, for sartin," the boy exclaims, "'cept that my hands is rather bigger than some I've seen."[6] After sneering at a lisping dandy with white kid gloves and a tortoise-shell walking stick, "a Broadway exquisite come to have his pretty face perpetuated," the metropolitan counterpart of the country rube, Roberts ends her account with the sentimental image of a boy, his little sister, and his dog Bruno who come to sit for a group portrait. Throughout the brief narrative, the operator, whose appearance is never limned, is a deft handler of human variety, able to listen patiently to country jabber and a dandy's prattle while posing his subjects in ways suited to their personalities. All leave the studio pleased with the result.

Most of these customers would have placed their portraits in the home. Accordingly, the parlor did much to insert images into Protestant domestic piety, particularly with regard to images of women and children. From the very beginning, daguerreotypes were understood to appeal to the sensibility of American women. An article in the New York *Morning Herald* of September 30, 1839 commented on the very first daguerreotype (now lost), which was then on exhibit in a shop on Broadway. Picturing St. Paul's Church in the city, the daguerreotype was described as "a most remarkable gem," and said to look like "fairy work." Apparently the author believed, and with amusement, that its enchanting delicacy recommended it to female appreciation. The author urged "ladies, if they are pretty, with small feet and delicate hands, [and] fond of science" to call on the shop and see the image. "It is the first time," the author continued, "that the rays of the sun were ever caught on this continent, and imprisoned, in all their glory and beauty, in a morocco case with golden clasps."[7] The precious and small character of the image was linked in the writer's mind with ladies perhaps because it recalled the miniature paintings that girls and young women were trained to create in finishing schools such as the ivory miniatures discussed in Chapter 3 (see Figure 24, p. 82). The leather case and clasp recall important artifacts of the antebellum material culture of the parlor: the embossed, gilt leather bindings of gift books and the jewel-like lockets and brooches that carried memorial art and portraiture. The themes of remembrance to which gift books were dedicated also provided the framework for daguerreotypes in the feminine sphere of the parlor. So it is not surprising that gift books and photographic cases were bound in identical ways for display there.[8] The uniqueness of daguerreotypes likely appealed to American consumers because it took the place of the miniatures. Most successful as portraits, daguerreotypes were one of a kind, faithful visual transcripts of their sitters. Such a portrait, neatly bound in leather and set beneath a protective pane of glass, was a kind of alter ego, an enduring facsimile of its original.

Death and photography

The churlish insinuation of the *Morning Herald* article seems to have been that ladies would find this new fad to conform to their parlor aesthetic. The anonymous author's wit aside, there is no reason to be surprised that women (as well as men) responded very enthusiastically to the daguerreotype. Women were, after all, in charge of the parlor. Working- and middle-class women found in the small portraits of husbands, lovers, family members, and friends commodities that fit the domestic cult of sentimentalism. (It is no less evident from the large number of daguerreotypes and paper photographs from mid-century that men enjoyed portraits of themselves with their men friends and associates.)[9] Among the religious subjects of photographic imagery in the 1850s and 1860s, which include churches, portraits of clergy, nuns, and treatments of biblical figures as fine art, the subject that corresponds most closely to the feminine sphere of Victorian womanhood was the angel. The stereographic image reproduced here (only one of the original pair forming the stereograph) shows a very young guardian angel hovering tenderly above the crib of a sleeping girl (Figure 40). The image was created, presumably by Philadelphia photographer William Rau who copyrighted it in 1897, as a double exposure that recalls the "spirit photography" of the nineteenth century.[10] The ethereal presence of the angel exploits the medium of photography, which joined the Victorian taste for the supernatural with one of the fondest of sentimental themes. Guardian angels also adorned daguerreotype cases that may have held images of departed children, mothers, and wives.[11] The angel was among the most potent symbols of maternal love and spiritual sensibility and was most frequently associated with the protection of children and the proximity of life and death. Quite commonly, guardian angels were portrayed as women or girls, feminine spirits devoted to the welfare of their earthly charges.

As part of the piety of child nurture, mothers were increasingly seen as supernatural figures – as angels and even as latter-day equivalents of Jesus.[12] Brought into Christian theology and practice from Greco-Roman belief in custodial angels that usher souls both into and out of this world, guardian angels were welcomed by mid-nineteenth-century American Christians who came to regard women as the maternal equivalent in the domestic ideology of the maternal sphere to which women were thought ideally to belong.[13] Rather than part of the rough-and-tumble world of business, politics, and public life, this ideology conceived of women as a spiritual force that "influenced" male behavior from the quiet distance of the home, that is, from the reach of memory installed in the childhood of men, when they were spiritually formed by their mothers. The ethereal presence of the angel, especially the guardian angel, struck Victorian Americans as an appropriate symbol of the effect that women exerted over men. In the cultural theology of sentimentalism, women were composed of a more spiritual substance, their heart and feelings constituting a

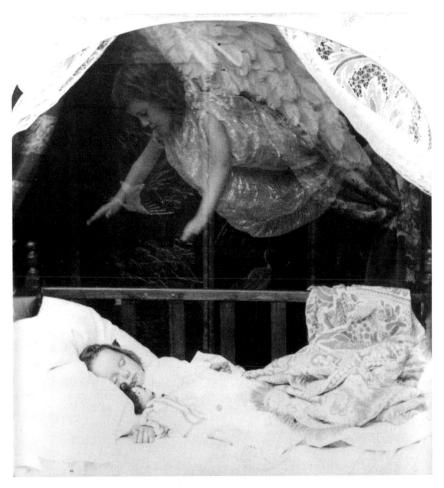

Figure 40 Her Guardian Angel, one half of stereographic image, copyrighted by William H. Rau, 1897. Courtesy Library of Congress.

higher sensibility than the worldly stuff of which men were made. Angels are typically shown attending children within or without the home.

In the history of Western culture, there are hundreds of different kinds of angels, many of them named and part of various cults and religious and arcane practices.[14] But the angels that popular Christian culture knew most fondly, beyond the many different angels mentioned in the bible and other than Mephistopheles in the story of Faust, was the guardian angel, which came to figure in fine art and popular imagery by the 1830s and continued to do so throughout the rest of the century. Angels perform a number of functions, chiefly perhaps as messengers and servants of God. They tend to appear at propitious moments, in crises, at junctures of the here and hereafter. Guardian angels keep children from danger, protect them from evil, and accompany them on their life journey. A central role was given to a guardian angel by the painter Thomas Cole in his cycle of paintings entitled *Voyage of Life* in 1839–40 (see Figure 68, p. 233), which was issued as a set of large engravings just over a decade later. In this suite of images, a guardian spirit attends the voyage of a boy from childhood to old age, in good times and bad. Cole, who was a fervent Protestant, portrayed the angel as visualized for centuries: ethereal, luminous, long-haired figures of effeminate grace, dressed in full-length white robes. In accord with their liminal sites of manifestation, angels in Victorian America are found at graveside, often adorning the memorial stones of the graves of the wealthy in cemeteries such as Laurel Hill in Philadelphia or Hollywood Cemetery in Richmond (see Figure 25, p. 86). More commonly in mass-produced imagery, angels for domestic use hover just above or behind children at play or appear at bedside to protect or to usher deceased children to heaven.

Whatever the case, angels were a spiritual means of dealing with the unknown, of marking difficult passages and securing supernatural assistance or protection at such junctures. Although this had long been one vital purpose of angels in Western culture, the profusion of angels in nineteenth-century America is fascinating. Why in an age of rapid industrialization, when technology was transforming modern life into something that resembled the pre-modern world less and less each day, would people redouble their reliance on supernatural devices like angels? As emblems of femininity, angels helped spiritualize women and locate them in the domestic sphere, the anchor in a tempest of social change. Angels also allowed Victorian Americans to baptize science and technology, to regard these potentially cataclysmic forces of change as benevolent. Many Americans in the nineteenth century were convinced of the harmony of spirituality and science. Such innovations as photography, steam power, and telegraphy were hailed as evidence of the spiritualization of matter, as the advance guard of a new religious character to modern life. Throwing aside the haunted restrictions of life in the mansion of his Puritan forebears, Clifford Pyncheon, Hawthorne's eccentric Romantic character in *House of the Seven Gables*, takes a ride on a locomotive and sings a paean to the spiritual glory of modern life. He classed mesmerism and spirit rapping with the train and telegraph. Though his hymnic remarks befuddled the Yankee train conductor who simply wanted to collect his ticket, Clifford expressed feelings that were celebrated by many in Hawthorne's day (including Hawthorne himself).[15] One need only think of the interest in photography as a medium able to capture the auras and wraithlike emanations of departed souls.[16]

Death and the dread of it provided the occasion for images of the guardian angel and the angel of deliverance who takes the departed to heaven. From the beginning, photography has been associated with death by those who have hailed it as well as those who have not. A broadside used to advertise the business of a

Massachusetts daguerreotypist pressed readers to become his customers for the ability of the new medium to anticipate the inevitable human fate:

> Words of warning to all! Now, ready, whether you be old or young, male or female, married or single, you should at once secure to those friends who may survive you a correct picture of your living self; that they, after you shall have been called away by death, may have this pleasant memorial always in their possession.

The broadside urged parents not to wait before obtaining an image of their children, then, mindful of the power of children at persuading their parents in matters of consumption, informed children that it was their duty "to prevail with them [parents] to sit for the Daguerreotypes."[17]

The death of a child was a most poignant occasion for daguerreotype portraits. Whether a portrait taken during the life of the child or just after he or she died, such images could become the focal point of a parent's grief. "The Little Daguerreotype," a poem by the Rev. J. G. Adams, published in a mid-century gift book, demonstrates how a memorial image could become a kind of Protestant icon able to evoke the felt presence of the deceased subject of the portrait. Adams wrote that he was comforted "as on that face I gaze," and that he was drawn into colloquy with the child through the intermediary image of the face:

> I seem to ask the spirit
>   Which through that face once shone,
> What of that world celestial,
>   To which though now hast gone?
> . . .
>
> And since thou hast departed,
>   We still would keep thy name,
> And hold thy new life's mysteries
>   In sacredness the same.
>
> And then *we* have *our* darling,
>   In that high home of light;
> Say, of her angel presence
>   Hast thou yet had the sight?
> Say, in communings holy,
>   Are ye not often near,
> When distant most we think thee
>   From this our mortal sphere?
>
> Those lips give us no answer
>   To these deep thoughts of thee,

That calm sweet face unchanging,
Hath still its mystery.[18]

The author is drawn into conversation with the spirit of his dead child through the face captured in the daguerreotype. He begins by asking the spirit about the heavenly realm it occupies, then tells the spirit that he and his wife wish both to remember the mortal life of their child, as portrayed in the image, and to celebrate its newly acquired life in heaven. He then asks the spirit of the child upon whose mortal face he looks if the child's soul has gazed upon its own angelic countenance in heaven, and if the child's soul is not near to them when its parents are caught up in sacred communion, presumably prayer and devotional meditation. The poem intermingles memory, image, soul, and angelic or celestial being, though not without some confusion. But the confusion is telling as it stresses a new ambivalence in a Protestant's response to images, particularly to daguerreotypes, whose relation to their referents seemed unusually compelling. The portrait of the child seems to bridge the divide of death and channel the father's grieving thoughts to the lost one who, it turns out, is not distant, but preserved mysteriously in or through the daguerreotype.

Adams opened his poem gazing at the image of his lost child by describing the face "Like one in softest slumber,/ with eyelids closed, it seems – / A slumber now unbroken/ By any earthly dreams." The child was dead when this picture was taken, though appearing only to sleep. This appearance helps account for its iconic power. In fact, the practice of taking postmortem photographs of children and other family members was not unusual in the nineteenth century. It was a practice used by both Protestants and Catholics, and was often done in the parlor of the home, where both prepared and displayed the body before burial, and where Catholics, especially Irish immigrants, displayed the body during the wake. Figure 41 is a Catholic postmortem portrait of a child daguerreotyped by a New York studio at mid-century. A cross stands beside the child, who is dressed in what may have been the baptismal gown. Surrounded by flowers and a wreath, the child is also accompanied by a lighted candle, which may mark the vigil of the wake or may be part of the last rites. Dimly visible on the far side of the crib may be a rosary.

The image suggests, consonant with Rev. Adams' daguerreotype, that the child has not died so much as gone to sleep, having passed in a peaceful state from the painful present to the better world of heaven. The image serves to mark the passage, assuring the Catholic parents of the child in Figure 41 as well as the Rev. Adams that the child is now at peace. Postmortem daguerreotype portraits were more than pictures to mourners. A brief note accompanying a daguerreotype of a dead infant named Jacob Noah, Jr., in the collection of the Historical Society of Pennsylvania delivers in telegraphic and poignant brevity the precarious nature of life and the significance of postmortem imagery: "My dead brother in his metallic coffin. Buried in Odd Fellows cemetery. Had a fall. Hurt his knee."[19] The metal-plate image itself is the coffin of

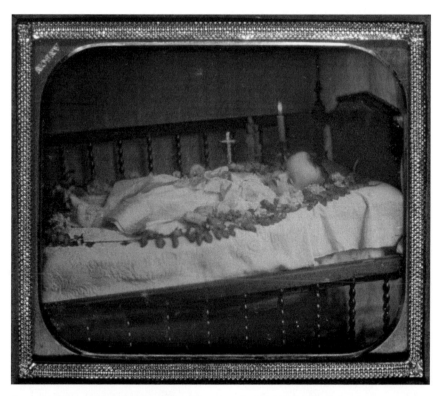

Figure 41 Postmortem daguerreotype of unidentified child in bed with flowers, a cross, and lit candles, Anson's Studio, New York City, ca. 1840–50s. Courtesy Strong – National Museum of Play®, Rochester, NY, copyright 1992.

Jacob Noah. The Harlem photographer James VanDerZee produced many postmortem photographic portraits well into the twentieth century for black parents grieving the loss of their children. VanDerZee's popular use of composite imagery was able to suggest a seamless join between the dead child and the hereafter (Figure 42). Though appearing to be asleep in bed, the stiff hands of the child in Figure 42 indicate that it is deceased. But by exposing the photographic page to two or more negatives, VanDerZee was able to merge overlapping images into a single visual field that imbued standard religious iconography with new meanings particularized for the mourning customer. The photograph shows a standing female figure, who appears to be lifted whole from a Baroque painting of the Assumption of the Virgin. The figure resembles several versions of the Immaculate Conception produced in the later seventeenth century by the Spanish painter Murillo. Mary, who bears the mantle and tunic of the Immaculate Conception, is surrounded by a cloudy company of cherubs as well as older angels. On the right side of the image, an angel

Figure 42 James VanDerZee, photographer, child with angels and Mary, New York, ca. 1935.
Copyright Donna Mussenden VanDerZee.

enshrouds the deceased child with its wing, appearing to gather up the child's soul into a billowing veil of flowers. The gesture ushers the deceased child into the upward sweep of the composition, leading toward Mary, who looks to heaven, her hands clasped in prayer as she intercedes for the young soul. The composite image appropriates the traditional motif of the Assumption to the pastoral task of comforting aggrieved parents by envisioning the Virgin's benevolent act of intercession.[20]

Catholic parents took great consolation in the power of baptism to spare their children the shadowy world of limbo (the eternal destination of unbaptized infants). The lighted candle in Figure 41 surely compounded the consoling power of the image by recalling a priest's application of the rite of extreme unction, which purged the soul of any final venial sin as it passed from this world to the next. And the cross bespoke the final resurrection, when the sleeping dead will awake to enter eternal bliss together. The daguerreotypist has elevated the bed on which the child rests in order to allow a better view of the face, but also to enhance the sense of light slumber by lowering the chin against the chest.[21] It was common practice in days before undertaking to place ice beneath the body to retard decomposition before burial. The result was a memorial image, the final image of the departed, the image that would endure in the minds of the child's family, who would display the photograph in the parlor, where they might gaze on it in the manner that Rev. Adams did on the daguerreotype of his child, musing about the loss and seeking out some enduring presence in the mysterious face at rest in the silver mirror before him.

As the profession of the undertaker emerged in the late nineteenth century and the funeral home in the early twentieth century, death in America moved from the private home and the responsibility of family members, typically women who prepared the body for display, to the "funeral parlor" and the work of the professional mortician. With these developments, the postmortem photograph began to decline. But it did not vanish until well into the twentieth century. Immigrant Catholic families continued to hold the wake in their homes and Blacks sought the sort of postmortem portraiture that James VanDerZee provided as late as the 1930s. Jay Ruby has investigated how the photograph of the body in a casket in the funeral home, surrounded by flowers and family members, took the place of the postmortem portrait by the 1940s.[22] Death was pictured as an ensemble, a kind of ambience outside of the home. The visual culture shifted from regarding the dead as sleeping to displaying photographs of them while alive. The surfeit of snapshots that Americans commonly took and saved in albums and boxes provided a wealth of images to help them remember their dead. Also common, particularly among Catholic and Protestant Blacks, was the use of mass-produced religious iconography. VanDerZee's use of neo-Baroque Catholic motifs stressed angels and Mary, as we saw, while black Baptists from the 1940s even to the present have made use of the familiar imagery of Warner Sallman, especially his ubiquitous *Head of Christ* (see Figure 61, p. 210).

The tableau vivant

Photographing the dead as if they were asleep may have been poignant for Victorian Americans because much of their visual culture turned on what was not incidentally called the "tableau vivant," or living picture. Tableaux vivants were essentially visual templates lifted from well-known paintings and sculptures. In addition to popular parlor entertainment, tableaux could take the form of public pageantry or pious edification, and were even a fundamental part of the world-famous Passion play in Bavaria, as we will see in Chapter 6 (see Figures 49 and 51, pp. 166 and 170).

An early compendium, William Fearing Gill's *Parlor Tableaux and Amateur Theatricals* (1867), offered over one hundred subjects for staging tableaux.[23] Gill provided the title of the piece, indication of the cast by age and gender, often a poetic text that might be read to the audience, suggestions for music to be performed during the tableau's presentation, a careful description of how to costume and arrange the figures, and directions on lighting the scene. It was a theatrical ensemble and the stage manager was encouraged to integrate all elements carefully in order to achieve the desired effect. In his introduction, Gill assured readers that staging tableaux was a "simple and elegant amusement" and "a favorite entertainment with persons of taste." Tableaux could be done privately in the home, but were staged publicly as "the principal attraction of many charitable exhibitions for the benefit of worthy objects."[24] The subjects described by Gill ranged from patriotic themes to sentimental topics familiar to Victorian iconography: homeless orphan girls, guardian angels, and a mother's grave. Biblical and religious subjects abounded: Hope and Faith, David's Lament over Absalom, Belshazzar's Feast, and the Crown of Glory. Many tableaux were lifted directly from paintings and sculptures. Washington Allston's unfinished canvas provided the source for a tableau of Belshazzar's Feast while John Rogers' popular ceramic figures of contemporary life were the inspiration for a tableau called "Home-Guard," which consisted of two ladies "keeping guard on the outskirts of one of our Western cities – a scene quite common during the late war."[25]

Recalling the memorial imagery produced by Currier & Ives, "A Mother's Grave" composed three children about a marble plinth with a wreath of flowers atop it. The children have brought flowers to the grave of their mother. As "some sacred hymn" is sung, the curtain is parted, "revealing a lady dressed in white, with her head inclined towards the children, her hands extended over them. A thick blue smoke should surround her."[26] We are not told if the female figure is an angel or the benevolent spirit of the children's mother. Her gesture recalls portrayals of the Madonna of the Protective Shroud in Catholic iconography, but the greater similarity to the tableau of the Guardian Angel suggests her likely identity. Gill described "The Guardian Angel" as a woman dressed in white, surrounded by blue smoke, and extending her arms toward a young girl below her. But his description offers a few more iconographical points of information: she wears "a long white robe, and drapery-sleeves, with an over-skirt; a silver band, with star in the centre, upon her head; and wings of paper or muslin on a wire frame."[27] Both images anticipate the costume selected by Aimee Semple McPherson (see Figure 64, p. 215), and worn as she preached in her Angelus Temple in Los Angeles in the 1920s and 1930s. In each case, consistent with Victorian ideology of the feminine ideal, the benevolent woman is seen as angelic, a divine messenger whose benevolence is keyed to her feminine and maternal qualities.

In another nineteenth-century publication on tableaux several angels appear, most notably one in a stage space that was designed to enhance the audience's sense of illusion. The angel and its stage were showcased as the frontispiece to the book, which consisted of forty-five tableaux gathered by Josephine Pollard and illustrated by the well-known artist and illustrator, Walter Satterlee (Figure 43).[28] When the heavy stage curtains were drawn on the elaborate setting of Pollard's stage, viewers were treated to a series of devices that successively framed its recession into space. Beginning with the curtains themselves, the eye moves next to potted plants flanking the central image of the figure posing as the Angel of Prayer. The poser stands in an opening cut in a screen appearing to be a wall. The opening is bordered by a varnished wooden frame. Behind the

Frontispiece.

Figure 43 Walter Satterlee, diagram of tableau vivant, frontispiece in Josephine Pollard, *Artistic Tableaux with Picturesque Diagrams and Descriptions of Costumes.* New York: White, Stokes, and Allen, 1884. Photo author.

figure is another screen, which creates the background of the fictive painting. Over the pictorial frame surrounding the scene is stretched a piece of dark tarlatan, a sheer cotton fabric, "which serves as an illusionizing medium,"[29] providing the atmospheric effect that many viewers admired in "Old Master" oil paintings. Pollard praised the tableau vivant over even the theatrical stage for its direct appeal "to the sensibilities of the audience" and for its capacity to foster the imagination and to cultivate taste. She was struck by the power of the tableau to enchant the audience: "There is something indescribably weird and witching about an effective tableau; the crude or incongruous accessories are completely lost sight of, and the audience is carried away by the picture upon which their gaze is riveted."[30] The Angel itself, like several others represented in the manual, resembles the Victorian angel (see Figure 25, p. 86): a winged lady wrapped in flowing drapery and a belt of stars. She carries a censor and palm leaf and "looks communing with the skies."[31]

The sensation of bringing a painting to life, of metamorphosing two dimensions into three, was something that the tableau vivant shared with a popular device that appeared in mid-century American parlors: the stereograph (see Figure 44). The stereographic image was composed of two nearly identical paper photographs mounted side by side on heavy card stock and placed in a device called a stereoscope, which isolated the eyes from one another. The stereoscopic effect was produced as the two photographs were merged by the brain into a single image, resulting in a striking three-dimensional appearance. (The brain seeks to reconcile the slight differences that describe two different points of view of the same object, integrating them into a single image that offers more spatial information than either single image.) Stereographs were viewed in hand-held or table-top stereoscopes, some of which were very elaborate contraptions developed for parlor display.[32]

Advertisers promoted the product for its verisimilitude. One early advertisement claimed of stereographic portraits that "the living subject seems to stand before the eye."[33] Religious subjects were produced in France, Germany, and eventually the United States, and included the life of Christ visualized in sets of cards numbering from ten to thirty-six. Sales grew dramatically after 1860.[34] Two stereographs of the Passion narrative produced by the Ingersoll View Company, of St. Paul, Minnesota, are typical of the many portrayals of the subject (Figure 44). One features the scourging of Christ; the other his appearance to Mary Magdalene at the tomb. Both cards, which belong to a single series sold as a set, are labeled "From the Passion Play" and were clearly intended for Christian consumers who might imagine they were looking upon individual scenes of the famous play staged at Oberammergau. The illusion enhanced by the stereoscope relied on the organization of the figures in each scene. Rather than a photographic reproduction of paintings or photographs of tableaux vivants, these cards, like many others, used sculpted figures set before a painted backdrop or modeled scene. Stereoscopic effects of depth worked best when an object occupied the middle ground of an image's spatial recession. The

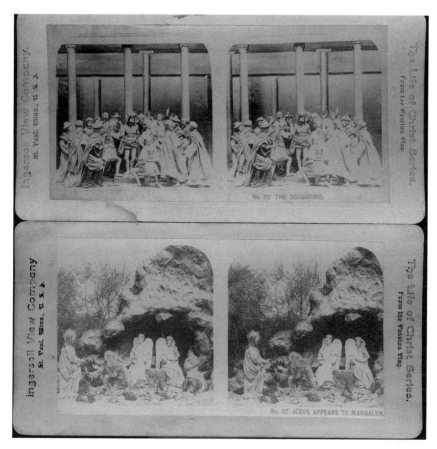

Figure 44 Two stereographic views of the Passion, Ingersoll View Company, of St. Paul, Minnesota, date unknown. Photo author.

effect depended on a contrast between near and far, and therefore favored the stark ordering of the image into planar relief. The portrayal of the biblical event glimpsed through the filter of the Passion play would have assured Victorian viewers of what might be called the "theatrical veracity" of the scene, that is, its reliability within the register of a reenactment of the biblical narrative, couched within the dramaturgy of a you-are-there pageantry.

The organization of figurative compositions in stereographic imagery consisted of discrete layers, usually three – foreground, middle, and back ground. Produced as black and white though sometimes hand-tinted, the stereographs arranged the succeeding levels in tonal terms, from darker to lighter, to indicate the recession of space from foreground to back. Human figures, as seen in Figure 44, were arranged isocephalically, that is, in a single plane that might throw them in relief against the background. The effect was stage-like and clearly reminiscent of the tableau as well as theater. Pointing to the visual disjuncture of levels in stereographic imagery, one scholar has noted that the strong planar effect tends to isolate features from one another as discrete projections that contrast with the uniform recession of space in theatrical scenography, which was grounded in the tradition of linear perspective.[35] Yet visual effects are a matter of historical relativity. In retrospect, stereographs look discontinuous, but in the context of their day, viewers responded to them as astonishing instances of verisimilitude that dwarfed the effect of paintings and other visual illusions.

Distant worlds brought near: tourism and religious spectacle

In 1859 and 1861, Oliver Wendell Holmes, physician in Harvard Medical School, published enthusiastic accounts of the stereograph and stereoscope in *The Atlantic Monthly*. In a prescient reflection on the larger cultural significance of photography in general and the stereograph in particular, Holmes characterized the medium of photography in curiously conflicting terms, as a "triumph of human ingenuity," but also as "miraculous" and as some manner of divine gift that has inaugurated "a new epoch in the history of human progress." God himself, Holmes grandly closed his essay, "took a pencil of fire from the 'angel standing in the sun,' and placed it in the hands of a mortal."[36] The trope inverts the myth of Prometheus to a strictly benevolent purpose: modern humanity has not stolen the divine fire, but by virtue of scientific ingenuity has merited its gift from God. This intermingling of science and religion suited the nineteenth century's fondness for the idea of progress, and Holmes' essays redound with optimism and futuristic zeal about the promise of photography for democratic institutions. Holmes called for the foundation of "a comprehensive and systematic stereographic library, where all men can find the special forms they particularly desire to see as artists, or as scholars, or as mechanics, or in any other capacity."[37] The new technology's divorce of form from matter assured Holmes of applications that would revolutionize human society.

In the world of immaterial images, nothing was ever really far away. Holmes and countless American consumers already enjoyed the tours of distant places that stereographic images offered them in the comfort of the parlor. Boxes of stereographs brought the most exotic sites to pleasant conversations around the center table. The article of 1861 took the reader on a virtual tour of Europe using stereographic images. Writing the essay on April 13, 1861, the very day that Fort Sumter was attacked and the Civil War began, Holmes invited readers to "turn our back on this miserable, even though inevitable, fraternal strife, and, closing our eyes for an instant, open them in London."[38] Proclaiming one apostrophe after another, Holmes worked his way through dozens of stereographs of the sites of London, England, the Lake District, and Scotland, pausing at Canterbury to register an awe that was surpassed only by the convenience of the new medium of the stereoscope, whose inversion of the process of pilgrimage underscores the difference between tourist and pilgrim:

> These old cathedrals are beyond all comparison what are best worth seeing, of man's handiwork, in Europe. How great the delight to be able to bring them, bodily, as it were, to our own firesides! A hundred thousand pilgrims a year used to visit Canterbury. Now Canterbury visits us.[39]

Stereographs juggled distance and nearness in a new way for visual consumers. Though it need not do so, tourism can reduce its object to the unreality of a picture, a gleaming surface that has far more to do with tourists' desire for divertissement than with any moral encounter with the culture and people they view and photograph. Convenience is often missing from pilgrimage, but rarely from tourism. Whereas the comfort sought by the pilgrim is spiritual, it is the psychological comfort of relaxation and diversion that is the tourist's aim. When images can accomplish the latter in the parlor hearth's warm glow, so much the better. Holmes ended his stereographic tour of Europe in Palestine. What may appear a geographical confusion was facilitated by the ease of rifling through stacks of photographs (he wrote that he'd looked at "perhaps a hundred thousand stereographs" and had formed a personal collection of one thousand).[40] But the leap from Europe to "the Holy Land" was powered by ideology. Christians had a keen interest in gazing upon the landscape of the bible. Looking at a stereograph of Nazareth set in its surrounding countryside, Holmes felt the image join his gaze to the gaze of another: "We know that these long declivities, beyond Nazareth, were pictured in the eyes of Mary's growing boy just as they are now in ours sitting here by our own firesides."[41] Tourism could morph quietly into parlor pilgrimage.

The term "Holy Land" is itself geographically ambiguous but generally meant contemporary Palestine as the latter-day equivalent of biblical Israel. The region corresponded in a hazy way to a very complex referent in the American Protestant imagination. From their arrival, the Puritans had likened their presence in the new world to the "city on a hill," an American Jerusalem, symbol of God's covenant with the Protestant remnant that many Americans over the next two centuries believed was providentially chosen by God to play an eminent role in the final age of history. Joseph Smith gave this millennial imagination a uniquely American form in the account of his excavation of artifacts that demonstrated the lost tribe of Israel had immigrated to North America. While the Mormons made an exodus of their own for a promised land in the West, American Protestants looked with growing fascination to a series of adventuresome archeological excavations throughout the Middle East that got underway in the 1840s and 1850s. American expeditions soon followed – scientific and otherwise. So it was in 1867 that Mark Twain took a steamer to Europe and then on to Greece and Syria in the company of sixty-seven "pilgrims" and "sinners," as he put it in his mammoth narrative, which established his national reputation, *The Innocents Abroad*. Leaving Damascus, which he deplored, and traveling southward toward the Holy Land "through the groves of the Biblical oaks of Bashan," Twain recorded his exasperation with the annoying tourist habits of the "the pilgrims," a portion of eight or so devout Protestants in the party to which his narrative regularly returned for comic relief as well as not a little spleen venting:

> The incorrigible pilgrims have come in with their pockets full of specimens broken from the ruins. I wish this vandalism could be stopped. They broke off fragments from Noah's tomb; from the exquisite sculptures of the temples of Baalbec; from the houses of Judas and Ananias, in Damascus; from the tomb of Nimrod the Mighty Hunter . . . and now they have been hacking and chipping these old arches here that Jesus looked upon in the flesh. Heaven protect the Sepulchre when this tribe invades Jerusalem![42]

Awed by the material traces of the sacred past, the pilgrims collected souvenirs of the places they visited, prying away bits of matter as if to harvest fossils of biblical heroes and the events of recorded scripture. But Twain was unable to negotiate the sharp difference between the mundane dust beneath his feet and the vaunted image of deity:

> It seems curious enough to us to be standing on ground that was once actually pressed by the feet of the Saviour. The situation is suggestive of a reality and a tangibility that seem at variance with the vagueness and mystery and ghostliness that one naturally attaches to the character of a god. I can not comprehend yet that I am sitting where a god has stood, and looking upon the brook and the mountains which that god looked upon, and am surrounded by dusky men and women whose ancestors saw him, and even talked with him, face to face, and carelessly, just as they would have done with any other stranger. I can not comprehend this; the gods of my understanding have been always hidden in clouds and very far away.[43]

Perhaps it would have been easier had he sat in Cambridge with Holmes and gazed at stereographs of Jerusalem. As the group entered Palestine, Twain was struck by the way that the pilgrims saw the landscape before them through the filter of a piety and a literary discourse established long in advance of their trip. "These men," he said of the pilgrims,

> had been taught from infancy to revere, almost to worship, the holy places whereon their happy eyes were resting now. For many and many a year this very picture had visited their thoughts by day and floated through their dreams by night.[44]

But as he looked at the rolling terrain of Northern Palestine – the hills of Capernaum, the lake of Galilee, the town of Magdala – Twain did not see the descriptions that he had read in American and European travel accounts. Writer and pilgrim alike saw what their veneration and affection moved them to see. Visitors brought their descriptions along and unloaded them on the land. They beheld a gaze that unfolded before them, a vista that had been fashioned before they left New York harbor.

> I am sure, from the tenor of the books I have read, that many who have visited this land in years gone by, were Presbyterians, and came seeking evidences in support of their particular creed; they found a Presbyterian Palestine, and they had already made up their minds to find no other, though possibly they did not know it, being blinded by their zeal. Others were Baptists, seeking Baptist evidences and a Baptist Palestine. Others were Catholics, Methodists, Episcopalians, seeking a Catholic, a Methodist, an Episcopalian Palestine. . . . Our pilgrims have brought *their* verdicts with them.[45]

Of course, Twain brought his own share of verdicts, which he did not spare his readers. Although he was no pilgrim in the Holy Land, he was a tourist with a mission of fashioning himself as an author. He succeeded by providing American readers with an engaging access to a subject for which, whether Protestant, Catholic, or Jewish, they had a voracious appetite. Americans could not get enough of the Holy Land. Twain rightly pointed out the effect of popular Holy Land literature on the American imagination. Because these travel accounts were so prevalent and absorbed so intently, the Holy Land was more an imaginative ideal than it ever was an actual destination for most Americans. Their tourism was visual and performed and there was a dizzying array of ways for Americans to undertake virtual visits to the land of the bible. One of the most celebrated and widely visited was a model of Palestine at Lake Chautauqua, New York. In the summer of 1874 Chautauqua opened as an inter-denominational Protestant camp dedicated to improving the operation and effectiveness of Sunday schools. Established as an institute for Sunday school teachers and administrators during the month of August each summer, Chautauqua immersed its participants in biblical history, geography, costume, language, and religious pedagogy in order to invigorate the national enterprise of Sunday school education. The founders, John Vincent and Lewis Miller, had long been involved in teaching and promoting Protestant Sunday schools.[46]

Vincent made sure that Chautauqua was able to compete among vacationers and tourists who were spending the summer at the lake and had little interest in Sunday school matters or the study of scripture. This local public "needed some other attraction to bring them to our Assembly" and the Assembly needed their "financial support" in order to pursue its larger goals. Vincent crafted a rationale that lured this potential clientele without compromising the mission of the project:

> To bring them up to an appreciation of our best, we must give them what would be to them their best, and, without catering to weakness or wrong, gradually improve their tastes and ideas by making Chautauqua a place of rest and delight to them.

He happily reported that this policy succeeded in bringing "tens of thousands every season to the sessions of the Chautauqua Assembly."[47] He listed lectures, concerts, impersonations, tableaux vivants, and travelogues as some of the popular forms of entertainment used to attract the casual tourist to the camp. In addition to these, visitors were engaged by museums and models of antiquities that quickly sprung up across the grounds. There were also "attractions for light-hearted youth and wearied but rational age, bonfires, banners, processions, fireworks, illuminated fleets." These spectacles appealed to those who were "simply recipients," those passive onlookers who came merely to see out of curiosity and the desire for amusement. But they paid to do so, and were at least exposed to sermons, lectures, or music, which Vincent hoped might open "the soul to the worlds all about it replete with marvel, beauty, and power."[48]

One of the attractions that visitors mentioned was something that Vincent had constructed from the beginning as a central tool for the instruction of students and teachers alike: Palestine Park, a more-or-less scale model of central Palestine. Once again, the image was understood to enhance learning in a way that reading alone could not. A long article in *Harper's Monthly Magazine* in 1879 claimed that Vincent suggested the model because people "could learn more from the topography of the Holy Land in an hour's study than by the use of any other means."[49] The success of the model moved Vincent and his colleagues to add several new features by the summer of 1875. These included a scale model of one of the pyramids at Giza, a half-scale Jewish tabernacle, an "Oriental House," which served as a museum for biblical antiquities, and a model of modern Jerusalem. Visitors could also see daily performances of impersonators of an Arab and a Jewish high priest. *Harper's* summarized the intent of the representations:

> By means of this collection of models, and with the aid of stereoscopic views of scenes in the Holy Land thrown in a magnified form on an immense screen at night, the student of Bible history is enabled to secure a more vivid comprehension of Eastern life than is attainable without making a transatlantic voyage to the Orient itself.[50]

In order to enhance learning even further and achieve "a thorough understanding of the life depicted in the Bible," the organizers merged entertainment with instruction by illustrating lectures with "*tableaux vivants* representing scenes in the daily life of dwellers on what Christianity calls holy ground."[51] Photographs, painted panoramas, and blackboard drawings and chalk talks were other visual media used for instruction and entertainment from the first meeting onward. The use of mass-produced imagery was beginning to capture the attention of American Protestants. Celebrated clergy such as Lyman Abbott and Henry Ward Beecher published illustrated lives of Jesus shortly before Chautauqua began. Interest in blackboard illustrations for religious education was growing by the early 1870s and was promoted by Vincent in the religious monthly that he edited, *The Sunday School Teacher*, in 1866–67.[52] Some visiting speakers who frequented Chautauqua during the early years may have drawn encouragement from the ambitious use of visual media that they experienced there to go on to publish books that foregrounded use of imagery in religious instruction and devotion.[53] Numerous staff members and visiting speakers were proponents of "blackboard work" or stereoscopes in the Sunday school, and published books or articles on the subject.[54]

When American Christians did go to Palestine it was, as Twain noted, to see what they had long read about. Once they got there, their experience was often either disappointing or passionate. Either they confronted a stark gap between their imagined expectations and the physical reality before them, or, happy to ignore what did not fit the templates that guided their vision, they did as Twain's pilgrims and gathered bits and pieces that served as material footnotes to their reading of the bible. When travel to Palestine or even Chautauqua was not possible, a more convenient method of virtual travel was the lantern slide presentation, which had the keen advantage of filtering out the underwhelming features of actual visits while projecting remarkably clear images the size of cinematic screens and also allowing one the enjoyment of an amusing evening in the parlor. Composed of large format photographic images printed on glass (3 ¼ × 4 inches), lantern slides were projected with powerful lamps fitted with large lenses. In a letter used as an advertisement in *The Magic Lantern*, a trade journal published in Philadelphia, a professional exhibitor of lantern slides from Evanston, Illinois, stated that when he showed lantern slides of scenes photographed in Europe, Egypt, and the Holy Land, his well-traveled audience members told him that they got "more satisfaction in studying these pictures . . . than they get in traveling over the same countries."[55]

Perhaps the most ambitious collections of lantern slides were those gathered on site in 1881–82 when Philadelphia photographers William Rau and Edward Wilson visited Egypt, Arabia, Palestine, and Syria, at the request of educators interested in using lantern slides in the classroom. Wilson was editor of *The Philadelphia Photographer*, a monthly trade journal for photographers, and Rau's employer. Rau did most of the shooting, but both kept diaries, whose entries formed the basis of two long series of columns that each man published from 1881 to 1883 in the journal. Comparing the diary accounts with the photography is instructive in making visible the difference between what tourists imagined and what they actually saw in Palestine. The pressing, menacing

crowd that Rau described in his diary account of his Easter visit to the Church
of the Holy Sepulchre in Jerusalem was completely eliminated in the photograph, taken from above, on the roof of a building across the street. It was the
crowds of beggars and residents that quickly formed about the American visitors almost wherever they went that drew Rau's ire as recorded in his diary and
his letters to his wife. "You must understand," he wrote his wife from Cairo on
January 8, 1882,

> that the streets are narrow and winding, with a sidewalk only about 30
> inches wide and the traffic, walking and carriage, is all done in the middle
> of the street. You can form no idea how very crowded they are, if you set up
> your camera you are at once surrounded with hundreds of Arabs, they
> seem to spring out of the ground.[56]

Rau indicated in his diary that he and Wilson spent a total of only two hours
one morning visiting Nazareth, where they were "very much bothered with
people in the streets."[57] The photograph of a street in Nazareth (Figure 45)
shows the source of Rau's frustration: ghostly gray masses of figures float
on either side of the street. The large format, glass-negative photographs that
Rau and Wilson took required exposures that did not accommodate moving
subjects.

Looking at the hundreds of photographs taken by Rau and Wilson during
their trip, one is struck by the absence of human figures, especially groups.
Picturesque single figures occur with some frequency, but always carefully
posed by the photographers, who selected them carefully for their picturesque
value as describing the typical "Bedouin" or "woman carrying water." What was
considered authentic about the Holy Land, what actual and virtual American
tourists found even more compelling in lantern slides, panoramas, and scale
models at Chautauqua than the real thing, were sites purged of the living
nuisance of inhabitants, none of whom suited the antique ideal of "the Holy
Land" unless they were seen through the filter of the picturesque pose. The lure
of the image was its power to cloak a humble and bothersome reality in order to
expedite the tourist-pilgrim's access to what was already in mind.

Jewish visitors understandably had a different set of reactions. For Zionist
advocates of a Jewish homeland, the material souvenirs they brought back for
display in their homes were intended as pieces of the desired homeland and
souvenirs of the *yishuv*, or Jewish settlement project that was already underway
in the late nineteenth century. For Orthodox religious Jews, the reason was yet
different again. As one study of American Jewish culture and the Holy Land
put it,

> While Christian travelers might bring back bottles of water from the Jordan
> River [in which Jesus had been baptized], religious Jews often returned
> home with bags of Holy Land soil, designed for use in Jewish burial, as a

Figure 45 William Rau, street scene in Nazareth, lantern slide, 1882. Courtesy The Library
    Company of Philadelphia.

way of preparing for the messianic age of restoration in the Land of
Israel.[58]

For Christians, especially Protestants, the Holy Land tended to be either a
decrepit signpost or an exotic relic. In either case, however, it was the avenue
to the past, not the present. Even the religious skeptic Twain closed his account
of his visit to the Holy Land with bitter words describing a wretched ruin:
"Palestine sits in sackcloth and ashes. Over it broods the spell of a curse that
has withered its fields and fettered its energies."[59] The Orientalist alternative
regarded the current inhabitants as frozen in the past: they were, wrote one
traveler, "the same to-day that they were two thousand and more years ago."[60]
For Jewish supporters of a homeland, the poverty and provinciality of Palestine
was a development issue, and for some a political one. American Zionists
welcomed images such as Rosh Hashanah cards that intermingled ancient

buildings and the Zionist flag, which eventually became the flag of the state of Israel. Jews sympathetic to settlement naturally saw an organic connection between the present and actual landscape, their historical identity as a scattered people, and the desired future homeland that might reverse the global Diaspora by anchoring it in a nation centered in Palestine.

Among the items that have served as universal signage of Israel and Judaism in the twentieth century is the menorah (Figure 46). One of the ceremonial

Figure 46 Menorah, souvenir purchased in Jerusalem, 2005. Photo author.

objects of ancient Judaism, even pictured on the arch of Titus among the booty carried off by the Roman army after destroying the temple in Jerusalem, the menorah attracted special attention as a symbol in the United States, as in the celebration of Hanukkah in proximity to Christmas. Moreover, the ceremony was important to Zionists since it represented armed Jewish resistance to a hostile invader of the homeland. As a result, the menorah is among favorite souvenirs for visitors to Israel. Figure 46 is an example of a mass-produced trinket, purchased in the street in Jerusalem near the Temple Mount. Jewish tourists bring such objects back to display in their homes as evidence of their having made pilgrimage to the Jewish homeland. The same object appeals to Christian visitors who might easily see in it a bronze replica of ancient biblical artifacts, the sort of item illustrated in the popular literature that prepares tourist-pilgrims for their trip to Palestine.

Because the public taste for biblical history and culture far exceeded the number of Americans who could afford to travel to Palestine, exhibits of the region were included in the series of world's fairs staged in the late nineteenth and early twentieth centuries in the United States and Europe. American Christians and Jews who attended the St. Louis World's Fair in 1904 encountered the major exhibit of a section of Jerusalem. Although organizers of such exhibits intended them for a broad public, the overarching framework was often Protestant in conception. Barbara Kirshenblatt-Gimblett has suggested that the exhibition model of the Holy Land may have suited Protestant sensibility far better than actual trips to Palestine, which so often resulted in an underwhelming impression. "The goal [for Protestants] was to make the Biblical text more 'real' and the experience of it as vivid and immediate as possible."[61] Like lantern slides purged of distractions, the model dispensed with irrelevant and possibly conflicting material and was experienced within the parenthesis of "model," which meant that scale was automatically dispensable. The model could therefore much more readily exemplify or illustrate what the Protestant already knew. Faithfulness to the sacred text and the elimination of the inessential welcomed the simulacrum's neat erasure of borders, scale, and sheer artifice, enhancing the fit between physical reality and pious imagination.

But for Jews, Kirshenblatt-Gimblett points out, the model would have meant something different:

> For Jews, in contrast, the attachment to the land of Israel was covenantal, and this was the determining factor in identifying holy places, the Wailing Wall chief among them, and creating models, most of the Tabernacle and the Temple.[62]

Jews used models to help them experience their relation to the actual sites of God's compact with Israel whereas Protestants used models to help them read the bible – and to do so as the unrivaled, secure source of spiritual authority. Historical research, literary criticism, and scientific theories about the age of the earth and the origin of life came to be viewed by conservative Protestants as an assault on the authority of "God's Word." Insofar as exhibition models and biblical artifacts could support a traditional understanding of the historical reliability of the biblical text, they were experienced with the tourist's awe of a brush with authenticity.

Word and image: Protestant preaching and the panorama

Tourists at the world fairs were commonly treated to a variety of costumed performances set in halls and streets that evoked faraway places. The American taste for sensational visual tourism had been indulged since the 1820s in New York and Boston in the form of panoramas and dioramas (long canvases or murals portraying several interconnected scenes) featuring aspects of the Holy Land. Early versions were paintings installed in rotundas or toured as dioramas. In the 1840s long stretches of continuously painted canvas had been mounted on two spools and were presented as a single visual narrative while an orator narrated a visual journey down the Mississippi or through Palestine.[63] These devices had the advantage of mobility and were therefore taken on the road by traveling raconteurs who rolled through cities in the South and Midwest. A reporter writing in a St. Louis paper in 1850 claimed that the practice of "taking long sea voyages for the recovery of health, or short trips for purposes of pleasure" had been replaced by "the modern introduction of panoramas." Audiences enjoyed the illusion of sitting on a boat or railroad car, watching the countryside pass them without "the annoyance of rail way porters, disagreeable traveling companions, and the perpetual losses of trunks and carpet bags."[64] Once again, a new visual medium was celebrated for making tourism convenient. As one of the most popular forms of popular visual entertainment, panoramas enjoyed a period of wide attention from mid-century until the 1890s, until the nickelodeon machine and the flickering screen eclipsed their appeal for the sense of verity and presence. Until then, however, the medium captured great attention for its realism. In addition to indulging popular taste for visual spectacle, the panorama worked out the rudimentary commercial apparatus that greeted the rise of film in the early twentieth century and remains very much in place today. It is important to understand that commerce and pious entertainment were not regarded as antithetical in principle by most nineteenth-century Americans, who had at least as much P. T. Barnum in their souls as they did Emerson or Thoreau.

Consisting of hundreds of yards of scenically painted canvas gathered on two rollers, moving panoramas were gigantic scrolls (from ten to fifteen feet high, and reportedly even larger) that were slowly rolled from one spool to the other as a speaker narrated a journey, often accompanied by a pianist or other musicians. American audiences were especially fond of the scenery of their country, and enjoyed the leisure of trips down the Mississippi, which numerous panorama producers took on the road during the middle decades of the century. The Overland Trail, Niagara Falls, the St. Lawrence River, and the Great Lakes were the subjects of other celebrated panoramas. If such spectacular features of the national landscape were the themes of most panoramas, there were some dedicated to religious subjects, which were also commercially successful. In 1875, the Rev. Edwin Long advertised his *New Course of Illustrated Sermons*, which offered preachers or speakers an apparatus (Figure 47) that mounted illustrations of biblical texts on spools that could be noiselessly advanced during the presentation. The device presented images designed expressly for Rev. Long's use and were touted as "biblical, soul-awakening, Christ-elevating, forming for eye and ear so many links in the chain of thought." The advertisement claimed that the images were "equal in size and artistic beauty to first-class panoramas."[65] Moreover, the images were meant for the vast interiors in which contemporary celebrity-preachers gathered huge audiences. Ad copy stated that the imagery was large enough to be seen "by crowded audiences in Rev. Henry Ward Beecher's church [Brooklyn], Tremont Temple, Boston, Bethany, Philadelphia, and many of the largest churches in Chicago, Cincinnati, Baltimore, Washington, etc., where Mr. Long has been invited to preach." The device was meant to be placed behind the pulpit, where it displayed "as many illustrations as may serve as HELPS to rivet the truth." If clergy had learned anything from contemporary visual culture, it was that images commanded attention and that preachers had good reason to couple word and image in their battle for the congregation's attention.

Although Long intended his apparatus to be tastefully installed in the nation's finest churches, it nonetheless shared the key interest of linking word and image with promoters of religious panoramas who took their show on the road to small towns in much less cosmopolitan places than Boston or New York. The Book of Revelation (Figure 48) was the subject of one traveling panorama, created in the late 1870s by an industrious man named Arthur Butt, who had studied art in Pennsylvania, then returned to his native Charlotte, North Carolina, to produce twenty-two scenes, each fifteen by twenty feet, on a single run of canvas several hundred feet long. In 1880, Butt took his moving panorama on tour through the South, receiving rave reviews and large crowds from Maryland to Indiana.[66] Butt's brother traveled to towns ahead of the show in order to work out advance arrangements and commence advertising. He posted placards and large lithographs, placed show cards in windows, and consulted with local clergy, newspapers, and journalists, and operators of opera houses, schools, churches, and theaters, where the panorama show was to be staged. In the performances, Butt himself narrated the complex Book of Revelation. But the enterprise quickly became a family business. He also employed his father, who was a clergyman, as speaker, while his wife provided musical accompaniment. Admission varied from 25 to 50 cents for adults and 10 to 25 cents for children.

Figure 47 Rolling panorama device, Rev. Edwin M. Long, *Illustrated History of Hymns and their Authors*. Philadelphia, PA: Joseph F. Jaggers, 1875, 427. Courtesy The Library Company of Philadelphia.

Figure 48 Whore of Babylon and dragon, section from panorama of the Book of Revelation by Arthur Butt, painting on canvas, 1880. Courtesy North Carolina Museum of History.

Newspaper accounts indicate that Butt frequently filled his houses and that long lines formed outside awaiting entrance. Churches were happy to sponsor the event since they took a cut of proceeds. Response to the shows indicates that audiences were "awestruck" and that they found the panorama's depiction of the dramatic events of the Book of Revelation "overwhelming," "stupefying," "sublime," and "exalted."[67] The large size and the exotic imagery certainly accounted for the spectacle, as did all of the advance work by Butt's brother. The Whore of Babylon (Figure 48) and the Pearly Gates of the New Jerusalem (for which he used a large number of real pearls, sewn to the canvas) "were greeted with hearty cheers," as a Charlotte newspaper put it. "So enraptured were a portion of the audience at the last scene of The New Jerusalem, that some of them lingered after the close of the entertainment to gaze upon it."[68] Butt used artificial lighting to spotlight the imagery during his oratory, which augmented the drama and which was frequently mentioned in press accounts. The result was a thrilling show. The Chattanooga *Daily Times* proclaimed that "the scenes present a succession of magnificent spectacles, each presenting some new feature to excite the admiration and applause of the spectators, culminating in two, which far surpass anything ever exhibited here."[69] Religious entertainment, at least among southern Protestants, could rival all forms of public amusement.

Protestants crowded into churches and public buildings to witness Butt's presentation for many reasons – for the fun of it, for moral edification, and for the sensation of a rousing visual experience. A press report about the exhibition of the panorama in a Baptist church in Lebanon, Tennessee, stated that, "when seen under the glare of a calcium light [the spotlight used by Butt]," the scenes of the Apocalypse of St. John "seem more like a real vision than a picture." Another report noted that the portrayal of one scene was so "magnificent" that "one would almost imagine that [the audience] witnessed this grandly sublime miracle."[70] The Atlanta *Daily Post* reported that the panorama's scene of the Vision of the Lamb was "so grand" that the audience "forgot to applaud and only looked on in silent wonder." A Lutheran pastor in Charlotte wrote that the artist "has transferred to canvas the wonderful word painting of the inspired Apostle so skillfully that [the biblical subjects] seem to live and move before us."[71]

No doubt much of this tone was part of the rhetoric of public hyperbole and advertisement. But what seems quite significant in the published reception of Butt's panorama is the willingness of conservative American Protestants to regard images of Scripture as rising in stature, even to the point of becoming the visual equivalent of Holy Writ. One clergyman assured readers that Butt's images were "faithful delineations" of their biblical texts, and even suggested that the authority directing the artist's work was spiritual in nature:

> If the one was inspired to write, the other must have been inspired to paint these visions. The chaste, sweet, refined and enraptured spirit of John glows on the living canvas as if he were present pointing the way from the deformities and discords of earth to the beauties and symphonies of Heaven.[72]

Observers often noted that words failed to convey the effect of the panorama. "It must be seen to be appreciated," claimed the clergyman just cited. Visual spectacle in the form of the panorama's popular version of the sublime rivaled, even surpassed, words, making access to the events portrayed in biblical text immediate and riveting. As one fan put it after seeing the panorama, recalling contemporary claims for lantern slides and other visual portrayals of the Holy Land: "a person can learn more of the Book of Revelation in one evening than he would from reading it in a life-time." Another viewer asserted that the panorama "ministers to the eye, and to the heart as no language can."[73] It seems clear that for many Protestant viewers of such sacred spectacles as Butt's panorama, *seeing* paintings of biblical subjects had joined *hearing* the biblical word as a celebrated (and even favored) channel of revelation. The lure of much new visual media in the second half of the nineteenth century was its apparent power to come alive, to leave its artificial character behind and address viewers with a spectacular effect they found irresistible.

Chapter 6

Seeing in public

America as imagined community

The subtitle of this chapter draws from a widely admired book by Benedict Anderson, which proposed as a definition of nationhood the shared practices of imagining national purpose and cohesion.[1] National identity is not to be understood in the first instance as a common language, geography, racial stock, religion, or even history, but as shared forms of thinking and feeling. Important as all those undeniably may be in any given instance, generally speaking it is the narratives, symbols, songs, and legends that Anderson felt provide the overarching linkages that hold a nation together. A nation is imagined, Anderson argued, because the symbolic sensations in the minds and bodies of its citizens are what they actually share since most never meet one another to exchange or agree on their beliefs. According to Anderson, the capitalist commodity of print – books, newspapers, journals, and broadsides – creates a new cultural domain in which readers share simultaneous access to ideas and symbols by means of which they commonly envision or otherwise experience their cultural and national unity.[2] Print and mass-produced imagery are a fundamental aspect of national imagination since these circulate widely and are viewed and consumed repeatedly. They find their way into almost every aspect of national and personal life, from the public school to government propaganda to mass entertainment. Anderson's claim applies very well to the case of the United States, where a variety of different visual media contribute importantly to the experience of American nationhood and often invoke religion as fundamental to imagining the national community and its purpose.

Passion plays

Visitors to Chautauqua experienced different visual media and a popular iconography that intermingled commerce, entertainment, instruction, and inspiration. As with the other visual media examined here, the point was to foster an emboldened sense of the life of Jesus and the Holy Land's significance for the welfare of the American republic. The experience drew on and served to disseminate the iconography of the Holy Land and the life of Jesus that were also found in a great variety of other visual media. Yet another popular source of imagery was the Passion play, as it was practiced in the United States, recreated during Lent in local congregations or on stage in major cities, or as it was presented every ten years in the village of Oberammergau in the south of Germany. Those who did not attend the play could peruse the travel literature or the official text issued by the play, both of which described and reproduced photographs of the event. The play was also a very popular theme on the Lyceum and Chautauqua lecture circuit during the first decade of the twentieth century, illustrated by lantern slides (Figures 45, 49 and 51). In every instance, pervading all of sacred visual media is the tableau vivant, which served Protestants and Catholics as a fundamental motif for visualizing the life and person of Jesus.

Passion plays were crucial because they served as the ongoing intertextual reinforcement of the tableau vivant, infusing the still image with a direct tie to public presence before the real thing, the original event. Simply put, the tableau vivant is how the Christian and especially the Protestant imagination made images real, in effect more real than representations. Passion plays theatricalized paintings and photographs, urging viewers to imagine that each still depiction of the life of Jesus was a frozen scene, an ideal translation of scriptural narrative onto a stage before which the Christian public sits and observes it.

Figure 49 "Joseph Sold into Slavery," Oberammergau Passion play, lantern slide from Charles and Katherine Bowden illustrated lecture, "A Trip to Oberammergau and the Passion Play," 1900, Bowden Papers, Valparaiso University. Courtesy of the Department of Special Collections, Valparaiso University.

Visual media that employed the tableau vivant concerted the gaze of viewers into a visual field in which the image represented the Gospel events to an audience that was self-conscious, aware of the public event of spectation. The visual field of the (Christian) public consisted of a mode of viewing that presupposed and reinforced the viewer's membership in a shared practice of looking. Seeing films, paintings, or panoramas of Jesus or the bible was not an impersonal act of observation, but a public participation, a collective visual piety for devout viewers. It did not simply place individuals before the real thing, but brought fellow believers into a common presence. The tableau vivant presumed a live audience, a discrete group of people sharing a space and a temporal experience, a common presence before the sacred presentation of the Story.

The sense of an audience enrapt in the event, transported to the first century as it watches the Passion play at Oberammergau, is conveyed by contemporary accounts of those who traveled to see it. A Catholic viewer who described his "pilgrimage" to Oberammergau in 1880 was impressed by the effect of the presentation on those assembled to witness it: "That all present were impressed I am confident. The perfect silence that prevailed, the stillness with which the audience sat out each act (some rather long, and the dialogue often tedious), the eager attention they gave throughout, proved this."[3] The writer even noted that a Protestant expressed approval of the play. Another travel account, recorded in a volume of Burton Holmes' popular *Travelogues*, offered an illustrated description of Holmes' visit to the famous Passion play in 1900:

> Four thousand people are around us, but we forget their presence, and they, too, are far away in the first century, witnesses of this sublimest sacrifice. What their impressions are we cannot tell. We see the tears in many eyes, some sobs are heard; we see faces pale and drawn, and other faces quite unmoved. But even those who see in the picture there revealed nothing but a spectacle, a play, recognize the solemnity and the intensity of its import; there is no scoffing save from the Priests and Pharisees of the stage, while the tears of Mary and of Martha are shared by many women, and the expressed agony of St. John is but an echo of that which tortures many strong men in the audience.[4]

The photographs in Holmes' volume as well as lantern slides used in a contemporary illustrated lecture on the play (Figures 45 and 51, pp. 157 and 170) show that the theatrical scenes shared the composition of the tableau vivant and the stereographic card (cf. Figures 43 and 44, pp. 147 and 149): a foreground of figures arranged parallel to the picture plane and silhouetted against a flat background, usually a painted scrim that recalls the standard practice of portraiture in studios of nineteenth-century photographers as well as the staging of tableaux vivants. In fact, the entire structure of the Bavarian Passion play was a series of tableaux describing Old Testament anti-types paired with key moments in Christ's passion. Twenty-five tableau subjects were presented by the cast while a choir sang a prologue for the corresponding scene from the Passion that followed immediately upon each tableau. For example, a tableau of the expulsion of Adam and Eve was paired with the scene of Christ entering Jerusalem (Act 1); the fiery serpents and brazen serpent was coupled with the Crucifixion (Act 16); a tableau of the Israelites crossing the Red Sea preceded the final scene of the play, the Resurrection (Act 18).[5] Joseph sold into slavery by his brothers (Figure 49) is paired with Caiaphas before the Sanhedrin, plotting the apprehension of Jesus.[6]

Among the audience with Burton Holmes at the 1900 presentation in Oberammergau were ten Protestants from Indiana who traveled there with their pastor to see the play. Like the "pilgrims" who had accompanied Twain to the Holy Land to trace the footsteps of their Master, the ten made their own pilgrimage to Oberammergau to behold the ancient events unfold. Two in the group, Charles and Katherine Bowden, came along in order to create an illustrated lecture of the entire event, including the trip, the town, and the play, with the intention of staging a program for the Lyceum and Chautauqua circuits back home. They took hundreds of photographs and bought dozens of official photographs for sale in Oberammergau. From these and a commercially available film they fashioned a nearly two-hour presentation of the ocean voyage to Europe, a tour of the village and its inhabitants, and the play itself (Figure 50). It was a *virtual* pilgrimage that the Bowdens performed for a decade thereafter to audiences around the country.[7] Culminating in the stage production, the lecture offered American audiences a "you-are-there" view not only of the play, but also of the pious world of the Bavarian villagers who performed it. Contemporary accounts of the Bowden lecture indicate that people were awed by the sense of immediacy the images created. A Minnesota newspaper lauded the presentation's realism in 1901: "The figures were natural and their movements life like and the scenery was of course exactly reproduced."[8]

The Passion play's scenes in Oberammergau and in the resulting illustrated lecture taken on the road by the Bowdens were designed to animate the history of visual representations, grounding the images on stage in the still imagery from the history of Christian art in order to secure the authenticity of the theatrical representation. The official text for the 1900 performance cited a French viewer's response to the scene of Caiaphas raging before the Sanhedrin. The viewer said "he could not better designate the method of representation than by saying it was to him as if pictures of medieval painters had become endowed with life."[9] Several tableaux and scenes in the play quote medieval, Renaissance, and Baroque religious paintings. The use of Leonardo's *Last Supper* is evident in the tableau struck at Oberammergau (Figure 51). Throughout the play, we see each moment minted by the history of European art from the Middle Ages to the Renaissance: Suffer the Little Children to Come unto Me, The Resurrection, The Ascension, The Descent from the Cross, The Crucifixion, Christ before Pilate, The Crown of Thorns, and the remainder of the Stations

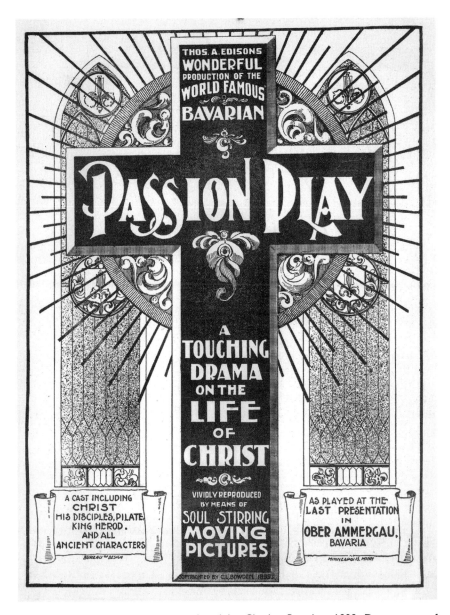

Figure 50 Passion Play, brochure produced by Charles Bowden, 1899, Department of Special Collections, Christopher Center, Valparaiso University. Courtesy of the Department of Special Collections, Valparaiso University.

Figure 51 "The Last Supper," Oberammergau Passion play, lantern slide from Charles and Katherine Bowden illustrated lecture, "A Trip to Oberammergau and the Passion Play," 1900, Bowden Papers, Valparaiso University. Courtesy of the Department of Special Collections, Valparaiso University.

of the Cross. The history of sacred art provided the pictorial framework in which to see the Passion. Whether tableau or scene, the setting on stage was treated as a backdrop against which the leading figures were silhouetted or accented in a dramatic visual manner.

The pictorial vocabulary of the history painting as tableau vivant and its avid reception among American viewers is well summarized by an enormous canvas produced in 1881 by Mihaly Munkácsy, a Hungarian painter whose *Christ before Pilate* (Figure 52) was exhibited in New York in 1886–87, where it was admired by many clergy in printed reviews and from the pulpit. Charles Kurtz, member of the National Academy of Design, assembled dozens of their notices, commentaries, sermon extracts, and editorial letters into a single volume and added an essay of his own in order to promote the American reception

Figure 52 Mihaly Munkácsy, *Christ before Pilate*, oil on canvas, 1881. Courtesy Library of Congress.

of the painting as it was publicly exhibited in the Twenty-third Street Tabernacle in New York. Kurtz noted that

> the first glance at the picture usually gives the spectator the impression that the scene is real, and that the figures before him are living persons; this feeling is one which it sometimes seems to require an effort to shake off.[10]

A Boston clergyman was also struck by the scene of the picture's exhibition:

> the effect, after one enters, is unique and startling; there seems a subdued and reverent atmosphere pervading the place. You feel as if suddenly carried back eighteen hundred years, and standing in the very presence of the dread reality which is there portrayed before you.

The clergyman recalled the touching effect of watching mothers bring their children before the image in order to explain it to them. "The little ones," he reported, "would look up and become awestruck. How real and how much the picture seemed to them, especially as they gazed so earnestly at the Redeemer, of whom they had so often heard!" The exhibition of the painting was a spectacle for children as well as adults. Many viewers observed, as did one New

York correspondent, that "the utmost stillness prevailed in the Tabernacle all afternoon."[11] To be sure, not everyone was taken by the picture or its theatrical presentation. Some critics objected to the exhibition in the Tabernacle as comparable to methods "used in the ordinary 'show' of a prodigy."[12] Most observations culled by Kurtz, however, mirrored that of a Philadelphia writer who proclaimed that "you feel as if you had really entered the Judgment Hall of Pilate, and were an actual spectator of the more than tragic event, which the artist has delineated."[13]

Viewers of Munkácsy's image repeatedly responded as if it were not an image at all, but a visual surface that dissolved into the very persons, place, and time that it depicted. It is often said that Protestants oppose images or have no use for them. Clearly, this was not the case among those clergy who went to see *Christ before Pilate* and wrote enthusiastically about it in the press afterwards. Protestants could overcome their scruples about sacred art insofar as images canceled their status as images by coming to life. Image as theater, as tableau vivant, was in no danger of becoming an idol. Seen as a living image, a sacred work of art could act as a window through which the devout peer in order to behold the sacred past or personage. The tableau vivant was not, therefore, the derivative of an image, but a Protestant way of seeing that transformed an image into what may be described as sacred spectacle. A tableau vivant was alluring because it operated as something of a stereoscopic transformation of a painting, causing it to morph into the appearance of three dimensions. But this virtual effect, which offered a dramatic sense of presence, remained spectacle, that is, a visual conjuration. By this I mean that the tableau was something other than the literal presence of the sacred, which would miss what was actually happening in Protestant experience. Protestants reported what amounts to a devotional mindfulness of the sacred, the evocation of its historical reality, a looking beyond the image to respond to what is called forth and performed by means of it, namely, the authority of the biblical narrative. Rather like viewing the frozen effigies in a wax museum, the magic was seeing an image come to life, traversing the fictive boundary between a flat image and the enactment of its story. It was something like the magic of the stereoscope, which morphed flat photographs into three-dimensional objects floating just before the eye, or seeming to do so. But the real frame of reference for measuring the reality of the image was the scriptural account that the image served to confirm. Oliver Wendell Holmes conveyed this sense of presence when he described a stereographic image of Jerusalem: "as we look across the city to the Mount of Olives, we know that these lines which run in graceful curves along the horizon are the same that He looked upon as he turned his eyes sadly over Jerusalem."[14] Holmes felt his gaze joined to that of Jesus by looking at the same landscape at a moment described in the New Testament (Luke 19: 41). The stereograph created the illusion of the landscape before his eyes – the landscape that Jesus saw. So it was not a direct communion, but one mediated by scripture and separated by the ages. Time distanced Holmes from Jesus, but by making the

Holy Land appear to him, it was as if the stereograph canceled time, as if the Holy Land had not changed since Jesus saw it. The photographic image mediated each viewer's gaze in a kind of optical contact at the point described in Holy Writ. The photograph could do so precisely because of its ontology, enhanced by the illusionism of the stereoscope: objects photographed, Holmes wrote, shed an airy layer of skin, a luminous effigy divorced from its material substrate.[15] Yet we should not limit this sense of presence to photography, as response to Munkácsy's painting suggests. It was the image's capacity to stand out from its surface fiction when it was informed by scriptural text. What mattered to Protestants was seeing what they believed the bible said. Images could accomplish that by behaving transparently, as tableaux vivants.

From still to moving images: Protestantism and the rise of motion pictures

The transition from still to moving imagery started long in advance of the cinema. Indeed, it might be said to have commenced already in the narration of a single image, when a speaker stood before an audience and pointed successively to the moments encapsulated in the image as a visual encoding of the biblical narrative. The effect was a cumulative one, assembling a series of moments into a singular experience of viewing. Closer to a cinematic effect, crank-operated stereoscopes had been developed about 1860, which held fifty or one hundred cards, allowing the operator to view a rapid succession of images. Though the result was not cinematic motion, it was described as capturing the passage of time by Oliver Wendell Holmes in 1861.[16] The use of the panorama, still, then moving, literalized the moving narrative, and took another step toward the cinematic image. Visual narratives in lantern slides serialized images, though rarely achieved the illusion of animation that is the hallmark of cinema. That illusion came closer in the 1870s with the high-speed photographic studies of locomotion in humans and horses by Marey and Muybridge among others.[17]

The Protestant reception of film in the first decade of the twentieth century, though varied, voiced a wide-ranging anxiety about the power and effect of the new medium. While many Protestants were able to embrace such visual media as panoramas, stereoscopes, Passion plays, lantern slides, scale models, and illustrated books, they were more likely to regard film with a certain apprehension. Why the difference? Film encouraged a different way of seeing. Like secular theater, it redeployed audiences as private consumers whose reason for viewing was personal entertainment in the form of visual absorption, not edification. The shift was significant: from public moral assent to private amusement or aesthetic enjoyment. At stake was the manner of viewing, that is, what happened in front of the image among the audience, what might be called the cultural work of seeing. Film historian Charles Musser studied the opposition among conservative American Protestants to staging the Passion play in professional, secular, and commercial theaters during the 1880s. Among other reasons, Musser noted that Protestants associated the theatrical stage with nightlife and profane entertainment. Such spaces as the commercial stage and its company were not considered conducive to the cultivation of devout thought and practice, and were therefore liable to sully and distort the sacred subject. The Passion play in Bavaria, by contrast, was set in a remote village and enacted by pious peasantry and local people of faith.[18]

Yet anxieties about film were neither universal nor constant, though they did linger. Betting on the spectacle and sensation of the new medium, the Bowdens integrated over 2,000 feet of film with lantern slides of art and scenes from the Passion play, according to press accounts. The film they used, as a brochure they issued in 1899 or 1900 indicates (see Figure 50, p. 169), was distributed by Thomas A. Edison & Company. Edison & Co. sold different versions, one based on a version of the play performed by the members of the village of Hortiz in Bohemia, produced in 1897, and premiered in Philadelphia.[19] But another version, produced by New York City's Eden Musee Films in the following year, was called *The Passion Play of Oberammergau*, though it was not produced on site in Bavaria but staged and filmed on the roof of Grand Central Palace in New York City.[20] Contemporaries described the Bowden lecture as a sensational interplay of film and lantern slides. One viewer wrote that "the dissolving of stereopticon [lantern slide] views into moving pictures was particularly pleasing and a feature that was entirely new to all who were present."[21] Far from alienating devout audiences, the effect was hailed as spell-binding and inspiring. But the Bowdens were apparently mindful of those clergy who had and would continue to express hostility toward the medium of moving pictures and the idea of stage presentations of the Passion. A writer who attended the Bowdens' presentation of their Passion play lecture in Dublin, Georgia, in June of 1903, noted that Katherine Bowden allayed anxieties among her audience:

> Some of those who went out to hear the lecture and witness the moving pictures were just a little fearful that there might be something sacrilegious about it, but this feeling wore away as the lecturer sweetly told the story of the sacred drama, "The Passion Play," and as picture after picture of the actors in the play, the village, the theater, and the play itself were given.[22]

Bowden was careful to stress the piety of the German villagers in order to defuse any sense among audience members that a theatrical portrayal of the story of Jesus might be sacrilegious:

> She gave a short history of Oberammergau and the people of that village, in which no crime involving moral turpitude has been committed in over three hundred years; where there are no policemen, sheriffs, jails or police barracks; where the inhabitants live the lives of Jesus, Mary . . . and all the other personages of sacred memory as nearly as possible.[23]

One was not watching professional actors perform theatrical roles, but real people presenting sacred characters with which they personally identified themselves. If that were not enough, the Bowdens collected a file full of written endorsements from clergy, Chautauqua managers, and university presidents, all of whom attested to the propriety of the presentation. As a Presbyterian pastor from Dubuque, Iowa, reassured potential bookings: "There is nothing objectionable in the exhibition. It is quite suitable to be given in the church."[24]

Mixing the sacred and the profane through commercial adaptation of the Passion play as some of the earliest films did during the late 1890s threatened to desecrate a subject that required a devout audience and a reverential form of representation. It seems likely, however, that the Bowdens' integration of Edison's motion picture version of the Passion play with lantern slides, couched within endorsements, publicity, and a lecture that stressed the piety of the event and its topic, may have helped many Americans reconcile their fears regarding the mixture of the new visual media with the sacred subject of the Passion play. Protestants objected to the perceived menace of restructuring the audience that secular amusement entailed in theatrical and, later, cinematic presentations. But once they learned that the setting of public, commercial entertainment could also serve as a venue sympathetic on its own terms to the propagation of the faith, many Protestants quickly warmed to films of the Passion. They were learning the same lesson as other media such as novels and theater, one which would shortly also be learned in radio and beyond. And it was not a new lesson for American Protestants, who had led the way in mass print publication in the early nineteenth century. Indeed, it would be difficult to point to a single subculture that more quickly negotiated initial anxieties about new media than Protestants. Again and again, the obstacle consisted of coming to terms with the impact of any medium on the structure of the audience, which, for Protestants, is a paradigmatic oral culture of preaching and hearing the Word of God. Once this ideal or baseline form of communication is imbricated in a new medium, that medium is enthusiastically endorsed and exploited. This pattern is evident in the early years of American Protestant attitudes toward film.

A crucial transitional device once again was the tableau vivant, which appeared in filmed versions of the Passion play. This *mise-en-scène* of successive moments in the narrative presented the subject in a way that mimicked the staged presentation of the Passion play, and thus reassured early film spectators that they were observing the older medium through the transparent form of the new. The familiarity of the biblical text, the Passion play, or other visualizations of the narrative affirmed the public character of the story as the gathering point of believers, as the shared or common site of belief. Herbert Reynolds has shown how individual images of the bible illustrated by artist James Tissot informed the 1912 film, *From Manger to the Cross*.[25] The tableau construction of scenes in even earlier films such as the Horitz Passion Play and the Eden Musee's *The Passion Play of Oberammergau* also emulated older visual media. Stills from these films confirm that the early cinematic representation of the

Passion play was a pageantry of tableaux vivants. "The Messiah's Entry into Jersusalem," a scene from the Eden Musee's 1898 production (Figure 53), shows the shallow, stage-like space across which figures move, silhouetted against the painted scrims behind them. An isocephalic arrangement of figures (all the heads occupy the same level) across the composition pulls them into the foreground, where they are displayed in full pageantry of dress. All action is parallel to the picture plane and unfurls at or toward the center, where the eye is led by all elements of the composition. Architectural setting is conceived as a backdrop, tinted with aerial perspective as it lightly sketches the location of the event. The flatness of the background serves to enhance the darker, more detailed foreground of the figures, recalling the visual dynamics of the stereograph (see Figure 44, p. 149). The same visual device is found at work in tableaux vivants (see Figures 43, 49 and 51, pp. 147, 166 and 170) and in Munkácsy's *Christ before Pilate* (see Figure 52, p. 171). The intertextuality of these media bolstered their power to endow scenes with a familiarity that early films of the Passion needed to employ in order to make them visually compelling and spiritually safe. For Protestant viewers the imbrication of film on the tableau vivant, stereograph, and history painting helped eschew or at least mitigate anxieties about compromising the public or communal function of representing the Passion.

Figure 53 Film still, "The Messiah's Entry into Jerusalem," from *The Passion Play of Oberammergau*, produced by Eden Musee Films, New York, 1898. Courtesy George Eastman House.

The self-conscious presentation of the biblical narrative helped construct a self-consciously Christian audience, a viewing situation composed of individual Christians who belonged to a Christian community. The problem with professional theater was that Christians in the audience dissolved into a profane public. One way of regarding Protestant opposition to film (or any other medium) stresses that it was a response to the threat of losing traditional forms of social control and cultural authority. Yet this overlooks the fact that even as Protestant church bodies such as the Episcopal Methodist Church prohibited its members from seeing commercial films in movie houses, Methodist clergy welcomed the exhibition of the very same films in their churches.[26] Why? Because there the conditions of viewing the film were conducive to the edification of the audience members as a community of faith. It is important therefore to focus on the medium's ability to structure the audience privately or communally as the reason for criticism or praise from religious quarters. American Protestants wanted to avoid the loss of community in the face of mass culture's anonymous and privatized mode of entertainment. The Christian audience seated before the Passion play was one that maintained a corporate identity as Christian. The public was a community. The crucial challenge for American Protestants was to realize how community could survive the new way of viewing that film entailed. The community was no longer to be affirmed as an assembled body of Christians simultaneously beholding an event that recognized and endorsed their real presence before one another. The new public medium of film as entertainment restructured the audience in a way that required Christians to become anonymous members of a public, which was no longer community in a Christian sense, but composed of members of a mass culture who privately experienced the edification of their faith. The challenge was a privatized experience of belief that was traditionally interpersonal, public, and testimonial.

Whether novels, theater, or film, the menace of the private experience of commercial media for Protestants was that private amusement placed such media beyond the purpose of moral instrumentation. I do not mean moral instrumentation in the blatant sense of authoritarian social control, but the power of media to cultivate the communal sense of an audience. The new medium of film as entertainment presented the capacity of media to cultivate an inner life of imagination, a private stage space in which media are not instruments for information delivery or moral influence or communal participation, but the raw material for private meaning construction. In 1924, one study of public relations divided film into two groups, the theatrical and non-theatrical:

> The first comprises those produced for houses operating on a commercial basis. The second classification consists of films that are most likely to find their opportunity for showing in clubs, community centers, school houses, Y.M.C.A.'s [Young Men's Christian Associations], church entertainments, conventions, and other organizations which do not expect to pay anything

for the use of the film beyond the cost of expressage. The motion picture public is not interested in instruction and will stand for only a limited amount of advertising slides, and resists most forms of visual education.[27]

The distinction, though understood in economic terms here, is comparable to the audiences under discussion. Each of the venues enumerated for the non-theatrical variety of film is a preeminently communal one. Clubs, schools, conventions, organizations, and churches all share the social feature of elective membership of individuals known to one another and belonging to a discrete social group. Theatrical film, according to this distinction, appeals to those viewers whose reasons for viewing are their own, which they service by virtue of purchasing access to the film, not by belonging to a group. Accordingly, a pastoral letter of December, 1925, from the Bishop of the Methodist Episcopal Church, pitted church and theater against one another and included most motion picture houses with theaters.[28] Not surprisingly, therefore, most American Protestant advocates of film in the first decades of its experience sought to exploit the medium's social value by deploying it within strictly communal circumstances – in church fellowship halls, at youth gatherings in the YMCA gymnasium, and so forth. When the medium enhanced the Christian sense of community, film was often applauded and enthusiastically put to use by Protestants. Both the menace and the promise of the medium were determined by the social fields of vision they helped construct.

Early Protestant commentators on film stressed the importance of limiting the frequency of viewing among children and called for regulation of theaters and producers. In 1911 a Protestant writer in Boston warned against motion pictures following the low road of vaudeville and burlesque theater. The proper task of "popular entertainment" lay in "molding character and in strengthening and sweetening life."[29] Although he recalled American Protestantism's old suspicion of theater, claiming that "the theater has too long been left to manage itself," the author believed that theater, and motion pictures as its latest manifestation, should be yoked to the moral needs of the public. "When *the people* begin to use [the theater] as a servant they will for the first time learn its value." He called therefore for "a stronger public demand for stage exhibitions which are clean and wholesome." Parents should make a point of determining the effect of theater upon their children. "And every good citizen for the honor of his community will do the same. Civic spirit will resent the stain upon the fair name of a community cast by a vulgar show."[30]

Protestant reformers, including many contributors to *Religious Education*, the organ of the Religious Education Association, a progressive, ecumenical Protestant association of clergy and educators founded in Chicago in 1903, believed that motion pictures could be made useful if they were not allowed to disturb the integrity of the public as a unified, civic body, a community that corresponded in will and moral commitment to the family.[31] Film appealed to the masses; biblical film should be made to reconnect with "the people," the great American public of people of faith. In addition to production, regulation of films and movie houses according to moral standards of character formation and civic virtue appeared to be the sure means of applying the new popular medium to the task of public edification. Mass audience was not to replace public will. The new medium of film was to contribute to the formation and maintenance of a civic polity. The commercial power of films needed to be controlled by moral frameworks applied by boards of review.

The creation of such boards occurred rapidly. The Board of Censorship was organized as part of the People's Institute of New York, which enlisted the voluntary cooperation of leading producers of motion pictures in 1909 to submit their work to review. Praising the effectiveness of this cooperation between censors and the film industry in 1911, a Congregationalist clergyman, Herbert Jump, celebrated the "social influence of the moving picture" on three counts. Motion pictures possessed the educational capacity to augment "the general intelligence of the common people." They promoted "the spirit and beauty of home life" by portraying "domestic happiness and comfort." And they fostered "decent moral standards" in the triumph of good over evil in the stories they dramatize.[32] Other contributors to *Religious Education* underscored the importance of programming the viewing of films – viewing portions of films during a sermon or lecture, viewing them in church buildings on Sunday afternoons or evenings, as part of larger programs that involved community singing and music, or as part of public forums. Congregations in neighboring communities might also collaborate to sponsor a "traveling operator" who could project films for "weekly or bi-weekly operations."[33]

In a pamphlet printed in 1910, Rev. Jump responded to critics of the ecclesiastical use of motion pictures, insisting that the medium "offers the most colossal opportunity for making a fresh moral and religious appeal to the non-churched portions of the community that has arisen in the history of recent Christianity."[34] He went so far as to claim that the motion picture was "the most wonderful invention which has come into existence since the invention of printing in the fifteenth century." Jump even implied that the new visual medium surpassed the eloquence of "the most enthusiastic orator" and advocated its use in "cities where there are large alien populations" because images transcended linguistic barriers: "A picture is a sort of graphic esperanto, a universal language."[35] Film was the new bible of the illiterate, in effect, speaking in a language "as needs no interpreter." Another contemporary advocate of film in religious venues, writing in an industry journal, regarded motion pictures as "an arm of the church" and proclaimed that "the moving picture machine has become a preacher and [that] its sermons are most effective because they are addressed to the eye rather than to the ear."[36] The claim recalls the response to Arthur Butt's biblical panorama thirty years before. In fact, the reception of film as a new religious medium among clergy and Christian enthusiasts recalls the rhetoric used to hail visual media from illustrated tracts to panoramas and stereographs. Rev. Jump believed that men and women who have ever shown interest in pictures, hanging them on the walls of our homes, seeking them in illustrated books and now in picture-postcards, should turn naturally to the motion picture sermon which puts the gospel in a pictorial form.[37]

Whereas early advocates of tracts in antebellum America had stressed the convenience of the print medium for far-flung evangelism, even surpassing the impact of the oral culture of preached sermons, promoters of film applied the same logic. Writing of the relevance of the motion picture for the church in the Nashville *Independent*, the head of the English Department at Vanderbilt University, Carl Halliday, noted that the medium's "universality of appeal" secured its superiority even over preachers themselves:

> All preachers are not equally effective or successful as orators or as social mixers; but here is an instrument that speaks the same language and the same lesson to all nations, and has more power in arousing feeling of kindliness and brotherhood than any one individual or group of individuals.[38]

Viewed under the proper conditions, film was able to construct the ideal discursive situation of church.

For an entire generation or more of American clergy committed to the social ideals of a "progressive church" and the moral reform pursued by a broad range of social service and philanthropic initiatives, film offered an exciting new tool for it was something to be consumed corporately and could achieve its moralizing ends on a public, even mass-public scale. This promised to secure the nation itself – the public that was the republic. Halliday assured his readers that

> in the battle against child labor, white-slavery, labor-conflicts, and vice development, in spreading knowledge of the Bible and biblical lands, in the teaching of patriotism and brotherhood, in the general education and developing of the public conscience, [the use of film by churches] apparently is destined to play an enormous part. Here then is a movement that cannot be ignored by the progressive church.[39]

A professor at the University of Chicago proclaimed that the medium of film "stands for a better Americanism because it is attracting millions of the masses to an uplifting institution, drawing them to an improving as well as amusing feature of city life."[40] Jump recommended film to all manner of charities and philanthropic efforts as the best way to address the "large alien populations" in American cities who did not speak English. As a universal visual language, film might do what many Christian, Jewish, and secular reformers hoped to accomplish: teach "social and domestic and personal hygiene."[41]

Within congregations, film was hailed as offering further resources. As "the highest type of entertainment in the history of the world," Rev. Jump claimed, film could attract the attention of the masses and overcome the principal resistance to attending church: dullness.[42] Jump encouraged clergy to integrate film into their sermons and worship services, promising "the motion picture preacher" that he would thereby enjoy "crowded congregations." Worship services could be built around three films, sandwiched between hymn singing and prayer and straddling a sermon on practical, reform-minded topics such as temperance, purity of the home, and self-sacrifice.[43] The result, Jump assured his readers, would be an interesting, engaging service that would go far to reverse the flight of Protestant congregations from such hot spots as the lower district of New York City, neighborhoods that were teeming with newly arrived immigrants. Jump targeted the rival theatrical medium of "low vaudeville" to be replaced by cinema in the reformer's zeal to take control of "the recreation of the poor." Ministering to the masses meant using film to revive congregational life and accommodate urban and immigrant populations to the community of the metropolitan congregation.[44] Although film was a mass medium, Jump labored to fit it to the existing religious culture, which still understood the church as a local community in a nation that consisted of local communities, each of which was believed to mirror a national unity, or at least the ideal of one. Film was to affirm national identity, the assimilation of immigrants, the Evangelical outreach of the church, and the appeal to the large numbers of Americans who did not attend church. Moreover, Jump argued that the film industry was submitting itself to a careful proscription of indecent and harmful topics. Film, in short, was the new mass medium that had the power to affirm community, to keep the "public" in the American re-public by advancing the national influence of Christianity.

This was understood to take place by a kind of benevolent coercion, enabled by the medium's subject matter as well as the conditions of its viewing. A contemporary writer urged churches to use films in order to attract boys, who, though they often avoided Sunday school, "do attend picture shows" and would be much more likely to remember bible stories seen on screen "than if the stories were told them by an indifferently interested teacher on a sunshiny Sabbath morning."[45] In 1913 Carl Halliday cited a municipal report which indicated that the popular appeal of motion pictures in the previous year had resulted in a precipitous drop in applications for saloon licenses in Washington, DC.[46] A Protestant minister in Vincennes, Indiana, introduced moving pictures in a Sunday evening program in the summer of 1912 in order "to compete in a friendly way with the Sunday evening entertainments which were drawing crowds in my town," and wrote another clergyman in the fall of the same year that he had "secured quadrupled attendance at my evening services."[47]

The number of authors who defended the use of films in religious settings before the First World War rarely failed to adduce such evidence, usually more anecdotal than statistical, to support the "progressive" utility of film in social and moral campaigns. Like tracts, which had been deployed in antebellum America for the same reason, the power of film consisted of its ability to address the masses, to appeal to broad classes of Americans who represented a challenge to moral order and character formation – boys, immigrants, the poor. Rev. Jump spoke for many when he put the matter this way:

> The problem of the poor man's leisure, someone has said, is the crux of the social problem. If only the motion picture ... could be carried on by the school and church and municipality so as to fill the poor man's and the poor boy's leisure with helpful instruction and clean entertainment, instead of being carried on by private individuals not always of the most refined type for gain, it would be a splendid thing.[48]

In step with the philanthropic and social service sensibility of the Progressive Era, Jump and other advocates of the religious utility of film promoted the self-regulation of the film industry, but regarded the use of films in churches as an indispensable complement to the commercial marketplace. In a lecture delivered at the University of California in the fall of 1912, Jump lauded the motion picture theater as the "most democratic thing which we have in American life today except the polls." No one interested in social conditions of the day, Jump insisted, could afford to overlook the importance of film and "its power for molding character."[49]

What did it mean to mold character? It is important not to conflate character with personality, which is the term that twentieth-century psychology used to replace the idea of character, which derived from nineteenth-century moral discourse.[50] Character was something that linked the individual to others, to a class, to a religious and moral set of ideals. Although individuals were said to possess their own character, to exhibit character meant to display the sense of judgment and self-restraint that was the mark of moral virtue. Character in that sense is what indicated the individual's membership within the class of respectability. Character, in other words, meant likeness to shared values and to those who also exhibited character. The definition, development, and display of character required a community and were meaningless without it. Behavior was the measure of one's acquiescence in the shared ideal. Rather than the nurturing of idiosyncratic personality, character was a communal affair. For advocates of character, democracy meant the communal affirmation of shared values more than it did the cultivation of personal peculiarities. Film was considered a powerful tool in achieving that community as a shared practice of imagination. By teaching morality, film promoted a uniform public code of conduct that was designed to strengthen character. To do so, according to Jump and many sympathetically disposed writers, the conditions of viewing film needed to be carefully constructed. He applauded the recent move from darkened theaters to half-lit movie houses, which eliminated inappropriate activities by exposing film audiences to the view of ushers as well as one another. Jump strongly advocated the reform or complete elimination of vaudevillian interludes between film screenings; and he urged the universal adoption and enforcement of laws "requiring that young children be attended by their parents or older guardians."[51] Film could not be expected to support American democracy if the conditions of its public consumption did not foster the formation of character.

From the republic to the masses: democracy, film, and public opinion

For proponents of film like Jump as well as liberal Protestant reformers such as Lyman Abbott and Washington Gladden "democracy" meant doing things together, in national unison, as a community.

> The seventy millions of people constituting the population of these United States [wrote Abbott in 1908] must learn how to feel, to think, and to plan together. They may be guided, but not controlled. There must be a corporate judgment, a corporate feeling, a corporate purpose, a corporate conscience.[52]

Gladden, like many other Protestants, looked to the schools as the saving constellation of religious forces in American life, as the preeminent institution from which a national unity should proceed. The nineteenth-century idea of a Christian republic persisted into the twentieth century, rivaling or tempering anything like a populist conception of democracy. The pluralist masses immigrating to the United States only intensified the longing of most Protestants for a system of assimilation that would prevent the loss of a deeply desired unity, which never existed beyond the ideological framework it was meant to bolster. Nativist Americanism and the nationalistic flag rituals and patriotic initiatives that were promoted by hereditary organizations such as the Daughters of the American Revolution responded to the changing demography, the growing pluralism, the dynamic urban scene, the ever shifting politics of immigration, and the mass culture that was plied by politicians, advertisers, educators, and entertainers to secure the attention and commerce of new Americans as well as old.[53]

By urging that films be selected for public screening "with a view to their educative uplift upon the masses of our population," clergy and religious educators signaled a new realization among Protestants and many others: film addressed "the masses." This became unusually clear after the war began in Europe. The editors of *Religious Education* signaled their opposition to the war when, in October of 1914, they reprinted a brief column by a professor of English at the University of Wisconsin, who invited film makers to use their medium as counter-propaganda:

more than any other agency the motion picture has in its power to let people know what war is. . . . Let us know by seeing before our eyes that war is not ideal glory; it is murder and maiming of men; it is rapine and theft.

The professor called on motion picture producers to use their access to a mass audience:

You have not created your audience for nothing. With such an audience as this, with such power as yours, it need never be again in our country that men shall fail to know what war really is.[54]

The war effort in the United States not only made quick use of film as a form of mass propaganda, but also stimulated recognition among advertisers, sociologists, psychologists, educators, and political theorists of the need to define and understand "public opinion." In the context of Americanism (the quest for racial hegemony among Anglo Protestants) and a nationalistic patriotism invested in flag rituals, many scholars focused on the troubling consequences of public opinion for the health of American democracy. Public opinion was often regarded as the unreasoned feelings that bound Americans into mass patterns that made up what some called "group mind" or herd instincts. For Walter Lippmann, whose *Public Opinion* (1922) is an enduring analysis of the formation of broadly shared perceptions, the task at hand was ultimately to show how democracy might survive the tyranny of unthinking public opinion.[55] Lippmann challenged the notion that democracy meant unity or uniform thought. He contended that American democracy had moved beyond the founding assumptions of a body politic that votes from wisdom and innate goodness. Having observed the effect of propaganda during the war, Lippmann knew that public opinion was not a rational formation. Noting the effect of self-interest in voter behavior, he argued that the motive power of democracy was the quest for liberty. Public opinion, he argued, was shaped by stereotypes, generalized symbols or vague images that stood in for careful reflection by appealing to fears, desires, taste preferences, and shared feelings of menace, or resentment.

Lippmann characterized the formation and operation of stereotypes in distinctly visual terms. A stereotype, he explained, is a picture in the mind, a model that precedes experience, to which sense data are subordinate, not unlike the mental imagery that Protestants carried to the Holy Land in actual or virtual pilgrimage. People tend to act on the basis of what they think they know, what in fact they care to have confirmed by experience, not impeached by it. "Human culture," Lippmann wrote, "is very largely the selection, the rearrangement, the tracing of patterns upon, and the stylizing of" ideas. The outside world is, he quoted William James, his favorite philosopher, "one great, blooming, buzzing confusion."[56] Human beings must rely on cultural constructions to apprehend their "real environment [which] is altogether too big, too complex, and too fleeting for direct acquaintance." We create what Lippmann called "pseudo-environments," useful fictions that reconstruct the world as a "simpler model" so that "we can manage with it."[57] The pseudo-environment is the domain of public opinion.

Lippmann's understanding of public opinion, which he formally defined as "those pictures which are acted upon by groups of people," constructed a visual field or gaze in which the image on the screen eclipsed the outside world, substituting itself for the more demanding and complex reality.[58] Public opinion was a theater of prejudices that replaced the actual environment with a pseudo-environment, a parade of fictions. The "public" of cinema audiences consists of the masses that gather to enjoy the affirmation of common knowledge, their prejudices or stereotypes, as a form of diversion. Lippmann took film and all mass media seriously precisely because they were mediums of communication in which the great diversity of the public consumed a common set of symbols that blurred their differences and worked toward creating a sense of unity. Such media even worked together:

> there can be little doubt that the moving picture is steadily building up imagery which is then evoked by the words people read in their newspapers. In the whole experience of the race there has been no aid to visualization [of stereotypes] comparable to cinema.[59]

This operation of mass-mediated stereotypic imagery threatened democracy, according to Lippmann, because it short-circuited critical reflection by direct appeal to irrationally held opinion. Such images were a menace because of the way they could be manipulated as propaganda to shape public opinion, thwarting the political process of a republic of citizens and resulting in pliant masses. Lippmann witnessed the power of visual propaganda in the formation of American public opinion in the First World War as well as the Second. Posters such as Figure 54 were issued by the government over the course of the Second World War in order to stoke public dedication to the war effort. "The enemy," the poster proclaims, is the Nazi assault on the bible, which is brutally impaled on a bayonet. Such propaganda affords no room for cogitation. The image was designed to penetrate to visceral feeling with the same force as the shank piercing the cherished tome. Indignation was the intended result, which would install this graphic image in the minds of American viewers where it might operate as the mental stereotype in the place of any sympathy for German soldiers, many of whom were less than a generation removed from German American immigrants.[60]

The better representation to inform political choice was textual information generated by scientific inquiry and assembled without partisan interest. Like Socrates in Plato's *Republic*, which he fondly quoted, Lippmann argued that image and opinion were untrustworthy; only scientific knowledge was reliable.

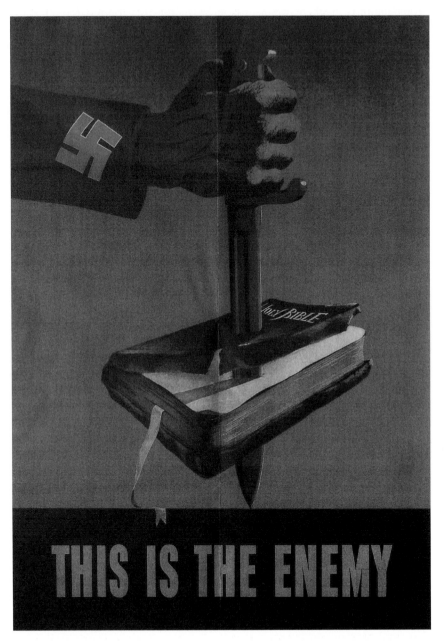

Figure 54 Barbara Marks, *This Is the Enemy*, 1943. Second World War poster issued by the United States Office of War Information. Courtesy Brauer Museum of Art, Valparaiso University.

The hope for democracy was to shift from preoccupation with the will of the people, which gave rise to the misleading idea of "public opinion" as some sort of a hovering spirit. The task of democratic government should be to see to the public good. To do that would require the reliable information provided by impartial experts who cared nothing about partisan politics or public opinion, but were dedicated to the pursuit of the "truth," which was "to bring to light the hidden facts, to set them into relation with each other, and make a picture of reality on which men can act."[61] It was a cultural critique of America brilliantly revived by Daniel Boorstin in 1961 in his book *The Image*, which lamented the power of mediated images in creating what Boorstin, indebted to Lippmann, called "the pseudo-event." Lippmann, and Boorstin after him, was inclined to regard images in entertainment and graphic media in a Platonic way: they were illusions that appealed to feeling and irrational desires, and the consensus they build should not be trusted. Pseudo-community, it might be said, is no substitute for a properly guided democratic government.

Seeing in groups: competing fields of vision and the visual practice of nationhood

Early film invited a way of looking that was not new – it had long been engaged in the visual arts – but was new to the field of mass entertainment. By characterizing the picture inside people's heads as the basis of public opinion, Lippmann identified a key distinction between mass culture and the local communal culture of Protestant ideology: the subjective gaze of the individual viewer/consumer versus the joint or communal experience of the visual spectacle as tableau vivant. The communal gaze gathers all viewers into a single arena of spectation to gaze together as a self-conscious body on the living picture that returns their gaze, acknowledging them as a single community joined together in a presence before the enacted Word. Together, the audience or public is edified as a congregation. Their presence is a public event, acknowledged by one another and sealed by the image that looks back at them. The result is the improvement of their collective Christian character. Being there is a public affirmation of who each person is in the midst of one another. The screen is the presentation of the historical origin of their collective identity. Thus, the faithfulness of what they see to the original is a matter of serious concern. It must be biblically accurate and morally reliable. The appeal to archeology and history and the quotation of famous paintings only enhanced this experience of authenticity.

The subjective or cinematic gaze of mass entertainment configured the visual field differently. The viewer was now a private individual, sitting in a darkened theater, watching the screen for the sake of personal enjoyment. Consequently, the image was less bound to its inspiring text. Film directors made all manner of changes to the screenplay for the sake of melodrama and visual engagement of the audience, which was not a community, but a mass public. The manner of relationship characterized by Lippmann is one of empathy, of individual identification with a hero, and revulsion at the villain.[62] Viewers become absorbed in the image and project their experiences into the roles performed on screen. The purpose of such spectacle was not to improve one's character, but to enthrall viewers in the stories of characters through vicarious and private identification with them.

Absorption was the pivotal feature identified by Harvard psychologist Hugo Münsterberg in a fascinating study of 1916. Münsterberg argued that cinema should be understood as an art form in its own right, distinct from the theatrical stage by virtue of the signature subjectivization or dematerialization of reality in the way film directed the viewer's attention, memory, and imagination. Münsterberg analyzed the visual language of film techniques to show how the medium manipulated time by intersplicing sequences that cut to the past; and how the close-up eliminated everything the director wished to have the audience disregard:

> The detail which is being watched has suddenly become the whole content of the performance, and everything which our mind wants to disregard has been suddenly banished from our sight and has disappeared. The events without have become obedient to the demands of our consciousness.[63]

As a result, a new visual field emerged, the absorptive nature of the cinematic gaze. The objective reality of the physical world of time and space was freely recast by film. "It is as if reality has lost its own continuous connection and become shaped by the demands of our soul."[64] Yet Münsterberg worried that the "intensity with which the plays [films] take hold of the audience cannot remain without the strong social effects . . . The sight of crime and vice may force itself on the consciousness with disastrous results."[65] He reported that one sociologist had exaggerated the claim that 85 percent of juvenile crime could be traced to movies. Yet Münsterberg did not doubt the premise that film could motivate some to commit crime since it was consistent with his account of the subjective operation of film. But the menace of the new medium could also be its great power. The same enthrallment might be used by reformers as "an incomparable power for the remodeling and upbuilding of the national soul."[66] The task, however, was not to produce "a dramatized sermon on morality and religion," but to engage Americans in "esthetic cultivation."[67] Art was not an imitation of nature, Münsterberg asserted, but a loosening of the hold of matter over mind, which is allowed thereby to indulge in the free play of its own faculties in the aesthetic fiction of film.

This mode of viewing had been endorsed by an early advocate of the use of fine art in religious education in the twentieth century, the Rev. Henry Spaulding, who applauded in a speech before the Religious Education Association "our *modern* attitude toward the Bible" and castigated the use of scripture "as an arsenal of proof-texts."[68] Spaulding urged his Protestant colleagues to read scripture for its relevance to modern experience, as "the story of the soul's inward struggles and . . . its conflicts with the world without." In order to learn how to do so and to bring it to the aid of religious education, he suggested that teachers consult the work of great painters: "They would have had little patience with the pietistic literalism which seeks to understand and interpret the New Testament by studying the altered scenery of the Holy Land and associating with the Arabs of modern Syria."[69] With this dig at the Chautauqua tradition, Spaulding quoted art connoisseur Bernard Berenson as authorizing the sort of projection that moderns required, concluding that Renaissance masters "detached ideas and ideals from the written records and brought them close to our common human sympathies."[70]

The way of seeing that Spaulding advocated shifted from public to private and the aesthetic experience from one of real presence to imagined narrative. Whereas panoramas and Passion plays put one in the presence of the biblical event and placed the viewer among other viewers as common witnesses, an act of vision in which a Christian (re)public was arrayed in a concerted gaze, film was properly (aesthetically) viewed when it constructed a subjective or private visual field whose reliance on feeling directed its subordination of biblical literalism. Film came increasingly to construe the viewer as the private eye for which the event was singularly represented. Protestants responded to this new relationship of the viewer to the viewed in a way that recalls their proscription of novel-reading, which had likewise operated on the basis of the inner gaze. The "cinematic gaze" made consumption interior, subjective, private, and therefore less controllable by the communal parameters of collective viewing. The corresponding concept of the public shifted: from a more or less uniform audience constituting a single, American public to a mass audience of individual consumers over whom one could not expect to exert any singular moral effect. Protestant moralists feared that the relationship of the visual medium or image to a Christian American audience, to which viewers belonged and toward which they had certain abiding responsibilities as members of the republic, was metamorphosing into individual acts of consumption in which viewers were anonymous instances of a shapeless mass audience, each of whom had nothing in common with the next and who attended films not for moral edification, but for entertainment or distraction, or private concerns such as personal interests.

For some Protestant critics, the older mode of spectation was clearly preferable because it kept viewing public and communal. Among Protestants associated with the Social Gospel's understanding of Christianity as fundamentally socially minded, dedicated to the institutional application of the Gospel of amelioration and redemption, the arts represented a vital resource for communal formation. H. Augustine Smith, on the faculty of Boston University, published a paper in *Religious Education* in 1922 in which he encouraged civic renewal, interdenominational cooperation, and municipal engagement through public choral performance, concerts, and pageantry. Castigating traditional "ecclesiastical worship" as resting on "tradition and smug prejudice," Smith championed "community ritual" as new forms of fellowship that should occupy

Christians. He cited such new occasions as Armistice Day and World Peace Brotherhood alongside of Church Federation Day and City Beautiful Week, and cited works by Percy MacKaye, playwright and wartime purveyor of ritualistic and inclusive patriotism.[71] For his part, Smith urged administrators of religious schools to make use of the arts and included "the fine arts of pageantry and visualization" on his list, pointing out that "pageantry and living pictures [tableaux vivants] are marvelous teachers of history, of biography, of social problems." The results, he felt certain, would be positive:

> The church would do well to make her shrine a home for Christian pageant masters and students. She will fill her auditoriums Sunday nights, she will vivify Sunday School lesson material, she will grip her restless adolescent life and save them from blind alleys, down whose foul stretches are questionable modern dances and free-love movies.[72]

When contained within fixed physical settings, crowds organize themselves in a number of ways. They may sit in the neat rows of a cinema's darkness, privately watching a film together; they may assemble in arenas and churches where they see and respond to one another while listening to a speaker; or they may fill bleachers or schoolrooms where they stand at attention to recite the Pledge of Allegiance or to sing the National Anthem in steady, mesmerizing cadences. Other forms of religious gathering relied on the structural feature of an audience arrayed before a speaker or stationary stage space. The staging of pageants and tableaux vivants to gather Christian students into a single audience for communal uplift and education recalls contemporary efforts to organize the collective and reverent viewing of the American flag – in public ceremonies in which new citizens swore loyalty to their new nation or each morning in public schools when school children recited the Pledge of Allegiance. One thinks, for instance, of such popular activities as assembling people in bleachers or on hillsides in colored patterns to create the image of a "Living Flag" (Figure 55). Their regimented organization was a ritualized performance of national unity – or at least the unity and nation that people wished to imagine on the occasion, in 1911, when the group of children was gathered before the audience in the foreground to dedicate a soldiers' monument.[73] Quite often the groups creating living flags were members of a patriotic organization such as the Grand Army of the Republic or the United Confederate Veterans.

Commemoration and civil rites of passage welcomed display as a public expression of the unity or passage, especially as regards patriotic occasions when visualizing the ideal unity or community could become part of the collective ritual imagination. Creations of such spectacles, which fashioned a single body of a gathering, were common practices in the late nineteenth and twentieth centuries. Percy MacKaye authored a civic ritual for immigrants to pledge their loyalty and celebrate their new citizenship. In 1915, MacKaye published

Figure 55 "The Living Flag," Soldiers' Monument Dedication, May 30, 1911, location unknown. Courtesy Library of Congress.

The New Citizenship, a script for staging a massive public ceremony in the City College Stadium of New York City, but which he presented to the public as a model to be adapted to much smaller circumstances as need be. MacKaye's design was to gather new citizens into a single space where they would collect-ively proclaim their allegiance and experience a rite of passage that conferred citizenship upon them in an event conducted by the Spirit of Liberty and per-formed by the Founding Fathers and the reigning luminaries in American civil religion – George Washington and Abraham Lincoln. For MacKaye the task was to balance the ideal face-to-face, oral culture of primitive democracy exemplified in the town-meeting with the contemporary reality of a burgeoning nation that consisted of a welter of ethnic strands. Set in a stadium for an audience of thousands, MacKaye nevertheless pointed out that "the form of the ritual developed itself in my mind from the simple precedents of the old American town-meeting: above on a platform, the presiding chairman; and speeches by citizens from the floor."[74] The declamatory model was for MacKaye the enduring paradigm of democracy and of public ritual. Citing such cele-brated orators as Samuel Adams, Patrick Henry, and Daniel Webster, MacKaye declared that "these citizen speakers have been the lay prophets of our civil religion."[75] Rothermel's familiar portrait of Patrick Henry (see Figure 1, p. 10) may even have been in MacKaye's mind as he imagined the ideal discursive situation of participatory democracy to be the iconic background for the oath of citizenship, which enacted the social contract of allegiance between citizen and the state that Henry conceived in his original act of protest. The duty of the rite of inducting new citizens grew all the more important "as our constrained town-meeting becomes crowded and overwhelmed by the multitudinous desires and colorful temperaments of the world races."[76] Accordingly, MacKaye directed that the background on the stage be painted "to suggest (below) the old colonial interior and (above) the balcony exterior façade of Independence Hall, Philadelphia."[77]

The challenge was to span the precipitous gap separating oral and mass culture in a way that preserved the spirit of the town-meeting, where oral culture corresponded to the ideal of one voice, one vote, where voice meant citizen. Americans responded differently to the challenge. Some were alarmed by the diversity of immigrants and stressed a strong model of assimilation. Others, like MacKaye, were progressive and resisted a melting-pot scheme of citizenship, considering homogeneity to sacrifice the virtues of cultural differences. Before the stage on which speakers addressed the thousands in the City College Stadium was situated the "civic altar" dedicated to the Spirit of Liberty, located on the main floor of the stadium, on the same level as the new citizens seated before the stage. "Here, then," wrote MacKaye, "at the altar of our English-speaking tradition of liberty gather the manifold cultures, languages, arts and crafts of all peoples in the persons of our new citizens."[78] The new citizens processed into the stadium wearing modern American clothing, but carried with them emblems of their homeland and were accompanied by folk dancers dressed in original costume and performing the ethnic dances of their original nations and singing "hymns of their native lands."[79] At the moment of dedication to their new country, the new citizens successively watched their former national flags placed at the civic altar below the central place of the American flag. The ceremony ends with the Spirit of Liberty sending forth the new Americans: "Citizens! You who came to my altar as separate groups depart now as a community of Americans."[80]

MacKaye's ceremony included a passage from a contemporary speech by President Woodrow Wilson, delivered in Philadelphia at the oath of new citizens:

> I certainly would not be one even to suggest that a man cease to love the home of his birth and the nation of his origin. These things are very sacred and ought not to be put out of your hearts.[81]

In the preface to his book, MacKaye asserted that the "enlightened ideals of the new citizenship" did not stand for

the leveling away of all world-cultures to leave bare an American medi-
ocrity, but for the welcoming of all world-cultures to create an American
excellence: not for a national melting-pot to reduce all precious heritages to
a cold puddle of shapeless ore, but for a national studio to perpetuate them
in new creative forms of plastic life.[82]

The aim of the rite of citizenship was to fashion a national work of art, whose
organic integrity thrived on distinction. Such liberal condescension to national
diversity was not something others were willing to allow. By 1922, the Pledge of
Allegiance was formally emended, adding "to the flag of the United States of
America" to the opening words "I pledge allegiance . . . " Advocates of homogeneity feared that immigrants might harbor in their minds the image of their
native flag, thus swearing allegiance to it.[83] The new Pledge sought to fix in
every American mind the picture that Walter Lippmann analyzed as the
medium of public opinion and group mind.

Efforts toward that end had begun in the final two decades of the nineteenth
century when rituals for the veneration of the national flag were prepared
for use in public schools. If MacKaye sought to preserve the communal gaze
with its appeal to patriotic heroes dedicated to liberty as the principal matrix
for making American citizens, the Pledge was used in more coercive ways by
American nationalists. The nationalistic use of the communal gaze was no less
forceful than Lippmann's apprehension about cinema in propagandistically
shaping public opinion. An early version of these was penned by Colonel
George T. Balch, Civil War veteran and member of the New York City Board of
Education. In his *Methods of Teaching Patriotism in the Public Schools* (1890),
Balch designed a set of rituals for the display of the flag and for the distribution of awards among students to recognize good citizenship.[84] His rationale
accented the importance of group solidarity and weighted the good of the
whole over the individual. "One of the fundamental principles on which civil
society is based," he wrote, is that "the interests of a single individual must ever
be subordinate to the general interest of the great body of individuals."[85] Balch
was harshly critical of Jewish and Christian denominations that operated private schools, arguing that for American solidarity to prevail, the public schools
should be the exclusive system for shaping young citizens.[86] Unity was (and
remains) the overriding goal of American nationalists, particularly in the wake
of the Civil War, when, as Robert Bellah perceptively wrote in a pivotal article
on American civil religion, the national cultus shifted from the courage and self-
denial in the example of George Washington to the themes of redemption,
sacrifice, and death associated with the writings and example of Abraham
Lincoln.[87] As the generation of Civil War veterans aged and died, some of its
members adopted the practice of giving regimental banners and flags to public
schools. For veterans like Balch, the institution of the public school was the
most important means of determining "the character of this nation" – more
important, he said, than churches or political parties.[88]

In contrast to MacKaye, Balch felt the national character was threatened by the large number of immigrants, who, Balch wrote, "bear in their physical and mental features the indelible impress of centuries of monarchical or aristocratic rule and oppression."[89] But both MacKaye and Balch believed in the shaping power of public rituals. If immigrant parents bore an ineradicable impression of non-democratic governance, Balch contended that their children were not beyond the re-minting power of the public school properly operated. He urged the Children's Aid Society of New York, before which he spoke in 1889, to engage in rigorous "methods for cultivating patriotism" which he devised.[90] The Society, which operated twenty-one public schools for poor, largely immigrant children, agreed to Balch's request, allowing him access to its nearly 5,000 students to put his plan to the test. As shown in a contemporary photograph from a New York industrial school during the 1890s (Figure 56), students were to gather before the flag in a formal manner each morning to recite the dedication to national ideals of loyalty and the corporate good. The aim was to inculcate in students the belief that "next to what we owe to God, nothing should be more dear or sacred than the love and respect we owe our country."[91] Balch anticipated the instrumental value of propaganda described by Lippmann:

Figure 56 Jacob Riis, photographer, Working-class children observe flag ritual in New York City school, ca. 1890. Courtesy Library of Congress.

it will be possible [Balch stated] to so direct the child's thoughts, to so surround it as it were with the atmosphere of patriotic feeling, that . . . [the pupil] will insensibly become interested in and permeated with the thought or impression you are essaying to convey.[92]

Making citizens meant training bodies in the collective exercises of group mind, imprinting in the surfaces of their faces and bodies, to use Balch's metaphor, by means of ritualized daily procedures of flag veneration. Belief in the sacred status and mission of the nation happened in groups, in the public ceremonies that impressed on students their collective identity as American citizens. Participation was compulsory and shaped by positive reinforcement, whereby children were selected on the basis of their achievements to receive shiny metallic badges, which were displayed on their classroom desks, no doubt to the envy of their classmates.

It would not be until 1943 that the Supreme Court would rule in favor of a Jehovah's Witness plaintiff who objected to a West Virginia state law that required public school children to salute the flag each morning and recite the Pledge of Allegiance.[93] The Supreme Court agreed, in effect, that the reverential gaze ensconced in a ritual of civil religion was indeed a religious practice that imbued the flag, according to the plaintiff, with an idolatrous status that violated his First Amendment right by allowing the state to endorse a religion. The flag, the Court decided, and the visual practice of its veneration with the Pledge, were part of a religion which the state could not force on students against their wishes without injuring their freedom of conscience. In the cause of liberty, the right to dissent overruled American nationalism's cult of unity.

Part III

The power and menace of images

Chapter 7

Facing the sacred
Image and charisma

A face attracts attention because it is rich with information about the person it images. Indeed, a face is commonly taken to be the imprint of the soul. According to the nineteenth-century Philadelphia photographer Marcus Aurelius Root, the human face is "the most perfect of all mediums of expression . . . the index of the soul."[1] In his writings promoting the new medium of photography Root invoked the popular Victorian fads of physiognomy and phrenology, which contended that the features of the face or the shape of the head responded physically to the nature of the soul (physiognomy) or the physical structure of the brain (phrenology). Phrenologist Samuel Wells published a plate of celebrated Protestant "Divines" (Figure 57) in his 1871 volume *New Physiognomy* as eminent examples of spiritual character registered in broad, high brows and large eyes that train themselves soberly on the viewer in several instances. Faces can powerfully convey what people think and feel. A face, Root proclaimed, is "the revelation of the real man."[2] The lesson was not lost on twentieth-century film makers and critics. Hugo Münsterberg underscored the face's emotional range, which "the close-up on the screen brings . . . to sharpest relief."[3] Grounded on the visual medium of the face, visual media in the twentieth century have been used to convey charisma – among living religious leaders and in the representation of figures from the past. The faces of countless evangelists filling television screens are latter-day examples of Wells' famous divines. This chapter examines the power of images in the generation and circulation of charisma among religious celebrities and quasi-religious figures portrayed in entertainment media.

Charisma and masculinity

Religious leaders have long recognized the power of images to shape public perception. While Walter Lippmann lamented the formation of public opinion around images, many of his contemporaries exploited it in the field of religious pedagogy. A prevailing perception among many religious educators in the early twentieth century was that the image of Christianity had suffered among Americans, particularly American boys, because of the emasculation of Jesus.

Figure 57 "Divines," in Samuel R. Wells, *New Physiognomy: Or, Signs of Character.* New York: American Book Company, 1871, 484. Courtesy The Library Company of Philadelphia.

The quest for the face of Jesus became the search for an image that would attract the admiration of boys and young men by envisioning the personal magnetism of Jesus – his charisma, the force or authority that radiated from his person and commanded respect and obedience.

Although charisma is a quality found in men and women, boys and girls, debate during the opening decades of the twentieth century regarding the likeness of Jesus fixed on the question of his masculinity. Many came to feel that popular representations of Jesus did not go far enough to envision a male personality that could command the respect of boys and men. One prominent intellectual who inveighed against the effeminate Jesus image was the psychologist G. Stanley Hall. Among the most prolific and widely read psychologists of his day and one of the founders of modern child psychology, Hall was also a Sunday school teacher, one-time seminary student, and an educator who collected images of Jesus for use in the classroom. Hall directed his attention to the role of Christian art in his study, *Jesus, the Christ, In the Light of Psychology* (1917). There he assigned to contemporary literature and the visual arts an immense task: "to reincarnate the risen Lord in the modern world."[4] Because critical methods of modern historical analysis had placed in doubt the unquestioned authority of biblical texts, Hall sought to base the legitimacy of Christ as a hero for the modern psyche on the power of the imagination to evoke what modern humanity required. He spoke of the "psychological Jesus Christ" as more important than the "historical Jesus" and insisted that the "true Christ is present in human hearts to-day and not merely in the ancient and very imperfect annals of incompetent recorders."[5] True religion was not a projection of God into a heavenly realm, the conjuring of an afterlife, or reliance on miracles, but a psychologization of all such needs: "there must be no craven, supine or neurotic flight from present now and here reality."[6] There is only the temporal formation of the self. Even the church threatened the vitality and this-worldliness of the modern soul:

> The church is a cult and no longer stands for the highest culture. It has become an idolater of its symbols, and lost the holy passion to penetrate ever deeper into their significance. It has lost control of, and often all vital touch with the leaders of mankind, and makes only a falsetto, sporadic appeal to educated youth.[7]

Hall called for "nothing less than a new Christianity," which is how he ended the second volume of *Adolescence*, which appeared in 1916. Psychology was to provide this new religion by demonstrating how Jesus, the heroic symbol of the world's highest religion, encompassed within his life the ideal formation of the self and offered a heroic model that could be used to transform the ancient creeds of Christianity into the symbolic confessions of today's "educated youth" (ever the concern of Hall). The "falsetto appeal," which was all the church could muster, signifies the great threat it posed: a feminization of the virile, passionate strength that adolescent boys and young men especially needed in the shaping of their souls. Hall scorned the corresponding state of much recent art: "Most pictures of Jesus during the last century give him a distinctly feminine look. The brow, cheek, and nose, if all below were covered, would generally be taken for those of a refined and superior woman."[8] Particularly telling in the physiognomy of Christ's emasculation in nineteenth-century art was the meagerness of his beard, which was often portrayed by artists as "light, exposing the upper part of the chin, and its scantiness, with the usually copious hair of the scalp and the feminine features, sometimes almost suggest[ing] a bearded lady."[9]

Hall feared that "the personality of Jesus is in some danger of paling into ineffectiveness."[10] He therefore stressed the importance of an artistic treatment that would infuse the image of Christ with "beauty, power, and sublimity." Hall was convinced of the power of mythic imagery to speak to the soul. Artists offered modern Christianity the ability to inspire the imagination rather than to constrain reason with uncompelling articles of belief. Inspired by Nietzsche's concept of a heroic "Uebermensch" to lead humanity beyond itself, Hall yearned for "a normative Jesus figure" and warned, "Without it man lacks orientation for the direction of growth and progress."[11]

The need for a hero dominated Hall's thinking about the formation of boys and young men, a hero with charisma or vital force that would be communicated to young males in the formative stages of their personalities as an ideal in which to invest the energy that modern civilization and urban life threatened to sap and misdirect. Hall considered the need for a compelling Jesus figure to depend on deploying the hero archetype in the costume and relevance of modernity:

> Could we not have Jesus as an athletic champion, illustrating perhaps the ideal of doing the prodigies that athletes so admire? Could Jesus be knight priest, banker, sailor, landed proprietor, society man, manufacturer, actor, professor, editor, etc.? and if so, how? and if not, why not?[12]

Although the heroic possibilities of the college professor seem clear enough, Christ as landed proprietor, society man, or manufacturer is surprising, that is, until one realizes such images comport with the perceived need to reclaim Christianity, or its charismatic founder, for modern urban, industrial society.

A similar set of concerns animated the advertising mogul and pioneer of public relations, Bruce Barton, another liberal Protestant who blamed the lack of interest among American boys and young men in the church on the excessive influence of women.[13] Like Hall, Barton was convinced that American men did not have available to them the real Jesus, who ought to be the ruggedly charismatic figure of a male cult of youth, an active young man who rightly inspired admiration and imitation. Barton faulted artists for creating feeble visual portrayals of Christ and he longed for a fitting picture of the Christ he knew. In his 1914 manifesto on Christian virility, A Young Man's Jesus, Barton excoriated painters who portrayed Christ as "soft-faced and effeminate." Speaking to his audience of likeminded young men and anticipating the male bonding that became a mark of later versions of bear-hugging, macho spirituality, Barton proclaimed: "We are His age: we know Him: He is ours."[14] Presaging his momentous career as one of the nation's most influential admen, Barton proffered in a frontispiece to his book a proper image of Jesus that seems calculated to have met Hall's criteria – at least insofar as evident masculinity and density of facial hair were concerned. Poised like a billboard, seeking out the viewer with a penetrating gaze, Darius Cobb's *The Master* (Figure 58) displays a copious beard and moustache and sports a heavy brow that recalls the "primitive" energies that Hall endorsed as the antidote to over-refinement. This

Figure 58 Darius Cobb, *The Master*, frontispiece in Bruce Barton, *A Young Man's Jesus*. Boston, MA: Pilgrim Press, 1914. Photo author.

Neanderthal Jesus was clearly immune to the emasculating neurasthenia and other nervous disorders that plagued modern men; and, judging from his hirsute visage and intense glare, he would appear to be a candidate for the heroic ideal of a modern "superman" that Hall called on artists to contribute to the revitalizing of Christianity.

Hall's invocation of a modern Jesus set the stage for Barton's characterization of Christ as business executive extraordinaire in his best-selling book, *The Man Nobody Knows* (1924). There Jesus was said to have radiated charismatic effulgence and exerted boundless influence over others not by virtue of miracles or supernatural intervention, but by sheer personal magnetism, the same vital force that captains of industry in corporate America commanded in their day-to-day ministries of executive influence. The importance of heroism and charisma occupied both Hall and Barton, as well as many others. Conducting a psychological analysis of heroes and gods, Hall had enumerated four inferences regarding Christ's "personal impressiveness." Jesus must have been large, strong, and beautiful; and he must have exhibited bearing and presence, or personal magnetism.[15] Barton's evocation of the man nobody knew conformed entirely to this image.

But liberal Protestants like Hall and Barton were not alone in harnessing the hope of Christian faith in modern America to the charisma of the hero. At the opposite end of the theological spectrum, revivalist preacher Billy Sunday was renowned during the years before and during the First World War for his masculinist rhetoric and jingoistic oratorical acrobatics, all of which projected a carefully cultivated image of the revivalist as a heroic athlete for Jesus. A former professional baseball player, Sunday swept through cities from Davenport to New York on a heroic mission to renew American spiritual life. Bristling at the heart of his message was a passionate concern for American masculinity. "Come on, boys, you've got a chance to show your manhood," he urged the hundreds and thousands of men who attended the special meetings for business and working men in all of his campaigns.[16] Showing manhood was very much what Sunday's revivals were about, as the many postcards picturing the evangelist himself make clear. As early as 1908 the religious celebrity began printing them for sale at his revivals, anticipating a trend that arose a few years later among commercial producers of postcards that pictured motion picture stars.[17] Damning booze in brusquely physical terms, Sunday promised he would "fight till Hell freezes over," and had the phrase inscribed on a postcard showing him about to hammer his imagined foe (Figure 59). For audience members with a living memory of evangelist Dwight Moody's restrained manner or the Victorian gentility of Christian manliness envisioned in Currier & Ives' portrait of Ira D. Sankey (see Figure 22, p. 79), Sunday's postcards would have signaled a new agenda.

Sunday effectively built on the importance of masculinity in American urban revivalism since Moody's day as a special attraction to male audiences by turning up the volume and acrobatics of his pulpit performances. No other

Figure 59 C. V. Williams, photographer, Billy Sunday preaching, *I'll Fight till Hell Freezes over*, postcard, 1908. Courtesy Archives of the Billy Graham Center.

evangelist, Bruce Barton claimed in a flattering essay on Sunday, "can number a larger proportion of men than women on his convert rolls."[18] No doubt that was due to Sunday's insistence that Jesus "was no dough-faced, lick-spittle proposition . . . [but] the greatest scrapper that ever lived."[19] Signaling his allegiance to the conservative, nationalistic politics of his friend, former President Theodore Roosevelt, Sunday fashioned an American middle-class Christianity with a militant, masculine appeal to American self-interest: "Moral welfare makes a man hard. Superficial peace makes a man mushy. . . . The prophets all carried the Big Stick."[20]

According to one of Sunday's early biographers, William T. Ellis, "The oldest problem of the Christian church, and the latest problem of democracy, is how to reach the great mass of people." For Sunday and Barton alike, that was a communication or public relations problem. Ellis believed that Sunday's revivals solved the problem. For Ellis, there was "no question that [Sunday] stirs a city as not even the fiercest political campaign stirs it."[21] Other sympathetic observers agreed. Writing in a Protestant Episcopal publication about Sunday's Pittsburgh campaign (the first city of over half a million inhabitants to host a Sunday crusade), one contemporary was struck by the city-wide impact of the event:

> City politicians came forward at the meetings and asked for prayer. The daily newspapers gave more space to salvation than they did to scandal, not for one day, but day after day and week after week. As a mere spectacle of a whole modern city enthralled by the Gospel it was astonishing, unbelievable, unprecedented, prodigious.[22]

The secret to this successful mass communication, according to Sunday, was a carefully controlled procedure. In order to achieve maximum impact for his campaigns, Sunday enthusiastically practiced "business methods" in religion, rigorously organizing each revival and commencing on-site planning as much as one year in advance. He made deliberate use of media and many forms of advertising. And at each revival he made a point of endorsing such "business methods" and encouraged his audience of businessmen to do the same in their congregations. Understanding his job as selling the ideal of the self-made man, Sunday cast the task of evangelism in terms of salesmanship and advertising. Although he was often criticized for the theatricality of his diction and gesticulation, dismissed by some as "offer[ing] himself as a substitute for a vaudeville show," Sunday and his publicity machine were careful to underscore (and often inflate) the numerical results of his flamboyant style of preaching.[23]

If the many remarks in the press as well as the caricatures both fond and spiteful are any indication, people recognized Sunday's vernacular manner of preaching as his trademark. Sunday capitalized on this "brand recognition" by using photographs and postcards to model the life of Evangelical belief. For years at revival meetings Sunday's personal secretary, Fred Seibert, sold tracts, Sunday's authorized biography, and postcards with images of Sunday striking

the trademark dramatic gestures and poses that animated his sermons. Typically, the postcards visualized an athletic figure hurling invective or grasping a
chair, which he might fling across the stage in the next instant. Some of the most
histrionic images show the evangelist standing on a chair with arms flailing or
curled over his lectern in the manner of a grappler, manhandling his audience
into submission. Still others present a well-dressed and eloquent speaker, snapshots of the self-made man, the fellow who started out in a slovenly wooden
shed in small-town Iowa, but made it big. As accoutrements of fame and celebrity status, the postcards documented and broadcast the truth about pulling
oneself up by one's own bootstraps.

By selling postcards at the meetings, Sunday fostered a cult of personality in
which religious charisma was converted into popular celebrity. Longing for
righteousness became desire for the American way. As a kind of evangelical
baseball card, postcards of Sunday's aggressive preaching style offered his
admirers icons of Christian heroism. While Max Weber contended that charisma was replaced in modern, secular society by rational bureaucratization,
Sunday proved the contrary.[24] His operation subtly blended routine and method
with personal magic in the attempt to maximize and to sustain his enchanting
appeal. The renewal of genuine religion, according to Sunday, centered on
the charismatic figure who performed it. The postcards were souvenirs of his
charismatic performances. The personalized commodities which audiences
purchased on site were calculated to promote and circulate his charisma.
"Charisma not only disrupts social order," one student of Weber has stressed,
"it also maintains or conserves it."[25] Weber's inclination to contrast charisma
and the process of secular institutionalization may reflect his view that the
modern world was disenchanted. Sunday's Evangelical efforts in the modern
American city might be seen as an attempt to reverse this secularization by
injecting religious institutions with a reviving power of charisma. Similarly,
Hall and Barton, despite their considerable theological distance from Sunday,
sought to revitalize an emasculated modern culture by invoking the charisma
of a manly Christ reclaimed from anachronism and feminine influence. It
was a mass-culture invention of icons of male heroism that could be cheaply
manufactured and easily distributed to the city-bound populations of American
men. Sunday was crucial in promoting awareness among twentieth-century
Evangelical revivalists of the power of the image to convey personal dynamism
or charisma.[26]

Commercial producers of Christian imagery paid attention to the contemporary commentary about the look of Jesus, though they varied markedly
in what they considered that look to be. For purveyors of Sunday school
instructional material, the look needed to be articulated according to the age of
children. For younger children, pictures of Jesus as a boy were especially
appropriate. But as Hall, Barton, and others advanced the view that Jesus must
stand out by virtue of his masculinity, others looked for the visual cues of
Christ's divinity. In May of 1941, Phillips Booth, then art director of Providence

Lithography Company, received a letter from Mrs. Hattie Allen, representative of the Baptist Sunday School Board, regarding the need for an appropriate image of Jesus in the children's curriculum. Booth had corresponded with an artist about the need and Mrs. Allen directed him to prefer a well-known painting by the German artist Heinrich Hofmann (Figure 60), of Christ in the temple speaking with learned teachers. Mrs. Allen took exception in her letter to another image that Booth had sent the artist:

> I do not like the characterization of Jesus which shows him with a face older than that of a twelve-year old boy, and lacking in that quality which, I feel, every characterization of Jesus ought to have, that is, the divine.
>
> That is, in my opinion, the chief objection to Elsie Anna Wood's pictures which I have seen. Jesus is no different from the other characters; they are all merely human. I have not found a single one of her pictures in which Jesus can be recognized by children without prompting, and I have made a good many tests. . . .
>
> I realize that there are many people in the religious education field who want Jesus to be "just like the others" and no more. They would like to strip him of his divinity because it cannot be explained. We want Jesus to be human, too, perfectly human, but we want him to be more. Jesus was

Figure 60 Heinrich Hofmann, *Boy Christ Teaching in the Temple*, Riverside Church, New York. Courtesy Riverside Church.

God living on the earth in the body of a man and, therefore, a picture of him should be more than "just like the others." We do not, of course, want a halo, but there should be in his characterization that indefinable something which we call the divine element. I think Hofmann's picture clearly has this.[27]

Mrs. Allen's letter is an attempt to visualize Christ's difference, to establish a recognizable iconography of his authority, his charisma. The halo, the most traditional device for marking the literal emission of divine glory, was unacceptable to the Baptist woman because that symbol was Catholic. She preferred the picture by Hofmann because the composition itself organized the sages around the boy, acknowledging his authority as divine.

The most successful and widely reproduced image of Jesus in the twentieth century, Warner Sallman's *Head of Christ* (1940; Figure 61), signaled divine authority without using the halo. That may help account for why Sallman's picture so quickly became ubiquitous among Protestants *and* Catholics. The luminous effect achieved by backlighting and vignetting performed the customary function of the halo without saying "Roman Catholic" to Protestants. It was savvy marketing. Moreover, Sallman was able to appease Sunday school teachers in search of a gentle, reassuring Jesus, and, at least for a time, advocates of Christian masculinity who, following Hall and Barton, complained of "wimpy" portrayals of Jesus. Sallman reported a dialogue that he had with a faculty member at Moody Bible Institute sometime during the artist's early career.[28] "There is a great need for Christian artists," Sallman's interlocutor told him. "Sometime I hope you give us your conception of Christ. And I hope it's a manly one. Most of our pictures today are too effeminate." "You mean to say you think Jesus was a more rugged type?" Sallman replied. "More of a man's man?" "Yes, according to the way I read my Bible."[29] The conversation was widely repeated in devotional literature during the 1940s. Many viewers admired Sallman's picture, regarding it as a compelling portrayal of Jesus. During the 1950s and beyond, however, others turned the masculinist discourse against Sallman's image, accusing it of perpetuating the tradition of effeminate images of Jesus. Most memorably, perhaps, is a Lutheran seminary professor's denunciation of the image as "a pretty picture of a woman with a curling beard who has just come from the beauty parlor with a Halo shampoo."[30] The remark gendered the luminous effect that Sallman had used as an ecumenical replacement of the Catholic halo, turning the image's aura from magnetic attraction to cross-gendered repulsion.

As if to correct the many images of a meek religious hero despised since Barton's day, Cecil B. DeMille cast the macho Charlton Heston as Moses in *The Ten Commandments* in 1956, and contrasted his mantled, bearded prophetic eminence with a bald and fleshy Yul Brynner as Rameses. Once the film's hero has seen the Burning Bush and been tasked by the Almighty to lead Israel from Egyptian bondage, he takes on a gray-haired and voluminous aura, speaking

Figure 61 Warner Sallman, *The Head of Christ*, oil on canvas, 1940. ©1941 Warner Press, Inc., Anderson, IN. All rights reserved. Used with permission.

with an amplified voice and moving with formal and solemn gestures. A publicity poster (Figure 62), issued when the film was promoted in Japan, pivots on the stark visual contrast of prophet and pharaoh. Though DeMille preserved the pageantry of the Passion play iconography, he infused a new masculinity as the basis of Moses' authority. The macho monumentality of Moses is clearly

Figure 62 The Ten Commandments, Japanese film poster, after 1956. Courtesy Brauer Museum of Art, Valparaiso University.

conveyed in the poster's juxtaposition of Moses and his enemy. An abrupt descent from Moses' terrible gesture (condemning the errant children of Israel, who had lapsed into idol worship during his absence on Mount Sinai) is linked to the dramatic parting of the Red Sea. The diagonal ends in the diminutive but menacing figure of Rameses in the lower right. The hoary-headed prophet wielding tablets of stone contrasts sharply with the hairless, bare, bejeweled pagan ruler. Austere, monotheistic judgment is pitted against sensuous pretense, deception, and false gods. The opposition was not without contemporary resonance. One of the principal exports of American culture then, as now, was film entertainment. Films like *The Ten Commandments* were avidly consumed around the world. The spectacle of DeMille's popular masterpiece carried abroad a kind of epic grandeur that placed American culture within a favorable light and promoted the triumph of a divinely appointed leader over tyranny that denied biblical monotheism and sought the enslavement of God's people. It is difficult to imagine a better script for American foreign policy during its long propaganda war with the Soviet Union.

But even if DeMille's Moses trumped Sallman's Jesus for machismo, many Protestants and Catholics continued to admire the image. Catholics used this picture of Jesus and others by Sallman, sometimes by photo-mechanically adding luminous effects and the motif of the Sacred Heart. For Protestant admirers of the *Head of Christ*, the image could even speak with an iconic authority. Some reported that the image was "a photograph of Jesus." Sallman himself frequently told the story that the image had originally come to him as a sudden and revelatory mental visualization one night in 1924, which he quickly transcribed as a sketch, later painting the image in oil for mass reproduction. As photograph or revelation, the image drew its origin from a higher source, not made by human hands. Other viewers consider it a reliable portrait of Jesus, a genuine representation of what he actually looked like. For some Protestants, the image is appropriately installed in devotional centers in the home and contemplated during prayer and bible study. It has widely been placed in children's bedrooms, in living rooms, and throughout the home as a reassuring image that protects, soothes, and encourages those who gaze adoringly upon it. These viewers have long cited the face's meek and tender expression as intimate and inviting, the steadfast gaze of the eyes heavenward as inspiring, and the glowing effects on the face as arresting. The vignette, which throws the face in warm light, recalls not only contemporary photographic portraiture, but also film close-ups from the 1920s. The visual rhetoric of the "portrait" invited a solemn and adoring gaze from viewers. The most common remark in discussing their fondness for the image and its beloved role in their personal lives is that the image visualizes their "best friend."[31] For many Protestants this matched an Evangelical Christology of friendship in which commitment to Jesus Christ as "personal savior" was commonly expressed in terms of a special intimacy between Jesus and the believer. The image also achieved the commercially lucrative status of a generic brand identity. Some admirers have told me that when they see the picture hanging in a church they visit, they know the congregation is a Christ-centered one. Such visual advertisement reached many religious consumers during the image's heyday. If sociologist Will Herberg was correct that by mid-century Americans had developed three equally American religions – Protestant, Catholic, and Jewish – then Sallman's *Head of Christ* was surely the logo for the Protestant side of this triad of national faiths.[32]

Herberg lamented the homogeneity of the three categories, regretting that vitality and particularity were the expense that each tradition paid for becoming a general rubric in American culture, the religions of consensus rather than resistance and prophetic justice. The victory seemed an empty one since it entailed an evisceration of each faith. Quite a different vision emerges in favorite images used by Mormons in literature published by the Church of the Latter-Day Saints, including the Book of Mormon itself. In the 1981 edition of the Book of Mormon eight color plates appeared, including the heroic image of Moroni burying the hallowed golden plates at Hill Cummorah in New York state (Figure 63), where Joseph Smith would rediscover them more than two thousand years later with the assistance of the Angel Moroni. Mormon artist Tom Lovell portrays Moroni, shortly before the end of his life, after his kinsfolk had been wiped out by the murderous Lamanites. He has used his sword to prepare a hiding place for the plates that bear the ancient history of the Nephites, who had come to the new world at God's direction as part of an epic history. Moroni's massive forearms and his monumental stature signal the valor of his cause in spite of his people's tragic end. Moreover, his masculinity seems to vouchsafe the survival of the sacred record as the single but sure link between the ancient epic and its modern continuation in the wandering and eventual triumph of the Latter-Day Saints. The heroic realism of Lovell's painting takes up where Charlton Heston leaves off, crafting a particularly American story from the ancient narrative of the Jews.

Pentecostalism and charisma

The success of Sallman's Jesus owed a great deal to the persistence of a Victorian ideal of women as the pure and righteous vessels of divine activity in modern life. This was grounded in the parlor cult of motherhood that situated women in the home, engaged in the care of children while men worked in the secular world, earning their family's livelihood. It was also reflected in the popular cult of female guardian angels. The feminine, or at least the tender and approachable features of Sallman's Christ, matched the qualities of maternal piety that surrounded the home life and religious upbringing of many children. As urban America mushroomed in the twentieth century, this backward-looking ideal of Jesus enjoyed special fondness among Protestants (Catholics were able to recognize the religion of mother focused on the Madonna).

Even as Billy Sunday performed a militantly masculine image of Christian manhood from one urban revival meeting to the next during the early decades

Figure 63 Tom Lovell, *Moroni Burying the Gold Plates*, oil on panel, 33 × 23 inches, 1968. ©
Intellectual Reserve, Inc.

of the twentieth century, a Canadian revivalist was building her ministry on the basis of a Jesus much closer to what Sallman would eventually visualize. Aimee Semple McPherson (Figure 64) began her career as the wife of an itinerant Pentecostal preacher in Ontario. When he died shortly after the couple arrived

Figure 64 Publicity photograph of Aimee Semple McPherson, ca. 1920s. Courtesy Billy Graham Center Museum.

as missionaries in China in 1910, her conflicted career as evangelist and woman began. McPherson struggled with the cultural role of conservative Christian woman and her invincible ambition to command a highly visible public career, eventually working out something of a compromise when her equally domineering mother agreed to help her raise her children, came to her aid in the wake of failed marriages, and managed the considerable business side of the evangelist's public ministry, particularly once it took root in Los Angeles with the construction of the Angelus Temple, which opened its doors in 1923.

McPherson's image of Christ suited her complex personality. In a sermon of 1922 on "The Vision of Ezekiel," the evangelist offered her own interpretation of the four faces of the prophetic image – man, lion, ox, and eagle – which Christian iconography has traditionally regarded as the four evangelists, Matthew, Mark, Luke, and John. McPherson saw them as the four faces of Jesus, which corresponded to the four corners of her "Foursquare Gospel." The lion was Jesus who baptized with fire, foretold by John the Baptist; the ox represented the savior who delivered humanity from sin; the eagle signified the coming King of Pentecostalism's apocalyptic expectations; and the face of the man pictured the "man of sorrows" who was humbled to death on the cross.[33] Each aspect belonged to her understanding of Christ, but the terms she used again and again to describe him were redolent of Victorian parlor piety: "Rose of Sharon," "Lily of the Valley," "Master," "King," "Great Physician," and "Bridegroom." Such terms invoked the popular names of women's gift books given at Christmas or New Year for parlor display in the mid-nineteenth century.

The erotic nature of bridal imagery was no mistake. In 1917 McPherson founded a magazine called *The Bridal Call*, which she continued to edit for the rest of her life. She often preached on the Song of Solomon and was prone to snag the attention of her large crowds with such assertions as she was "head over heels in love with Jesus."[34] Erotic imagery allowed her an intimacy and, if her own relationships with her husbands are any indication, certain liberties with male authority. Aimee Semple McPherson combined the passion of Methodist hymnody from her youth with her mother's enthusiastic engagement in the Salvation Army and her own Pentecostal experience in order to come to terms with the limits imposed by her culture on women. Setting aside the emphasis on sin and damnation that played a central role in the masculinist revivalism of Billy Sunday, McPherson stressed instead the inviting and affirming nature of Jesus. She applied it to her own life and spoke autobiographically with great frequency in her sermons. In one of her three autobiographies she recounted the prayer that issued in her baptism of the Holy Spirit at the Pentecostal Revival Mission in 1908, where she met her first husband: "Oh, Master, I love Thee," she prayed.

> Take me, use me, have Thine own way with this poor life of mine; I am only a school girl, dear Lord, I live on a Canadian farm but such as I am I give to

Thee. Oh, Jesus, let me be an empty vessel for the Master's use made meet, fill me with Thy Spirit, take me up in Thine own hand and pour me out upon the dry and thirsty land![35]

Over the years she retold stories like this, narrating her call and evangelist experiences again and again, investing her life with the manifestation of divine favor and power. In autobiography and sermon she often compared key moments in her life to those of biblical prophets and Jesus. Heading to a revival meeting, passing through ripe wheat fields, she felt like the biblical Ruth setting out to harvest a crop of souls. After resisting God's call to preach, she likened her return to the evangelist's field to Jonah heading to Nineveh or Moses crossing the Red Sea. When she gazed over Paris from the height of the Eiffel Tower and longed for a city-wide revival there, she thought of Jesus weeping over the city of Jerusalem.[36] Much of Aimee Semple McPherson's message was couched in the package of herself. Her story was the story of a struggle to respond to God's call and the resulting manifold blessing poured out upon a servant dedicated to divine work.

It is difficult to imagine a ministry and religious life more amenable to the experience and deployment of charisma. McPherson lived it out and managed it masterfully in diverse media. Deeply shaped by a theatrical sensibility, she engaged in a media-rich ministry of preaching during her early itinerant years as well as later when her center of operations had become the Angelus Temple. She made banners, displayed mottoes and bible passages on her "gospel car," the automobile that she drove from meeting to meeting around the nation, wrote and distributed tracts, and edited *The Bridal Call*. The Angelus Temple served as a carefully crafted stage for her weekly multi-media productions, which included illustrated lectures (using colored lantern slides) presenting her trip to the Holy Land in 1926, daily radio broadcasts from her station at the Temple, and her "illustrated sermons," elaborate stage sets with costumed actors and exotic props that played to packed houses and were widely discussed in local newspapers. McPherson was a publicity master. She brought celebrities to the Temple, courted journalists, posed for photo opportunities, even represented the Temple with ambitious, prize-winning floats in Pasadena's annual Tournament of the Roses Parade.[37]

Not surprisingly, the evangelist took care to manage her own image. Like Sunday, she had photographs of herself produced and offered for sale at her services. The image was unforgettable thanks to her photogenic quality and her distinctive costuming (see Figure 64) in a white, ankle-length dress with a sequined cross on her chest and a dark, flowing cape. She appeared to draw simultaneously from numerous nineteenth-century sources: nurse's uniform, choir robe, Salvation Army uniform, and the luminous, full-length robes of guardian angels found everywhere from funerary monuments to fine art to devotional illustrations. The look appealed to the thousands and thousands among her admirers who responded to her softer, more positive Christianity.

She presented an image of purity, trustworthiness, and care. The packaging of her charisma was necessary, not only for the conflicted McPherson, but also for her public, which needed to know that her public calling and assertive ministry were not a violation of feminine respectability.[38] She was allowed to stray from the Victorian parlor only when dressed for the role of the guardian angel.

Charisma matters in most religious settings, though it varies considerably from one situation to the next. The aged Catholic priest, the well-educated suburban Protestant minister, the Buddhist master, and the storefront priestess or Holiness preacher will evoke different genders, ethnicities, ages, and demeanors as charismatic figures. Authority takes many forms and invests itself differently in media. Although Aimee Semple McPherson's career represents the apex of what most Pentecostal and Holiness preachers at work in storefront churches aspire to in terms of media exposure, financial success, and grand building campaigns, most never achieve it. Their experience of charisma in small, storefront interiors is not immediately about celebrity, but engaged in establishing and maintaining the structure of religious community, which turns on the vision and leadership of a prophet or preacher. It is instructive, therefore, to consider how charisma is conveyed and practiced in the setting of the storefront church, where face-to-face orality prevails rather than mass media.

Most Evangelicals understand the bible not as a textual document compiled and written by many authors and editors over time, but as the actual utterance of God. To read the scriptures is to hear God speaking. The bible is an oral transcription rather than a literary composition. Scripture consists of the verbally inspired traces of divine speech that were "infallibly" recorded by divinely selected amanuenses, according to conservative Protestant belief. Among Pentecostal Christians the bible is an act of divine speech that flows directly into the discourse of the preacher, singer, prayer, and testifier. The charismatic orality of inner-city Pentecostal and Holiness Protestantism among Anglos, Blacks, and Latinos is especially inclined to regard the bible as a divine speech act, a proclamation of authority that can be harnessed by quotation and invocation, resulting in human speech acts in which saying is more than describing or stating. It is doing. I take this operative distinction from the work of J. L. Austin, whose pioneering set of lectures, *How to Do Things with Words* (1955), generated a rich stream of thought among philosophers of language from its day to the present. Austin called those acts of speech "performative utterances" that accomplish something by virtue of being said. One of his examples of a performative utterance is the statement "I give and bequeath my watch to my brother," as in the case of a last will and testament. By virtue of saying this, the act is done, even if the watch has not yet been handed over by the executor of the estate to the deceased's brother. The written document of the will is a transcription of the testator's final desire, the graphical deposit of his personal act of willing. The utterance makes the act a reality by pronouncing the testator's desire. The signed will confirms the uttered action.

Speech act theory, which is the nomenclature given to the philosophical inquiry inaugurated by Austin, can help us understand the power of charismatic orality among storefront Evangelicals (and many more) since this religious subculture invests great energy in oral performance and employs visual culture to enhance the effect of the spoken word. Preachers use printed texts on walls to amplify their utterances. Austin prescribed several rules that ensure the effective (or what he called the "felicitous") operation of the performative utterance. These may be conveniently summarized for our purpose as follows. First, for performatives to function effectively, "there must exist an accepted conventional procedure having a certain conventional effect," which will involve specific words uttered by certain persons on prescribed occasions. Second, "the procedure must be executed by all participants both correctly and completely." Finally, those who utter the performative must conduct themselves subsequently in accord with it lest the act be nullified.[39] Austin's account is far more subtle and articulated than this, and the line of thought that issued from it has taken up all manner of technical exceptions and nuances. Yet these need not concern us here since the aim is not to indulge in the fine points of linguistic philosophy, but to put in place a conceptual scheme that can illuminate the lived religion of storefront churches.[40]

Applying Austin's example to these rules, we note that a person's will is a speech act. The last will and testament performs what it says when it is created in obedience to legal conventions, that is, when the will is composed by the testator under sound mind, signed in the presence of a proper witness, and not usurped by a subsequent will. The conditions may be applied to the many speech acts or performative utterances conducted in Evangelical practice. I have in mind here those utterances of various kinds that perform spiritual work by exerting the power of the divinity that animates scripture qua divine speech. The pastoral call itself is such an act of divine speech. God speaks to individuals and in doing so makes them a preacher, elder, overseer, healer, minister, or bishop. The call itself endows the individual with a new status. The pronouncement of the call, heard or discerned by the individual, is a revelation that enacts a new way of being.

Invoking the name of Jesus is another pervasive practice among those Evangelical groups engaged in healing and exorcism – speech acts which are held to deliver believers from illness and demonic possession. The miracle in each case is spoken in ritual performance. Uttering the name of Jesus is powerful in these circumstances because spirits of illness and possession must obey it. Some Evangelicals believe that Satan, who controls all evil spirits, is himself unable to say Jesus' name. The Apostle Ernest Leonard directed his commands at the forces of darkness at work among those attending his services at Provision of Promise Ministries in Newark:

We command the power of demonic forces to loose their forces. We come against the spirit of confusion, the spirit of distortion, the spirit of witchcraft. Go now in Jesus' name; go now in the name of Jesus. I break the power of mind-control spirits, of spirits of divination; I release the anointing to cast out devils. Start that anointing; every tie of witchcraft is broken. The east wind! There is something in the east wind.[41]

The Apostle's final reference to the east wind signaled the efficacy of his speech act, perhaps that the evil spirits were fleeing or that the spirit of God was arriving.[42] To command the removal of evil and to invoke Christ's name in the setting of the ritual, to conduct the procedure with scriptural warrant, and to do so among a gathering of the faithful joined in prayer converge to satisfy Austin's prescriptive conditions for the performative utterance, rendering it effective, at least insofar as those healed walk the right path and do not suffer a relapse of evil or illness. Not only can the speech act banish physical or spiritual maladies, but it can also call down blessing. In a sermon entitled "Increasing in Favor," Houston megachurch pastor Joel Osteen boldly tutors his audience in the confidence of releasing "our faith through our words" as an assertive message of what has come to be known as the "prosperity gospel":

> I believe one of the main ways that we grow in favor is by declaring it. It's not enough to just read it; it's not enough to just believe it. You've got to speak it out. Your words have creative power.[43]

Laity and clergy alike experience divine speech in many ways – in the songs they sing, in the oral performance of sermons and testimonies, in the study of scripture, in occasional dreams and visions. They also commonly cover the walls of their churches and homes with placards, mottoes, bible verses, paintings, posters, and painted inscriptions of the bible. Rather than regarding these "images" as mere illustrations or reminders, however, I would like to explore their relationship to the charismatic orality of Evangelical piety. How may these artifacts, which I propose to call "image-texts," evince the power of speech in Evangelical practice? Do they themselves act as graphic versions of the performative utterance? The preacher delivers what God has given him or her. And this deliverance is not uncommonly inscribed on the walls of the church. One founder of a chapel in New Haven recorded in a text placed within the church that "The Lord gave the pastor this passage from the Bible [Colossians 3: 23, 'And whatsoever you do, do it heartily as to the Lord and not onto (sic) man'] before she started the church."[44] By placing the inspirational text on the wall of the church, the pastor posted the authority of her revelation. In a sense, the text is a kind of speech act itself: it publicly proclaims the mandate of God that authorizes the pastor's ministry and forms the foundation and mission of her church.

Biblical inscriptions speak to readers just as the bible speaks to readers and just as preachers exhort their listeners. Texts appear throughout the interior and on the exterior of storefront churches in the manner that

devotional images and icons populate the walls and altars of Catholic, Orthodox, and some liturgical Protestant churches. These texts may be characterized
as "image-texts" inasmuch as they combine the features of textuality with
visuality, creating a visual artifact that is neither purely text nor image, but
both.[45] Rather than operating as icons that visualize the appearance of a sacred
figure, the Evangelical image-text visualizes the Word of God – the bible as a
living text, as the holy spoken word, the speech of God. And it visualizes the
authorizing utterances of the pastor, the charismatic leader of the community
whose speech conveys the anointing of the Spirit of God. Few image-texts in
inner-city Pentecostal-Holiness and mission churches are as fascinating as visual
artifacts as John B. Downey's many sign paintings (Figure 65). Little biographical information survives regarding Downey (active during the 1970s in
Los Angeles).[46] Works such as Figure 65 clearly suggest the craft of the professional sign painter. But Downey's work also recalls the domestic tradition of
pious mottoes that Christians display in homes, where texts are intended to
serve as devotional reminders that might curb misbehavior and nurture the
practice of Christian virtues. Figure 65 quotes a bible passage and includes
quotation marks and the citation of the passage (Acts 16: 31) to certify the
origin of the text. If that were not enough, he places the text on the visual field
of an open bible. But Downey does not merely quote scripture. He visually
performs it by enhancing the lettering. This infuses the text with an oral or
performative quality. The key portion of the inscription, "Lord Jesus Christ," is
enlarged and colored red, which enunciates the ritual invocation of the name of

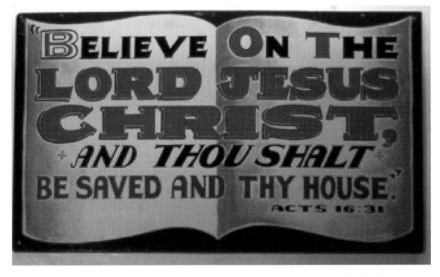

Figure 65 Camilo José Vergara, photographer, hand-painted sign by John B. Downey at
Emmanuel Baptist Rescue Mission, Fifth Street, Los Angeles, CA, 2003. Courtesy
of the photographer.

Jesus in sermons and in rites of healing and exorcism and also corresponds to the oratorical qualities of emphasis and intonation. The variation of color, style, and size of typography may reflect several intentions. In addition to making the text easier to read and more visually engaging, and recalling the nineteenth-century lithographic mottoes issued by Currier & Ives and Louis Prang among many others, the use of rubricated letters brings to mind so-called "red letter" bibles, which place the spoken words of Jesus in red type. Red lettering is intended to turn the written text into the oral and aural word. Downey's portrayal of scripture text is a visual articulation of the spoken utterance, the verbal revelation of divine will in the bible. In other words, his motto is an image-text that engages readers in a visual performance of what is heard. Seeing is reading is hearing.

Charismatic orality is grounded in the body and understands speech as a performative action, a movement of the Spirit of God through the body and person of the inspired, anointed preacher. Face-to-face encounter is the primary register of charismatic orality, where spoken words are heard directly and such transmissions of spiritual power as the laying on of hands and spiritual anointing occur. When mass media disembody charisma by removing the preacher from the immediate presence of the people, they are subject to fakery or dissimulation. This is one reason why image-texts are a common form of communication within the church interiors. As a medium of communication they remain close to the body and performative practices of the speaker. For instance, word and image sometimes are shown to intermingle, to refer to one another as a conjoint act of speech. A mural on the front of the First Bethel Missionary Baptist Church in Newark (Figure 66) demonstrates the proximity of text and speaker. The words are from Matthew 11: 28, where Christ addresses the public gathered to hear him. Beside the text appears an African figure of Jesus in biblical dress. It is noteworthy that the figure does not gesture toward the viewer, as if he were enacting the words of invitation and consolation as he does in other artistic portrayals of the subject. Instead, Jesus motions toward the words themselves, bearing witness with his bodily presence to what he says. In the text appears the first- and second-person address, "I will give you rest." Rather than looking at the addressee, however, thereby identifying the "you" of the invitation, the figure of Jesus gazes upon what he says, suggesting not only an underlying unity of figure and speech, but also a priority of word in which the body is present, but subordinate. Word and image corroborate one another in order to signal the preeminence of the spoken word. In this instance, as in many others such as Evangelical imagery noted in Chapter 1, one should recognize that the purpose of imagery is to enact the *iconicity of the text*. Imagery operates to endorse the transparency of text to the spoken word, whose breath emanates from the spirit-filled speaker.

Figure 66 Camilo José Vergara, photographer, Mural of Christ inviting passersby to come to him for rest, First Bethel Missionary Baptist Church, 19th Avenue, Newark, NJ, 2003. Courtesy of the photographer.

Television and the charisma of being there

Charisma is obviously not just a category of authority applying to religious leaders, but a quality of desirability or appeal as well as force and authority commanded by leaders in business, military, and political life as well as by professional athletes and entertainers. Indeed, any social setting organized according to the "star system" is in the business of generating and managing charisma on the stage of public representations. Charisma is a kind of energy that is akin to electricity: it requires a circuit and a form of manifestation to put its power to work. The fundamental medium of charisma is the human body. In circulating and (re)presenting charisma to a mass audience, television, radio, and film are constructed on the analogy of human speech and vision, indeed operate as extensions of them. This is evident in the use of these media in religious practice. In the days of radio broadcast, evangelist Oral Roberts asked his listeners to place their hands on their radio sets as they listened from afar in their parlors to pray with him and receive a special blessing which he would send by touching the microphone through which he broadcast his sermon. His son, Oral Roberts, Jr., applied the same practice in his televised services, asking viewers to place their hands on their television sets to touch his own palm raised before the camera.

Americans have long regarded modern media as magical, infused with spiritual energy or power, whether it is spirit photography or spiritualist interpretations of telegraphy or radio dimly rationalized as extensions of human sensory organs.[47] Often the power of media inspires fear – as in conspiracy theories of state spying or harm caused by new media like television or computers, which cause addiction, injury to eyes, exposure to radiation, and so forth. These intuitions and fears have been dramatized and exaggerated in horror films like *Poltergeist* (1982), *The Ring* (2002), and *White Noise* (2005), which portray television or video as a visual portal that opens up to supernatural realms beyond, providing contact with dimensions that threaten mortal life. In each case, the television or video screen becomes an entrance into another world or the gateway through which evil enters this world. Whether it is film, as we saw in Chapter 6, or television or internet, new visual media invariably annoy or threaten the conventional moral sensibilities of older generations, who find that youth adapt to new media far too easily.[48]

These very anxieties become the fare for a good deal of popular entertainment. *The Ring* makes this point with unusual effect. The danger it dramatizes is the very act of looking at a mysterious video, which results in the death of the viewer seven days later. The grotesque corpse of a murdered girl crawls from a well on television and then through the television screen to bare her Medusa-like face before killing her voyeur-victims. The film implicates viewing itself as somehow complicit in the death of the girl, who was drowned in a well, which forms the arcane "ring" shape that animates the film's iconography and is left imprinted on the bodies of her victims in the distended shape of their mouths. Images are dangerous, the film demonstrates: seeing some things results in death. The linkage of seeing and death was made by the God of Israel when Moses asked to look upon him: "man shall not see me and live" (Exodus 33: 20). *The Ring*, as well as the caution raised by scripture, asserts that media are lethal because they are easily transformed from communication to forms of immediate contact. This transformation enables them to rival the embodied presence of the world at hand and its community of moral influence. Rather than reshaping the world in imagination, as Münsterberg had analyzed the effect of film, the medium threatens to invade the real world. Horror films, like many dark fairy-tales before them, may deliver the most traditional of moral messages: curiosity and hubris are hazardous. For parents the threat of much entertainment is losing their children to the chimerical world of movie stars, fictional heroes whose charisma is so intoxicating that children are unable to look away.

The power of charisma is precisely its infectious, non-rational capacity to capture attention and to rivet it to the person who radiates it – whether it is Luke Skywalker or Darth Vader, good or evil; Princess Diana or Princess Leia, real or fictional. Television and film are the visual mass media that make this happen. They do this by enacting the enchantment of an immediate connection. With film the concentrated gaze of viewers sitting in darkened interiors – theaters or their dens at home – allows them to forget everything but the faces filling the screens before them. Although television can operate as a video screen, as a live medium it attracts the viewer's attention on different terms. The magnetic or charismatic pull of live television is the sheer presence or immediacy of the medium. Televised sermons are one way this happens for religious viewers, who sit before televisions whose screens convey the glowing image of a talking head, such as a priest or rabbi at a lectern, who gazes into the camera as if it were the steady eye of his or her audience. Viewers listen as if they were seated in a church or synagogue. Other speakers practice a much more dynamic form of delivery, gesturing broadly, moving about the stage, walking among their audience. Rather than one camera trained frontally on their heads, these speakers understand their stage presence as a performance. Their presentations are produced, composed from several camera angles, including cuts to the audience so that the effect of their words may be registered in the rapt faces of those listening to them. Evangelists such as Billy Graham or T. D. Jakes take their show on the road, filling stadiums and vast arenas around the world. But even lesser religious celebrities such as those featured in the weekly productions of so-called mega churches still find large regional and national audiences for their carefully choreographed worship services. These are produced from on-site production facilities with large staffs of camera operators and editors who produce live feed for televisual audiences across the country.

Religious television viewers tune into live talk shows as well as worship programs for the same reason that most people respond to live television as a medium: live production allows viewers to see from afar, as if television were telescopic, bringing the far near as if its presence were not produced or mediated. Viewers do not like gaps or discontinuities, or anything that betrays the artifice of image production. The medium is supposed to be invisible, the stagecraft concealed. The mechanics of television production should not be obtrusive especially if live television is to deliver immediate access to what is happening. Live television purports to be just this transparent immediacy: we are watching it happen, present in time with it, free to make of it what we will, untouched and unthreatened, consuming it with the convenience of private viewing and comfortable seating. Television is about comfortable chairs and the privacy of the home. It is the electronic hearth that one turns on and off at will. Its abundance of channels means a surfeit of choice instantly gratified. It is difficult to imagine a visual medium more ideally suited to consumption.

In order for live television to hide its means of production, it commonly relies on a host or an anchor on whom the viewer's attention is fixed. This focal figure maintains an overarching narrative or commentary, which knits multiple cuts into a seamless fabric. The news anchor's voice and face secure the many strands, providing a kind of center of gravity. The anchor addresses the viewer as if directly, gazing into one's eye through the camera and screen. He or she tells viewers each evening what they need to know, particularly when images shape a story. The anchor's words frame what viewers see, making the images intelligible, part of a narrative. When live feed on the scene is not claiming the viewer's attention, the familiar personality in the studio is. The recognizability of the anchor or host is crucial since viewers develop relationships with them, tuning in regularly to enjoy the daily rhythm of their presence. For this reason, news organizations invest considerable effort in promoting their news anchors in advertisements that stress their personality, reliability, and authority.[49] The reliability of the news is enhanced by the conferral of the anchor's charisma. Even in talk shows that are taped, as they almost always are, the show is produced as if it were live, with a live studio audience to augment the illusion.

Live television and web broadcasts are able to launch what media scholars have called "media events," that is, mediated experiences that are not otherwise capable of being experienced because they are constructed by news organizations or production companies for access on the television or computer screen.[50] Media events of the most "pseudo-eventual" proportions include televised coverage of Emmy and Academy awards ceremonies, which feature Hollywood glitterati arriving, sashaying, chatting, posing, and displaying their fashion ware for the cameras and crowd, oozing glamor, which is the film or television star's brand of charisma. Although commentators on the scene feign spontaneity, the entire event is scripted and carefully choreographed to create a total impression. The event itself exists fully only in mediation. Daniel Dayan and Elihu Katz studied epic events that transfixed a nation by arresting mass-viewer attention to televised coverage of an occasion as it happened. Many such events enacted mass rites of passage or classic clashes of mythic forces such as battles, the burial of monarchs or presidents, the marriage of prince and princess, the inauguration of a president or crowning of a king. The cultural work of media events, according to Dayan and Katz, is to achieve a national sense of shared unity around a common center. Although this has been criticized as illusory, or even dangerous, its actual basis is mythical rather than empirical. The mythic power of a nation's center corresponds to the perceived need for one as the inherent force that will resist disintegration. The appearance of homogeneity or unity serves the ideological needs of the nation-state.[51] Being there, in the mediated moment of television, seeing close from afar, is experienced by massive audiences as obligatory, a binding or cohering experience consumed privately, but occurring in the present and thereafter in memory and conversation as formative for a generation, a nation, or a world. Not all such media events focus on charismatic personae, but many do, and are often responsible for amplifying the stature of individuals to legendary proportions.

Charisma, religion, and film

The charismatic person is a dominant feature in religious epics from the early days of film during the late 1890s to such popular sensations as *The Ten Commandments* (1956), *The Greatest Story Ever Told* (1965), *Jesus Christ Superstar* (1973), *Jesus of Nazareth* (1977), DreamWork's *Prince of Egypt* (1998), and Mel Gibson's *The Passion of the Christ* (2004).[52] Virtually every film about

Jesus or Moses or Buddha (such as Bernardo Bertolucci's *The Little Buddha*, 1993) is a treatment of a charismatic leader who exerts mysterious power over his followers and his detractors by virtue of the force of his person apart from whatever supernatural powers he may command over nature or the spirit world. But religion in film and television is not restricted to the stories of explicitly religious figures or events. David Carradine's portrayal of a renegade Chinese priest of the Shaolin sect (Ch'an Buddhism) in the 1970s television hit, *Kung Fu*, demonstrated that vaguely defined Asian spirituality could sell in prime time, as long as it offered the hard-hitting acrobatics of the martial arts that Bruce Lee had begun to sensationalize during the early 1970s in a string of martial arts films that quickly gathered a cult following.[53] From 1994 to 2003 the tender uplift of *Touched by an Angel* succeeded in appealing to a broad swathe of American television viewers, offering a feel-good storyline that stressed reconciliation and forgiveness, and regarded the divine in the work of a female angel in the reassuring terms set out by Frank Capra's persistently appealing film, *It's a Wonderful Life* (1946), and by Victorian guardian angels before that.

With the exception of most Jesus films, which are typically bathed in dramatic piety, or *The Little Buddha*, which is clearly an homage, most film and television treatments of religion avoid specificities. Anything too clearly defined in denominational or sectarian terms risks the appearance of bigotry or narrow-mindedness, on the one hand, and incommunicability on the other. A Southern Baptist preacher or an Ultramontanist priest comes with too much specificity: television viewers will not understand the subtle theological features distinguishing one sect or another, and will therefore code such distinctive figures as irrelevant or obscure. Generically Catholic priests or homogenously Protestant parsons or quaintly ethnic rabbis are the rule if the role is to be appealing to large audiences. The well-worn stereotypes of clergy only reinforce the fact that most portrayals of clergy in mainstream entertainment could not be less charismatic. They are company men in the service of ecclesiastical bureaucracies or personifications of traditional moral codes. Exceptions include Robert Duval in *The Apostle* (1997) or Burt Lancaster in *Elmer Gantry* (1960), but they only prove the rule. Portrayals of women as religious figures are not very different. An abundance of kindly nuns outnumbers the distinctive portrayals of strong women (exceptions are noteworthy, such as *Babette's Feast*, (1987) or *Like Water for Chocolate* (1992)). But in recent years, and often in the science fiction genre, women have played robust lead characters in films that accord them powerful spiritual roles: Princess Leia in the *Star Wars* epic, Ripley in the *Alien* films, or Trinity in the *Matrix* trilogy. Prominent examples of women wielding spiritual power or struggling successfully with spiritual forces in recent television programs include the lead characters of such successful shows as *Medium, Charmed, Buffy the Vampire Slayer*, and *Xena*.[54] It would seem that the guardian angels of the Victorian era have developed into sword-wielding, karate-kicking dynamos dedicated to vigilant protection of the innocent. Buffy, for example, despite her physical prowess as a warrior, remains a guardian of her fellow high school students who are beset by demons, vampires, and werewolves – all monstrous symbols of youthful anxiety and alienation that are defeated by the watchful intervention of a benevolent if lethal female protector.

The quest for autonomy or self-determination that moves through American popular as well as high-brow entertainment is strongly inclined to regard the hero as the one who marches to his or her own drum, unperturbed by the constraints of the crowd. Science fiction and fantasy have seized on this theme in their valorization of the individual's struggle with the ethos of conformity. The scramble for charisma has also served as the plot in numerous films dealing with youth, whose lives are plagued by peer pressure and the struggle for popularity, by finding one's place in the pecking order, and generally by avoiding the taint of stigma in the social hothouse of high school. Religion, visuality, and charisma come together around the theme of social acceptance in *The Craft* (1996), a film about four girls who practice witchcraft as students at a California Catholic high school in which they are social outcasts. A familiar plot about the anxiety of adolescent alienation and the volatile social lives of teenage girls, *The Craft* opens with the arrival of a new student, Sarah, who must quickly sort out her allegiances between rival cliques: the jocks and their cheerleader girl friends versus a band of black-clad, outsider girls who recognize in the newcomer the missing fourth member of their small coven. Witchcraft serves as a means of creating a counterculture that will empower the girls to avenge the insults they have suffered. Yet, like the Sorcerer's Apprentice, magic gets out of hand. Defensive measures turn offensive; the victims turn into the bullies.

Charisma is what all the students at the high school seek in the form of desirability or social acceptance. In one scene, the four young witches perform an incantation for glamor since each is plagued by a personal stigma that she wants the glamor to overcome. They gather about candles and pentagrams, levitate, chant liturgically, experiment with spells to enhance their beauty or appeal, and move inexorably toward rituals with greater and darker power. But only Sarah really possesses charisma as an inborn power. As the group's abuse of witchcraft becomes apparent to her, she seeks out the counsel of the film's single positively portrayed adult, the female proprietor of an occult shop who befriends Sarah, recognizing in her a genuine or "natural witch." She tells Sarah that she must "invoke the spirit" to fight the dark application of its power by Nancy, the imperious leader of the group, who has turned the power of Satanic invocation to tyranny and self-aggrandizement. Yet the film appears of two minds. The sympathetic older female has informed the girls that true witches use spells with ethical concern since the effect of every enchantment comes back to them threefold. She even quotes the golden rule (which Jesus taught in the New Testament): "Do unto others as you would have them do to you."

But the ethical, communitarian message is lost on the girls, who use witchcraft for selfish reasons. In the end, the logic of charisma in teenage culture is even too strong for Sarah to resist. Besieged by the murderous Nancy, Sarah is told by her dead mother (also a witch) to "reach inside yourself." After invoking the spirit and killing Nancy in violent battle, Sarah confronts the other two friends who had turned against her. When they apologize and confess that their powers are gone, she spurns them. When they respond by questioning her power, signaling the return of the normal regime of adolescent petulance, Sarah demonstrates her potency by causing a thunderbolt to fell a tree branch before them. The film ends there, suggesting that the lead character has solved the problem of social stigma by becoming a charismatic loner, someone set apart from the social set by virtue of her indwelling power. This adolescent solution ensures her desirability or envy. As it does throughout the film, the camera settles on Sarah's face, filling the screen with its blond-haired and broad white surfaces, which contrast to the dark, ethnic and very Goth features of Nancy. Sarah herself is the face of the blond-haired, Caucasian cheerleader, the visual ideal of the all-American white girl, the very gold standard of charismatic desirability. Rather than creating friendships of genuine concern on the model of the golden rule, Sarah plays the charisma game better than everyone by cultivating her own, inborn power at it. Competitive self-realization is the ethic, not communitarianism. The way to deal with the torments of the pecking order is to climb to the top of the heap and stay there by the command of charismatic force. That is certainly not a practical solution for virtually any teen caught up in the social vagaries of high school life and adolescence, but it remains the ideal that keeps kids watching television and film, avidly consuming the illusion of personal well-being as the solution to all social ills.

The Craft is finally a story about the revenge of the loner who rises above the life of cliques to find within herself the treasure that the gospel of self-realization preaches as paramount. Sarah is a charismatic loner whose powers of enchantment set her apart, delivering her from the humiliation of social stigma and infusing her with desirability or envy. But if her solution works for a Hollywood feature film, it did not for the television program it inspired, Charmed (1998–2006). Prime-time television accents the enduring communal value of sisterhood in the program's three sisters who fight evil with witchcraft. The charismatic loner works better in the film medium than on prime-time television, where sixty-minute moral lessons on communal life are a happier glow in the electronic hearth than the hauteur of a sexy adolescent schoolgirl. In either case, however, film and television program displace the older pre-ponderance of charisma among male religious figures. If Aimee Semple McPherson would have shuddered at their witchcraft, she would have surely envied the power of the young witches to do good in a world far larger than the upholstered compound of the Victorian parlor.

Chapter 8

Back to nature

In 1789 Daniel Boone told a friend that he was leaving Kentucky for "some point beyond the bounds of civilization and spend the remnant of my days in the woods." Penniless from his failed business of digging ginseng root, Boone complained that civilization appeared to him as "nothing more than improved ways to overreach your neighbor."[1] But Boone did not vanish into the wild. He moved up the Ohio River to a small settlement that had been established fifteen years before through a military defeat of local Shawnee Indians. By 1791 Boone was serving in the Virginia Assembly. From the earliest years of the national period, the American "wild" has been a powerful idea in the national mythology. Even though it never existed in the sense of an unpopulated realm of pure nature, Americans want to believe that it did, and still does. Wilderness remains the focus of serious American philanthropy, scientific research, and popular hobbies and entertainment. Organizations like Sierra Club, National Geographic Society, Boy Scouts of America, and the Audubon Society are committed to preserving wilderness as part of the nation's heritage, and some of these and other, more radical groups to reversing the incursion posed by industrialization, pollution, residential sprawl, and the municipal annexation of ecologically significant areas. The undiminished tide of novels, first-hand accounts, films, journalistic reporting, and television interviews about climbing dangerous mountains or exploring harsh places like the polar regions might be attributed in part to the American need to find wilderness that cannot be domesticated. The danger and difficulty of such ascents or treks mark the boundaries of nature and civilization, wilderness and culture. Captured in dramatic photographs and documentaries, their images create a liminal gaze that defines the nation.

The great popularity of nature photographs by Ansel Adams certainly reflects the American romance with nature as wilderness in the sense of an unpopulated, undomesticated domain. Adams' photographs, like the one reproduced here, *Monolith, Face of Half Dome* (Figure 67; 1927) in Yosemite National Park, have enjoyed a secure place in the canon of popular American imagery since their appearance, perhaps because the visual archetypes of the national imagination and collective memory gravitate strongly toward the

Figure 67 Ansel Adams, *Monolith, Face of Half Dome*, Yosemite National Park, 1927. Courtesy Brauer Museum of Art, Valparaiso University.

sublime and monumental. In her perceptive study of American nature religions, Catherine Albanese rightly called attention to the appeal of the sublime in many traditions of belief – Calvinist, Native American, Transcendentalist, and the preservationist movement launched by John Muir during the late 1860s in the awesome shadow of California's Yosemite Valley.[2] Proud as Americans are of their technological wonders, places like Yosemite dwarf human ingenuity, and that is perhaps one of the most compelling reasons why American tourist-pilgrims flock to such sites each year. They seem drawn to immensity in part because many wish to regard it as the imprint of a higher reality – providence or Great Spirit, Mother Earth or the spirit of the nation.

Nature and redemption in America

Americans have often regarded the national terrain as infused with special significance, a kind of physical epistle from God to the nation. What do "amber waves of grain" and "fruited plain" and "purple mountains' majesty" mean if not to recall the biblical theme of a land of milk and honey set aside by the Lord for his chosen people? As the New Canaan for the New Israel, the American continent bears benevolent markers of divine intention. The fertile regions are what people rely on for food production; the terrifying sites are where they ritually visit to be awed, to be reminded of the wildness that prevailed when the New Israel crossed the frontier to populate the land bestowed upon them. At least this seems to be the view of the dominant culture. In fact, of course, Native Americans have lived for centuries throughout the "wilds" of the country. But they are not visible in the dominant national ideology of the land. The purpose of liminal vision is to conceal them. So Native Americans do not appear in Adams' photographs of places like Yosemite.

What Adams saw, and what many viewers affirm in his images, is the sublime evacuation of human presence from nature. The looming face of granite, the dark sky, the untouched falls of snow seem to register in their size and pristine antiquity some sort of awful gesture, the trace of something before humanity, an agency whose age and power dwarf American civilization. Some viewers will deify this power, others will not. Sometimes Adams included a moon in the sullen skies, which renders the landscape itself lunar in emotional desolation, no human place. Humankind has no rightful claim here. The primordial process that heaved the mountains into the heavens in photographs like Figure 67 was terrifying and devoid of human purpose. Humans are late arrivals and passing ghosts, of no consequence, and therefore invisible in such images, which bespeak a scale of time and space and force that is fully inhuman. If Adams shows no Native Americans, neither does he show any forest rangers, campers, or tourists.

The sublime admits of many varieties. One is avowedly Evangelical – furiously portraying divine wrath and judgment in the purge of human vanity as seen in the final panels of Thomas Cole's suite of images, *Course of Empire* (1836).

Another example is Cole's series of paintings called *Voyage of Life* (1839–40), which was also issued as four engravings between 1853 and 1856. In the third of this series (Figure 68), called *Manhood*, the protagonist in the barque, formerly accompanied by a guardian angel who now watches from above, the man enters a stormy region of life. A tempest looms and the river descends into vicious rapids as blasted trees and dark rocks confront the lone figure. In the grip of forces that dwarf him, he is left with nothing to do but pray and trust blindly in a distant goodness. The scene bodes danger, which is alluring in itself, but the angel peaking downward hints at redemption, which indeed follows in the final image of the suite (*Old Age*), where the barque floats peacefully in plangent waters and is rejoined by the benevolent guardian.

The mystical sublime, another variety, hovers at the misty summit of self-transcendence and union with the divine. The Transcendentalist experience that Emerson described so well in the opening pages of *Nature* (1836) captures the mystical dissolution of the self within the woods, where "the plantations of God, a decorum and sanctity reign." It was in that larger presence that Emerson felt himself dissolve:

> Standing on the bare ground – my head bathed by the blithe air, and uplifted into infinite space – all mean egotism vanishes. I become a transparent eye-ball; I am nothing; I see all; the currents of the Universal Being

Figure 68 James Smillie, *Manhood*, from *Voyage of Life*, 1853–56, engraving after Thomas Cole, *Voyage of Life*, 1839–40. Courtesy Bronck Museum of the Green County Historical Society.

circulate through me; I am part or particle of God. The name of the nearest friend sounds then foreign and accidental.[3]

But if Emerson's mystical dissolution began in nature, it ended in the Soul, which transcended nature altogether. The inhuman sublime, by contrast, jettisons all human sentiment as presumption. The human presence is no more than a passing glimpse, a momentary capacity to register grandeur and perhaps, in that instant, be delivered from the smallness and busyness of one's place in a scheme that has no special need or message for the human animal. It is the decentering perspective of modern evolutionary science rather than Emerson's Romantic humanism. Viewed in this way, Ansel Adams' work may represent an alternative reading of nature within the American national mythology. Nature does not need us, does not offer us any purpose but the opportunity of escaping ourselves in moments of a transfixed gaze where art becomes a kind of meditation, if not a religion. Adams' photographs can offer a passing antidote to mortality, pointing to an abiding boundary even as they allow its momentary aesthetic transgression.[4]

All forms of the sublime constitute ways of seeing that position viewers both beneath and above what they see, and therefore in some way outside of themselves, stretching or shrinking the psyche or surpassing it altogether. As an aesthetic mode, the sublime usually serves as some form of antidote, the head-clearing prescription for a people engrossed in smallness or busyness or excessive refinement. As a bracing departure from pusillanimous routine, the sublime is meant to redraw the boundaries of self, people, nation, or nature as various kinds of landscapes defining "nature" or "wilderness." Boundaries are very important in the American psyche, in the national mythos that is told and retold in all manner of visual media, from story books to films, postcards to paintings. Landscapes take shape as complex forms of representation where civilized life is understood to brush up against or confront the wild. Fundamentalist Christians have recently created "Creation Centers" and "Creation Museums" that display exhibits designed to show the primeval continental past as harmonious with a literalistic reading of the bible's opening chapters in the book of Genesis.[5] In this case, the boundary is temporal and the task is to show that what looks wild and divergent in fact conforms to a certain interpretation of the scriptures. In another genre of representation, scenic views positioned along interstate highways allow travelers the opportunity to gaze upon choice vistas in the short span of a stop. Untold numbers of photographs follow, commonly with the travelers posing before a distant mountain range, forest, desert, or river valley that is framed for view by the very site and design of the roadside pull-over. The boundary is the stone wall or promontory that frames the view. Such images show the comfortable proximity of humanity and nature, which is a consoling visual lesson for Americans who are fond of landscapes that reassure them of where they belong. Mount Rushmore is perhaps an obvious example, where the natural formation of a mountain is altered to merge culture and nature into a landscape of national identity.

For newcomers to America, colossal monuments like Rushmore may signal the capacity of size and natural setting to establish their presence. For example, Indian immigrants in the Chicago metropolitan region built a large complex of two temples between 1985 and 1994, perched on a bluff overlooking a suburb. Placed on the way up the hill is a large bronze portrait of Swami Vivekananda, who was the first Hindu adept to come to the United States and teach his religious philosophy. Influenced by Rammohan Roy's reformist vision of Hindu monotheism as a young man, Vivekananda read widely in Hindu and Western scriptures and philosophy, which he combined with the mystical influence of his teacher, Sri Ramakrishna. In 1893 he participated in the Parliament of World Religions in Chicago and impressed many with his passionate case for a universal Hinduism, one which avoided caste and tensions between different religions.[6] In his first address to the Parliament he sounded his most essential point, quoting Lord Krishna in the *Bhagavad Gita*: "Whosoever comes to Me, through whatsoever form, I reach him. All men are struggling through paths which in the end lead to Me."[7] Enshrined in a large baldachin (Figure 69), Vivekananda's figure fits into the landscape as visitors wend their way toward

Figure 69 Canopy enclosing sculpture of Swami Vivekananda, Hindu Temple of Greater Chicago, 1998. Photo courtesy of Gretchen Bugglen.

the bluff's summit and the temples. He stands there as if to welcome all to a practice that transcends sectarian distinctions of any kind. In fact, Vivekananda's highly inclusive view of all religions suits the immigrant community of Indians associated with the temple since they come from across India.[8] The physical harmony of the temples and Vivekananda's monument in the landscape visually and spatially conveys the unity of his message and the salutary cooperation of different Hindu devotions to form an enduring community of immigrants in the Chicago region.

The intermingling of nature and culture in American landscapes has also incorporated non-Western influences such as the Zen garden; this sometimes appears in botanical settings as at Brooklyn's Botanical Garden, which includes a garden modeled on Kyoto's Ryoanji. Another example is the Zen monastery Zenshinji (Zen mind-heart temple), otherwise known as the Tassajara Zen Mountain Center in California's Santa Lucida Mountains, begun in 1966 and operated by the California Zen Center in San Francisco.[9] The intention of these subtle forms of representation is to suggest a thorough harmony between mind and matter, between human culture and nature. Zen Buddhism seeks to overcome the dualist separation that structures human consciousness, fueled by the illusory formation of a self driven by fear, greed, and lust and sustained by patterns of anger, shame, and ignorance. The role of art in the design of Zen gardens is to suggest not a balance of nature and culture, but their identity as something called "suchness." Zen monasteries commonly exhibit this in the practice of building structures that conform to the contours and existing features of the surrounding site. A pastoral or rustic quality evokes a rural simplicity and lack of presumption.[10] But Buddhism in the United States need not simply mean escape from the hubbub of modern life. The appeal of a Buddhist treatment of space is part of an ethos of wellness. For example, an office building in Boulder, Colorado (Figure 70), includes a Zen-style rock garden designed by Japanese archery master Onyumishi Kanjuro Shibata, who founded a school in Boulder. The garden he designed is surrounded by a variety of offices, which are psychotherapy, massage, trauma recovery, and health and wellness firms. Visitors are invited to meditate on the garden, which provides a décor tailored to the businesses, many of which promote alternative forms of healing.

The significance of getting away, of going to an isolated place that has sequestered itself from the temptations and abuses of ordinary life, especially life in the city, is a pervasive pattern in American religious history. It informs something of the Puritans' story of pilgrimage to the new world; it is found at work in the camp meeting revivals of Methodists and Baptists in the late eighteenth century and first decades of the nineteenth century; it drove the decision to create a vast park in New York City and the establishment of Chautauqua in upstate New York. And the mythic ideal of starting over in the protecting embrace of segregated life has motivated countless utopian communities and spiritual retreats dotting the countryside – such as Christian and Socialist communities in New Harmony, Indiana, the spread of Shaker communities

Figure 70 Zen rock garden designed by Onyumishi Kanjuro Shibata, Crossroad Gardens office building, Boulder, CO, 2006. Photo courtesy of Stewart Hoover.

from the northeast to the Midwest, the Mormon migration to Utah, and the ill-fated fortress of communal living belonging to the Branch Davidian outside of Waco, Texas.[11] In every case, a religious community sought to establish an alternative to a decadent or unsympathetic and often antagonistic social reality, often by moving into the wilderness, on the durable model of ancient Israel liberated from bondage in Egypt to wander in the wilderness in more intimate communion with its God. Or at least that is how it is supposed to happen. Even a cursory reading of the story of the forty years of Israel's long trek to the Promised Land shows how unhappy the sojourn beyond civilization can be. Likewise, when segregated communities did last more than a few years in the American wilderness they did so by sinking roots and evolving the very bureaucratic and institutional inertia that spurred its original abandonment of the world.

Yet the springs powering the myth of rebirth beyond the confines of a decadent and oppressive society are deeply sunk in the human constitution. If social life can account for human debauchery and brokenness, radical reformers such as Robert Owen or the Fourierist Albert Brisbane insisted that the re-engineering of society into small agrarian modules of common life governed by collectivist practices could generate a purified community. It is an idea as old as

Plato's ideal republic. To start over meant to slip the bonds of one form of social life for another. The spirit to begin again continued to inform twentieth-century Americans in a spate of new religious movements in mid-century such as the collective communities formed by various Indian adepts, including the Maharishi Mahesh Yogi, founder of Transcendental Meditation, whose organization has begun a "vedic city" in Fairfield, Iowa, site of its university; and Bhagwan Shree Rajneesh, who operated a very controversial ranch in Wasco County, Oregon, where large numbers of young people gathered for a collective style of life engaged in farming, communal living, and spiritual practice directed by their master.[12] Although reverently pressed palms and bowing at the feet of Hindu gurus struck a new look on the American religious landscape, the impulse to seek refuge in an agrarian life and engage in creating an alternative community was nothing new.

One thing the nineteenth century did not lack was an abundance of cultural mythology. Hence the long list of those who struggled to realize their aims for alternative communities across the country: Robert Dale Owen and Fanny Wright, George Ripley of Brook Farm, Oneida founder John Humphrey Noyes, Mormon patriarchs Joseph Smith and Brigham Young, and the Shaker leader Joseph Meacham. Many Americans headed West, urged by a prevailing sense of providence or national destiny to find their place under the sun on a continent the government had declared open for settlement. The aboriginal residents were already being displaced, indeed had long been regarded as passing away before the juggernaut of a new dispensation. If Americans considered the vast tracts of territory in the West to be uninhabited wilderness that awaited their colonization and ownership, the Indian nations that had lived there for centuries possessed a very different understanding of relationship to the land. The culminating clash of cultures during the second half of the nineteenth century coincided with the rise of American nationalism, which was energized by the Mexican–American War and by the American Civil War and was part of a larger process of national formation. Locating Indians in this emergent national landscape took place in tandem with the developing commerce of tourism and the conquest of the West as the realization of a "manifest destiny." Reservations were the answer the US government pursued, peacefully, duplicitously, and forcefully. Historian Mark David Spence has pointed out that "the creation of the first national parks coincided with efforts to restrict Indians to reservations and assimilate them into American society."[13] Ironically, in order to preserve "nature" in national monuments such as Yosemite and Yellowstone, it was considered necessary to remove Indian residents from the lands. According to the dominant ideology, the national landscape that was the "nature" that God bestowed on white Americans was an originally uninhabited domain. Spence prudently observes:

> Such a conception of wilderness forgets that native peoples shaped these environments for millennia, and thus parks like Yellowstone, Yosemite, and

Glacier are more representative of old fantasies about a continent awaiting "discovery" than actual conditions at the time of Columbus' voyage or Lewis and Clark's adventure.[14]

One result was the iconography of the vanishing Indian (Figure 71), glimpsed in the image of Hiawatha gliding into the distance on the back cover of the program for Chautauqua speaker Katherine Bowden's illustrated lecture, "Pictorial Story of Hiawatha," which she and her husband presented around the country from 1904 to 1910. Like Longfellow's long poem, *The Song of Hiawatha* (1855), on which it was based, the Bowden presentation ended with the departure of the hero, who leaves when a Jesuit missionary arrives to evangelize the Indians. As Hiawatha bids farewell to his people, he urges them to listen to the missionary's party, "For the Master of Life [Gitche Manito, or Great Spirit] has sent them,/ From the land of light and morning."[15] Significantly, he heads off into the sunset, "To the land of the Hereafter." His departure had been prophesied by his father, the West Wind, and comes when life among the Indian nations had degenerated. Hiawatha's leave-taking is an acquiescence to the new religion and culture that echoed the broadly felt sentiment among white Americans that the indigenous population was destined to vanish – by warfare, intermarriage, or attrition. Horace Bushnell had given a bluntly racist expression to the view in 1861 when he predicted that white Americans were inevitably going to "out-populate" red Americans. The "Christian body," he confidently proclaimed,

> stands among the other bodies and religions, just as any advanced race, the Saxon for example, stands among the feebler, wilder races, like the Aborigines of our continent; having so much power of every kind that it puts them in shadow, weakens them, lives them down, rolling its over-populating tides across them, and sweeping them away, as by a kind of doom.[16]

Longfellow's poem echoes the sentiment. The ethnological material from which he drew his tale, Henry Rowe Schoolcroft's *Algic Researches: Indian Tales and Legends* (1839), included an account of Manabozho, Longfellow's Hiawatha, but his character was quite different. "He affected to be influenced by the spirit of a god," Schoolcroft wrote, "and was really actuated by the malignity of a devil."[17] Manabozho's story did not end with a wistful Götterdämmerung, but stood as a small number of discrete narratives characterized by violence, trickery, warfare, daring, and petulance. Longfellow, by contrast, gathered up several stories from Schoolcroft, many of which had nothing to do with Manabozho, and crafted a melancholy harmony between Hiawatha's end and the "destiny" of Native Americans in his own lifetime. Manabozho the belligerent legend became Hiawatha the tragic hero. Longfellow had Hiawatha testify to the decline of native peoples and the arrival of a

Figure 71 Hiawatha's Departure, illustration on back cover of promotional booklet, Katherine Bowden, illustrated lecture, "Pictorial Story of Hiawatha," 1904. Bowden Papers, Valparaiso University. Courtesy of the Department of Special Collections, Valparaiso University.

superior religion. Hiawatha announced a vision of "our nation scattered,/ All forgetful of my counsels,/ Weakened, warring with each other."[18] At the same time, he countenanced the appearance of the Europeans as instruments of the Great Spirit, who "sends them hither on his errand."[19] Longfellow's poem ascribed the doctrine of manifest destiny to the Gitche Manito of all Native Americans. And the irony only compounded. In order to write his poem, Longfellow studied several of Schoolcroft's assembled legends, some of which were Ojibwa stories. As retold by Longfellow, these in turn became an important source for latter-day Ojibwa who, though Christian, used the poem to celebrate their ancestral identity in the late nineteenth century by creating a play based on the poem, which they performed annually on an island in Lake Huron off the coast of Ontario, in the heart of the Ojibwa's traditional homeland.[20] Bowden, who based her illustrated lecture on the Ojibwa production, later referred to it as "the Oberammergau of America," making Hiawatha a kind of Christ figure who sacrifices himself for the redemption of his people.[21]

But the motif of the vanishing Indian did not mean the same thing to all white Americans. A counterculture of spiritual seekers in quest of what is real is a venerable American tradition in its own right, and one that has sought to affirm the Indian presence in a landscape best rid of dualism. The countercultural experience is not supposed to focus on nature as a cultural artifact, but on the harmony of mind and body, human and non-human as a singular expression of nature. One of the most outspoken voices in this tradition belongs to Henry David Thoreau. In March of 1845 the self-possessed New Englander borrowed an axe and walked into the woods a mile from Concord, Massachusetts, to begin work on a small cabin that would house him as he conducted an experiment in honest living. "I went to the woods," he wrote in his incomparable memoir, "because I wished to live deliberately, to front only the essential facts of life, and see if I could not learn what it had to teach, and not, when I came to die, discover that I had not lived."[22] Thoreau's testimony appears to reveal a twofold motive: the desire to jettison from his life all that was not necessary in order to experience precisely what was indispensable, and therefore natural and right, and the fear of realizing at death that he had lived an inauthentic life. But perhaps they are not so very separate, for Thoreau was rigorously fixed on the present life, refusing to defer its import to another world, to a register beyond the immediate smell and make of things about Walden Pond. "I wanted to live deep and suck out all the marrow of life, to live so sturdily and Spartan-like as to put to rout all that was not life." Sparing life no quarter, he determined to live alone and from only what his own labor might produce in order to take the full measure of a human's span, mean or sublime, the better "to give a true account of it in my next excursion." Thoreau diagnosed an other-worldliness among his fellows that prevented their living deliberately, and precluded their learning from this life what it had to say for itself.

For most men, it appeared to me, are in a strange uncertainty about it, whether it is of the devil or of God, and have *somewhat hastily* concluded that it is the chief end of man here to glorify God and enjoy him forever.[23]

His quotation of the Westminster Catechism was not a flourish of unbelief, but aimed at a theological predisposition to exchange this world for the next, which amounted to substituting a dualism of ascetic theocentrism for the monistic concentration on the here and now that Thoreau evinced so well in his sharply hewn prose. Thoreau left Calvinism and Unitarianism behind for the earthy pursuit of a simultaneously grander and firmer spirituality. Self-reliance was neither misanthropy nor narcissism, but a refusal to take another's word for it, to submit to the authority of tradition or institution. To hearken to nature meant the nature without as well as within: "No law can be sacred to me," his friend and mentor Ralph Waldo Emerson uttered in a manifesto on self-reliance, "but that of my nature."[24] The point of *Walden* seems to be to demonstrate the rustic, providential fit between the two, self and nature.

Thoreau was convinced that humankind had lost something vital in modern society. He looked repeatedly to American Indians as proof of the fact. In modern society

> the life of the individual is to a great extent absorbed, in order to preserve and perfect that of the race. But I wish to show at what a sacrifice this advantage is at present obtained, and to suggest that we may possibly so live as to secure all the advantage without suffering any of the disadvantage.[25]

Why is it, he wondered, citing the words of Jesus, "that, though the birds of air have their nests, and the foxes their holes, and the savages their wigwams, in modern civilized society not more than one half the families own a shelter"?[26] No friend of factories or industrial capitalism, Thoreau contrasted the economic injustices of modernity with the serviceable simplicity and elegant economy of Indian life. When he gazed at newspapers and banks and stores and finery and social pretenses, Thoreau shuddered, ruing the loss of the real thing. He was drawn to the woods and the rustic life there to reclaim the real and prove it was enough.

> Let us settle ourselves, and work and wedge our feet downward through the mud and slush of opinion, and prejudice, and tradition, and delusion, and appearance ... till we come to a hard bottom and rocks in place, which we can call *reality*, and say, This is, and no mistake.[27]

Native America as culture and commodity

Thoreau's passionate search for the rock bottom, for the irreducible real thing, probably resonates with most Americans, however differently they may define that reality. For Thoreau and for many since, Native American cultures have represented an alternative to the mainstream view of nature and spiritual authenticity in experiencing what nature is and what it means for one's life. According to this view, Native Americans never lost touch with nature because they remained part of it. They did not own it, but were its children. This represents a very different relationship to the land, with a correspondingly different understanding and experience of "nature." It also betokens a different cultural economy. The land does not represent money, is not the equivalent of economic power, is not the material base of capital, not an abstraction more compelling than the land. Thoreau's pilgrimage can be seen as an attempt to invert the dominant scheme, to return to the land and to human life grounded in it the priority that capitalism has turned on its ear.

This, to be sure, is not to morph Thoreau into a Native American, to ignore the clear differences that remain. He never left the modern race of white men and women. He wanted to reinvigorate them by reclaiming the simplicity of life and direct relation to the natural world that he admired in Indians. But returning to nature did not mean "going native." "The civilized man," he averred, "is a more experienced and wiser savage."[28] Many Americans see public and private property when they look at the land around them, parsing it as zones of control under various forms of ownership. So did Thoreau. It was his timber he felled, his animals he raised, slaughtered, and ate. He did not enter nature without possessions. And he did not sojourn there without the legal advantages of ownership and property. As many Native American scholars have noted, contact with white Americans, their proprietary economy, and the government that enforced its culture of appropriation, forcefully and subtly challenged Native ways of thought by disseminating the view that land is about legal and financial status and its complicated network of relations, about earning power, about economic security, about a hedge against insecurities, in other words, about the cultural construction of identity in capitalist terms. The cultural economy of Native life was grounded in belonging to the land rather than owning it, which stresses ontological continuity with material things rather than their objectification in instrumental epistemologies where things are defined as inanimate extensions of human will and knowledge. This cultural economy collided violently with capitalism's transformation of nature into material wealth, which is not an intrinsic good, but the base for capital. If the national park system resists the capitalization of land, it does not fail to enforce appropriation since it turns the land into government-controlled public property.

Although he was earthier than Emerson, as a Transcendentalist Thoreau ultimately cared more about the ideas and intuitions that grasp the meaning of things and structure the human apprehension of order and value than he did for things themselves. "Mind is the only reality," according to Emerson, "of which men and all other natures are better or worse reflectors. Nature, literature, history, are only subjective phenomena."[29] The task is to learn to exercise the self's rightful autonomy, its inborn freedom. The materialist, according to Emerson, sees "sensible masses" where the idealist "reckons the world an appearance." As idealists, both writers regarded nature as a phenomenon, and therefore less real than mind. "Nature is thoroughly mediate," Emerson insisted.

> It is made to serve. It receives the dominion of man as meekly as the ass on which the Saviour rode. It offers all its kingdoms to man as the raw material which he may mould into what is useful.[30]

It was the desired assertion of this manful dominion over nature that led Thoreau to Walden Pond where he might in relative solitude recapture a sense of empowerment. He would not reason his way to the priority of mind, correcting the encroachments of an eviscerated society, but fish, axe, build, and eat his way there.

Although Emerson's hymn to the virtue of self-determination, entitled "Self-Reliance" (1841), is not a brief for New Age spirituality or the men's movement, nor is it by any means a call to return to a (white) conception of Indian primitiveness, it is part of a larger American project of celebrating individual sovereignty by stressing the creative, constructive power of human consciousness. Yet Emerson did gender the quest by recognizing in boys and men the privileged audience for his diatribe against conformity and tradition:

> A boy is in the parlour what the pit is in the playhouse; independent, irresponsible, looking out from his corner on such people and facts as pass by, he tries and sentences them on their merits, in the swift, summary ways of boys, as good, bad, interesting, silly, eloquent, troublesome.[31]

Emerson adored the self-absorbed vitality of boys and praised aversion to group conformity as the virtue of great individuals like Socrates, Jesus, Luther, Copernicus, Galileo, Wesley, Fox – all of whom were followed by institutions that were nothing more than "the lengthened shadow of one man."[32] He clearly sounded the modern American call for the Self, the active principle and core measure of existence that imitation acted only to imprison. The "nature" that this very American path of thinking recognizes as ultimately most important is not the physical terrain, but the soul or spiritual self of the individual seeker. Emerson's essay articulates a New World vision of the self as rightfully unhitched from the burden of tradition, from the determinative momentum of the past. By locating power in the mind rather than in society or material reality, Emerson was instrumental in directing a tradition of thought and practice that has continued to authorize individuals with the duty to liberate themselves. The individual's responsibility for formation and liberty is principally his or her own. Like many who came after him in the American marketplace of spirituality, Emerson assembled his view from a wide scope of sources – from Hinduism, Platonism, Christianity, British Romanticism, and German Idealism, to name a few. This self-entrepreneurship appeals broadly to the American Dream's ideal of self-made stature, of upward mobility, and to the bricoleur instead of the genealogical model of identity. But by withdrawing from primary reliance on a single community and body of beliefs, the seeker regards all beliefs as cultural resources, as packages or units of equal value preserved in a cultural library, where they await the browser-consumer. Although this way of thinking empowers the individual, stressing personal liberty in the pursuit of the lost or under-realized self, it is an ideal that operates at the expense of the autonomy or sovereignty of traditions and communities, particularly those that feel victimized by the dominant culture of white, affluent, well-educated American men and women who no longer identify with their Jewish or Christian backgrounds, but wish to act as independent entrepreneurs in search of self-created cultural identities.

The distinction between the Transcendentalist view of nature and Native American perception is important to make because for many today, especially but not only those who admire and practice what is generally called "New Age spirituality," it is very easy to collapse the clearly Western notion of a perennial philosophy, which bears much in common with popular Idealism, with what are taken to be perspectives of American Indian culture. In the 1980s and 1990s, Robert Bly, the men's movement, and the New Age took droves of white urban males to the woods donning masks, paint, and buckskins for drumming and chanting in order to heal the self and get back in touch with their primal, repressed nature as men, to stoke the "fire in the belly," and reclaim the "warrior," something perhaps akin to Thoreau's quest for the real lost to modern city life. Bly's method of thinking and writing is aptly described as Jungian or mythopoetic, that is, relying on metaphorical or figurative rhyming in the search for symbols of the psyche's enduring archetypes.[33] *Iron John*, Bly's poetic treatise on the male soul and its thwarted search for the inner wild man, is an energetic reflection on the woes of men in modern America, unweaned from mothers, frustrated and weakened warriors, deprived of the rites of initiation and male bonding that tribal cultures once enjoyed.[34] Like Freud and Jung, Bly makes extensive use of mythic imagery and fairy tales as well as religious rites and characters to assay the descent of modern man into a state of shamed spiritual alienation. Recalling the laments of moralists, clergy, and educators about the sapping of American masculinity by the modern city, by the alienation of boys and men from the strenuous life in nature, and by the feminization of Christianity, Bly's account invokes a broad range of pagan mythology and ritual to help men imagine what they have lost and how they might go about reclaiming it. To his critics, Bly's expansive invocation of sources is not literary richness, but a "welter of babble concerning the value of assorted strains of imagined primitivism and warrior spirit."[35] But for Bly and his admirers, the wide-ranging mythopoetic gestures are a potent way of thinking and feeling. Like Carl Jung, Mircea Eliade, and their American popularizer, Joseph Campbell, Bly regards myths as a single psychological language, versions of the same thing, common stock of the human experience. Native American belief is part of this mythopoetic mix. Although *Iron John* makes few references to Native American practices or beliefs, the practical side of the men's movement that Bly helped launch has made deliberate use of sweat lodges as part of its male rites designed to bring participants into a deeper awareness of their identities as men.

Two visual devices that have been especially popular among admirers of Native American culture, New Age proponents, and consumers generally are mass-produced versions of authentic Indian artifacts: kachina dolls and sand paintings (Figure 72). To this list might be readily added medicine bags, pipes, shields, dream catchers, basketry, headdresses, weaponry, clothing, drums, and paintings of the Sun Dance. We may confine our attention to kachina dolls and sand paintings, however, since these are objects that are widely collected as

Figure 72 Souvenir version of Navajo sand painting of yei, purchased in Sedona, Arizona, 1984; souvenir version of Hopi badger kachina, purchased at Grand Canyon in 1984. Courtesy Ed and Paul Senne. Photo author.

objets d'art, as genuine artifacts, as high-grade simulacra, and as inexpensive tourists' souvenirs. In fact, many are made and sold by Native American artists or artisans, available on the internet no less than at reservations, national parks, and in tourist shops along interstate highways throughout the West and southwest. The cultural fields in which these objects are variously produced and consumed are complex and overlapping, and merit nuanced analysis. Kachina dolls were originally part of the annual liturgy of Hopi rituals involving crops and weather, representing the spiritual being impersonated and invoked by men who danced in the rituals. They gave small effigies of the supernatural power they impersonated to women and children, who displayed them in their pueblo homes. When Hopi makers of the figures learned that ethnographers and collectors would pay for them, a new market emerged.[36] The image reproduced here, purchased for $7.00 at the Grand Canyon in 1984, loosely stylizes the features of the badger kachina doll.

A very helpful example of how the variety of objects and their production is to be approached is Nancy Parezo's *Navajo Sand Painting: From Religious Act to Commercial Art* (1983), in which the author charts the historical development from the Navajo ritual production of sand images to the creation and spectacular rise of sand painting as a commercial enterprise valued by tourists as well as collectors. Parezo demonstrates how an ancient ceremony, dedicated to healing, protection, and purification in the indigenous community, became a visual commodity. Because the primal powers of creation were summoned in the substance of the particular colors and the imagery in the ritual making of the sand image, the Navajo sand painting could not be allowed to remain intact.[37] Doing so might result in harm to anyone who was unaware of the image's power. The person undergoing treatment actually sits on the sand image to receive its benefit. Other participants in the ritual may apply some of the sand to themselves before leaving in order to acquire its beneficial effect. The very substance of the consecrated sand is charged with power that drawing the images of the supernatural figures brings to the whole. Partially erased in the process of its ritual use, the remaining imagery is fully effaced at the end of the rite as a precautionary iconoclasm.

Not surprisingly, since it was not intended to be permanent, the Navajo sand painting as work of art, that is, as an enduring object intended for aesthetic contemplation, not spiritual use, violated the traditional taboo against leaving the imagery even partially intact. Yet the demand from collectors and the promise of significant income (performers of the traditional rite were and are still rewarded with money for their curative services) pressed native makers to pursue permanent forms of the imagery – colored sands glued to a surface, jewelry, and weavings. The Navajo weavers and sand image makers accommodated tradition and demand by modifying or omitting features of the images they made on "the belief that completeness and accuracy were the crucial factors in the sanctification of sand paintings."[38] Deprived of the right details, the images were rendered impotent and therefore safe for commodification and public display. Navajo tradition was preserved and a lucrative form of income secured. The result was an industry in sand paintings like the one in Figure 72. The image employs the visual vocabulary of the yei, or divine figures, portrayed as masked dancers – in this case a female yei, as indicated by the rectangular shape of the mask. The image was produced by a Native woman named Gloria, and was purchased in Sedona, Arizona, in 1984 for $4.00.

Many Native Americans today continue to experience what they describe as cultural genocide, living in a constant state of siege that takes the form of legacies of alcoholism, poverty, and economic exploitation as well as more subtle cultural manifestations of an ongoing state of colonialism. This will seem a radical or "political" assertion to some, but the case has been so articulately made by many Native Americans, especially with reference to the material and visual culture of religion, that it bears consideration here. The Native American critique of the wholesale appropriation of Native artifacts exposes not only the plight of Indians in the Anglo ideology of national wilderness, but also the widespread appropriation of Native culture by more recent spiritualities in the United States.

In a widely quoted article Native American poet and anthropologist Wendy Rose focused on the cultural incursions of "whiteshamans," or non-Indians who purport to speak "in the guise of an American Indian medicine man."[39] Rose and other Native American critics such as Vine Deloria, Jr. contend that popular books including Carlos Castaneda's bestselling *Teachings of Don Juan* (1968) and Lynn Andrews' *Medicine Woman* (1981) have displaced genuine Native American voices by offering sensational but bogus accounts of vision quest, shamanic rituals, dreaming, and mystical learning from Native teachers. The danger posed to Native Americans, Rose and others argue, is the neo-colonial continuation of the pilfering of Native culture and history conducted by Whites since first contact with indigenous peoples in the Americas. Moreover, "most whiteshamans," many of them trafficking in the vast market-place of New Age books, tapes, retreats, and lecturing, "have demonstrated a profound ignorance of the very traditions they are trying to imitate or subsume."[40] Indeed, their very purpose seems to be to appropriate the rites and symbols of Native culture in fabricating "their own myths" as an avenue to lucrative non-Indian interest in self-help, therapeutic spirituality.

If, as Philip Deloria pointed out, New Age arose in the 1970s and 1980s as "a movement for an aging counterculture," producing what another scholar of religion has called "a generation of seekers," it is a movement and a cohort of participants that have thrived on consumption as an essential aspect, arguably even parts of their spiritual quest.[41] Deloria echoes Rose's key point about the whiteshaman's fascination with inventing personal mythology. New Age participants commonly understand spirituality as an individual quest, a creative search deliberately unhitched from social and religious institutions, indeed often occurring after church or synagogue of one's early years seems to fail to address an abiding sense of emptiness or despair. The quest takes the form of transgressing the cultural boundaries that come to appear identical with conventional social life or with traditional religions of the Western dominant culture – Jewish and Christian belief. Lynn Andrews' novelistic account of her tutelage under a Cree medicine woman named Agnes Whistling Elk is a paradigm of personal mythologizing and questing. Leaving her cosmopolitan world of art collecting and high society literati in Los Angeles at the encouragement of real-life guru and author, Hyemeyohsts Storm, Lynn travels to a Cree reservation in Canada, driven by a dream and the mysterious vision of an Indian artifact, a marriage basket. Her first impulse is to acquire the basket for her collection. But upon apprenticing to the medicine woman, a larger quest unfolds.

The mixing and matching and fictionalizing of Andrews' tale is apparent as she relates a conversation with Agnes. One day, sitting on the reclining seeker's chest, the Cree medicine woman rolls a cigarette from a medicine pouch and gives it to her apprentice to smoke while she encourages her to find in her dreams "the guarded [Pueblo] kivas where you have hidden your heart."[42] The intermixture of distinct Native traditions throughout the novel was likely missed by many non-Indian readers and is typical of New Age syncretistic practice since the common feature and driving force of ritual and storytelling is the person seeking illumination. Hyemeyohsts Storm had introduced her to the Cheyenne medicine wheel, which is a place to perform rituals, especially during the summer solstice among some modern Plains Indian groups. To Cree, Pueblo, and Cheyenne beliefs, Agnes added the wisdom of the therapeutic, self-questing syncretism of New Age:

> Dream your passion. Fly away. Go through the hoop of your innermost fears and desires. Meet them and conquer them. Come through your own reflection and be free of Red Dog [the malevolent sorcerer who possesses the marriage basket that Lynn seeks to steal from him to complete a mystical rite of passage].[43]

She encounters Red Dog when he appears in her dreams as a fierce Hopi kachina amidst visions of Mayan temples!

Andrews' technique of appropriation is hardly unique. Indeed, it was already at work in Longfellow's intermingling of stories from many different Indian traditions as he found them in Schoolcroft's collection. But even wilder borrowings and retelling is evident in latter-day entertainment. The mixture of elements is also at work in George Lucas' *Star Wars* epic, deeply inspired by Joseph Campbell's Jungian reading of world mythology. The quest for personal consciousness familiar in the many Indian gurus who came to the United States beginning in the 1960s recalls in particular Luke's apprenticeship to the Jedi master, Yoda, as the student prepares to face his evil nemesis, Darth Vader. The taste for this kind of laundry list mythology in the present day is virtually limitless and comports very well with the ultimately Idealist epistemology of modern spirituality from Transcendentalism and New Thought in the nineteenth century to New Age and Neo-Paganism in the twentieth and twenty-first centuries. Whether it is Emerson or Mary Baker Eddy, Pentecostal faith healers or scientologist Tom Cruise railing against the use of pharmaceuticals to treat psychological disorders, the conviction that the mind or faith in God overcomes physical reality is a firm conviction among many Americans. The emphasis of mind or spirit over matter certainly appeals to the self-help industry since regarding the self as each individual's personal work in progress invites new therapies, diets, techniques, and an unceasing stream of products that promise self-empowerment. The belief that reality is accessible only as a projection of ideas, feelings, or perceptions also accounts for the avid reception of Hindu and Buddhist practices from yoga and Transcendental Meditation to weekend meditation retreats at Buddhist centers and the voracious American appetite for books on Zen.[44]

The ambivalence of images

The power of images to trump material reality by shaping perception is apparent in many different religious traditions, and is not simply an invention of the highly personalized therapeutic consumerism of New Age. Santeria is an Afro-Caribbean religious practice that incorporates imagery from several religions (Figure 73) to invoke the power of spirits or Orishas to protect, heal, or bless. Santeria is known for its wide appropriation of figures from other religions, including Buddhism, Hinduism, and Christianity. A Native American shaman in Figure 73 demonstrates yet another instance of the diffusion of Native American culture. Images facilitate the practice of Santeria and Voodoo, among other related practices, by performing symbolic action, acting as a kind of analog system for acting at a distance. The visual language of Santeria relies on images, vestments, and other material forms to interface with invisible realms. Metaphor prevails in a liturgy that takes on a life of its own. Nothing is simply what it appears to be, but is connected to something else that it evokes or suggests. The power of images is precisely their ambivalence. Physical features correspond to the powers of the unseen, operating with a logic of association activated by need and ritual incantation conducted by an adept.

Because the mind is considered by many religious seekers in the United States as the organizing principle of reality, images and ideas become its extension, serving as figurations that can be doffed and donned as needed. A visual and intellectual economy of free trade emerges in the cultural marketplace that encourages a robust traffic in ideas that are exchanged for their value to reconfigure the self or mind. The result is a skimming of images as an exportable surface that recalls Oliver Wendell Holmes' discussion in 1859 of photography as sun-engraved currency. In order to expedite the formation of public and private collections of stereographic images, Holmes had urged "a comprehensive system of exchanges" that would foster an economy of images, "something

Figure 73 Camilo José Vergara, photographer, Elizabeth Valentin's bedroom with Santeria objects, Longwood Avenue, Bronx, NY, 1991. Courtesy of the photographer.

like a universal currency of these bank-notes, or promises to pay in solid substance, which the sun has engraved for the great Bank of Nature."[45] Mass reproduction encourages the abstraction of imagery from its concrete setting. Image, song, dance, poetry and other art forms facilitate appropriation because they detach motifs from one cultural setting and transpose them to a new context to be reenchanted as part of a new way of seeing or feeling. The ambivalence of images accommodates this migration of motif and reassignment of meaning. Tarot cards are among the most familiar uses of ambivalent images drawn from a wide variety of iconographical sources to create a system of visual suggestion. Christian, Roman, Greek, Babylonian, and Egyptian symbols are appropriated and incorporated into a set of pliant meanings that are successively read in registers keyed to the client's past, present, and future. A tarot reading unfolds as a succession of cards that enables an interactive narrative between reader and client. The elasticity of the imagery facilitates the cumulative narration of the cards as touchstones, triggers to association. A modern guide to popular use of tarot points out that tarot today is a "mirror," which "implies that personal insight plays a major role in the process" of a reading.[46] Far from operating as a rigid code of meanings to be applied uniformly, reading tarot cards for oneself stresses the role of the individual. For all of its arcane baggage, modern tarot is an occult version of modern psychotherapy's use of Rorschach ink-blots. Many techniques used in New Age spirituality such as tarot, astrology, and reading tea leaves are forms of divination that assist a person in achieving distance from himself or herself in order to renarrate the self. Ritualized uses of imagery performing as oracles enable people to transcend one story and find themselves in another. Practitioners do not consider the practice to be an unethical appropriation of another culture since the mind is more real than anything and all cultures are its manifestation.

The occult power of images pivots on their fascinating operation as ciphers, as symbols whose meanings must be puzzled out. Dan Brown's blockbuster novel *The Da Vinci Code* (2003), relied on this understanding of images, transforming Leonardo's fresco of *The Last Supper* into an arcane puzzle whose interpretation might appear certain to those dazzled by the author's facile invocation of arcana. Comparable uses of esoteric signification are found in the storm of conspiracy literature that lines shelves in popular bookstores. Whether it is books like *The Secret Symbols of the Dollar Bill*, which purports to show the multitude of "hidden magic and meaning" in American currency or the Christian Fundamentalist charts that construe figures in certain books of the Hebrew and Christian bibles as disclosing the date of the end of the world (see Figure 27, p. 90) or the esoteric imagery of Masonic charts (see Figure 26, p. 88), the hermeneutic of occult meaning gravitates toward emblems, images, and symbols precisely because of their alluring polyvalence.[47] Things are not what they seem, but, to quote the slogan of the television classic, *The X-Files*, the answers one seeks are out there, concealed by those who do not want the innocent to know. The lure of such images is the prospect of breaking their code to discover what they hide. This was also the message and fascination of *The Matrix* series, which self-consciously indulged viewers in a wildly syncretistic mesh of Buddhist, Gnostic, Platonic, and biblical motifs that hooked viewers in a game of allusion and decipherment. Various mythic and religious elements operated as tags, or clues, inviting the viewer to assemble them into a coherent but unconventional interpretation. Neo, a messianic computer geek, hacks his way through the wall of illusory appearances in search of the real world concealed behind the lies of a secretive state apparatus. He is Buddha, Bodhisattva, Socrates, and Jesus since they are all versions of one another, grist in the spiritual mysteries mill.

The quest for the self on which Neo is engaged in his attempt to break free of the mental restraints imposed by the matrix is taken up in a feature-length, compact disc tract promoting the perspective of New Age's keen interest in post-Newtonian science, quantum physics, *What the Bleep Do We Know?* (2004). The film seeks to combine the common New Age claim for universal human divinity with a radically subjectivist epistemology bolstered by a speculative science, or scientism, that supports the insights garnered by "sudden transformational experiences" known simply as "quantum."[48] In a series of personal appearances, the film's producers and writers speak with audiences about the spiritual significance of creative thinking. "You create your reality," states producer William Arntz. "Thought alone can change the body," announces one of the many talking heads interviewed in the film. Because thought controls the body, the task is to take control of thought rather than being controlled by it in the form of cultural conventions that construct our perception of reality. Overcoming the limits placed on one's thought is the therapeutic, spiritual task confronting the seeker. The film exemplifies the signature intertextuality of New Age thought when one speaker states "in fact, reality is like *The Matrix* – we make reality by repeating it, by locking in one paradigm." Christianity is one of those mind-forged manacles. The producers and speakers in the film repeatedly identify strait-jacketed Christians as critics of the quantum way of thinking.

By endorsing what Philip Deloria has observed is a postmodernist playful borrowing and performing of Indianness, New Age adherents indulge what amounts to a neo-colonial appropriation of Indian culture. Raiding its artifacts and practices in the interest of personal self-realization is made easy by reading books and periodicals, viewing films and videos, or attending lectures or weekend retreats. One Native writer notes that many

> non-Native Americans seem to feel an entitlement regarding Native American ceremonial and cultural traditions, artifacts, and gravesites, including ancestral bones, that can only be understood in the context of the original entitlement the first colonizers felt toward this land by "right of conquest" and soon after, "Manifest Destiny."[49]

Lakota and scholar Vine Deloria, Jr. registered the objection of many fellow Indians to the "wholesale appropriation of Indian rituals, symbols, and beliefs" by the host of "luminaries," including Lynn Andrews, who crowd "the New Age-Indian medicine man circuit."[50] The print and media available in book stores, by mail order, and now online make borrowing much easier because the seeker is freed from the inconvenience of time-consuming travel and research.

To be sure, many of the authors and speakers providing access to Native American belief and practice are Indians themselves. In 1992, Vine Deloria published an essay on the appropriation of sun dance, sweat lodge, and sacred pipe by non-Indians, and laid part of the blame on his own people – "Sioux Indians and their intense desire to act as hosts for the wide variety of people who beat their way to the Pine Ridge and Rosebud reservations." He wondered if "a clear statement by traditional people . . . and a disavowal of authorization for people outside the respective tribal traditions to perform [the sun dance] is in order."[51] In the following year an assembly of Canadian and American Lakota, Dakota, and Nakota nations officially endorsed a statement signed by three Lakota leaders and entitled "Declaration of War Against Exploiters of Lakota Spirituality."[52] One of the resolutions of the document was "to prevent our own people from contributing to and enabling the abuse of our sacred ceremonies and spiritual practices by outsiders." The declaration directed itself at the "expropriation" of Native culture, especially "individuals and groups involved in 'the New Age Movement,' in 'the men's movement,' in 'neo-paganism' cults and in 'shamanism' workshops" that "have exploited the spiritual traditions of our Lakota people by imitating our ceremonial ways and by mixing such imitation rituals with non-Indian occult practices in an offensive and harmful pseudo-religious hodgepodge." The declaration lamented the desecration of the Sacred Pipe "through the sale of pipestone pipes at flea markets, powwows, and 'New Age' retail stores."

Media were part of the lament, too. The Declaration deplored the way in which

> the television and film industry continues to saturate the entertainment media with vulgar, sensationalist and grossly distorted representations of Lakota spirituality and culture which reinforce the public's negative stereotyping of Indian people and which gravely impair the self-esteem of our children.

Yet media are also talismans to be used to the opposite end, as a way to heighten Native American identity by enhancing the experience of community and conveying knowledge of ritual and practice. Steven Leuthold has studied the role of documentary videos among Native Americans, a form of media produced by Native Americans for members of the community and dedicated to documenting, preserving, and revitalizing the heritage and sense of community.[53] Leuthold points out that Indians themselves argue for the historical importance of visual images from ancient petraglyphs to modern photographs. Leuthold stresses that the concern among Native Americans is to maintain control over visual representations, which brings to mind the efforts of Christian clergy at the opening of the twentieth century at ensuring wholesome films for public consumption. By maintaining a communal gaze on their culture, viewed in the home and together on other occasions, Native groups will preserve it as a living community and tradition.

The Lakota Declaration indicates the reason why vigilance is necessary: the long history of negative stereotypes in film, television, novels, and popular culture from cigar store Indians to professional sports mascots presents views of Indian culture that tacitly or even explicitly promote its subjugation or extinction. Even films with characters as sympathetic as the Indians in Michael Mann's *The Last of the Mohicans* (1993) are instances of conventions that nod to the inevitability of the vanishing Indian. Loosely based on James Fenimore Cooper's (1826) novel of the same name, *The Last of the Mohicans* narrates the beginning of the end for Native Americans as a prelude to the American Revolution. By pitting Hawkeye, the white adopted son of Chingachgook, the last Mohican, against a snobbish British colonel who is the rival for Hawkeye's love interest, Cora, Mann's film underscores racial difference. Hawkeye's Indian brother, who falls in love with Cora's sister, dies after she does, trying to save her. Afterward, Hawkeye and Cora join Chingachgook on the peak of a mountain to remember the lost Indian son and brother. They mourn, looking out over a majestic landscape. But the camera dwells on the white couple whose salvation is their romance, an American Adam and Eve in a natural paradise, the future nation of America. This scene closes the epic film in which Indians murder one another in order for white Americans to claim liberty from the French, but also to foreshadow revolutionary victory over the British. Mann's script considerably modified Cooper's story. Cooper had drawn on the life and lore of Daniel Boone to portray Hawkeye, or Natty Bumppo. In the film, Boone is morphed into a foster child and ally of Indians rather than their fearsome opponent. The film's Hawkeye is antagonistic to British rule, regarding himself as subject to none but himself. Like the novel, however, the film violently pits one Indian group against another and hails as hero the white "Indian" who saves the innocent Cora from ritual slaughter.[54]

From Emerson to contemporary New Age the concern to define nature appears to proceed from one of a few motives. First, Americans have yearned in religious terms for a direct experience of selfhood when they have suffered the press of identity crisis, which they have widely expressed in terms of alienation, victimization, and impotence. Whether it was Emerson's longing to throw off the shackles of tradition, in particular the restraints of institutional Christianity, or the purist ideal of Utopian communities, or Robert Bly's prevailing sense of the obsolescence of contemporary images of manhood, the pursuit of nature meant discovering the real self or a primordial form of communal self in fellowship with others seeking selfhood. Like Protestantism's historical and ongoing campaign to return *ad fontes* to the apostolic age's pure reception of the gospel of Jesus Christ that had been lost to medieval accretions and ecclesiastical impurity, modern American questing often takes the form of transcending the corruption by recovering the original nature of gender, self, or society.

American nationhood and landscapes of redemption

Geography is an unavoidable element in any definition of nationhood. While the actual borders of a nation may be unstable, offering occasions for cultural and even military conflict, citizens commonly imagine their collective identity by seeing its material expression in the features of a terrain. Landscape is more than physical dimensions – it is the boundary of a larger self. If king, language, or a religious polity such as "Christendom" served as the pivot around which peoples orbited in eras before modernity, the modern nation-state relies on forms of collective imagination, among which landscape – in painting, song, and story as well as national parks and roadside scenery – serves as an enduring deposit of national destiny.[55] Landscape roots imagination in time and place, provides the meeting point of past and present, divine and mortal. It is among the most pervasive and most powerful forms of national mythology and imagined community since landscape combines the mundane and the dramatic in a single range of common experience. For many Americans, mountains, oceans, and forests bear the imprint and intent of divinity while farm and land ownership secure the material base for individuality, citizenship, and liberty. The American landscape is also infused with collective memory – the heroic stories of battles, discoveries, adventures, courage, and leadership that children learn in schoolrooms as the basis for imagining their national community, their shared identity as American citizens.

The significance of images of nature for Americans as different as Mormons, Buddhists, and Evangelical Christians is that they operate as a kind of external scaffolding for the imaginative construction of a place that tells people who they are as believers. The epic narrative of the Book of Mormon gives an important place to wilderness – in the first instance, the Judean wilderness into which the patriarch Lehi leads his family at the Lord's behest. He left Jerusalem under the duress of having prophesied the destruction of the city and the coming of the messiah, which did not endear him to his fellow Israelites. In the wilderness for eight years, the group experienced great blessings such that the sojourn was presented by Lehi's son, Nephi, as an enduring example.[56] But the more dramatic wilderness of Mormon belief is the uninhabited continent of the new world first colonized by the patriarch about the year 589 BC.

The Lord instructed Nephi to build a ship, which he did, though not without suffering the same mockery that Noah had endured. Mormon artist Minerva Teichert illustrated the provisioning of the ship in a painting of 1935 (Figure 74). Poised in scaffolding, the ship awaits launching as its sails already fill with the air that would drive them "towards the promised land" (1 Nephi 18: 8). When the vessel was completed, Nephi and his family sailed under divine guidance to the Western hemisphere, where they "went forth upon the land, and did pitch our tents; and we did call it the promised land" (1 Nephi 18: 23). Once ashore, they planted the seed they had brought and found "all manner of wild animals, which were for the use of men." In addition to wildlife, they found something more important for Mormon history: "we did find all manner of ore, both of gold, and of silver, and of copper" (18: 25). From this material Nephi fashioned metal plates and set down on them in the language of Egypt "the record of my people" (19: 1). It was these plates and Nephi's prophetic visions recorded by his son, Lehi, that connected the ancient American colony to the world of the Latter-Day Saints. Foreseeing "a land of liberty," "a land which is choice above all other lands; a land which the Lord God hath covenanted with me should be a land for the inheritance of my seed" (2 Nephi 1: 5), Nephi charted out a long future that would culminate in the founding of the Mormon Church.

Figure 74 Minerva K. Teichert, *Loading the Ship*, oil on panel, 1935. Courtesy of Brigham Young University Museum of Art. All rights reserved.

Five hundred years later the ancient chapters of the epic come to an end with Moroni, the righteous and last descendant of Nephi. Not long after arriving in the New World, the sons of Laman (a son of Nephi), or Lamanites, had rebelled and were cursed by God, the outward sign of which was a "blackness of skin" (2 Nephi 5: 21–23). At the end of Moroni's life, his people were hunted down and slaughtered by the Lamanites. According to church teaching, the Lamanites were the ancestors of modern Native Americans, who would in later days be reconciled with the sons of Nephi and become white once again (3 Nephi 2: 14–16). Minerva Teichert dramatically portrayed the *Last Battle between Nephites and Lamanites* (Figure 75) as a galloping rout of the righteous beneath the mounted sons of Laman, who bear the dress and weaponry of nineteenth-century Plains Indians. Facing the end of his line with stoic determination, Moroni completed the ancient account with his own additions and then buries the plates: "I will write and hide up the records in the earth; and whither I go it mattereth not" (Mormon 8: 4). But Moroni did not exit the stage just yet. In the new age of antebellum America he returned, appearing to Joseph Smith in 1823 to show him the location of the buried records. A new dispensation in the sacred history of the American wilderness and the violent suffering of the saints it hosted was shortly to follow.[57]

Figure 75 Minerva K. Teichert, *Last Battle between Nephites and Lamanites*, oil on panel, 1935. Courtesy of Brigham Young University Museum of Art. All rights reserved.

If Mormonism presents a religion born on American soil, it is handily pre-dated by Zen Buddhist and poet Gary Snyder's "Smokey the Bear Sutra" (1969), which recounts the sermon of the Great Sun Buddha during the Jurassic Period, 150 million years ago, when the Buddha (an early predecessor of Siddartha Gautama, the Buddha of the current age) foresaw

> . . . a continent called
> America. It will have great centers of power called
> such as Pyramid Lake, Walden Pond, Mt. Rainier, Big Sur,
> Everglades, and so forth; and power nerves and channels
> such as Columbia River, Mississippi River, and Grand Canyon.
> The human race in that era will get into troubles all over
> its head, and practically wreck everything in spite of
> its own strong intelligent Buddha-nature.

The Great Sun Buddha said that he would enter a new form in that time "to cure the world of loveless knowledge." That form would be Smokey the Bear.

Wrathful but Calm. Austere but Comic. Smokey the Bear will
Illuminate those who would help him; but for those who would hinder or
   slander him,
HE WILL PUT THEM OUT.[58]

With a degree of humor characteristic of some Zen practitioners and masters, Snyder redeploys the National Forest Administration's mascot, Smokey the Bear, a television and poster cartoon character who urged a generation of American youth to help prevent forest fires by exercising care during campouts and hikes. Keenly interested in the idea of the wild, Snyder argued in many essays and poems for the recovery of experiencing the land as alive and sacred. He invited his readers to seek the knowledge of the "paysan," or people of the land, that was rooted out or repressed by the city-dwelling cultures of religion and science and industry. "The world is watching," he proclaimed in one essay,

> one cannot walk through a meadow or forest without a ripple of report spreading out from one's passage. The thrush darts back, the jay squalls, a beetle scuttles under the grasses, and the signal is passed along. Every creature knows when a hawk is cruising or a human strolling. The information passed through the system is intelligence.[59]

Snyder regarded nature as a form of consciousness, an animate reality the knowledge of which, as a way of being in the world, has been repeatedly forgotten in the ancient world, the medieval world, and in the modern world's oppression of Native American culture. He urged his contemporaries to attend to "the worldview of primitive peoples," especially the Native American legacy that he admired, in order to learn what Western culture had eclipsed by alienating itself "from the wilderness outside (that is to say, wild nature, the wild, self-contained, self-informing ecosystems) and from that other wilderness, the wilderness within."[60] Moreover, Buddhism, he believed, held the way to recover the sense of "mutual interdependence" practiced by life in the wild. The peaceful nature of Smokey, who walks upright, dressed in denim jeans and a ranger's hat, represents what the ancient Buddha prophesied would be "the age of harmony of man and nature," though Smokey's way would not be entirely pacifist since he would undertake, in fine millennial fashion, the "smashing [of] the worms of capitalism and totalitarianism."[61] If Smokey the Bear represents a secular totem of the national parks and monuments that were once the dominion of Native Americans, such as Yellowstone, the Black Hills, and Yosemite, Snyder wishes to suggest that he marks the iconic return of an animated nature that speaks wisely to human beings, teaching them how to respect the land.

Evangelical Christians have found in the enormously popular pictures of Thomas Kinkade a fond affirmation of the American nature they recognize as providentially blessed. The wide appeal of his landscape imagery owes much to

Kinkade's ability to intermingle piety with national pride by envisioning landscapes that are glorious and inviting, magnificent and intimate. Where Cole warned his contemporaries with Evangelical zeal, threatening divine retribution in *Course of Empire* or the ominous moments of *Voyage of Life* (see Figure 68, p. 233), Kinkade charts a different path through the American imaginary. His version of the national landscape prefers the flush of patriotic celebration to the gloom of prophetic lament. Kinkade's pictorial hymns vouch for the possibility of reclaiming what remains for a large number of American Christians a divinely insured national trust. The commercial success of his imagery depends on his keen insight into popular taste and his ambitious marketing. But the history of mass-produced and mass-marketed religious imagery noted in previous chapters also constitutes an additional framework for understanding the production, distribution, and reception of Kinkade's work. The religious imagery produced by Currier & Ives, the Providence Lithography Company, and Warner Sallman clearly anticipated the national market for mass-produced images among pious consumers. On the acknowledged model of Currier & Ives and Norman Rockwell, Kinkade issued a number of prints in the 1990s that celebrate the country dwelling as well as the small town as the cherished location of domestic values, the origin of American identity, and the womb of family tradition. Kinkade has straddled the landscape tradition of the sublime, represented by Thomas Cole and Albert Bierstadt in the nineteenth century and Ansel Adams in the twentieth, and the Protestant desire to read clearly legible pious symbols and emblems, which the artist embeds in his landscapes. "The natural world," Kinkade has commented, "is rich with allegories of profound spiritual truth."[62] Whole series of coastal scenes from the mid-1990s commonly pair Kinkade's favorite motif, the country cottage with gabled, slate-shingled roof and stone walls, with a rocky shore and a sturdy lighthouse rising into a sunset sky to achieve what the artist regards as "an allegory of faith," "a symbolic scene charged with a joyous message."[63]

In the signature painting entitled *Warmth of Home*, for example, which was first published in 1994, Kinkade offers viewers the subject that is as endearing to the artist as it to his many admirers: a "wilderness cabin," as he calls it, nestled in a snowy landscape over which looms a luminous, snow-covered mountain resembling Mt. Rainier in Washington.[64] The day is ending as a figure dressed in a red coat – in which the artist has depicted himself in several of his paintings – holds a lantern as he approaches the cabin, whose windows glow with the incandescent color that they do in virtually all of Kinkade's paintings since the 1990s. The figure appears to be returning home, perhaps after visiting one of the cabins glimpsed in the distance, along the thin ribbon of a pathway that vanishes in the middle distance. In this fond vision of America, every person has a home, set comfortably apart but gathered into a happy community resting quietly beneath the majestic countenance of the mountain. This rural idyll promotes a certain concept of "wilderness." By no means an uninhabited wild, the landscape's wilderness appears to mean something far more benevolent: the soothing and abiding proximity of divine goodness. Like all of Kinkade's landscapes, this picture is about a reassuring relationship between God and Americans, sung in the restful tones of a vespers hymn. Wilderness here denotes a providential nature which belongs to the New Israel. The green foothills part reverently before the central mountain, which the evening clouds encircle in a vignette that allows the eye to rest nowhere but on the monumental presence of this American Mt. Sinai. If there were any doubt about a Christian reading of his pictures, the artist is careful to sign each with an iconic scripture reference: John 3: 16.

Conclusion

Kinkade offers Americans a beguiling vision. Those who respond appreciatively prefer the imagery as a model for transfiguring the world around them. They acquire in the print reproductions of his paintings enchanting conjurations that match their idea of nationhood – the way America ought to be, the landscape of divine intent hanging fondly on their living room walls. Sometimes the lure of images resides in their capacity to conceal what would otherwise disillusion. Thomas Cole or Ansel Adams or Daniel Boorstin might accuse Kinkade of dissemblance or sentimentalism. What most of his detractors really object to, however, is the power of his pictures over those who admire them. If so, the best they might hope for is a counter lure, an alternative visual appeal. The lure of images is also their capacity to transcend the prison house of the ordinary, the conventional, or the tradition-bound. Images sometimes allow people to see their way toward new possibilities of self, community, or nationhood. That is certainly why northern abolitionists circulated images of outrageous cruelty toward slaves (see Figure 15, p. 56) or why immigrants visualized religious practice taking root in the novel setting of the new world (see Figures 12, 38 and 39, pp. 51, 130 and 133). Images may take hold of the future by renovating the past, as in the case of Fred Carter's black Christ (see Figures 29 and 66, pp. 102 and 223), who is the same, but different, or by radically re-visioning it, as in the millennial chart of Millerism, which foretold the sudden end of everything familiar (see Figure 27, p. 90), or by re-tasking an image to mean something altogether new like Smokey the Bear as Buddha. The lure of images resides not only in their promise of continuity or renewal, but also in transformation. In every case, the lure answers to a deep longing, which it is the undying business of religious belief to engage.

One evening in search of a shower nozzle at a local home improvement store, I happened across rows of buddhas molded in resin or ceramic, lining a shelf in the garden department. At first it struck me as incongruous: why, I wondered, do American consumers spend a few dollars to place mass-produced, orna-mental versions of an Asian deity in their back yards? The answer no doubt has to do with the history of gardens and the decorative arts, from Wedgwood to Japonisme, with how Orientalism and the occidental imagination have long fueled the consumption of imported luxury goods and their inexpensive imitations. Without rehearsing that history, it seems clear that in the very bosom of consumption resides the quest for release – if not from what Buddhists and Hindus consider the grueling cycle of rebirth, then at least from what Americans call "the grind." Not that Buddha would have approved. To the contrary. He would have said consumption only begets more consumption; the desire to possess only leads to more desire, and therefore to greater suffering. But most Americans probably are not interested in the regimen of ascetic self-denial that Buddha counseled. Still, if the inexpensive effigies are not the enlightened sage from northern India to most of the Americans who buy them, the polished, glistening busts and figures nevertheless offer a less demanding relief. Owning them may tender an exotic accent that helps make the American back yard a suburban refuge. The impassive gaze and knotted hair, the distended ears and shiny smallness of the contemplative images endow hedges and flowerbeds with a striking touch, one that contributes to the blissful distance that deck chairs, cocktails, and weekends deliver as a welcome haven from the cycle of weekly labor. It will not save their souls or detach them from the tight grip of craving, but sitting in the garden may at least reassure American consumers that toil is not or should not be the sum of their comfortable, yet restless lives. The lure of images is bound up with the stubborn quest for something better. However fragmented it may be in the labyrinthine refractions of want and fear, this something smiles if dimly even in the plastic cast of a god unknown.

Notes

1 The aura of print

1 Harlow Giles Unger, *Noah Webster: The Life and Times of an American Patriot* (New York: John Wiley & Sons, 1998), 45–54.
2 Noah Webster, *A Compendious Dictionary of the English Language: A Facsimile of the First (1806) Edition* (New York: Bounty Books, 1970).
3 As he wrote to Carey on March 11, 1822:

> If we can't get the Fair & Flush now in their teens to read the Bible & imbibe the spirit of Christian, i.e. Republican Simplicity, frugality, Honesty, Industry, & all such virtues that make men love one another we shall soon be a divided & a Ruined People.

Emily Ellsworth Ford Skeel, ed., *Mason Locke Weems: His Works and Ways in Three Volumes. Letters 1784–1825*, 3 vols (New York: privately published, 1929), vol. 3, 340.
4 Letter to Carey, received July 26, 1811, ibid., vol. 3, 52.
5 Paul C. Gutjahr, *An American Bible: A History of the Good Book in the United States, 1777–1880* (Stanford, CA: Stanford University Press, 1999), 20–21. For a good overview of American bible production see David Daniel, *The Bible in English: Its History and Influence* (New Haven, CT: Yale University Press, 2003), 590–658.
6 Caleb Bingham, *The Columbian Orator*, ed. David W. Blight (New York: New York University Press, 1998), 28.
7 Ibid., 261; see Michael Warner, *The Letters of the Republic: Publication and the Public Sphere in Eighteenth-Century America* (Cambridge, MA: Harvard University Press, 1990); Christopher Looby, *Voicing America: Language, Literary Form, and the Origins of the United States* (Chicago, IL: University of Chicago Press, 1996), 224–29; and Kenneth Cmiel, *Democratic Eloquence: The Fight over Popular Speech in Nineteenth-Century America* (New York: William Morrow, 1990), 39–49.
8 Bingham, *Columbian Orator*, 8.
9 Ibid., 15.
10 For a discussion of Rothermel's painting and reproductions of it, see Gail E. Husch, *Something Coming: Apocalyptic Expectation and Mid-Nineteenth-Century American Painting* (Hanover, NH: University Press of New England, 2000), 144–49.
11 See, for example, the image of Christ's Sermon on the Mount in John Fleetwood, *The Life of Christ* (New York: Virtue and Yorkston, n.d. [ca. 1861]), frontispiece of part 5; reproduced and discussed, along with the image of the printing press, in David Morgan, *Protestants and Pictures: Religion, Visual Culture, and the Age of American Mass Production* (New York: Oxford University Press, 1999), 26–28.

12 *The Third Annual Report of the Religious Tract Society of Baltimore* (Baltimore, MD: printed by William Warner, 1819), 10. This society became a branch of the ATS in 1826.

13 For a good overview of religion in the early national period, see Edwin S. Gaustad, *Neither King nor Prelate: Religion and the New Nation 1776–1826* (Grand Rapids, MI: Eerdmans, 1993).

14 David Bogue, *The Diffusion of Divine Truth: A Sermon Preached before the Religious Tract Society, on Lord's Day, May 18, 1800* (London: printed by S. Rousseau, Wood Street, Spa Fields, for the Religious Tract Society, and sold by T. Williams, 1800), 10.

15 Ibid., 11.

16 *An Address to Christians, Recommending the Distribution of Cheap Tracts: With an Extract from a Sermon by Bishop Porteus. Before the Yearly Meeting of the Charity Schools, London* (Charleston, MA: printed and sold by Samuel Etheridge, 1802), 3.

17 *The Publications of the Virginia Religious Tract Society* (Harrisonburg, VA: Davidson & Bourne, 1813), 11–24. The first annual meeting of the Society took place on October 30, 1812, when the Rev. Andrew B. Davidson, president of the Society, delivered a sermon entitled "The Necessity and Inducements to Do Good," 1–11. Davidson and the Rev. George Bourne, who served as secretary to the Society, were the publishers of the volume. The American reliance on British RTS material would remain the practice for tract societies in the United States over the next decade and more.

18 [David Bogue], *An Address to Christians, on the Distribution of Religious Tracts* (London: printed by P. Applegath and E. Cowper; and J. Nisbet [1799]), 3.

19 Ibid., 4.

20 "Address," *Publications of the Virginia RTS*, 5.

21 Andrew B. Davidson, "The Necessity and Inducement to Do Good: A Sermon, preached before the Virginia Religious Tract Society, October 30, 1812," *Publications of the Virginia RTS*, 2 [pagination in the volume begins again with Davidson's sermon].

22 For a discussion of the post-Puritan life of the American jeremiad, see Andrew R. Murphy, " 'One Nation Under God,' September 11 and the Chosen Nation: Moral Decline and Divine Punishment in American Public Discourse," *Political Theology* 6, no. 1 (2005), 9–30.

23 Davidson, "The Necessity and Inducement to Do Good," 2.

24 "Address," *Publications of the Virginia RTS*, 6.

25 Davidson, "The Necessity and Inducement to Do Good," 3.

26 *The American Tract Magazine [ATM]* 1, no. 1 (June 1824), 18.

27 For an authoritative and very instructive study of the technological, economic, and social history of the antebellum Evangelical print enterprise, especially the American Tract Society, see David Paul Nord, *Faith in Reading: Religious Publishing and the Birth of Mass Media in America* (New York: Oxford University Press, 2004).

28 Letter of February 11, 1834, from R. Baird, Augusta, to Frederick A. Packard, in Letters to Frederick A. Packard, 1829–1842, bound volume of unpublished letters in the Historical Society of Pennsylvania (HSP), Samuel C. Perkins Letters, 1829–1885.

29 Skeel, ed., *Mason Locke Weems*, letter to Carey, April 12, 1802, vol. 1, 233; for additional admonitions, see the letters to Carey of March 4, 1801, vol. 1, 175; April 7, 1802, vol. 1, 232, and April 26, 1802, vol. 1, 236.

30 Letter of October 14, 1800, ibid., vol. 1, 145.

31 Letter to Carey, February 15, 1816, ibid., vol. 3, 155.

32 "From a Mother in Fairfield County, Connecticut," *ATM* 1, no. 9 (October 1825), 213.

33 Autobiographical note, dated May 17, 1858, to Messrs. Childs and Peterson, 602 Arch Street, in the Historical Society of Pennsylvania. See also the preface to the first volume of James W. Alexander, *Forty Years' Familiar Letters*, ed. John Hall, 2 vols (New York: Charles Scribner, 1860), vol. 1, vii–viii.

34 See letters of December 18, 1840; July 12, 1841; and September 12, 1842. In a letter to Packard dated January 23, 1835, HSP, Alexander wrote: "If a good picture of any part of the lake Tiberias [in Palestine] can be got, I think I could cook up a decent article to match it."

35 Letter of February 11, 1840, from James W. Alexander to Frederick Packard, HSP.

36 On the Harper's Bible, see Gutjahr, *An American Bible*, 70–76.

37 Gutjahr, *An American Bible*, 71. The price did not include binding since the bible was issued in fifty-four parts at 25 cents each and binding was left to the customer.

38 Davidson, "The Necessity and Inducement to Do Good," 4.

39 Ibid., 7.

40 "Address," *Publications of the Virginia RTS*, 11.

41 Davidson, "The Necessity and Inducement to Do Good," 3.

42 *The Third Annual Report of the Religious Tract Society of Baltimore*, 7.

43 "African Female Auxiliary Tract Association of New-York City," *ATM* 2, no. 5 (February 1827), 114. Note that *ATM* became the publication of the American Tract Society in New York in 1825, when the Boston and New York tract societies merged to create the national organization. An authoritative study of women's benevolence groups and antebellum reform is Anne M. Boylan, *The Origins of Women's Activism: New York and Boston, 1797–1840* (Chapel Hill, NC: University of North Carolina Press, 2002).

44 Formation of the Female Branch of the New-York Religious Tract Society, pamphlet (1822), 4.

45 *Second Annual Report of the Religious Tract Society of the City of Washington* (Washington, DC: printed by Davis and Force, 1821), 8; *Fifteenth Annual Report of the Religious Tract Society of Baltimore* (Baltimore, MD: printed by John D. Toy, 1830), 21–28.

46 "To Female Friends of the American Tract Society," *ATM* 2, no. 2 (August 1826), 44.

47 *Female Influence and Obligations*, no. 226 (New York: Publications of the American Tract Society, [1842]), vol. 7, 393.

48 See Ann Braude, "Women's History *Is* American Religious History," in Thomas A. Tweed, ed., *Retelling U.S. Religious History* (Berkeley, CA: University of California Press, 1997), 88–92.

49 *Seventh Annual Report of the New England Tract Society* (Boston, MA: New England Tract Society, 1821), 10; *Fifteenth Annual Report of the Religious Tract Society of Baltimore*, 10.

50 Tract societies even regarded their annual reports as tracts in their own right, sometimes printing several thousand copies for distribution. See, for example, *The Third Annual Report of the Religious Tract Society of Baltimore*, an extra five thousand copies of which, along with the organization's constitution and the list of its subscribers, were printed "and circulated in the form of a Tract" (13).

51 *The Third Annual Report of the Religious Tract Society of Baltimore*, 8.

52 See "$80, For a Tract for New Settlements," *ATM* 1, no. 5 (February 1825), 115; *ATM* 1, no. 10 (December 1825), 237, and *ATM* 2, no. 5 (February 1826), 261; and "Time for Presenting Premium Tract on Christian Education Extended," *ATM* 2, no. 3 (October 1826), 91; "Award of Premium for Tract on Christian Education," *ATM* 2, no. 6 (April 1827), 138.

53 The colportage system has been carefully studied by Nord, *Faith in Reading*.

54 Rev. Mr. Malcolm, "Extracts from the Addresses before the American Tract Society," *ATM* 1, no. 9 (October 1825), 201.
55 *Utility of Religious Tracts*, no. 1 (New York: published by J. Emory and B. Waugh for the Tract Society of the Methodist Episcopal Church, n.d. [1826]), 1.
56 *ATM* 2, no. 8 (August 1827), 191.
57 "On Distributing Religious Tracts," *ATM* 1, no. 11 (February 1826), 283.
58 *Seventh Annual Report of the New England Tract Society*, 11.
59 "New York Religious Tract Society," *ATM* 1, no. 7 (June 1825), 165–66.
60 John S. J. Gardiner, "A Sermon Preached at Trinity-Church, Boston, before the Prayer-Book and Religious Tract Association, January 1, 1816" (Boston, MA: Munroe, Francis & Parker, Printers, 1816), 14, 22.
61 Quoted in an *American Tract Magazine* extra, December 1838, "Immediate Wants of the American Tract Society," pp. 5–6.
62 "How Tracts Were Successfully Used in a Revival of Religion," *ATM* 2, no. 9 (October 1827), 223.
63 *ATM* 1, no. 9 (October 1825), 201; "Appendix," *Third Annual Report of the Religious Tract Society of Baltimore*, 1819, 18.
64 "Use Made by a Missionary of a Single Tract," *ATM* 1, no. 7 (June 1825), 164.
65 "Usefulness of Tracts," no. 104, in *Tracts of the American Tract Society*, vol. 3 (New York: American Tract Society, n.d. [ca. 1826]), 3, 14–15.
66 Walter Benjamin, "The Work of Art in the Age of Mechanical Reproduction," in *Illuminations*, trans. Harry Zohn, ed. Hannah Arendt (New York: Schocken, 1968), 217–51. In the first edition of his book, *The Tourist* (1976), Dean MacCannell pointed out the fallacy of Benjamin's much repeated assertion, *The Tourist: A New Theory of the Leisure Class* (Berkeley, CA: University of California Press, 1999), 48.
67 *ATM* 1, no. 7 (June 1825), 165.
68 Rev. L. Ives Hoadly, "Extracts from Addresses at the Anniversary of the American Tract Society, Boston, May 25, 1825," *ATM* 1, no. 9 (October 1825), 205.
69 "Address of the Rev. Samuel Eastman," *ATM* 2, no. 7 (June 1827), 168.
70 "Colporteur Reports, Pennsylvania Branch," *Thirty-Sixth Annual Report* (New York: American Tract Society, 1861), 94.

2 Religious visual media and cultural conflict

1 *Fashionable Amusements*, no. 73 (New York: American Tract Society, n.d. [ca. 1833]); Nathan S. S. Beman, *Public Reformation. A Sermon Delivered May, 1817, at the anniversary of the Tract Societies of Mount Zion and Washington* (Augusta, GA: printed by William J. Bunce, 1817).
2 [James W. Alexander], *Frank Harper; or, The Country-Boy in Town* (Philadelphia, PA: American Sunday School Union, 1847), 26–28.
3 Ibid., 43–44.
4 James W. Alexander, "The Young Men of Cities, Urged to the Work of Mental Improvement," in *Words in Earnest* (New York: Edward H. Fletcher, 1851), 20.
5 Alexander, *Frank Harper*, 144–45.
6 *Pictures and Lessons for Little Readers* (Boston, MA: American Tract Society, n.d.), 54.
7 Alexander, *Frank Harper*, 106.
8 W. W. Everts, "The Social Position and Influence of Cities," in *Words in Earnest*, 9.
9 Ibid., 9.
10 Ibid., 12.
11 In a breathless rant, Rev. Everts (ibid., 11) had identified the adverse conditions of city life that exhaust the resources of inhabitants:

The unremitted cares of business, the rage of passions, the fury of politics, the restlessness of ambition, the thirst of gold, the struggles of competition, over-tax the physical, intellectual, and nervous constitution, and doom it to the depressive horrors and enfeebled state of reaction; and fast wear out human life.

12 Alexander, "The Young Men of Cities," 6–7.
13 Alexander, *Frank Harper*, 59.
14 Alexander, "The Young Men of Cities," 16.
15 "The Sabbath School and its Graduates," *The Well-Spring* 19, no. 48 (November 28, 1862), 1.
16 Ibid.
17 Horace Bushnell, *Christian Nurture* (Grand Rapids, MI: Baker Book House, 1979), 211.
18 *Proceedings of the National Convention of Colored People and Their Friends, Held in Troy, N.Y., on the 6th, 7th, 8th, and 9th October, 1847*, reprinted in *Pamphlets of Protest: An Anthology of Early African-American Protest Literature, 1790–1860*, ed. Richard Newman, Patrick Rael, and Philip Lapsansky (New York: Routledge, 2001), 166–77.
19 Ibid., 172.
20 Ibid., 173.
21 Ibid., 174.
22 Ibid., 175.
23 "Debate over Garnet's 'Address to the Slaves of the United States of America'," reprinted in *Pamphlets of Protest*, 158. A compelling study of the evolution of black political and religious thought during the antebellum period, particularly with regard to black national consciousness, is Eddie S. Glaude, Jr., *Exodus! Religion, Race, and Nation in Early Nineteenth-Century Black America* (Chicago, IL: University of Chicago Press, 2000).
24 David Walker, "Appeal to the Colored Citizens of the World," reprinted in *Pamphlets of Protest*, 97.
25 "To the Senate and House of Representatives, in Congress Assembled," in *Narrative of Sojourner Truth with "Book of Life" and "A Memorial Chapter,"* introduction and notes by Imani Perry (New York: Barnes & Noble Classics, 2005), 145.
26 Morris U. Schappes, *A Pictorial History of the Jews in the United States*, rev. edn (New York: Marzani & Munsell, 1965), 125–26.
27 John Tracy Ellis, ed., *Documents of American Catholic History*, 2 vols (Chicago, IL: Henry Regnery, 1967), vol. 1, 265–69.
28 See Henry J. Browne, "Archbishop Hughes and Western Colonization," *Catholic Historical Review* 36, no. 3 (October 1950), 262; and Ellis, *Documents of American Catholic History*, vol. 1, 311–14.
29 Browne, "Archbishop Hughes and Western Colonization," 275, 267–68.
30 J. L. Spalding, *The Religious Mission of the Irish People and Catholic Colonization* (New York: Catholic Publication Society, 1880; reprint, New York: Arno Press, 1978).
31 Ibid., 145.
32 Ibid., 39.
33 Ibid., 61.
34 An excellent discussion of the topic is Robert D. Cross, "The Changing Image of the City among American Catholics," *Catholic Historical Review* 47 (April 1962), 33–52.
35 Rt. Rev. John Lancaster Spalding, *Religion and Art and Other Essays* (1905; reprint, Freeport, NY: Books for Libraries Press, 1969).

36 Ibid., 16.
37 Ibid., 43, 33.
38 Ibid., 50–52.
39 For a discussion of Benziger Brothers, see Saul Zalesch, "The Religious Art of Benziger Brothers," *American Art* 13, no. 2 (Summer 1999), 58–79; David Morgan and Sally M. Promey, *Exhibiting the Visual Culture of American Religions* (Valparaiso, IN: Brauer Museum of Art, Valparaiso University, 2000), 99.
40 "An Explanation of the Grotto of the Redemption," a pamphlet produced by the Grotto, West Bend, Iowa; Duane Hutchinson, *Grotto Father: Artist-Priest of the West Bend Grotto* (Lincoln, NB: Foundation Books, 1989). A helpful case study of several Christian grottoes in the twentieth-century United States, including Father Dobberstein's West Bend grotto, is Susannah Koerber, "Signs of the Times: Context and Connection in Southern Conservative Evangelical Protestant and Midwestern Roman Catholic Grassroots Art Environments," Ph.D. dissertation, Emory University, 2004.
41 James W. Alexander, *Forty Years' Familiar Letters*, ed. John Hall, 2 vols (New York: Charles Scribner, 1860), vol. 1, p. 307, June 22, 1840; vol. 1, 308, July 1, 1840.
42 Ibid., letter of December 19, 1842, vol. 1, 361.
43 Ibid., March 10, 1842, from Ingleside, Charolotte County, Virginia, vol. 1, 351; March 21, 1842, 353.
44 Ambrose Serle, Esq. *The Happy Negro*, Tract no. 7 (New York: American Tract Society, 1825), 1.
45 Alexander, *Forty Years' Familiar Letters*, May 28, 1846, vol. 2, 52.
46 Ibid., May 11, 1846, vol. 2, 51.
47 "The American Tract Society," *Atlantic Monthly* 2, no. 9 (July 1858), 246.
48 *Pictures and Lessons*, 68.
49 For a discussion of some of these, see David Morgan, "For Christ and the Republic: Protestant Illustration and the History of Literacy in Nineteenth-Century America," in David Morgan and Sally M. Promey, eds., *The Visual Culture of American Religions* (Berkeley, CA: University of California Press, 2001), 49–67.
50 Harriet Beecher Stowe, *Uncle Tom's Cabin* (Boston, MA: John P. Jewett; Cleveland, OH: Jewett, Proctor, and Worthington, 1853).
51 Ibid., 517, 516.
52 *Martyrdom of Polycarp*, in *The Apostolic Fathers*, ed. and trans. Bart D. Ehrman (Cambridge, MA: Harvard University Press, 2003), 369.
53 Daniel Coker, "A Dialogue between a Virginian and an African Minister," in *Pamphlets of Protest*, 52–65.
54 Ibid., 60.
55 Frederick Douglass, "Address to the People of the United States," in *Pamphlets of Protest*, 216.
56 Frederick Douglass, *Narrative of the Life of Frederick Douglass, an American Slave* (New York: Penguin, 1986), 83.
57 "Proceedings of the National Convention of Colored People," in *Pamphlets of Protest*, 168.
58 Ibid., 167.
59 Mary Still, "An Appeal to the Females of the African Methodist Episcopal Church" (1857), in *Pamphlets of Protest*, 260.
60 T. Morris Chester, "Negro Self-Respect and Pride of Race," in *Pamphlets of Protest*, 308.
61 Ibid., 308.
62 Ibid., 310.
63 See Michael D. Harris, *Colored Pictures: Race and Visual Representation* (Chapel Hill, NC: University of North Carolina, 2003), 62–65.

64 *Proceedings of the Quarto-Centennial Conference of the African M. E. Church, of South Carolina,* at Charleston, SC, May 15, 16, and 17, 1889, ed. Bishop Benjamin W. Arnett, D.D., presiding bishop of the States of South Carolina and Florida, 1890.

65 On the history of Chinese immigration to the United States, see Erika Lee, *At America's Gates: Chinese Immigration during the Exclusion Era, 1882–1943* (Chapel Hill, NC: University of North Carolina Press, 2003); for a thoughtful discussion of images of Chinese religions among American Protestants in the late nineteenth and early twentieth centuries see Laurie Maffly-Kipp, "Engaging Habits and Besotted Idolatry: Viewing Chinese Religions in the American West," *Material Religion* 1, no. 1 (March 2005), 72–97.

66 On the Magdalen Society, see Carroll Smith-Rosenberg, *Religion and the Rise of the American City: The New York City Mission Movement, 1812–1870* (Ithaca, NY: Cornell University Press, 1971), 100–101.

67 *Orthodox Bubbles, or A Review of the First Annual Report of the Executive Committee of the New York Magdalen Society* (Boston, MA: printed for the publishers, 1831), 9.

68 Ibid., 13.

69 Rev. E[zra] S[tiles] Ely, *Visits of Mercy; being the Journal of the Stated Preacher to the Hospital and Almshouse, in the City of New York, 1811* (New York: John Jones, 1813), 71; the second volume printed Ely's journal of 1813, but was not published until 1829 by Samuel R. Bradford in Philadelphia, PA.

70 Cornelia S. King, "Women's History: Straying from the Path," *Annual Report of the Library Company of Philadelphia for the Year 2002* (Philadelphia, PA: Library Company of Philadelphia, 2003), 47. The print offers incorrect spellings for the names of the well-known figures it lambastes, presumably in order to avoid the charge of slander, though the device was all but transparent. However, if "Eli" is spelled correctly, it is likely Eli Wainwright, vice-president of the Magdalen Society, who is listed as a merchant at 52 Wall Street in New York in *Longworth's American Almanac, New-York Register, and City Directory* (New York: Thomas Longworth, 1832), 685.

71 See Benjamin Rush, *An Inquiry into the Effects of Spiritous Liquors on the Human Body and the Mind. To which is added, A Moral and Physical Thermometer* (Boston, MA: Thomas and Andrews, 1790).

72 Princeton Seminary was targeted since it was a former student there, John McDowall, who, as a volunteer for the ATS, had come to New York City to become shortly later the leading missionary of the Magdalen Society. The controversial McDowall is discussed by Smith-Rosenberg, *Religion and the Rise of the American City,* 98–102.

73 Ibid., 23.

74 In 1831, the paper published an article critical of the Magdalen Society and regularly printed pieces that targeted the tract, bible, and missionary societies – *Free Enquirer* (July 23, 1831), 313–14.

75 Isaac Leeser, "To the American Tract Society: A Warning," reprinted in Abraham J. Karp, ed., *The Jews in America: A Treasury of Art and Literature* (Westport, CT: Hugh Lauter Levin Associates, 1994), 81.

76 See Ray Allen Billington and other sources. For a study of anti-Catholicism and Protestant church architecture see Ryan K. Smith, *Gothic Arches, Latin Crosses: Anti-Catholicism and American Church Designs in the Nineteenth Century* (Chapel Hill, NC: University of North Carolina Press, 2006).

77 Ellis, ed., *Documents of American Catholic History,* vol. 1, 263–65.

78 Pope Gregory XVI, *Mirari vos,* August 15, 1832, para. 14 and 15.

79 Pius IX, *Quanta Cura*, in Anne Fremantle, ed., *The Papal Encyclicals in their Historical Context* (New York: New American Library, 1963), 137.

80 Ibid., 152.

81 An instructive study of the Cincinnati controversy is Robert Michaelson, "Common School, Common Religion? A Case Study in Church–State Relations, Cincinnati, 1869–1870," *Church History* 38, no. 2 (June 1969), 201–17. More recent studies are Tracy Fessenden, "The Nineteenth-Century Bible Wars and the Separation of Church and State," *Church History* 74, no. 4 (December 2005), 784–811; and R. Laurence Moore, "Bible Reading and Nonsectarian Schooling: The Failure of Religious Instruction in Nineteenth-Century Public Education," *Journal of American History* 86, no. 4 (March 2000), 1,581–599.

82 Eugene Lawrence, "Hunter's Point – Romish Politics," *Harper's Weekly* (August 17, 1872), 637.

83 Orestes Brownson, "Education and the Republic," in *Brownson's Quarterly Review* 2 (1874), 44.

84 Ibid.

85 Ibid., 54.

86 Orestes Brownson, "The Papacy and the Republic," *Brownson's Quarterly Review* 1 (1873), 18.

87 Robert Anthony Orsi, *The Madonna of 115th Street: Faith and Community in Italian Harlem, 1880–1950* (New Haven, CT: Yale University Press, 1985), 191.

88 Susan A. Phillips, *Wallbangin': Graffiti and Gangs in L.A.* (Chicago, IL: University of Chicago Press, 1999). On the history of the image of Guadalupe see D. A. Brading, *Mexican Phoenix: Our Lady of Guadalupe. Image and Tradition across Five Centuries* (Cambridge: Cambridge University Press, 2001); and Jacqueline Orsini Dunnington, *Viva Guadalupe! The Virgin in New Mexican Popular Art* (Santa Fe, NM: Museum of New Mexico Press, 1997).

89 Jorge Durand and Douglas S. Massey have produced an illuminating and visually rich study of the Mexican votive retablos, *Miracles on the Border: Retablos of Mexican Migrants to the United States* (Tucson, AZ: University of Arizona Press, 1995).

90 Durand and Massey provide a table indicating the geographical distribution of destinations of Mexican migrants who mention source and destination in their retablos, *Miracles on the Border*, 80. Not surprisingly, given the location of the farmland where migrant workers are employed, 35 percent of the destinations are in California and Texas. Their data show a nearly even split in the genders of those who commission retablos.

91 Ibid., 59.

92 "Dedico este retablo a Nuestra Señora de Talpa por haberme hecho una grande maravilla que le pedi el dia 19 de Marzo de 1924. Silveria Camarena." My thanks to Juan Carlos Henriquez for discussing the translation of the inscription with me.

93 Thomas A. Tweed, *Our Lady of the Exile: Diasporic Religion at a Cuban Catholic Shrine in Miami* (New York: Oxford University Press, 1997).

94 Ibid., 83–98.

95 The strongly localized and ethnic devotion to Mary has been formally recognized by the church and unified in another Marian monument, also studied by Tweed – the Basilica of the National Shrine to the Immaculate Conception, whose construction began in Washington, DC, in 1920. See Thomas A. Tweed, "America's Church: Roman Catholicism and Civic Space in the Nation's Capital," in David Morgan and Sally M. Promey, eds., *Visual Culture of American Religions* (Berkeley, CA: University of California Press, 2001), 68–86.

3 Consumption and religious images

1 The essays by several authors compiled by Arjun Apadurai in *The Social Life of Things: Commodities in Cultural Perspective* (Cambridge: Cambridge University Press, 1986) have been very helpful to me in understanding consumption and commodity.

2 The literature on the history of consumption is large. I have found very helpful Woodruff D. Smith's *Consumption and the Making of Respectability 1600–1800* (New York: Routledge, 2002). Major studies include: Neil McKendrick, John Brewer, and J. H. Plumb, eds., *The Birth of a Consumer Society: The Commercialization of Eighteenth-Century England* (Bloomington, IN: Indiana University Press, 1982); Carole Shammus, *The Pre-Industrial Consumer in Britain and America* (Oxford: Clarendon Press, 1990); John Brewer and Roy Porter, eds., *Consumption and the World of Goods* (London: Routledge, 1993); and Maxine Berg and Helen Clifford, eds., *Consumers and Luxury: Consumer Culture in Europe 1650–1850* (Manchester: Manchester University Press, 1999).

3 See Smith, *Consumption and the Making of Respectability*, and Richard L. Bushman, *The Refinement of America: Persons, Houses, Cities* (New York: Alfred A. Knopf, 1992).

4 T. J. Jackson Lears, "From Salvation to Self-Realization: Advertising and the Therapeutic Roots of the Consumer Culture, 1800–1930," in Richard Wightman Fox and T. J. Jackson Lears, eds., *The Culture of Consumption: Critical Essays in American History, 1800–1980* (New York: Pantheon, 1983), 1–38; Andrew R. Heinze, *Adapting to Abundance: Jewish Immigrants, Mass Consumption, and the Search for American Identity* (New York: Columbia University Press, 1990); R. Laurence Moore, *Selling God: American Life in the Marketplace of Culture* (New York: Oxford University Press, 1994); Colleen McDannell, *Material Christianity: Religion and Popular Culture in America* (New Haven, CT: Yale University Press, 1995); Leigh Eric Schmidt, *Consumer Rites: The Buying and Selling of American Holidays* (Princeton, NJ: Princeton University Press, 1995); Paul Gutjahr, *An American Bible: A History of the Good Book in the United States, 1770–1880* (Stanford, CA: Stanford University Press, 1999); John M. Giggie and Diane Winston, eds., *Faith in the Market: Religion and the Rise of Urban Commercial Culture* (New Brunswick, NJ: Rutgers University Press, 2002); and Heather Hendershot, *Shaking the World for Jesus: Media and Conservative Evangelical Culture* (Chicago, IL: University of Chicago Press, 2004), 17–51.

5 Harry T. Peters, *Currier & Ives: Printmakers to the American People* (Garden City, NY: Doubleday, Doran, 1942), 5.

6 For discussion of Currier's use of lithographs as visual news items see Walton Rawls, *Currier & Ives' America* (New York: Abbeville Press, 1979), 22–23, and Bryan F. Le Beau, *Currier & Ives: America Imagined* (Washington, DC: Smithsonian Institution Press, 2001), 11–13; Rawls, *Currier & Ives' America*, 23–25. For a study of illustrations and the penny press in antebellum New York City, see Isabelle Lehuu, *Carnival on the Page: Popular Print Media in Antebellum America* (Chapel Hill, NC: University of North Carolina Press, 2002), 36–58.

7 For a discussion of the pricing, organization, and marketing at Currier & Ives, see Rawls, *Currier & Ives' America*, 37–39.

8 Elizabeth Gilmore Holt, "Revivalist Themes in American Prints and Folksongs 1830–50," in *American Printmaking before 1876: Fact, Fiction, and Fantasy* (Washington, DC: Library of Congress, 1975), 34–46.

9 For consideration of the replacement of traditional forms of Catholic imagery among Latinos in the southwestern United States, see Claire Farago, "Transforming Images: New Mexican Santos between Theory and History," in David Morgan and

Sally M. Promey, eds., *The Visual Culture of American Religions* (Berkeley, CA: University of California Press, 2001), 192–96.

10 See Robert Rosenblum, *Transformations in Late Eighteenth Century Art* (Princeton, NJ: Princeton University Press, 1967), 50–85, on the death scene as neoclassical *exemplum virtutis*; and Hugh Honour's *Neo-classicism* (London: Penguin, 1968), 141–46, for a discussion of the relationship between the "language of the heart" or sensibility, a precursor of "sentiment," and neoclassicism. For a discussion of the neoclassical style and subject matter of mourning art in the early nineteenth century, see Anita Schorsch, *Mourning Becomes America: Mourning Art in the New Nation*, exhibition catalogue (Philadelphia, PA: Main Street Press, 1976).

11 Quoted in Brian Dolan, *Wedgwood: The First Tycoon* (New York: Viking, 2004), 240.

12 Quoted in Schorsch, *Mourning Becomes America*, unpaginated (p. 9); for a discussion of the range of objects and commodities associated with mourning art, see Martha V. Pike and Janice Gray Armstrong, *A Time to Mourn: Expressions of Grief in Nineteenth Century America*, exhibition catalogue (Stony Brook, NY: The Museums at Stony Brook, 1980).

13 Karen Haltunen, *Confidence Men and Painted Women: A Study of Middle-Class Culture in America, 1830–1870* (New Haven, CT: Yale University Press, 1982), 57. The prevailing study of sentimentalism in nineteenth-century America remains Ann Douglas' polemic, *The Feminization of American Culture* (New York: Doubleday, 1977).

14 Haltunen, *Confidence Men and Painted Women*, 57.

15 See Schorsch, *Mourning Becomes America*, for discussion of the production of mourning art. A very fine study of ivory miniatures on brooches and pendants is Robin Jaffee Frank, *Love and Loss: American Portrait and Mourning Miniatures*, exhibition catalogue, Yale University Art Gallery (New Haven, CT: Yale University Press, 2000).

16 Instances of the memorial print motif issued by Currier & Ives are nos. 3336, 3337, 5731–734, 6584–591 in the Gale Catalogue Raisonné, *Currier & Ives: Catalogue Raisonné* (Detroit, MI: Gale Research Company, 1984). Another print issued by Currier & Ives shows two young girls admiring the miniature pendant bearing the image of their mother, entitled "The Sisters Prayer," Gale cat. no. 5938.

17 See Harriette Merrifield Forbes, *Gravestones of Early New England and the Men Who Made Them* (Boston, MA: Houghton Mifflin, 1927); Francis Y. Duval and Ivan B. Rigby, *Early Modern Gravestone Art in Photographs* (New York: Dover, 1978); Allan I. Ludwig, *Graven Images: New England Stonecarving and its Symbols, 1650–1815* (Middletown, CT: Wesleyan University Press, 1966). Haltunen provides a very instructive discussion of mourning and sentimentalism, *Confidence Men and Painted Women*, 124–52; see also Douglas, *Feminization of American Culture*, 200–26, for a discussion of mourning and death in the cult of sentimentalism. I am indebted to Louis Nelson's fascinating study of eighteenth-century tombstones regarding the shift circa 1750, Louis P. Nelson, "Word, Shape, and Image: Anglican Constructions of the Sacred," in Louis P. Nelson, ed., *American Sanctuary: Understanding Sacred Spaces* (Bloomington, IN: Indiana University Press, 2006), 173–76.

18 On the rural cemetery movement and new practices of burial and graveside commemoration, see McDannell, *Material Christianity*, 103–31; and Gary Laderman, *The Sacred Remains: American Attitudes toward Death, 1799–1883* (New Haven, CT: Yale University Press, 1996), 39–50.

19 *Catalogue of Colored Prints*, published by E. C. Kellogg, 87 Fulton Street, New York, and 73 Main Street, Hartford, CT. Horace Thayer & Co., 127 Main Street, Buffalo, NY. My thanks to Nancy Finley, Connecticut Historical Society, for sharing

the catalogue list with me. The document is undated, but one print entitled "Thirteen Presidents" suggests a date during the office of Millard Fillmore (1850–53), the thirteenth president. Franklin Pierce, the fourteenth president, was not listed. Moreover, "Little Emma" is another title. Since Harriet Beecher Stowe's *Uncle Tom's Cabin* did not appear until 1852, it is possible that this date serves as the post-quem and the final year of Fillmore's presidency as the ante-quem.

20 Robert Freke Gould et al., eds., *A Library of Freemasonry*, 5 vols (London: John C. Yorston, 1911), vol. 5, 436.

21 Ibid., 493.

22 See, for example, Robert Morris, *The Lights and Shadows of Freemasonry: Consisting of Masonic Tales, Songs, and Sketches*, 5th edn (Louisville, KY: J. F. Brenan, for the author, 1853), 197–238, where Morris (founder of the Order of the Eastern Star and hailed as the "poet laureate of American Freemasonry" in *A Library of Freemasonry*, 429) describes the life of John Callis, a beloved Mason, whose dedication to Christian benevolent causes was second to none. His home featured three rooms decorated according to the three degrees of Masonry comprised in the chart reproduced here. Masonry's system of moral perfection may have appealed to the perfectionist sensibility of Methodists, who were well represented among Lodges. The emphasis on secrecy and occult learning in Masonry also appealed to Mormons; see Clyde R. Forsberg, Jr., *Equal Rites: The Book of Mormon, Masonry, Gender, and American Culture* (New York: Columbia University Press, 2004).

23 *Library of Freemasonry*, vol. 5, 437.

24 On the artistic aspects of Freemasonry see James Stevens Curl, *The Art and Architecture of Freemasonry: An Introductory Study* (Woodstock, NY: Overlook Press, 1993); and David Bjelajac, *Washington Allston, Secret Societies, and the Alchemy of Anglo-American Painting* (Cambridge: Cambridge University Press, 1997).

25 For discussion of Millerite and Seventh-Day Adventist imagery and visual practices, see David Morgan, *Protestants and Pictures: Religion, Visual Culture, and the Age of American Mass Production* (New York: Oxford University Press, 1999), 123–98.

26 L. Prang & Co.'s Catalogue. Season 1879–80. Art and Educational Publishers, 286 Roxbury Street, Boston, MA, no pages (3). My thanks to Sandy Brewer for the gift of this catalogue.

27 On the critical attack on chromolithography, see Peter C. Marzio, *The Democratic Art: Chromolithography 1840–1900: Pictures for a 19th-Century America* (Boston, MA: David R. Godine, 1979), 205–10.

28 L. Prang & Co.'s Catalogue, 1879–80. See Schmidt, *Consumer Rites*, 224–31, for discussion of Prang's imagery on Easter cards.

29 Schmidt, *Consumer Rites*, 227.

30 Rawls, *Currier & Ives' America*, 453, states that Currier & Ives "published some 350 lithographs on religious and moralistic themes."

31 My count using the subject index of the *Currier & Ives: Catalogue Raisonné*.

32 Rawls, *Currier & Ives' America*, 242.

33 Roger Daniels, *Coming to America: A History of Immigration and Ethnicity in American Life* (New York: HarperCollins, 1990), 124, 129, 146, 189. Jewish immigration, overwhelmingly Russian by country of origin, got seriously underway in the 1880s (224). Asian immigration, largely Chinese and Japanese, was comparatively smaller and focused on the Pacific Coast, reaching its peak years in the 1880s and 1890s for Chinese, and 1920s and 1930s for Japanese (240, 250).

34 For historical information about Providence Lithography Company I am indebted to an anonymous, unpublished typescript entitled "History of the Providence Lithography Company," dated September 26, 1954, in the collection of the Rhode Island Historical Society, pp. 4–24.

35 For a summary of the history of the Sunday school movement as it relates to national goals and visual materials, and for relevant bibliography, see Morgan, *Protestants and Pictures*, 303–309.

36 On the lesson cards see "History of the Providence Lithography Company," 32–33.

37 Ibid., 59.

38 Letter of May 29, 1901 from the Presbyterian Board of Publication and Sabbath-School Work to Providence Lithography Company, Miscellaneous Correspondence, 1880–1908, folder 1, box 1, Providence Lithography Company, Mss 1028–1–1, Rhode Island Historical Society.

39 Arthur E. Becher, letter of August 1, 1931, to Providence Lithography Company, folder 28, American Artists 1, box 3, Mss 1028–3–28.

40 William H. Levering, letter of December 18, 1885, Miscellaneous Correspondence, 1880–1908, folder 1, box 1, Providence Lithography Company, Mss 1028–1–1, Rhode Island Historical Society.

41 Among the most developed discussions of visual religious curricula were Frederica Beard, "The Use of Pictures in Religious Education," in John T. McFarland and Benjamin S. Winchester, eds., *Encyclopedia of Sunday Schools and Religious Education*, 3 vols (New York: Thomas Nelson, 1915), vol. 3, 794–95; and Beard, *Pictures in Religious Education* (New York: George H. Doran, 1920).

42 Statistic cited in "History of the Providence Lithography Company," 72. For further discussion of the graded lesson plan, see 71–82.

43 Ms. Robbie Trent, Letter of April 11, 1936, Baptist Sunday School Board, Correspondence 1931–1937, folder 16, box 1, Providence Lithography Company, Mss 1028–1–16, Rhode Island Historical Society. For a memo that lists by name the several women who composed the editorial group and their specific responses to another image by Copping, see "Comments," dated September 24, 1930, folder 28, American Artists 1, box 3, Providence Lithography Company, Mss 1028–3–28.

44 Phillips Booth (art director), letter of July 1942 to (artist) T. Victor Hall (New York City), folder 28, American Artists 1, box 3, Mss 1028–3–28.

45 Letter of August 8, 1932 from Mr. Nelson to Arthur E. Beecher, folder 28, American Artists 1, box 3, Mss 1028–3–28.

46 Letter of June 27, 1940, from Phillips Booth to John Clymer, Westport, Connecticut, folder 29, American Artists 2, box 3, Mss 1028–3–29.

47 Letter of April 22, 1941, Phillips Booth to John Clymer, Mss 1028–3–29; letter of April 19, 1942, to Victor Hall, Mss 1028–3–28.

48 Mr. Nelson, memo of November 18, 1935, on correspondence with Samuel J. Brown, folder 28, American Artists 1, box 3, Mss 1028–3–28.

4 Parlors and kitchens

1 On the history of the American parlor, see Katherine C. Grier, *Culture & Comfort: People, Parlors, and Upholstery, 1850–1930* (Rochester, NY: The Strong Museum, 1988), esp. 62–66, for discussion of the early phase of parlor history; Thomas J. Schlereth, *Victorian America: Transformations in Everyday Life, 1876–1915* (New York: HarperPerennial, 1991), 118–24. Colleen McDannell offers a helpful overview of the Protestant material culture of the American parlor into the early twentieth century, "Parlor Piety: The Home as Sacred Space in Protestant America," in Jessica H. Foy and Thomas J. Schlereth, eds., *American Home Life, 1880–1930: A Social History of Spaces and Services* (Knoxville, TN: University of Tennessee Press, 1992), 162–89, which draws on her helpful study of the religious understanding and practices defining the nineteenth-century American home, *The Christian Home in Victorian America, 1840–1900* (Bloomington, IN: Indiana University Press,

1986); see also McDannell, *Material Christianity: Religion and Popular Culture in America* (New Haven, CT: Yale University Press, 1995). Another important discussion is Kenneth L. Ames, *Death in the Dining Room and Other Tales of Victorian Culture* (Philadelphia, PA: Temple University Press, 1992).

2 Richard L. Bushman, *The Refinement of America: Persons, Houses, Cities* (New York: Alfred A. Knopf, 1992), 273.

3 Bushman has explored the importance of refinement for the parlor and for religious consumers (ibid., 353–401). Lawrence W. Levine's *Highbrow Lowbrow: The Emergence of Cultural Hierarchy in America* (Cambridge, MA: Harvard University Press, 1988) examines the shift in taste in tandem with the formation of imposing cultural institutions.

4 Caroline M. Kirkland, *The Evening Book, or, Fireside Talk on Morals and Manners* (New York: Scribner, 1852), 14.

5 Ibid., 17.

6 Ibid., 18.

7 Ibid., 19.

8 On gift books, see Benjamin Rowland, Jr., "Popular Romanticism: Art and the Gift Books 1825–1865," *Art Quarterly* 20 (Winter 1957), 365–81; Ann Katharine Martinez, "'Messengers of Love, Tokens of Friendship': Gift-Book Illustrations by John Sartain," in Gerald W. R. Ward, ed., *The American Illustrated Book in the Nineteenth Century* (Winterthur, DE: Henry Francis du Pont Winterthur Museum, 1987), 89–112; and Isabelle Lehuu, *Carnival on the Page: Popular Print Media in Antebellum America* (Chapel Hill, NC: University of North Carolina Press, 2000), 76–101.

9 S. G. Goodrich, *Recollections of a Lifetime, or Men and Things I Have Seen*, 2 vols (New York: Miller, Orton and Mulligan, 1857), vol. 2, 260–61.

10 Ibid., vol. 2, 260.

11 Ibid., vol. 2, 261.

12 Ibid., vol. 2, 262, 383. Harper Brothers published their mammoth *Illuminated Bible* in the mid-1840s; Appleton issued *Women of the Bible* in 1849 and *Our Saviour with Prophets and Apostles* in 1851.

13 "Devotion," *The Parlor Annual and Christian Family Casket. 1846.* Edited by an Association of Clergymen (New York: J. E. D. Comstock, 1845), 173–74.

14 Edward E. Hale, *The Ingham Papers: Some Memorials of the Life of Capt. Frederic Ingham, U.S.N.* (Boston, MA: Fields, Osgood, 1869), 109. Stuart M. Blumin has examined probate records in 1860s Philadelphia, finding, among other things, that engravings were often included in the households of the middle and upper middle classes, *The Emergence of the Middle Class: Social Experience in the American City, 1760–1900* (Cambridge: Cambridge University Press, 1989), 159–63; for a helpful description of the material culture of urban housing from working class to upper class, see 146–63.

15 Hale, *The Ingham Papers*, 111.

16 Ibid., 115.

17 Ibid., 120.

18 Mary I. Hoffman, *Alice Murray: A Tale* (New York: P. O'Shea, 1859?), 50.

19 Thomas Butler Gunn, *The Physiology of New York Boarding-Houses* (New York: Mason Brothers, 1857), 65–66.

20 Ruth Parthington (B. P. Shillader), *Knitting Work: A Web of Many Textures* (Boston, MA: Brown, Taggard, and Chase; New York: Sheldon, 1859), 111.

21 Mary W. Janvrin's *Peace, or, The Stolen Will!* (Boston, MA: J. French, 1857), 178.

22 Ibid., 179.

23 Maria J. McIntosh, *Violet, or, The Cross and the Crown* (Boston, MA: J. P. Jewett, 1856), 78.

24 Horace Bushnell, *Christian Nurture*, introduced by John M. Mulder (Grand Rapids, MI: Baker Books House, 1979), 30.

25 Ibid., 31.

26 Ibid., 56.

27 Ibid., 63.

28 Ibid., 91.

29 Karen Haltunen, *Confidence Men and Painted Women: A Study of Middle-Class Culture in America, 1830–1870* (New Haven, CT: Yale University Press, 1982), 59.

30 A reference to a picture by Benjamin Robert Haydon (1786–1846) entitled *Reading the Scriptures* appeared in the *Mirror of Literature, Amusement, and Instruction*, vol. 19, 537 (March 10, 1832), 150. My thanks to Nancy Finlay for this information. I have been unable to find such an image in the known corpus of works by Haydon or any reference to it in the artist's memoirs. An undated lithograph of Haydon's *Reading the Scriptures* was produced by Alfred E. Baker in New York; for a reproduction of Baker's lithograph, see Grier, *Culture & Comfort*, 14. Another lithographic version of the motif, allegedly Haydon's, published in Philadelphia by A. Hoffy and printed on P. S. Duval's lithographic press in Philadelphia sometime between 1847 and 1852 is now in the collection of the American Antiquarian Society.

31 Thomas J. Schlereth, *Victorian America: Transformations in Everyday Life, 1876–1915* (New York: HarperPerennial, 1992), 122.

32 See *Reading the Scriptures* by Kellogg and Thayer, who were in business together in the mid-1840s. The print, a copy of which may be found in the Billy Graham Museum (accession no. 80.3734), also lists two other publishers: E. B. and E. C. Kellogg, 136 Main Street, Hartford, CT, where the two were in business only through 1848. A final publisher is listed on the print at D. Needham, 223 Main Street, Buffalo, NY, in business in the 1840s. The title of the print appears on a "Catalogue of Colored Prints" issued by E. C. Kellogg and Horace Thayer in 1852 or 1853. But this catalogue was the list of stock acquired from the earlier firm of Kellogg and Thayer. Hence a date of ca. 1848 for the Kellogg and Thayer seems quite likely. In other words, since Currier was in the habit of responding immediately to events and competition in issuing prints, his two versions of *Reading the Scriptures* reproduced here may both date from 1848. My thanks to Nancy Finlay and Georgia Barnhill for their generous assistance with the problem of dating the prints.

33 Currier & Ives hand-colored all of their production, preferring not for the most part to engage in chromolithography.

34 Kirkland, *The Evening Book*, 13.

35 Ibid., 16.

36 [Mrs. A. M. Richards] A Lady of Massachusetts, *Memories of a Grandmother* (Boston, MA: Gould and Lincoln; New York: Sheldon, Lamport & Blakeman, 1854), 94.

37 Ibid., 95.

38 The print (Gale no. 5841) is undated, but carries Nathaniel Currier's name and the address of 2 Spruce Street. The same image appeared as a metal-plate engraving in *Godey's Lady's Book* in 1851 (p. 206), and is reproduced in McDannell, *The Christian Home*, p. 131. The hand-painted version of the Currier lithograph in the collection of the Billy Graham Center (no. 80.3840) casts the curtain in a deep green, the sofa as light mauve, and the young woman's dress dark violet accented by a yellow scarf.

39 Harriet Beecher Stowe, *House and Home Papers* (Boston, MA: Ticknor and Fields, 1865), 310.

40 Ibid., 319, 311.

41 Ibid., 312.

42 Ibid., 313.

43 Ibid., 313.

44 Ibid., 314, 318.

45 See Jonathan D. Sarna, "The Debate over Mixed Seating in the American Synagogue," in David G. Hackett, ed., *Religion and American Culture: A Reader* (New York: Routledge, 1995), 273–90; and Karla Goldman, *Beyond the Synagogue Gallery: Finding a Place for Women in American Judaism* (Cambridge, MA: Harvard University Press, 2000).

46 For a description of Schechter's apartment in New York, see Jenna Weissman Joselit, *The Wonders of America: Reinventing Jewish Culture, 1880–1950* (New York: Hill and Wang, 1994), 151–52.

47 I have benefited from the expertise of several scholars in the study of American Jewish history, commerce, and material culture. Jenna Weissman Joselit has produced a number of insightful investigations of the history of Jewish culture in the United States, in which she trains a careful eye on the importance of consumption and material culture; see especially "A Set Table: Jewish Domestic Culture in the New World, 1880–1950," in Susan L. Braunstein and Jenna Weissman Joselit, eds., *Getting Comfortable in New York: The American Jewish Home, 1880–1950* (New York: The Jewish Museum, 1990), 19–73; and *The Wonders of America*, esp. 135–69; see also Barbara Kirshenblatt-Gimblett, "Kitchen Judaism," in *Getting Comfortable*, 75–105; and Andrew R. Heinze, *Adapting to Abundance: Jewish Immigrants, Mass Consumption, and the Search for American Identity* (New York: Columbia University Press, 1990).

48 *The Junior Jewish Encyclopedia*, 11th edn, ed. Naomi Ben-Asher and Haim Leaf (New York: Shengold, 1991), 169.

49 Esther J. Ruskay, *Hearth and Home Essays* (Philadelphia, PA: Jewish Publication Society of America, 1902), 15, 53. The emblem visualized an age of peace expressed in Isaiah 11: 6. A lion, symbol of Judah, was long used by Christians and Jews alike instead of a lamb.

50 Bertha M. Smith, "The Gospel of Simplicity as Applied to Tenement Homes," *The Craftsman* 9 (October 1905), 83–90. For a discussion of ethnicity in the early period of immigration, see Naomi W. Cohen, "The Ethnic Catalyst: The Impact of the East European Immigration on the American Jewish Establishment," in David Berger, ed., *The Legacy of Jewish Migration: 1881 and its Impact* (New York: Social Science Monographs, Brooklyn College Press: distributed by Columbia University Press, 1983), 131–48. A fine study of the material culture of working-class housing is Lizabeth A. Cohen, "Embellishing a Life of Labor: An Interpretation of the Material Culture of American Working-Class Homes, 1885–1915," in Dell Upton and John Michael Vlach, eds., *Common Places: Readings in American Vernacular Architecture* (Athens, GA: University of Georgia Press, 1986), 261–78. Cohen's essay was first published, under the same title, in *Journal of American Culture* 3, no. 4 (Winter 1980), 752–75.

51 See, for instance, many papers delivered at the Jewish Women's Congress at the Columbian Exposition in 1893, especially Goldie Bamber, response to Carrie Shevelson Benjamin, "Woman's Place in Charitable Work – What It Is and What It Should Be," 157–62, and Rebekah Kohut, response to Minnie Louis, "Mission-Work among the Unenlightened Jews," 187–95, in *Papers of the Jewish Women's Congress* (Philadelphia, PA: Jewish Publication Society of America, 1894).

52 Minnie Louis, "Mission-Work Among the Unenlightened Jews," in *Papers of the Jewish Women's Congress*, 183–84. Louis cites the Three Ds on p. 177.

53 Ibid., 185.

54 Ibid., 191.
55 Kohut, response to Louis, ibid., 194. See Heinze, *Adapting to Abundance*, 89–104, for a good discussion of the role of clothing in the Americanization process among Jewish immigrants.
56 See Joselit, *The Wonders of America*; Kirshenblatt-Gimblett, "Kitchen Judaism"; Heinze, *Adapting to Abundance*.
57 Ruskay, *Hearth and Home Essays*, 53.
58 Ibid., 92–96.
59 Ibid., 40–41.
60 Ibid., 58–59.
61 Ibid., 9.
62 Ibid., 40.
63 Ibid., 63–64.
64 On the house beautiful, see David P. Handlin, *The American Home: Architecture and Society, 1815–1915* (Boston, MA: Little, Brown, 1979), 290–329; and Schlereth, *Victorian America*, 123.
65 See, for instance, Betty D. Greenberg and Althea O. Silverman, *The Jewish Home Beautiful* (New York: The Women's League of the United Synagogue of America, 1941).
66 Smith, "The Gospel of Simplicity," 84. For a very practical guide to outfitting and maintaining the tenement, see Mabel Hyde Kittredge, ed., *Housekeeping Notes: How to Furnish and Keep House in a Tenement Flat. A Series of Lessons Prepared for Use in the Association of Practical Housekeeping Centers of New York* (Boston, MA: Whitcomb & Barrows, 1911).
67 Smith, "The Gospel of Simplicity," 86.
68 Ibid., 83.
69 Ibid., 88.
70 Kittredge, *Housekeeping Notes*, 18.
71 Cohen, "Embellishing a Life of Labor."
72 For a reproduction of the ad, see Braunstein and Joselit, eds., *Getting Comfortable in New York*, 34.
73 For a discussion of Rosh Hashanah postcards in the collection of the American Jewish Historical Society, see Ellen Smith, "Greetings from Faith: Early-Twentieth-Century American Jewish New Year Postcards," in David Morgan and Sally M. Promey, eds., *The Visual Culture of American Religions* (Berkeley, CA: University of California Press, 2001), 229–48.
74 Cohen, "Embellishing the Life of Labor," 272.
75 Ibid., 275.
76 Heinze, *Adapting to Abundance*, 6.
77 Irving Howe, *World of Our Fathers* (New York: Harcourt Brace Jovanovich, 1976), 171.
78 Heinze, *Adapting to Abundance*, 108.
79 At the time of the publication of his study, Yosef Hayim Yerushalmi reported that there were over 3,500 catalogued editions of the Haggadah – *Haggadah and History: A Panorama in Facsimile of Five Centuries of the Printed Haggadah from the Collections of Harvard University and the Jewish Theological Seminary of America* (Philadelphia, PA: Jewish Theological Seminary of America, 1974), 13.
80 See *The Seder Service for Passover Eve in the Home*, arranged by Mrs. Philip Cowen, 11th edn (New York: Philip Cowen, 1918), 128; *The Seder Service*, 17th edn (Philadelphia, PA: Julius H. Greenstone, 1935), 128; *The New Haggadah for the Pesah Seder*, ed. Mordecai M. Kaplan, Eugene Kohn and Ira Eisenstein (New York: Behrman House, 1942), 176.

81 *Haggadah Passover Seder Service*. Prepared by Joseph Jacobs Organization, no date (1940s–50s).

82 *The Haggadah of Passover*, translated by Abraham Regelson, illustrated by Siegmund Forst (New York: Shulsinger Brothers, 1951).

83 According to Yerushalmi, *Haggadah and History*, 45, the four sons first appeared together in the same image in a Dutch edition of the Haggadah published in 1695 (see his plate 60). Apparently that remained unusual. The only other images Yerushalmi indicates as doing so were a Chicago edition of 1883 (plate 115) and a German edition of 1923 (plate 134). Four sons appeared in other Haggadah illustrations, but either separately (plate 138) or, if as a group, then undifferentiated (see his plates 84, 98, 109).

84 Heinze, *Adapting to Abundance*, 65.

85 Ibid., 66.

86 Ibid., 77.

87 Ibid., 78.

5 Pictorial entertainment and instruction

1 Matthew R. Isenburg, "The Wonder of the American Daguerreotype," in Richard S. Field and Robin Jaffee Frank, eds., *American Daguerreotypes from the Matthew R. Isenburg Collection* (New Haven, CT: Yale University Art Gallery, 1989), 12.

2 Sarah Roberts, "An Hour in a Daguerrian Gallery," in Emily Percival, ed., *The Amaranth; or, Token of Remembrance. A Christmas and New Year's Gift for 1855* (Boston, MA: Phillips, Sampson; New York: J. C. Derby, 1855), 211.

3 Harriet Beecher Stowe, *Uncle Tom's Cabin, or Life Among the Lowly* (London: J. Cassell, 1852).

4 Roberts, "An Hour in a Daguerrian Gallery," 212.

5 Ibid., 216.

6 Ibid., 218.

7 Quoted in Richard Rudisill, *Mirror Image: The Influence of the Daguerreotype on American Society* (Albuquerque, NM: University of New Mexico Press, 1971), 52–53.

8 A. W. "Christmas Albums and Photographic Cases," *History of Photography* 5, no. 1 (January 1981), 20.

9 See, for example, Jon Ibson, *Picturing Men: A Century of Male Relationships in Everyday American Photography* (Washington, DC: Smithsonian Institution Press, 2002).

10 See Clément Chéroux et al., *The Perfect Medium: Photography and the Occult* (New Haven, CT: Yale University Press, 2005).

11 Discussed by Heinz K. Henisch and Bridget A. Henisch, *The Photographic Experience 1839–1914: Images and Attitudes* (University Park, PA: Pennsylvania State University Press, 1993), 124–29, 187–88.

12 For a discussion of the iconography of the Victorian mother as Jesus, see David Morgan, *The Sacred Gaze: Religious Visual Culture in Theory and Practice* (Berkeley, CA: University of California Press, 2005), 199–206.

13 For an overview of angels in the history of religions, see Andrea Prias, "Angels," *Encyclopedia of Religion*, 2nd edn (Detroit, MI: Thomson Gale, 2005), 343–49.

14 See Gustav Davidson, *A Dictionary of Angels* (New York: The Free Press, 1967).

15 Nathaniel Hawthorne, *The House of the Seven Gables* (New York: New American Library, 2001), 227: "These railroads . . . give us wings; they annihilate the toil and dust of pilgrimage; they spiritualize travel!" For consideration of Hawthorne's own beliefs, see Samuel Chase Coale, *Mesmerism and Hawthorne: Mediums of American Romance* (Tuscaloosa, AL: University of Alabama Press, 1998).

16 See Chéroux et al., *The Perfect Medium*; James Coates, *Photographing the Invisible: Practical Studies in Spirit Photography, Spirit Portraiture, and Other Rare but Allied Phenomena* (New York: Arno Press, 1973 [original, 1911]).

17 Quoted in Isenburg, "The Wonder of the American Daguerreotype," 10.

18 Rev. J. G. Adams, "The Little Daguerreotype," in Mrs. C. M. Sawyer, ed., *The Rose of Sharon: A Religious Souvenir for 1855* (Boston, MA: A. Tompkins and B. B. Mussey, 1855), 252–53. Emphasis in original.

19 Note with portrait of dead baby, post 1850, Cased Photograph Collection, box 2a, Historical Society of Pennsylvania.

20 For several other examples and discussion of VanDerZee's mortuary portraits see Deborah Willis-Braithwaite, *VanDerZee: Photographer 1886–1983* (New York: Harry N. Abrams, 1993), 16–18, 148–53.

21 For very fine studies of postmortem American photography in the nineteenth century see Jay Ruby, *Secure the Shadow: Death and Photography in America* (Cambridge, MA: MIT Press, 1995), and Henisch and Henisch, *The Photographic Experience*, 179–93.

22 Ruby, *Secure the Shadow*, 75–9.

23 [William Fearing Gill], *Parlor Tableaux and Amateur Theatricals* (Boston, MA: J. E. Tilton, 1867). The tableau vivant garnered widespread success during the 1860s. The author of an early guide to domestic entertainment, published in 1858, felt it necessary to introduce popular American readers to the device: "The Tableaux Vivants may be new to many of our readers, although they have been popular for some years, in polite society, both in Europe and this country, and especially in the South," Anonymous, *The Sociable; or, One Thousand and One Home Amusements* (New York: Dick & Fitzgerald, 1858), iii. By 1869, however, Sarah Annie Frost was able to write in another handbook, produced by the same publisher, that there "is scarcely any way of passing a social evening more delightful and popular than that offered by the performers of Tableaux Vivants to their audience," *The Book of Tableaux and Shadow Pantomimes* (New York: Dick & Fitzgerald, 1869), 9.

24 Gill, *Parlor Tableaux*, 5.

25 Ibid., 95.

26 Ibid., 92.

27 Ibid., 278.

28 Josephine Pollard, *Artistic Tableaux with Picturesque Diagrams and Descriptions of Costumes* (New York: White, Stokes, and Allen, 1884).

29 Ibid., 6.

30 Ibid., 5.

31 Ibid., 22.

32 William Culp Darrah, *Stereo Views: A History of Stereographs in America and their Collection* (Gettysburg, PA: William Culp Darrah, 1964).

33 Advertisement from *Scientific American*, August 1856, reproduced in Paul Wing, *Stereoscopes: The First One Hundred Years* (Nashua, NH: Transition, 1996), 54.

34 Darrah, *Stereo Views*, 177–79; for price and production history of American stereographs see pp. 3–17.

35 Jonathan Crary, *Techniques of the Observer: On Vision and Modernity in the Nineteenth Century* (Cambridge, MA: MIT Press, 1990), 124.

36 Oliver Wendell Holmes, "The Stereoscope and the Stereograph," *The Atlantic Monthly* 3, no. 20 (June 1859), 82.

37 Ibid., 81.

38 Oliver Wendell Holmes, "Sun-Painting and Sun-Sculpture; with a Stereoscopic Trip across the Atlantic," *The Atlantic Monthly* 8, no. 45 (July 1861), 18.

39 Ibid., 23.

40 Ibid., 15–16.
41 Ibid., 28.
42 Mark Twain, *The Innocents Abroad, or The New Pilgrims' Progress* (Hartford, CT: American, 1869; facsimile reproduction, New York: Oxford University Press, 1996), 471.
43 Ibid., 472.
44 Ibid., 496.
45 Ibid., 511.
46 On Miller and Vincent in the context of the history of American Sunday schools, see Anne M. Boylan, *Sunday School: The Formation of an American Institution, 1790–1880* (New Haven, CT: Yale University Press, 1988), 90–92.
47 Ibid., 30.
48 Ibid., 54.
49 D. H. Post, "Chautauqua," *Harper's New Monthly Magazine* 59, no. 351 (August 1879), 353. Two instructive studies of Chautauqua's visual culture are John Davis, *The Landscape of Belief: Encountering the Holy Land in Nineteenth-Century American Art and Culture* (Princeton, NJ: Princeton University Press, 1996), 88–97; and Burke O. Long, *Imagining the Holy Land: Maps, Models, and Fantasy Travels* (Bloomington, IN: Indiana University Press, 2003), 7–41. Burke's study is especially good at discussing Chautauqua's understanding and use of biblical geography, esp. 28–37. For a fascinating study of Holy Land theme parks and the long history of replicating Jerusalem, see Annabel Jane Wharton, *Selling Jerusalem: Relics, Replicas, Theme Parks* (Chicago, IL: University of Chicago Press, 2006).
50 Post, "Chautauqua," 353.
51 Ibid., 353–54.
52 Lyman Abbott, *Jesus of Nazareth: His Life and Teachings* (New York: Harper & Bros., 1869); Henry Ward Beecher, *Life of Jesus, the Christ* (New York: J. B. Ford, 1871). For a discussion of this new genre of religious publication in the United States, see David Morgan, *Protestants and Pictures: Visual Culture, and the Age of American Mass Production* (New York: Oxford University Press, 1999), 292–304.
53 Two clergy who preached sermons during the first Chautauqua summer, Charles F. Deems and T. Dewitt Talmage, both published illustrated lives of Christ. The Methodist writer Edward Eggleston, who lectured on childhood in 1875 and thereafter, published an early collection of fine art portrayals of Jesus in that year. Charles F. Deems, *The Light of the Nations* (New York: Gay Brothers, 1884); Rev. T. Dewitt Talmage, *From Manger to Throne: Embracing a New Life of Jesus the Christ* (Philadelphia, PA: Historical Publishing, 1890); Edward Eggleston, *Christ in Art: The Story of the Words and Acts of Jesus Christ* (New York: J. B. Ford, 1875). Eggleston contributed several columns on blackboard illustrations to *The Sunday School Teacher* in 1867–68.
54 Advocates of blackboard drawing and chalk talk included Edward Eggleston, John Vincent himself, and A. O. Van Lennep. Van Lennep was the eccentric fellow who dressed as an Arab and performed a Muslim call to prayer each morning at Chautauqua. In an 1873 issue of *The American Sunday School Worker* he advertised as publisher a periodical called *The Sunday School Blackboard Magazine*, which is said to have begun publication in 1869. The magazine was touted as offering illustrations for every lesson of the International Series of the uniform Sunday school lesson for 1873. For a description of the comical use of chalk talks see Jesse Lyman Hurlbut, *The Story of Chautauqua* (New York: G. P. Putnam's Sons, 1921), 41. Hurlbut himself published *Traveling in the Holy Land through the Stereoscope* (New York: Underwood and Underwood, 1900).
55 Ad for Benerman & Wilson Lantern Slides, *The Magic Lantern* 1, no. 3 (November

1874), 19. The "Wilson" in Benerman & Wilson was Edward Wilson, publisher of *The Philadelphia Photographer*, who traveled to Egypt with William Rau in 1881–82 to take photographs for use as commercial lantern slides. Wilson had hoped to visit Egypt for the same purpose in 1874, but was unable to do so.

56 Letter from William H. Rau to his wife. Written from Cairo, Sunday, January 8, 1882. Library Company of Philadelphia.

57 Tiberias, Saturday, April 22, 1882, p. 83, William H. Rau Diary, Library Company of Philadelphia.

58 Jeffrey Shandler and Beth S. Wenger, " 'The Site of Paradise': The Holy Land in American Jewish Imagination," in Jeffrey Shandler and Beth S. Wenger, eds., *Encounters with the "Holy Land": Place, Past and Future in American Jewish Culture* (Philadelphia, PA: National Museum of American Jewish History; the Center for Judaic Studies, University of Pennsylvania; and the University of Pennsylvania Library, 1997), 19.

59 Twain, *Innocents Abroad*, 607.

60 Quoted in Shandler and Wenger, *Encounters*, 31.

61 Barbara Kirshenblatt-Gimblett, "A Place in the World: Jews and the Holy Land at World's Fairs," in Shandler and Wenger, *Encounters*, 74.

62 Ibid.

63 For a detailed and beautifully illustrated history of panoramas and related devices in Europe and the United States, see Stephan Oettermann, *The Panorama: History of a Mass Medium*, tr. Deborah Lucas Schneider (New York: Zone Books, 1997), with the history of American panoramas treated on pp. 313–44; on American panoramas of the Holy Land, see Davis, *Landscape of Belief*, 53–72; for a very fine discussion of photography and panoramas of the West, see Martha A. Sandweiss, *Print the Legend: Photography and the American West* (New Haven, CT: Yale University Press, 2002), 48–86. For a very helpful bibliography of major studies of panoramas, see Sandweiss, 349, n. 9.

64 Quoted in Sandweiss, *Print the Legend*, 53.

65 The advertisement appears in Rev. Edwin M. Long, *Illustrated History of Hymns and their Authors* (Philadelphia, PA: Joseph F. Jaggers, 1875), 428.

66 *Comments on Arthur L. Butt's Panorama* (Charlotte, NC: Standard Printing Company, n.d. [ca. 1898]. This publication reprints fifty-two pages of commentary drawn from newspaper accounts from 1880 to 1898, from North Carolina to Indiana.

67 See *Comments*, 6, 12.

68 "Butt's Paintings Wednesday Night," Durham *Plant*, April 1880; reprinted in *Comments*, 27.

69 "The Apocalyptic Vision," Chattanooga *Daily Times*, August 2, 1880; reprinted in *Comments*, 30.

70 "The Exhibition at the Baptist Church," Lebanon, Tennessee, in *Comments*, 33; *The Literary World*, March 10, 1883, in *Comments*, 9.

71 Atlanta *Daily Post*, June 15, 1880, reprinted in *Comments*, 4; E. A. Wingard, Charlotte, NC, no date, in *Comments*, 12.

72 J. J. Renn, Pastor, Methodist Episcopal Church, Salisbury, NC, no date, in *Comments*, 12.

73 Brookhaven *Ledger*, 1881, in *Comments*, 35; "Exhibition," *Economiss*, Elizabeth City, NC, June 14, 1881, in *Comments*, 41.

6 Seeing in public

1 Benedict Anderson, *Imagined Communities: Reflections on the Origin and Spread of Nationalism*, rev. edn (London: Verso, 1991).

2 Ibid., 37–46.
3 Rev. James Hayes, "The Passion-Play at Ober-Ammergau," *The Ave Maria* 19, no. 9 (March 3, 1883), 162.
4 Burton Holmes, *Travelogues*, 12 vols (New York: McClure, 1910), vol. 7, 201–202. For a study of the play, see James Shapiro, *Oberammergau: The Troubling Story of the World's Most Famous Passion Play* (New York: Vintage, 2001).
5 Hayes, "The Passion-Play," 163. See also the official text for 1900: John P. Jackson, *The Oberammergau-Passion Play* (New York: American Photo., 1900), which offers the full script and organization of successive tableaux and scenes.
6 It is just this pairing that raises the enduring issue of the Passion play's anti-Jewish character – see Shapiro, *Oberammergau*; and Marcia Kupfer, ed., *The Passion Story: From Visual Representation to Social Drama* (University Park, PA: Pennsylvania State University Press, 2007).
7 Information on the Bowdens and their illustrated lectures is found with their lantern slides in Bowden Papers, the Department of Special Collections, Christopher Library and Information Center, Valparaiso University.
8 *Owatonna* (Minnesota) *Evening Journal*, November 4, 1901; unpaginated news clipping, Bowden Papers, Valparaiso University.
9 Quoted in Jackson, *The Oberammergau-Passion Play*, 59.
10 Charles M. Kurtz, *Christ Before Pilate: The Painting by Munkacsy* (New York: published for the Exhibition, 1887), 9.
11 Rev. William Butler, from *Zion's Herald*, Boston, March 30, 1887, in Kurtz, *Christ Before Pilate*, 42; *The New York Star*, November 18, 1886, reprinted in Kurtz, 49.
12 From *Beck's Journal of Decorative Art*, January 1887, reprinted in Kurtz, *Christ Before Pilate*, 54.
13 *Philadelphia North American*, March 2, 1887, reprinted in Kurtz, *Christ Before Pilate*, 55.
14 Oliver Wendell Holmes, "Sun-Painting and Sun-Sculpture," *The Atlantic Monthly* 8, no. 45 (July 1861), 28.
15 Oliver Wendell Holmes, "The Stereoscope and the Stereograph," *The Atlantic Monthly* 3, no. 20 (June 1859), 747–48.
16 Holmes, "Sun-Painting and Sun-Sculpture," 29.
17 For a discussion of new media and the emergence of cinema, see Anthony R. Guneratne, "The Birth of a New Realism: Photography, Painting and the Advent of Documentary Cinema," *Film History* 10 (1998), 165–87.
18 Charles Musser, "Passions and the Passion Play: Theater, Film, and Religion in America, 1880–1900," *Film History* 5 (1993), 426.
19 Ibid., 435–37. For further discussion see Charles Musser, *Before the Nickelodeon: Edwin S. Porter and the Edison Manufacturing Company* (Berkeley, CA: University of California Press, 1991), 120–25.
20 Musser, "Passions and the Passion Play," 440.
21 Galen A. Merrill, public school official from Owatonna, Minnesota, unidentified and undated newspaper clipping, Bowden Papers, Valparaiso University. The Bowdens presented their lecture in Owatonna in November of 1901. Musser points out that the combination of slides and film was quite common at this time, *Before the Nickelodeon*, 123.
22 "[Chautauqua] Has Been a Great Success," *Dublin (Georgia) Currier-Dispatch* (June 25, 1903), 1, Bowden Papers, Valparaiso University.
23 Ibid.
24 Letter of March 23, 1900, from W. O. Ruston, Pastor, First Presbyterian Church, Dubuque, Iowa, to Charles L. Bowden, in Correspondence File, Bowden Papers,

Valparaiso University. A Minnesota newspaper carried an endorsement of the play and the signatures of thirty-four Protestant and Catholic clergy and public school officials, assuring the public that the Bowdens' presentation scheduled for a Catholic church in Austin, Minnesota, on November 4–5, 1901, was safe, "The Only Genuine Oberammergau Passion Play of 1900 in America," unidentified news clipping, Bowden Papers.

25 Herbert Reynolds, "From Palette to the Screen: The Tissot Bible as Sourcebook for From Manger to the Cross," in Roland Cosandey, André Gaudreault, and Tom Gunning, eds., *Une invention du diable? Cinéma des premiers temps et religion* (Sainte-Foy, France: Les Presses de l'Université Laval, 1992), 275–310.

26 See Charles Musser in collaboration with Carol Nelson, *High-Class Moving Pictures: Lyman H. Howe and the Forgotten Era of Traveling Exhibition, 1880–1920* (Princeton, NJ: Princeton University Press, 1991), 72.

27 J. C. Long, *Public Relations* (New York: McGraw-Hill, 1924); quoted in W. Brooke Graves, ed., *Readings in Public Opinion: Its Formation and Control* (New York: D. Appleton, 1928), 398.

28 Cited in Graves, *Readings in Public Opinion*, 401.

29 Edward H. Chandler, "The Moving Picture Show: The Child and the Theater," *Religious Education* 6, no. 4 (October 1911), 346.

30 Ibid., 349, emphasis added; 348.

31 For discussion of the Religious Education Association, see David Morgan, *Protestants and Pictures: Visual Culture and the Age of American Mass Production* (New York: Oxford University Press, 1999), 311–16.

32 Rev. Herbert A. Jump, "The Child's Leisure Hour – How It Is Affected by the Motion Picture," *Religious Education* 6, no. 4 (October 1911), 352–53.

33 Herbert F. Sherwood, "Motion Pictures for Church Use," *Religious Education* 13, no. 6 (December 1918), 422.

34 Herbert A. Jump, "The Religious Possibilities of the Motion Picture," reprinted in Terry Lindvall, ed., *The Silents of God: Issues and Documents in Silent American Film and Religion, 1908–1925* (Lanham, MD: Scarecrow Press, 2001), 57. Jump privately printed the pamphlet in December of 1910.

35 Jump, "Religious Possibilities," 60–61, 58, 71.

36 K. S. Hover, "Motography as an Arm of the Church," *Motography* 5, no. 5 (May 1911), 84; reprinted in Lindvall, *Silents*, 48.

37 Jump, "Religious Possibilities," 57.

38 Carl Halliday, "The Motion Picture and the Church," *The Independent* 74 (February 13, 1913); reprinted in Lindvall, *Silents*, 95.

39 Ibid., 96.

40 Professor Frederick K. Starr, quoted by Jump, "Religious Possibilities," 65.

41 Jump, "Religious Possibilities," 71.

42 Ibid., 57.

43 Ibid., 72.

44 Ibid., 69.

45 Hover, "Motography," 49.

46 Halliday, "The Motion Picture and the Church," 95.

47 Rev. Edgar Fay Daugherty, minister of First Christian Church, quoted in Rev. E. Boudinot Stockton, "The Picture in the Pulpit," *Moving Picture World* 14, no. 4 (October 26, 1912), 336; reprinted in Lindvall, *Silents*, 79.

48 Jump, "Religious Possibilities," 59.

49 Quoted in Rev. E. Boudinot, "The Picture in the Pulpit," *Moving Picture World* 14, no. 7 (November 16, 1912), 642; reprinted in Lindvall, *Silents*, 83.

50 Warren I. Sussman, " 'Personality' and the Making of Twentieth-Century Culture,"

in John Higham and Paul K. Conkin, eds., *New Directions in American Intellectual History* (Baltimore, MD: Johns Hopkins University Press, 1979), 212–26.

51 Jump, "Religious Possibilities," 60.

52 Lyman Abbott, "The Significance of the Present Moral Awakening in the Nation," in Henry Churchill King, Francis Greenwood Peabody, Lyman Abbott and Washington Gladden, *Education and National Character* (Chicago, IL: Religious Education Association, 1908), 28.

53 David Morgan, *The Sacred Gaze: Religious Visual Culture in Theory and Practice* Berkeley, CA: University of California Press, 2005), 220–55.

54 Thomas H. Dickinson, "War and Motion Pictures," *Religious Education* 9, no. 5 (October 1914), 418.

55 Walter Lippmann, *Public Opinion* (New York: Harcourt, Brace, 1922).

56 Ibid, 16, 80.

57 Ibid., 15–16.

58 Ibid., 29.

59 Ibid., 91. Lippmann desired that film producers be freed from commercial constraints in order to create films whose contribution would be "to enlarge and to refine, to verify and criticize the repertory of images with which our imaginations work," 166.

60 For a discussion of the poster and its setting in wartime America's book campaigns, see Matthew Hedstrom, "Seeking a Spiritual Center: Mass Market Books and Liberal Religion in America, 1921–1948," Ph.D. dissertation (Austin, TX: University of Texas, 2006), 239–40.

61 Lippmann, *Public Opinion*, 313, 358.

62 Ibid., 163.

63 Hugo Münsterberg, *The Photoplay: A Psychological Study* (New York: D. Appleton, 1916), 87.

64 Ibid., 95.

65 Ibid., 221.

66 Ibid., 223.

67 Ibid., 228.

68 Rev. Henry S. Spaulding, "The Educative Value of the Art of the Great Painters," in *The Aims of Religious Education, The Proceedings of the Third Annual Convention of the Religious Education Association, Boston, February 12–16, 1905* (Chicago, IL: Religious Education Association, 1905), 416. Emphasis added.

69 Ibid.

70 Ibid., 417.

71 H. Augustine Smith, "The Fine Arts in the Curriculum," *Religious Education* 17, no. 3 (June 1922), 217–18. Smith cited two titles by Percy MacKaye: *The New Citizenship: A Civic Ritual Devised for Places of Public Meeting in America* (New York: Macmillan, 1915) and *The Will of Song: A Dramatic Service of Community Singing* (New York: Boni and Liverright, 1919).

72 Smith, "Fine Arts in the Curriculum," 218.

73 Scot M. Guenter, *The American Flag, 1777–1924: Cultural Shifts from Creation to Codification* (Cranbury, NJ: Associated University Presses, 1990), 148; n. 37, 232. For another example of a living flag, see Cecilia Elizabeth O'Leary, *To Die For: The Paradox of American Patriotism* (Princeton, NJ: Princeton University Press, 1999), 126. The pageantry of street theater had long been associated with the public display of militias in American cities – see Susan G. Davis, *Parades and Power: Street Theater in Nineteenth-Century Philadelphia* (Philadelphia, PA: Temple University Press, 1986), 49–72.

74 MacKaye, *The New Citizenship*, 11.

75 Ibid., 12.
76 Ibid., 12–13.
77 Ibid., 28.
78 Ibid., 14.
79 Ibid., 34.
80 Ibid., 86.
81 Ibid., 81.
82 Ibid., 14.
83 Guenter, *The American Flag*, 178.
84 Colonel Geo[rge] T. Balch, *Methods of Teaching Patriotism in the Public Schools* (New York: D. Van Nostrand, 1890). For more on Balch, see O'Leary, *To Die For*, 151–55; Guenter, *The American Flag*, 114–20; and Morgan, *The Sacred Gaze: Religious Visual Culture in Theory and Practice*, 233–37.
85 Balch, *Methods of Teaching Patriotism*, 46.
86 Ibid., xviii.
87 Robert Bellah, "Civil Religion in America," *Daedulus* (Winter 1967); reprinted in Russell E. Richey and Donald G. Jones, eds., *American Civil Religion* (New York: Harper & Row, 1974), 25.
88 Balch, *Methods of Teaching Patriotism*, v.
89 Ibid., viii.
90 Ibid., xxxvii.
91 Ibid., 5.
92 Ibid.
93 *West Virginia State Board of Education v. Barnette*; reprinted in Robert Justin Goldstein, ed., *Desecrating the American Flag: Key Documents of the Controversy from the Civil War to 1995* (Syracuse, NY: Syracuse University Press, 1996), 74–75. A fine study of the history of the Pledge of Allegiance is Richard J. Ellis, *To the Flag; The Unlikely History of the Pledge of Allegiance* (Lawrence, KS: University Press of Kansas, 2005).

7 Facing the sacred

1 Marcus Aurelius Root, *The Camera and the Pencil or The Heliographic Art* (Philadelphia, PA: M. A. Root, 1864; reprint, Pawlet, VT: Helios, 1971), 84–85.
2 Ibid., 89.
3 Hugo Münsterberg, *The Photoplay: A Psychological Study* (New York: D. Appleton, 1916), 113.
4 G. Stanley Hall, *Jesus, the Christ, In the Light of Psychology*, 2 vols (Garden City, NY: Doubleday, 1917), vol. 1, viii. All page references in the text hereafter are to volume 1 of this publication.
5 Ibid., viii.
6 Ibid., xiv.
7 Ibid., xvi.
8 Ibid., 22.
9 Ibid., 23.
10 Ibid., 28.
11 Ibid., 32.
12 Ibid., 34–35.
13 For insightful studies of Barton, see Warren Susman, "Piety, Profits, and Play: The 1920s," in *Men, Women, and Issues in American History*, vol. 2, rev. edn, ed. Howard H. Quint and Milton Cantor (Homewood, IL: Dorsey Press, 1980), 202–27; and T. J. Jackson Lears, "From Salvation to Self-Realization: Advertising

and the Therapeutic Roots of the Consumer Culture, 1880–1930," in *The Culture of Consumption: Critical Essays in American History, 1880–1980*, ed. Richard Wightman Fox and T. J. Jackson Lears (New York: Pantheon, 1983), 1–38.

14 Bruce Barton, *A Young Man's Jesus* (Boston, MA: Pilgrim Press, 1914), xvii.

15 Ibid., 35–38.

16 Quoted in Bruce Barton, "Billy Sunday – Baseball Evangelist," *Collier's* 51 (July 26, 1913), 7.

17 See Q. David Bowers, "Souvenir Postcards and the Development of the Star System, 1912–1914," *Film History* 3, no. 1 (1989), 39–45.

18 Barton, "Billy Sunday," 8.

19 Quoted in William G. McLoughlin, Jr., *Billy Sunday Was His Real Name* (Chicago, IL: University of Chicago Press, 1955), 179. For a helpful study of masculinity and Protestant revivalism in Sunday's day, see Gail Bederman, " 'The Women Have Had Charge of the Church Work Long Enough': The Men and Religion Forward Movement of 1911–1912 and the Masculinization of Middle-Class Protestantism," *American Quarterly* 41 (1989), 432–65. This movement attracted the support of Protestant intellectuals and mainline churchmen, such as Washington Gladden, who sneered at Sunday's revivalism. Bederman notes that an increase in male membership occurred in the Episcopal Church as well as the Congregationalist (p. 454), both of which included many clergy who castigated Sunday in the press.

20 McLoughlin, *Sunday*, 141.

21 William T. Ellis, *Billy Sunday: The Man and His Message* (Philadelphia, PA: John C. Winston, 1914), 299.

22 Quoted in "Billy Sunday in Big Cities," *Literary Digest* 48 (April 4, 1914), 761.

23 Quoted in ibid.

24 Max Weber, *On Charisma and Institution Building: Selected Papers*, ed. S. N. Eisenstadt (Chicago, IL: University of Chicago Press, 1968).

25 Edward Shils, "Charisma, Order, and Status," *American Sociological Review* 30, no. 2 (April 1965), 203. The following observation is Shil's.

26 Helpful studies of Evangelicalism, television, and film include Heather Hendershot, *Shaking the World for Jesus: Media and Conservative Evangelical Culture* (Chicago, IL: University of Chicago Press, 2004); Bruce David Forbes and Jeffrey H. Mahan, eds., *Religion and Popular Culture in America* (Berkeley, CA: University of California Press, 2000); Eithne Johnson, "The Emergence of Christian Video and the Cultivation of Videovangelism," in Linda Klintz and Julia Lesage, eds., *Media, Culture, and the Religious Right* (Minneapolis, MN: University of Minnesota Press, 1998), 191–210; Quentin J. Schultze, ed., *American Evangelicals and Mass Media* (Grand Rapids, MI: Zondervan, 1990); Gregor T. Goethals, *The Electronic Golden Calf: Images, Religion, and the Making of Meaning* (Cambridge, MA: Cowley, 1990); and Stewart M. Hoover, *Mass Media Religion: The Social Sources of the Electronic Church* (Newbury Park, CA: Sage, 1988). The most celebrated evangelist in the second half of the twentieth century was Billy Graham, who achieved global recognition through the deft use of television to build and transmit his charisma – see Michael R. Real, *Mass-Mediated Culture* (Englewood Cliffs, NJ: Prentice-Hall, 1977), 150–205.

27 Letter of May 7, 1941, from Mrs. (Hattie Bill) Clifton J. Allen to Booth, folder 17, Baptist Sunday School Board, 1938–1941, Mss 1028–1–17, Providence Lithography Company, Rhode Island Historical Society.

28 For a discussion of the conversation, see David Morgan, *Visual Piety: A History and Theory of Popular Religious Images* (Berkeley, CA: University of California Press, 1998), 119–20.

29 Quoted in Sylvia E. Peterson, "The Ministry of Christian Art," *Lutheran Companion* 55, no. 14 (April 2, 1947), 11.

30 Robert Paul Roth, "Christ and the Muses," *Christianity Today* 2, no. 11 (March 3, 1958), 9.

31 For further discussion of the popular reception of Jesus among twentieth-century Americans, see Stephen Prothero, *American Jesus: How the Son of God Became a National Icon* (New York: Farrar, Straus, Giroux, 2003); Richard Wightman Fox, *Jesus in America: Personal Savior, Cultural Hero, National Obsession* (New York: HarperSanFrancisco, 2004); and David Morgan, ed., *Icons of American Protestantism: The Art of Warner Sallman* (New Haven, CT: Yale University Press, 1996).

32 Will Herberg, *Protestant, Catholic, Jew: An Essay in American Religious Sociology*, rev. edn (Garden City, NY: Anchor, 1960).

33 Aimee Semple McPherson, *The Story of My Life* (Waco, TX: Word Books, 1973), 111–12.

34 Quoted in Edith L. Blumhofer, *Aimee Semple McPherson: Everybody's Sister* (Grand Rapids, MI: William B. Eerdmans, 1993), 216.

35 Aimee Semple McPherson, *The Personal Testimony of Aimee Semple McPherson* (Los Angeles, CA: Foursquare, reprinted by B. N. Robertson Printshop, 1973), 14. Blumhofer, *Aimee Semple McPherson*, 120, observed that during the 1920s McPherson preached on the Song of Solomon more even than she did on the key doctrine of Christ's Second Coming.

36 Semple McPherson, *Story of My Life*, 80, 75–76, 139.

37 For discussion of McPherson's use of various media and her sense of publicity, especially with regard to the Angelus Temple, see Blumhofer, *Aimee Semple McPherson*, 224–80; for instructive consideration of her pioneering use of radio see Tona J. Hangen, *Redeeming the Dial: Radio, Religion, and Popular Culture in America* (Chapel Hill, NC: University of North Carolina Press, 2002), 57–79.

38 For a study of the theatricality of Salvation Army practices, see Diane Winston, "All the World's a Stage: The Performed Religion of the Salvation Army, 1880–1920," in Stewart M. Hoover and Lynn Schofield Clark, eds., *Practicing Religion in the Age of the Media: Explorations in Media, Religion, and Culture* (New York: Columbia University Press, 2002), 113–37; and the importance of uniforms and fashion among Salvation Army women evangelists, Diane Winston, "Living in the Material World: Salvation Army Lassies and Urban Commercial Culture, 1880–1918," in John M. Giggie and Diane Winston, eds., *Faith in the Market: Religion and the Rise of Urban Commercial Culture* (New Brunswick, NJ: Rutgers University Press, 2002), 13–36.

39 J. L. Austin, *How to Do Things with Words*, 2nd edn, eds. J. O. Urmson and Marina Sbisà (Cambridge, MA: University of Harvard Press, 1975), 6, 14–15.

40 For consideration of speech act theory as it relates to religious language see a pioneering work by the student of Austin, Donald D. Evans, *The Logic of Self-Involvement: A Philosophical Study of Everyday Language with Special Reference to the Christian Use of Language about God as Creator* (London: SCM Press, 1963). One set of considerations of the relevance of speech act theory for the study of the bible is *After Pentecost: Language and Biblical Interpretation*, ed. Craig Bartholomew, Colin Greene, and Karl Möller (Carlisle, UK: Paternoster Press, 2001). Beyond the realm of academic theology and religious philosophy, anthropologist Simon Coleman has studied the oral performance of Pentecostals in Sweden, "Words as Things: Language, Aesthetics, and the Objectification of Protestant Evangelicalism," *Material Culture* 1, no. 1 (1996), 107–28.

41 Quoted in Camilo José Vergara, *How the Other Half Worships* (New Brunswick, NJ: Rutgers University Press, 2005), 178.

42 The "east wind" is a natural force deployed by God in several instances in prophetic

books of the Hebrew bible either to punish an errant servant, as in the case of Jonah (Jonah 4: 8), or to punish faithless members of God's chosen, such as the tribe of Ephraim (Hosea 13: 15), or all of Israel (Ezekiel 17: 10).

43 See http://www.cultlink.com/ar/osteen.htm

44 Quoted in Vergara, *How the Other Half Worships*, 243.

45 The term has been used by W. J. T. Mitchell, *Picture Theory* (Chicago, IL: University of Chicago Press, 1994), 83–107 et passim; and Allen F. Roberts and Mary Nooter Roberts, *A Saint in the City: Sufi Arts of Urban Senegal* (Los Angeles, CA: UCLA Fowler Museum of Cultural History, 2003), 92–96.

46 For several examples of Downey's work, see Vergara, *How the Other Half Worships*.

47 For a historical examination of spiritualized media, see Jeffrey Sconce, *Haunted Media: Electronic Presence from Telegraphy to Television* (Durham, NC: Duke University Press, 2000).

48 An insightful discussion of American Protestant anxieties about television in the mid-twentieth century is Michele Rosenthal, " 'Turn it off!' TV Criticism in the *Christian Century* Magazine, 1946–1960," in Hoover and Clark, eds., *Practicing Religion in the Age of the Media*, 138–62.

49 Helpful texts for the analysis of television are John Fiske, *Television Culture* (London: Routledge, 1989); Horace Newcomb, ed., *Television: The Critical View*, 5th edn (New York: Oxford University Press, 1994); and Cat Celebrezze, "The Birth of American Televisual Spectatorship," in David Holloway and John Beck, eds., *American Visual Cultures* (London: Continuum, 2005), 125–32.

50 Daniel Dayan and Elihu Katz, *Media Events: The Live Broadcasting of History* (Cambridge, MA: Harvard University Press, 1992). For insightful studies of media as ritual and religious experience, see Stewart M. Hoover and Knut Lundby, eds., *Rethinking Media, Religion, and Culture* (Thousand Oaks, CA: Sage, 1997); and Stewart M. Hoover, *Religion in the Media Age* (London: Routledge, 2006).

51 For the critique of the putative centralizing effect of media events, see Nick Couldry, *Media Rituals: A Critical Approach* (London: Routledge, 2003).

52 The critical and historical literature on this aspect of religion and Hollywood is quite large; a brief sample of recent studies of American film and religion from a variety of perspectives: Peter W. Williams, "Review Essay: Religion Goes to the Movies," *Religion and American Culture* 10, no. 2 (Summer 2000), 225–39; Margaret R. Miles, *Seeing and Believing: Religion and Values in the Movies* (Boston, MA: Beacon Press, 1996); Joel W. Martin and Conrad E. Ostwalt, Jr., eds., *Screening the Sacred: Religion, Myth, and Ideology in Popular American Film* (Boulder, CO: Westview, 1995); John R. May, ed., *New Image of Religious Film* (Kansas City, MO: Sheed & Ward, 1997); and John R. May, ed., *Images and Likeness: Religious Visions in American Film Classics* (Mahwah, NJ: Paulist Press, 1991).

53 Jane Naomi Iwamura has studied the American fascination with Asian monks and gurus, "The Oriental Monk in American Popular Culture," in Bruce David Forbes and Jeffrey H. Mahan, eds., *Religion and Popular Culture in America* (Berkeley, CA: University of California Press, 2000), 25–43.

54 The literature in media studies on media, religion, and youth is recent and sophisticated; see, for example, Lynn Schofield Clark, *From Angels to Aliens: Teenagers, the Media, and the Supernatural* (Oxford: Oxford University Press, 2003); on media uses in the home, which provide some religious sources for youth and family members, see Stewart M. Hoover, Lynn Schofield Clark, and Diane F. Alters, *Media, Home, and Family* (New York: Routledge, 2004).

8 Back to nature

1 John Mack Faragher, *Daniel Boone: The Life and Legend of an American Pioneer* (New York: Henry Holt, 1992), 262.
2 Catherine L. Albanese, *Nature Religion in America from the Algonkian Indians to the New Age* (Chicago, IL: University of Chicago Press, 1990). On Muir's use of the sublime to promote the preservation of American wilderness, see Christine Oravec, "John Muir, Yosemite, and the Sublime Response: A Study in the Rhetoric of Preservationism," *Quarterly Journal of Speech* 67 (Autumn 1981), 245–58. For an insightful discussion of Muir, Emerson, and Ansel Adams, see William Deverell, " 'Niagara Magnified': Finding Emerson, Muir, and Adams in Yosemite," in Amy Scott, ed., *Yosemite: Art of an American Icon* (Los Angeles, CA: Autry National Center in association with University of California Press, 2006), 9–21.
3 Ralph Waldo Emerson, *Nature; Addresses, and Lectures*, in *Essays and Lectures*, ed. Joel Porte (New York: Library of America, 1983), 10.
4 For discussion of the sublime in American landscape art, see Barbara Novak, *Nature and Culture: American Landscape and Painting 1825–1875*, rev. edn (New York: Oxford University Press, 1995), 34–44; Andrew Wilton and Tim Barringer, *American Sublime: Landscape Painting in the United States 1820–1880* (London: Tate, 2002).
5 The following website lists no fewer than sixteen different creation science museums in the United States: http://www.nwcreation.net/museums.html
6 For a helpful introduction to Vivekananda's life and thought, see Thomas J. Hopkins and Brian A. Hatcher, "Vivekananda," *Encyclopedia of Religion*, 2nd edn (Detroit, MI: Macmillan Reference USA, Thomson Gale, 2005), vol. 14, 9,628–631. For a good introduction to the large literature on Emerson and Hindu thought, see Russell B. Goodman, "East-West Philosophy in Nineteenth-Century America: Emerson and Hindusim," *Journal of the History of Ideas* 51, no. 4 (October 1990), 625–45.
7 Swami Vivekananda, "Response to Welcome at the World's Parliament of Religions, Chicago, September 11, 1893," reprinted in Swami Nikhilandanda, ed., *Vivekananda: The Yogas and Other Works*, rev. edn (New York: Ramakrishna-Vivekananda Center, 1953), 183.
8 Diana L. Eck has pointed out that the decision of Indian immigrant communities to build temples in various American cities such as Chicago "forced immigrant Hindus to negotiate their identities anew – both as Hindus and as Americans," *Darśan: Seeing the Divine Image in India*, 3rd edn (New York: Columbia University Press, 1998), 80.
9 Paul Kagan, *New World Utopias: A Photographic History of the Search for Community* (New York: Penguin, 1975), 158–75.
10 See several readings on Zen and Zen gardens excerpted in S. Brent Plate, ed., *Religion, Art, and Visual Culture: A Cross-Cultural Reader* (New York: Palgrave, 2002), 134–58.
11 For discussion of many of these see Mark Halloway, *Heavens on Earth: Utopian Communities in America 1680–1880* (New York: Dover, 1966); Sally M. Promey, *Spiritual Spectacles: Vision and Image in Mid-Nineteenth-Century Shakerism* (Bloomington, IN: Indiana University Press, 1993); Richard Francis, *Transcendental Utopias: Individual and Community at Brook Farm, Fruitlands, and Walden* (Ithaca, NY: Cornell University Press, 1997).
12 Jack Forem, *Transcendental Meditation: Maharishi Mahesh Yogi and the Science of Creative Intelligence* (New York: E. P. Dutton, 1973); James S. Gordon, *The Golden Guru: The Strange Journey of Bhagwan Shree Rajneesh* (Lexingon, MA: S. Greene Press, 1988).
13 Mark David Spence, *Dispossessing the Wilderness: Indian Removal and the Making of the National Parks* (New York: Oxford University Press, 1999), 4.
14 Ibid., 5.

15 Henry Wadsworth Longfellow, *The Song of Hiawatha*, ed. Daniel Aaron (London: J. M. Dent, Everyman's Library, 1993), 159.

16 Horace Bushnell, *Christian Nurture* (Grand Rapids, MI: Baker Book House, 1979), 213. For discussion of the "vanishing Indian" motif in photography of the nineteenth-century West, see Martha A. Sandweiss, *Print the Legend: Photography and the American West* (New Haven, CT: Yale University Press, 2002), 217–19, 249–54, 260–66.

17 Henry Rowe Schoolcroft, *Algic Researches: Indian Tales and Legends*, 2 vols (Baltimore, MD: Genealogical Publishing for Clearfield, 1992), vol. 1, 172.

18 Longfellow, *Song of Hiawatha*, 153.

19 Ibid., 152.

20 William E. Brogham, " 'Hiawatha' in Ojibway," *Boston Evening Transcript* (July 19, 1902), unpaginated news clipping, Bowden Papers, Valparaiso University. Theresa Strouth Gaul has examined the ongoing performance of the "Song of Hiawatha Pageant" by white Americans in the small town of Pipestone, Minnesota, "Discordant Notes: Longfellow's *Song of Hiawatha*, Community, Race, and Performance Politics," *Journal of American Culture* 27, no. 4 (December 2004), 406–14.

21 Roberta Ihde, Valparaiso University, September 12, 1951, memo to the Chicago *Tribune*, Bowden Papers, Valparaiso University.

22 Henry David Thoreau, *Walden and Civil Disobedience*, ed. Owen Thomas, Norton Critical Edition (New York: W. W. Norton, 1966), 61.

23 Ibid. Emphasis in original.

24 Emerson, "Self-Reliance," *Essays and Lectures*, 262.

25 Thoreau, *Walden*, 21.

26 Ibid., 20.

27 Ibid., 66. Emphasis in original.

28 Ibid., 27.

29 Emerson, "The Transcendentalist," *Essays and Lectures*, 195.

30 Emerson, *Nature*, in *Essays and Lectures*, 28.

31 Emerson, "Self-Reliance," in *Essays and Lectures*, 261. For a discussion of the importance of masculinity in Emerson's thought see Susan L. Robertson, " 'Degenerate Effeminacy' and the Making of a Masculine Spirituality in the Sermons of Ralph Waldo Emerson," in Donald E. Hall, ed., *Muscular Christianity: Embodying the Victorian Age* (Cambridge: Cambridge University Press, 1994), 150–72.

32 Emerson, "Self-Reliance," 267.

33 For a discussion of Bly and the "mythopoetic men's movement" see Michael A. Messner, *Politics of Masculinities: Men in Movements* (Thousand Oaks, CA: Sage, 1997), 16–24.

34 Robert Bly, *Iron John: A Book about Men* (Reading, PA: Addison-Wesley, 1990).

35 Ward Churchill, "Indians Are Us?", in Churchill, *Indians Are Us? Culture and Genocide in Native North America* (Monroe, ME: Common Courage Press, 1994), 215.

36 An instructive introduction to kachina imagery and a useful source of iconographical information is Barton Wright, *Hopi Kachinas: The Complete Guide to Collecting Kachina Dolls* (Flagstaff, AZ: Northland Press, 1977).

37 Nancy J. Parezo, *Navajo Sand Painting: From Religious Act to Commercial Art* (Tucson, AZ: University of Arizona Press, 1983), 20. A more recent study of the ritual and world view in which the sand paintings operate is Trudy Griffin-Pierce, "The Continuous Renewal of Sacred Relations: Navajo Religion," in Lawrence E. Sullivan, ed., *Native Religions and Cultures of North America: Anthropology of the Sacred* (New York: Continuum, 2000), 121–41.

38 Parezo, *Navajo Sand Painting*, 75.
39 Wendy Rose, "The Great Pretenders: Further Reflections on Whiteshamanism," in M. Annette Jaimes, ed., *The State of Native America: Genocide, Colonization, and Resistance* (Boston, MA: South End Press, 1992), 403.
40 Ibid., 417. For a discussion of the relationship between spiritual seeking and plundering, see Myke Johnson, "Wanting to be Indian: When Spiritual Searching Turns into Cultural Theft," in Joanne Pearson, ed., *Belief Beyond Boundaries: Wicca, Celtic Spirituality and the New Age* (Milton Keynes: The Open University and Aldershot, UK: Ashgate, 2002), 277–93. For Ward Churchill's critique of Castaneda, see Churchill, "Carlos Castaneda: The Greatest Hoax since Piltdown Man," in Ward Churchill, *Fantasies of the Master Race: Literature, Cinema and the Colonization of American Indians*, ed. M. Annette Jaimes (Monroe, ME: Common Courage Press, 1992), 43–64.
41 Philip J. Deloria, *Playing Indian* (New Haven, CT: Yale University Press, 1998), 170. Wade Clark Roof, *A Generation of Seekers: The Spiritual Journeys of the Baby Boom Generation* (New York: HarperCollins, 1993), 22, includes among his ethnographic informants a woman from a traditional religious heritage (Jewish) who embraced the counterculture of the 1960s, then explored afterward a number of "spiritual and human potential alternatives," including "New Age in its many versions," eventually finding her way to Native American spirituality.
42 Lynn V. Andrews, *Medicine Woman* (New York: Harper & Row, 1981), 155. For a blistering denunciation of the hybrid promiscuity of pseudo-Indian spirituality, including Andrews and Storm by name, see Ward Churchill, "Spiritual Hucksterism: The Rise of the Plastic Medicine Men," in *Fantasies of the Master Race*, 215–25. Vine Deloria, "Is Religion Possible?" (p. 38), was no less dismissive:

> Can anyone take Lynn Andrews' books seriously? Of course. It is standard operating procedure for Indian medicine women to give ancient religious secrets to art collectors from Rodeo Drive in Hollywood – that was written into the structure of the universe from the very beginning.

43 Andrews, *Medicine Woman*, 155.
44 For consideration of the role of subjectivist epistemology, Asian religions, and New Age, see several essays in James R. Lewis and J. Gordon Melton, eds., *Perspectives on the New Age* (Albany, NY: State University of New York Press, 1992): J. Gordon Melton, "New Thought and the New Age," 15–29; Andrea Grace Diem and James R. Lewis, "Imagining India: The Influence of Hinduism on the New Age Movement," 48–58; and Suzanne Riordan, "Channeling: A New Revelation?", 105–26. On the importance of borrowing or appropriation among Neo-Pagan practitioners, see Sarah M. Pike, *Earthly Bodies, Magical Selves: Contemporary Pagans and the Search for Community* (Berkeley, CA: University of California Press, 2001), 123–54.
45 Oliver Wendell Holmes, "The Stereoscope and the Stereograph," *The Atlantic Monthly* 3, no. 20 (June 1859), 81.
46 Evelin Burger and Johannes Fiebig, *Tarot Basics* (New York: Sterling, 2006), 9.
47 David Ovason, *The Secret Symbols of the Dollar Bill* (New York: HarperCollins, 2004).
48 *What the Bleep Do We Know?* was produced, written, and directed by William Arntz, Mark Vincente, and Betsy Chasse. The "quantum" of *What the Bleep* as well as its epistemological restructuring of knowledge-making and its implications for personal transformation are not new, but related to several classic presentations of New Age thought such as Fritjof Capra, *The Tao of Physics: An Exploration of the*

Parallels between Modern Physics and Eastern Mysticism (Berkeley, CA: Shambhala, 1975); Gary Zukav, *The Dancing Wu Li Masters: An Overview of the New Physics* (New York: Morrow, 1979); and Marilyn Ferguson, *The Aquarian Conspiracy: Personal and Social Transformation in the 1980s* (Los Angeles, CA: J. P. Tarcher, 1980).

49 Inés Hernández-Ávila, "Meditations of the Spirit: Native American Religious Traditions and the Ethics of Representation," in Lee Irwin, ed., *Native American Spirituality: A Critical Reader* (Lincoln, NB: University of Nebraska Press, 2000), 25.

50 Vine Deloria, Jr., "Is Religion Possible? An Evaluation of Present Efforts to Revive Traditional Tribal Religions," *Wicazo Sa Review* 8 (Spring 1992), 35. For an overview of the controversy of Native American culture and the New Age, see Susan Mumm, "Aspirational Indians: North American Indigenous Religions and the New Age," in Pearson, ed., *Belief Beyond Boundaries*, 103–28.

51 Deloria, "Is Religion Possible?", 36.

52 The authors of the Declaration are Wilmer Stampede Mesteth, Darrell Standing Elk, and Phyllis Swift Hawk. The document has been posted by Professor Raymond Bucko, S.J. at http://puffin.creighton.edu/lakota/war.html. It has also been reprinted in Pearson, ed., *Belief Beyond Boundaries*, 129–31.

53 Steven Leuthold, "Native Media's Communities," in Duane Champagne, ed., *Contemporary Native American Cultural Issues* (Walnut Creek, CA: AltaMira Press, 1999), 193–216.

54 In contrast to this and countless other portrayals, which are often much less artful, a number of documentaries have been produced by Native American film makers who "put forth a model of community different than that found in middle-class America," a model that emphasizes "togetherness, interdependence, and mutual accountability," according to Leuthold, "Native Media's Communities," 197.

55 I depend on the very influential thesis of Benedict Anderson, *Imagined Communities: Reflections on the Origin and Spread of Nationalism*, rev. edn (London: Verso, 1991).

56 1 Nephi 17: 3, *The Book of Mormon. An Account written by the hand of Mormon upon plates taken from the plates of Nephi*, translated by Joseph Smith, Jr. (Salt Lake, UT: The Church of Jesus Christ of the Latter-day Saints, 1981).

57 An important survey of twentieth-century Mormon painting and iconography is Noel A. Carmack, "Images of Christ in Latter-day Saint Visual Culture, 1900–1999," *BYU Studies* 39, no. 3 (2000), 19–76.

58 Gary Snyder, "Smokey the Bear Sutra," published as a broadside in 1969, reprinted in Thomas A. Tweed and Stephen Prothero, eds., *Asian Religions in America: A Documentary History* (New York: Oxford University Press, 1999), 342–45.

59 Gary Snyder, "The Etiquette of Freedom," in *The Practice of the Wild* (San Francisco, CA: North Point Press, 1990), 19.

60 Gary Snyder, "The Wilderness," in *Turtle Island* (New York: New Directions, 1974), 106.

61 Snyder, "Smokey the Bear Sutra," 344. Ironically, Snyder was taken to task by some Native American activists for appropriating Native beliefs in his Pulitzer Prize winning book of poetry, *Turtle Island*, which opened with a poetic address to the Anasazi – see Rose, "The Great Pretenders," 403 and 418, n. 2, where she refers critically to Snyder's *Turtle Island*.

62 Rick Barnett, *The Thomas Kinkade Story: A 20-Year Chronology of the Artist* (Boston, MA: Bulfinch Press, 2003), 130.

63 Ibid., 112, 150. I requested permission of the Thomas Kinkade Company to reproduce the image discussed here, but my request was denied without explanation. Readers may find *Warmth of Home* reproduced in Barnett's book on page 109.

64 Barnett, *The Thomas Kinkade Story*, 109.

Select bibliography

Albanese, Catherine L. *Nature Religion in America from the Algonkian Indians to the New Age.* Chicago, IL: University of Chicago Press, 1990.

Ames, Kenneth L. *Death in the Dining Room and Other Tales of Victorian Culture.* Philadelphia, PA: Temple University Press, 1992.

Anderson, Benedict. *Imagined Communities: Reflections on the Origin and Spread of Nationalism,* rev. edn. London: Verso, 1991.

Austin, J. L. *How to Do Things with Words,* 2nd edn, ed. J. O. Urmson and Marina Sbisà. Cambridge, MA: Harvard University Press, 1975.

Balch, Colonel Geo[rge] T. *Methods of Teaching Patriotism in the Public Schools.* New York: D. Van Nostrand, 1890.

Barnett, Rick. *The Thomas Kinkade Story: A 20-Year Chronology of the Artist.* Boston, MA: Bulfinch Press, 2003.

Barton, Bruce. *A Young Man's Jesus.* Boston, MA: Pilgrim Press, 1914.

Barton, Bruce. *The Man Nobody Knows: A Discovery of Jesus.* Indianapolis, IN: Bobbs-Merrill, 1924.

Berger, David, ed. *The Legacy of Jewish Migration: 1881 and its Impact.* New York: Social Science Monographs; Brooklyn College Press: distributed by Columbia University Press, 1983.

Blumhofer, Edith L. *Aimee Semple McPherson: Everybody's Sister.* Grand Rapids, MI: William B. Eerdmans, 1993.

Boorstin, Daniel J. *The Image, or, What Happened to the American Dream.* London: Weidenfeld & Nicolson, 1961.

Boylan, Alexis, ed. *Thomas Kinkade: The Artist in the Mall.* Durham, NC: Duke University Press, 2007.

Boylan, Anne M. *Sunday School: The Formation of an American Institution, 1790–1880.* New Haven, CT: Yale University Press, 1988.

Boylan, Anne M. *The Origins of Women's Activism: New York and Boston, 1797–1840.* Chapel Hill, NC: University of North Carolina Press, 2002.

Braunstein, Susan L. and Jenna Weissman Joselit, eds, *Getting Comfortable in New York: The American Jewish Home, 1880–1950.* New York: The Jewish Museum, 1990.

Bushman, Richard L. *The Refinement of America: Persons, Houses, Cities.* New York: Alfred A. Knopf, 1992.

Bushnell, Horace. *Christian Nurture.* Grand Rapids, MI: Baker Book House, 1979.

Carmack, Noel A. "Images of Christ in Latter-day Saint Visual Culture, 1900–1999," *BYU Studies* 39, no. 3 (2000), 19–76.

Champagne, Duane, ed. *Contemporary Native American Cultural Issues*. Walnut Creek, CA: AltaMira Press, 1999.

Chéroux, Clément, ed. *The Perfect Medium: Photography and the Occult*. New Haven, CT: Yale University Press, 2005.

Churchill, Ward. *Fantasies of the Master Race: Literature, Cinema and the Colonization of American Indians*, ed. M. Annette Jaimes. Monroe, ME: Common Courage Press, 1992.

Clark, Lynn Schofield. *From Angels to Aliens: Teenagers, the Media, and the Supernatural*. Oxford: Oxford University Press, 2003.

Cohen, Lizabeth A. "Embellishing a Life of Labor: An Interpretation of the Material Culture of American Working-Class Homes, 1885–1915," in Dell Upton and John Michael Vlach, eds., *Common Places: Readings in American Vernacular Architecture*. Athens, GA: University of Georgia Press, 1986, 261–78.

Coleman, Simon. "Words as Things: Language, Aesthetics, and the Objectification of Protestant Evangelicalism." *Material Culture* 1, no. 1 (1996), 107–28.

Crary, Jonathan. *Techniques of the Observer: On Vision and Modernity in the Nineteenth Century*. Cambridge, MA: MIT Press, 1990.

Currier & Ives: Catalogue Raisonné, 2 vols. Detroit, MI: Gale Research Company, 1984.

Daniel, David. *The Bible in English: Its History and Influence*. New Haven, CT: Yale University Press, 2003.

Darrah, William Culp. *Stereo Views: A History of Stereographs in America and their Collection*. Gettysburg, PA: William Culp Darrah, 1964.

Davis, John. *The Landscape of Belief: Encountering the Holy Land in Nineteenth-Century American Art and Culture*. Princeton, NJ: Princeton University Press, 1996.

Dayan, Daniel and Elihu Katz. *Media Events: The Live Broadcasting of History*. Cambridge, MA: Harvard University Press, 1992.

Deloria, Philip J. *Playing Indian*. New Haven, CT: Yale University Press, 1998.

Douglas, Ann. *The Feminization of American Culture*. New York: Doubleday, 1977.

Dunnington, Jacqueline Orsini. *Viva Guadalupe! The Virgin in New Mexican Popular Art*. Santa Fe, NM: Museum of New Mexico Press, 1997.

Durand, Jorge and Douglas S. Massey. *Miracles on the Border: Retablos of Mexican Migrants to the United States*. Tucson, AZ: University of Arizona Press, 1995.

Eck, Diana L. *Darsan: Seeing the Divine Image in India*, 3rd edn. New York: Columbia University Press, 1998.

Ellis, John Tracy, ed. *Documents of American Catholic History*, 2 vols. Chicago, IL: Henry Regnery, 1967.

Emerson, Ralph Waldo. *Essays and Lectures*, ed. Joel Porte. New York: Library of America, 1983.

Fessenden, Tracy. "The Nineteenth-Century Bible Wars and the Separation of Church and State," *Church History* 74, no. 4 (December 2005), 784–811.

Field, Richard S. and Robin Jaffee Frank, eds. *American Daguerreotypes from the Matthew R. Isenburg Collection*. New Haven, CT: Yale University Art Gallery, 1989.

Forsberg, Jr., Clyde R. *Equal Rites: The Book of Mormon, Masonry, Gender, and American Culture*. New York: Columbia University Press, 2004.

Fox, Richard Wightman. *Jesus in America: Personal Savior, Cultural Hero, National Obsession*. New York: HarperSanFrancisco, 2004.

Fox, Richard Wightman, and T. J. Jackson Lears, eds. *The Culture of Consumption: Critical Essays in American History, 1800–1980*. New York: Pantheon, 1983.

Frank, Robin Jaffee. *Love and Loss: American Portrait and Mourning Miniatures*. New Haven, CT: Yale University Press, 2000.

Giggie, John M. and Diane Winston, eds. *Faith in the Market: Religion and the Rise of Urban Commercial Culture*. New Brunswick, NJ: Rutgers University Press, 2002.

Graves, W. Brooke, ed. *Readings in Public Opinion: Its Formation and Control*. New York: D. Appleton, 1928.

Grier, Katherine C. *Culture & Comfort: People, Parlors, and Upholstery, 1850–1930*. Rochester, NY: The Strong Museum, 1988.

Gould, Robert Freke, ed. *A Library of Freemasonry*, 5 vols. London, Philadelphia, PA: John C. Yorston, 1911.

Guenter, Scot M. *The American Flag, 1777–1924: Cultural Shifts from Creation to Codification*. Cranbury, NJ: Associated University Presses, 1990.

Gunning, Tom, ed. *Une invention du diable? Cinéma des premiers temps et religion*. Sainte-Foy, France: Les Presses de l'Université Laval, 1992.

Gutjahr, Paul C. *An American Bible: A History of the Good Book in the United States, 1777–1880*. Stanford, CA: Stanford University Press, 1999.

Hall, Donald E., ed. *Muscular Christianity: Embodying the Victorian Age*. Cambridge: Cambridge University Press, 1994.

Hall, G. Stanley. *Jesus, the Christ, In the Light of Psychology*, 2 vols. Garden City, NY: Doubleday, 1917.

Haltunen, Karen. *Confidence Men and Painted Women: A Study of Middle-Class Culture in America, 1830–1870*. New Haven, CT: Yale University Press, 1982.

Handlin, David P. *The American Home: Architecture and Society, 1815–1915*. Boston, MA: Little, Brown, 1979.

Hangen, Tona J. *Redeeming the Dial: Radio, Religion, and Popular Culture in America*. Chapel Hill, NC: University of North Carolina Press, 2002.

Harris, Michael D. *Colored Pictures: Race and Visual Representation*. Chapel Hill, NC: University of North Carolina, 2003.

Heinze, Andrew R. *Adapting to Abundance: Jewish Immigrants, Mass Consumption, and the Search for American Identity*. New York: Columbia University Press, 1990.

Hendershot, Heather. *Shaking the World for Jesus: Media and Conservative Evangelical Culture*. Chicago, IL: University of Chicago Press, 2004.

Henisch, Heinz K. and Bridget A. Henisch. *The Photographic Experience 1839–1914: Images and Attitudes*. University Park, PA: Pennsylvania State University Press, 1993.

Hoover, Stewart M. *Mass Media Religion: The Social Sources of the Electronic Church*. Newbury Park, CA: Sage, 1988.

Hoover, Stewart M. *Religion in the Media Age*. London: Routledge, 2006.

Hoover, Stewart M. and Lynn Schofield Clark, eds. *Practicing Religion in the Age of the Media: Explorations in Media, Religion, and Culture*. New York: Columbia University Press, 2002.

Hoover, Stewart M., Lynn Schofield Clark, and Diane F. Alters. *Media, Home, and Family*. New York: Routledge, 2004.

Howe, Irving. *World of Our Fathers*. New York: Harcourt Brace Jovanovich, 1976.

Ibson, Jon. *Picturing Men: A Century of Male Relationships in Everyday American Photography*. Washington, DC: Smithsonian Institution Press, 2002.

Irwin, Lee, ed. *Native American Spirituality: A Critical Reader*. Lincoln, NB: University of Nebraska Press, 2000.

Iwamura, Jane Naomi. "The Oriental Monk in American Popular Culture," in Bruce David Forbes and Jeffrey H. Mahan, eds. *Religion and Popular Culture in America*. Berkeley, CA: University of California Press, 2000, 25–43.

Jaimes, M. Annette, ed. *The State of Native America: Genocide, Colonization, and Resistance*. Boston, MA: South End Press, 1992.

Joselit, Jenna Weissman. *The Wonders of America: Reinventing Jewish Culture, 1880–1950*. New York: Hill and Wang, 1994.

Karp, Abraham J., ed. *The Jews in America: A Treasury of Art and Literature*. Westport, CT: Hugh Lauter Levin Associates, 1994.

Koerber, Susannah. "Signs of the Times: Context and Connection in Southern Conservative Evangelical Protestant and Midwestern Roman Catholic Grassroots Art Environments." Ph.D. dissertation, Emory University, 2004.

Kupfer, Marcia, ed. *The Passion Story: From Visual Representation to Social Drama*. University Park, PA: Pennsylvania State University Press, 2007.

Kurtz, Charles M. *Christ Before Pilate: The Painting by Munkacsy*. New York: published for the Exhibition, 1887.

Le Beau, Bryan F. *Currier & Ives: America Imagined*. Washington, DC: Smithsonian Institution Press, 2001.

Lehuu, Isabelle. *Carnival on the Page: Popular Print Media in Antebellum America*. Chapel Hill, NC: University of North Carolina Press, 2002.

Lewis, James R. and J. Gordon Melton, eds. *Perspectives on the New Age*. Albany, NY: State University of New York Press, 1992.

Lindvall, Terry, ed. *The Silents of God: Issues and Documents in Silent American Film and Religion, 1908–1925*. Lanham, MD: Scarecrow Press, 2001.

Lippmann, Walter. *Public Opinion*. New York: Harcourt, Brace, 1922.

McDannell, Colleen. *The Christian Home in Victorian America, 1840–1900*. Bloomington, IN: Indiana University Press, 1986.

McDannell, Colleen. "Parlor Piety: The Home as Sacred Space in Protestant America," in Jessica H. Foy and Thomas J. Schlereth, eds., *American Home Life, 1880–1930: A Social History of Spaces and Services*. Knoxville, TN: University of Tennessee Press, 1992, 162–89.

McDannell, Colleen. *Material Christianity: Religion and Popular Culture in America*. New Haven, CT: Yale University Press, 1995.

MacKaye, Percy. *The New Citizenship: A Civic Ritual Devised for Places of Public Meeting in America*. New York: Macmillan, 1915.

McPherson, Aimee Semple. *The Story of My Life*. Waco, TX: Word Books, 1973.

Maffly-Kipp, Laurie. "Engaging Habits and Besotted Idolatry: Viewing Chinese Religions in the American West." *Material Religion* 1, no. 1 (March 2005), 72–97.

Martin, Joel W. and Conrad E. Ostwalt, Jr., eds. *Screening the Sacred: Religion, Myth, and Ideology in Popular American Film*. Boulder, CO: Westview, 1995.

Marzio, Peter C. *The Democratic Art: Chromolithography 1840–1900. Pictures for a 19th-Century America*. Boston, MA: David R. Godine, 1979.

Moore, R. Laurence. *Selling God: American Life in the Marketplace of Culture*. New York: Oxford University Press, 1994.

Moore, R. Laurence. "Bible Reading and Nonsectarian Schooling: The Failure of

Religious Instruction in Nineteenth-Century Public Education." *Journal of American History* 86, no. 4 (March 2000), 1,581–599.

Morgan, David. *Visual Piety: A History and Theory of Popular Religious Images.* Berkeley, CA: University of California Press, 1998.

Morgan, David. *Protestants and Pictures: Religion, Visual Culture, and the Age of American Mass Production.* New York: Oxford University Press, 1999.

Morgan, David. *The Sacred Gaze: Religious Visual Culture in Theory and Practice.* Berkeley, CA: University of California Press, 2005.

Morgan, David and Sally M. Promey, eds. *The Visual Culture of American Religions.* Berkeley, CA: University of California Press, 2001.

Musser, Charles. *Before the Nickelodeon: Edwin S. Porter and the Edison Manufacturing Company.* Berkeley, CA: University of California Press, 1991.

Musser, Charles, in collaboration with Carol Nelson. *High-Class Moving Pictures: Lyman H. Howe and the Forgotten Era of Traveling Exhibition, 1880–1920.* Princeton, NJ: Princeton University Press, 1991.

Musser, Charles. "Passions and the Passion Play: Theater, Film, and Religion in America, 1880–1900," *Film History* 5 (1993), 419–56.

Nelson, Louis P., ed. *American Sanctuary: Understanding Sacred Spaces.* Bloomington, IN: Indiana University Press, 2006.

Newcomb, Horace, ed. *Television: The Critical View*, 5th edn. New York: Oxford University Press, 1994.

Newman, Richard, Patrick Rael, and Philip Lapsansky, eds. *Pamphlets of Protest: An Anthology of Early African-American Protest Literature, 1790–1860.* New York: Routledge, 2001.

Nord, David Paul. *Faith in Reading: Religious Publishing and the Birth of Mass Media in America.* New York: Oxford University Press, 2004.

Novak, Barbara. *Nature and Culture: American Landscape and Painting 1825–1875*, rev. edn. New York: Oxford University Press, 1995.

Oettermann, Stephan. *The Panorama: History of a Mass Medium*, tr. Deborah Lucas Schneider. New York: Zone Books, 1997.

Orsi, Robert Anthony. *The Madonna of 115th Street: Faith and Community in Italian Harlem, 1880–1950.* New Haven, CT: Yale University Press, 1985.

Parezo, Nancy J. *Navajo Sand Painting: From Religious Act to Commercial Art.* Tucson, AZ: University of Arizona Press, 1983.

Pearson, Joanne, ed. *Belief Beyond Boundaries: Wicca, Celtic Spirituality and the New Age.* Milton Keynes: The Open University and Aldershot, UK: Ashgate, 2002.

Peters, Harry T. *Currier & Ives: Printmakers to the American People.* Garden City, NY: Doubleday, Doran, 1942.

Pike, Martha V. and Janice Gray Armstrong. *A Time to Mourn: Expressions of Grief in Nineteenth Century America.* Stony Brook, NY: The Museums at Stony Brook, 1980.

Pike, Sarah M. *Earthly Bodies, Magical Selves: Contemporary Pagans and the Search for Community.* Berkeley, CA: University of California Press, 2001.

Plate, S. Brent, ed. *Religion, Art, and Visual Culture: A Cross-Cultural Reader.* New York: Palgrave, 2002.

Promey, Sally M. *Spiritual Spectacles: Vision and Image in Mid-Nineteenth-Century Shakerism.* Bloomington, IN: Indiana University Press, 1993.

Prothero, Stephen. *American Jesus: How the Son of God Became a National Icon.* New York: Farrar, Straus, Giroux, 2003.

Rawls, Walton. *Currier & Ives' America*. New York: Abbeville Press, 1979.

Richey, Russell E. and Donald G. Jones, eds. *American Civil Religion*. New York: Harper & Row, 1974.

Roof, Wade Clark. *A Generation of Seekers: The Spiritual Journeys of the Baby Boom Generation*. New York: HarperCollins, 1993.

Root, Marcus Aurelius. *The Camera and the Pencil or The Heliographic Art*. Philadelphia, PA: M. A. Root, 1864; reprint, Pawlet, VT: Helios, 1971.

Ruby, Jay. *Secure the Shadow: Death and Photography in America*. Cambridge, MA: MIT Press, 1995.

Rudisill, Richard. *Mirror Image: The Influence of the Daguerreotype on American Society*. Albuquerque, NM: University of New Mexico Press, 1971.

Ruskay, Esther J. *Hearth and Home Essays*. Philadelphia, PA: Jewish Publication Society of America, 1902.

Sandweiss, Martha A. *Print the Legend: Photography and the American West*. New Haven, CT: Yale University Press, 2002.

Schappes, Morris U. *A Pictorial History of the Jews in the United States*, rev. edn. New York: Marzani & Munsell, 1965.

Schlereth, Thomas J. *Victorian America: Transformations in Everyday Life, 1876–1915*. New York: HarperPerennial, 1992.

Schmidt, Leigh Eric. *Consumer Rites: The Buying and Selling of American Holidays*. Princeton, NJ: Princeton University Press, 1995.

Schorsch, Anita. *Mourning Becomes America: Mourning Art in the New Nation*. Philadelphia, PA: Main Street Press, 1976.

Schwain, Kristin. *Signs of Grace: Religion and Early Modern Art in America*. Ithaca, NY: Cornell University Press, 2007.

Shandler, Jeffrey and Beth S. Wenger, eds. *Encounters with the "Holy Land": Place, Past and Future in American Jewish Culture*. Philadelphia, PA: National Museum of American Jewish History; the Center for Judaic Studies, University of Pennsylvania; and the University of Pennsylvania Library, 1997.

Shapiro, James. *Oberammergau: The Troubling Story of the World's Most Famous Passion Play*. New York: Vintage, 2001.

Smith, Woodruff D. *Consumption and the Making of Respectability 1600–1800*. New York: Routledge, 2002.

Smith-Rosenberg, Carroll. *Religion and the Rise of the American City: The New York City Mission Movement, 1812–1870*. Ithaca, NY: Cornell University Press, 1971.

Snyder, Gary. *Turtle Island*. New York: New Directions, 1974.

Snyder, Gary. *The Practice of the Wild*. San Francisco, CA: North Point Press, 1990.

Sontag, Susan. *Regarding the Pain of Others*. New York: Farrar, Straus, Giroux, 2003.

Spalding, John Lancaster. *Religion and Art and Other Essays* (1905); reprint, Freeport, NY: Books for Libraries Press, 1969.

Spence, Mark David. *Dispossessing the Wilderness: Indian Removal and the Making of the National Parks*. New York: Oxford University Press, 1999.

Sullivan, Lawrence E., ed. *Native Religions and Cultures of North America: Anthropology of the Sacred*. New York: Continuum, 2000.

Sussman, Warren I. " 'Personality' and the Making of Twentieth-Century Culture," in John Higham and Paul K. Conkin, eds., *New Directions in American Intellectual History*. Baltimore, MD: Johns Hopkins University Press, 1979, 212–26.

Thoreau, Henry David. *Walden and Civil Disobedience*, ed. Owen Thomas, Norton Critical Edition. New York: W. W. Norton, 1966.

Twain, Mark. *The Innocents Abroad, or The New Pilgrims' Progress*. Hartford, CT: American, 1869; facsimile reproduction, New York: Oxford University Press, 1996.

Tweed, Thomas A. *Our Lady of the Exile: Diasporic Religion at a Cuban Catholic Shrine in Miami*. New York: Oxford University Press, 1997.

Tweed, Thomas A., ed. *Retelling U.S. Religious History*. Berkeley, CA: University of California Press, 1997.

Tweed, Thomas A. and Stephen Prothero, eds. *Asian Religions in America: A Documentary History*. New York: Oxford University Press, 1999.

Vergara, Camilo José. *How the Other Half Worships*. New Brunswick, NJ: Rutgers University Press, 2005.

Wacker, Grant. *Heaven Below: Early Pentecostals and American Culture*. Cambridge, MA: Harvard University Press, 2001.

Wharton, Annabel Jane. *Selling Jerusalem: Relics, Replicas, Theme Parks*. Chicago, IL: University of Chicago Press, 2006.

Weber, Max. *On Charisma and Institution Building: Selected Papers*, ed. S. N. Eisenstadt. Chicago, IL: University of Chicago Press, 1968.

Williams, Peter W. "Review Essay: Religion Goes to the Movies." *Religion and American Culture* 10, no. 2 (Summer 2000), 225–39.

Willis-Braithwaite, Deborah. *VanDerZee: Photographer 1886–1983*. New York: Harry N. Abrams, 1993.

Wing, Paul. *Stereoscopes: The First One Hundred Years*. Nashua, NH: Transition, 1996.

Winston, Diane. *Red-Hot and Righteous: The Urban Religion of the Salvation Army*. Cambridge, MA: Harvard University Press, 1999.

Zalesch, Saul. "The Religious Art of Benziger Brothers," *American Art* 13, no. 2 (Summer 1999), 58–79.

Index

Abbott, Lyman 183
abolitionism 55, 57; *see also* emancipation
Adams, Ansel 230, 232–34, 260–1; *Monolith, Face of Half Dome* 231
Adams, Rev. J.G. 141
Adventism 23, 89–91; *see also* millennialism
African Americans 50–61, 100–2; separatism 45
African Methodist Episcopal Church (AME) 58–61, 77; bishops of 60
Albanese, Catherine 232
Alexander, James W. 20–1, 23, 37–9, 42; and slavery 50, 52–4, 57
Allen, Hattie 208–9
Allen, Richard 58–9, 77, 94
Allston, Washington 146
America: colonial 8; early republic 9; and national identity 32; as new Israel 232, 260; as Protestant republic 66
American Bible Society (ABS) 21, 50
American Protestant Association 65
American Philosophical Society 21
American Preceptor 8
American Sunday School Union (ASSU) 18, 20–1, 23, 29, 41, 50, 95
American Tract Magazine (ATM) 18, 26, 28–30, 32, 265n43
Americanization 61, 126
Ames, Kenneth 104
Anderson, Alexander 11; illustrations: *Address* 25; *Female Influence and Obligations* 27; Missionary preaching 12
Anderson, Benedict 165
Andrews, Lynn 248–9, 253, 292n42; *Medicine Woman* 248

angels: 138–40, 147–8, 213; guardian 138–40, 146; in tableaux vivant 146; illustrations: Angel at prayer 86; Angel of Prayer 147; Her Guardian Angel 139
Angelus Temple 216–17, 288n37
anti-Semitism 45, 125, 168; and Oberammergau 283n6
Arntz, William 253
audience 160, 167, 225; as American republic 181; as community 165, 176–9; as local 181; and mass culture 179; as mass public 187; visual piety of 167
Austin, J.L. 218–19, 288n40

Babel 14
Baird, Robert 18
Balch, George T. 193–5
Barnum, P.T. 160
Barton, Bruce 202–4, 206–7, 286n13
Beecher, Catherine 84, 105
Beecher, Henry Ward 155, 161
benevolence 15–16, 26, 29
Benjamin, Walter 33, 266n66
Benziger Brothers 48–9
Bhagavad Gita 235
Bhagwan Shree Rajneesh 238
bible: as divine speech 221–2; *Illuminated Bible* 22; and illustration 19, 21–2; images of 12, 14, 22, 41, 54, 60, 61, 66, 98, 107, 114, 115, 116, 118, 120, 162, 215, 221; and inspiration 218; in public schools 18, 65–8; publication 19; red letter 222; and tracts 16, 32
Bierstadt, Albert 260
Bill of Rights 15
Bingham, Caleb 8–9

blackboard illustration 155, 281n54
Blumhofer, Edith L. 288n37
Blumin, Stuart M. 275n14
Bly, Robert 245–46, 255; *Iron John* 245–6
Bogue, David 15–16, 24, 29
Book of Revelation 161, 163–4
Boone, Daniel 230, 255
Boorstin, Daniel 187, 261
Booth, Phillips 99–100, 207–8
Bowden, Katherine 168, 174–5; Hiawatha lecture 239, 241
Boylan, Anne M. 265n43
Brady, Matthew 135–6
Brisbane, Albert 237
Brownson, Orestes 67–8
Brynner, Yul 209
Buddha 252, 258–9, 261–2
Buddhism 227, 236, 250, 252, 258–9, 261–2
Bufford, John 87
Bushman, Richard 104, 275n3
Bushnell, Horace 44, 112–13, 239; *Christian Nurture* 112
Butt, Arthur 161, 163–4, 179

Calvin, John 31, 77
Calvinism 15, 31, 62, 242
Campbell, Joseph 246, 249
capitalism 242–3, 259
Carey, Mathew 7, 19
Carter, Fred 101–2, 261; *Christ in Gethsemane* 102
Castaneda, Carlos 248; *Teachings of Don Juan* 248
character 182, 187, 193
charisma 3, 199–229; and adolescence 228–9; and business methods 206; and celebrity culture 223; as glamour 228; and Jesus 200–4; and Pentecostalism 213–23; and print 32; and religious celebrities 199–200, 204–7, 213–18; and the social order 207; in television and film 223–9
Chautauqua 95–6, 153–5, 165–6, 168, 189, 236, 281n49, 281n53
Chester, Thomas Morris 58–9
Chick, Jack T. 101
Christian union 50, 54–5
Christmas 92, 127, 133
chromolithography 91, 273n27, 276n33
church and state 15, 62, 64–5

Church of Jesus Christ of Latter-Day Saints: *see* Mormonism
creationism 234
city, menace of 37–44, 266n11
civil religion 189–95; *see* flag ritual
Clark, Lynn Schofield 289n54
class: aristocracy 74, 103; bourgeoisie 104; images and class distinctions 109–12; middle 24, 74, 103–4, 109, 112–13, 126; upper 24; working 24, 108, 129–31, 194
Cobb, Darius 203–4; *The Master* 203
Cohen, Lizabeth 129–30
Coker, Daniel 57
Cole, Thomas 140, 260–1; *Course of Empire* 232; *Voyage of Life* 140, 233
colporteurs 29, 34
Columbian Exposition 277n51
Columbian Orator 8–9, 57
commodity 73; print 165
commerce 2–3, 13, 73–5; and panorama 160
communalism, religious 236–8, 255
consumerism 74
consumption 73–4, 262, 271n2, n4; and home 105–6; middle class 74; and parlor 106–9
Cooper, James Fenimore 254–5
Copping, Harold 97, 99–100
country life 37–8; and migration 44–7; and rural piety 43
Cruise, Tom 250
culture: mass 33, 179; 187; oral 9, 175; popular 1; print 36
Currier, Nathaniel 41, 76–7, 84–5, 92–3, 115–16
Currier & Ives 75–7, 222; racist imagery 59; religious output 92–4

daguerreotype 119, 135–7; postmortem portraiture 142–5; as Protestant icon 141–2
Daughters of the American Revolution 183
Davidson, Andrew 16–18, 23
Dayan, Daniel 226
Declaration of War against Exploitation of Lakota Spirituality 253–4
Deloria, Philip 248, 253
Deloria, Vine, Jr. 248, 253
DeMille, Cecil B. 209–12
Democratic Party 67

Dobberstein, Father Paul Matthias 48, 50–1
Doddridge, Philip 29, 120
Douglas, Ann 272n13
Douglass, Frederick 44–5, 57–8
Downey, John 221–2, 288n46

Eck, Diana L. 290n8
Eddy, Mary Baker 250
Edwards, Jonathan 29
Eliade, Mircea 246
Ellis, William T. 206
eloquence 9
Ely, Ezra Stiles 62
emancipation 53, 55, 101
Emerson, Ralph Waldo 160, 233–4, 242–5, 250, 255; and masculinity 291n31; on mind and nature 244; "Self-Reliance" 244
empathy 187
entertainment 2, 38, 146, 160–1, 173, 175, 177–8, 181
Everts, W.W. 39
exorcism 219–21
eye of God 2, 87

Federalists 7, 8
feminization 201
film: and aesthetic contemplation 188; censorship 179; conditions of viewing 177–9; and democracy 182; integration with lantern slides 175; Passion play 174–6; Protestant reception 173–83; as religious instrument 179–83; as universal language 179
films, discussed: The Craft 228–9; The Da Vinci Code 252; It's a Wonderful Life 227; Last of the Mohicans 254–5; Little Buddha 226–7; The Matrix 227, 252–3; The Ring 224; The Sorcerer's Apprentice 228; Star Wars 224, 227, 249; The Ten Commandments 209–12; What the Bleep Do We Know? 252–3
flag ritual 183, 190, 192, 194–5
Frank Harper 37–9
The Free Inquirer 64
Freemasonry 87–9, 252, 273n22; chart 88
Freud, Sigmund 245

gaze 1–2, 117–19, 141–2, 145, 172, 184–5, 227, 234; cinematic gaze 187–9; communal gaze 187, 189, 193, 254;

liminal gaze 230; mutual gaze 151; subjective gaze 187; television and film 224; unilateral gaze 2; visual absorption 173, 188
gender roles 41; see also masculinity
gentility 104–5
gift books 106–9, 113, 137, 275n8
Gladden, Washington 183
Glaude, Eddie S. 267n23
Goodrich, Samuel 106–8
Goethe, Johann Wolfgang 83; Sorrows of the Young Werther 83
Graham, Billy 225, 287n26
Grand Army of the Republic 190
Grant, Ulysses S. 67
Gray, Thomas 83
grottoes 48, 50; Grotto of the Redemption 51

haggadah 131–3, 278n79, 279n83
Hale, Edward Everett 109–10
Hall, G. Stanley 201–4, 207
Halliday, Carl 180–1
Haltunen, Karen 83–4, 113
Hanukkah 121, 159
Harper's Monthly Magazine 154
Harper's Weekly Magazine 66–7
Hawthorne, Nathaniel 140, 279n15
Haydon, Benjamin Robert 276n30
Hedstrom, Matthew 285n60
Heinze, Andrew 131, 133
Henry, Patrick 9, 11; Patrick Henry Before the Virginia House of Burgesses 10
heroines 227–8
Heston, Charles 209, 213
Heywood, DuBose 101
Hiawatha: illustrated lecture 239–41; Hiawatha's Departure 240; play 291n20; The Song of Hiawatha 239, 241
Himes, Joshua 89
Hinduism 235–6, 238, 245, 250, 262
Hofmann, Heinrich 97, 99–100, 208–9; Boy Christ teaching in the Temple 208
Hollywood Cemetery 85–6
Holmes, Burton 167–8
Holmes, Oliver Wendell 150–1, 172–3, 250–1
Holy Land, The 151–60, 165
home 74–5, 105, 126–8, 131–2, 260; see also parlor
Hoover, Stewart M. 289n54

Howe, Irving 131
Hughes, Bishop John 46, 65

iconoclasm 58
Idealism 245
idolatry 172, 195
imagery: ambivalence 250–3; esoteric
    251–2; eye over ear 179; as lure 1–2, 13,
    94, 150, 173, 261–2; performative 1;
    power of 2, 13, 34, 112, 178, 185; and
    taste distinctions 109–12; and touch 2;
    as universal language 179–80
imagination 153, 155, 159, 166
immigration 68–9, 93–4; Asian 269n65,
    273n33; and children 194; Protestant
    fears of 183
information 15, 30
The Innocents Abroad: see Mark Twain
Irish Catholic Colonization Association
    47
Iwamura, Jane Naomi 289n53

Jakes, T.D. 225
James, William 184
Jefferson, Thomas 8, 15, 23, 81
Jehovah's Witnesses 195
Jesus: aspects of representation 208–9;
    and charisma 200–4; and emasculation
    199, 201; as hero 201; and masculinity
    201–7, 209; psychological and
    historical 201; second coming 89; as
    Victorian mother 279n12
Jesus images: Boy Christ Teaching in the
    Temple 208; Christ before Pilate 171;
    Christ in Gethsemane 102; Head of
    Christ 210; The Last Supper 170;
    The Master 203; Messiah's Entry into
    Jerusalem 176; Mural of Christ 223;
    Nativity 51; Passion of Christ 149;
    Whipping a slave 56
Jewish Publication Society of America
    123
Jewish Theological Seminary 121–2
The Jew 40
Jews 38–40, 121–34; and
    Americanization 125–6, 129, 277n55;
    colonization 44, 45; consumption 127;
    home 126–8, 131–2; immigration
    123–6; patriotism 132; women's
    activism 123, 125–8; see also Judaism
Jonah 217
Joselit, Jenna Weissman 277n47

Judaism 277n45n47; Conservative 121–2;
    Orthodox 122, 156; Reform 122;
    Zionism 156–9
Jump, Rev. Herbert 179–83
Jung, Carl 245–6

kachina dolls 246–7
Katz, Elihu 226
Kinkade, Thomas 259–61, 293n63;
    Warmth of Home 260
Kirkland, Caroline 105–6, 113, 117
Kirshenblatt-Gimblett, Barbara 159
Kittredge, Mabel Hyde 128–30
Koerber, Susannah 268n40
Kohut, Rebekah 125
Krishna 235
Kurtz, Charles 170

Lamanites 213, 257; Last Battle between
    Nephites and Lamanites 258; see also
    Mormonism
landscape 160–1; and providence 3, 23,
    259–60
lantern slides 153–6, 159, 164, 173, 175
Lee, Erika 269n65
Leeser, Rabbi Isaac 64
Leonardo 21, 168
Leuthold, Steven 254, 293n54
Library Company of Philadelphia 58
Lincoln, Abraham 191, 193
Lippmann, Walter 184–5, 187, 199
living flag 190–1
lithography 75–7; commercial aspects
    76–7, 80; process 75–6; rival firms 76
Long, Rev. Edwin 161–2
Longfellow, Henry Wadsworth 239–41
Louis, Minnie 123, 125
Lovell, Tom 213; Moroni burying the
    Gold Plates 214
Luther, Martin 31, 244

McDannell, Colleen 274n1
MacKaye, Percy 190–4
McPherson, Aimee Semple 147, 215–18,
    229; and charisma 217–18; dress 217;
    portrait 215; use of media 217
Madison, James 15
Maffly-Kipp, Laurie 269n65
Magdalen Society 62–4, 269nn70 72, 74
Maharishi, Mahesh Yogi 238
Manabozho 239
Mann, Michael 254

Martyrdom of Polycarp 56–7
masculinity 42–3, 201–9, 213; and men's
    movement 245–6, 287n19
Massachusetts Sabbath School Society
    42
media: definition 1; and faces 199; film
    224–29; imbrication 175–6;
    intertextuality 176; lithography 75; old
    and new 175; paper 18, 33, 34; radio
    217, 223; steel engraving 108;
    telegraphy 140, 223; television 223–6,
    287n26
media events 226
memorial image 80–4, 141, 146
memory 85; as aesthetic contemplation
    85; and domestic piety 117; and images
    119–20
Millennial Chart 90, 261
millennialism 17, 28, 50, 54, 89–91, 259;
    see also post-millennialism *and*
    Adventism
Miller, William 89–90
Millerism 261; *see also* William Miller
Moody Bible Institute 209
Moody, Dwight 77, 94, 204
Mormon, Book of 213, 256–7
Mormonism 23, 77, 151, 213; ancient
    narrative 256–7; migration 237;
    see also Joseph Smith *and* Brigham
    Young
Moroni 213, 257; *Moroni burying the
    Gold Plates* 214
Moses 16, 209–12, 217, 224, 226
motherhood 75, 147, 213, 279n12
mottoes 222
Mount Rushmore 234–5
mourning 80–5; Memorial for Werter 82;
    Memorial Image 80
Münsterberg, Hugo 188, 199, 224
Muir, John 232, 289n2
Munkácsy, Mihaly 170, 172; *Christ
    before Pilate* 171
Münzer, Thomas 31
Murillo, Bartolomé Esteban 143
Muscular Christianity 42–3
Musser, Charles 173

Nast, Thomas 66–7; Romish Politics 66
national parks: Yellowstone 238–9, 259;
    Yosemite 230, 232, 238–9, 259
nationalism: American 193–5, 232;
    Cuban 70

nationhood, American 24, 187;
    imagining 165; landscape 260; mission
    60–1; mythic center 226
Native Americans 14, 54, 243–50, 253–5;
    commoditization of artifacts 246–9,
    253–4; critique of New Age 248, 253–4,
    292n42; land 232, 238–9, 243;
    Mormonism 257; Thoreau 242–3;
    see also vanishing Indian
Native American groups: Cheyenne 249;
    Cree 249; Hopi 247; Lakota 253–4;
    Navajo 247–8; Ojibwa 241; Pueblo
    249; Shawnee 230
National Convention of Colored People
    44, 57–8
Navajo sand painting 247
Nelson, Louis P. 272n17
neoclassical style 81, 272n10
Neo-Paganism 250, 254, 292n44
Nephi 256–7; *see also* Mormonism
New Age 245–6, 248, 250, 252–4, 292n48
New Thought 249–50
Nietzsche, Friedrich 202
Nord, David Paul 264n27

orality 30–1, 175, 180, 191, 218–22
oratory 9, 11, 191, 219–21
Orientalism 156–7
Orsi, Robert 68
Osteen, Joel 220
Owen, Robert 64, 237, 238

Packard, Frederick 18, 20–1
pageantry 149, 189–90, 285n73
Palestine 151–60; *see also* Holy Land
Palestine Park 154
panorama 1, 154, 156, 160–4, 282n63;
    moving 160
Parezo, Nancy 247
Parliament of World Religions 235
parlor 74–5, 229, 274n1; Christian
    103–21; decoration and display 104–5,
    109–12, 117; as electronic hearth 135;
    furniture 104, 116, 130; Jewish 121–34;
    and mourning 84–5; as public face of
    the home 104
Passion plays 146, 148–9, 165–70, 174–6;
    Oberammergau 148, 166–8
Passover 121, 127–8, 131–3
Payne, Daniel 58–9
Pentecostalism: *see* Protestant groups
photography: and death 138; spirit 138

phrenology 199
physiognomy 104, 199
Pike, Sarah M. 292n44
pilgrimage 70, 151–60, 167–8, 236;
    virtual 168
A Pilgrim's Progress 11, 29
Pledge of Allegiance 190, 193, 195
Plockhorst, Bernhard 97, 99–100
Pollard, Josephine 147
Popes: Gregory XVI 65; Leo XIII 48, 77,
    193; Pius IX 47, 65, 77, 93; *see also*
    Roman Catholicism *and* Syllabus of
    Errors
Porgy 101
postcards 129–30, 204, 207
post-millennialism 23, 54; *see also*
    millennialism
practices 1, 120, 195; character formation
    182; child nurture 112, 138;
    commemoration 80–5, 140–45;
    communion 141–2; communal
    formation 187–9; divination 251;
    domestic display and visual
    consumption 74–5, 104, 109–13;
    ex-voto 68–70; gifting 92, 94, 96;
    instruction 94–102; intercession 48–50,
    68–70; invocation 250; proselytism
    24–8, 34–6, 61–3; protection 2, 138–40;
    and women 83, 85; *see also* gender
    roles, iconoclasm, mourning,
    pilgrimage, propaganda, religious
    souvenirs, *and* tourism
Prang, Louis 76, 91–2, 95, 222
Princeton Theological Seminary 20, 64
print: and aura 14, 16, 31–6, 61; and
    children 20; Evangelical-secular rivalry
    13, 18; power of 30; Protestant ideology
    of 28–36, 52; surpassing orality 33,
    180; stabilizing effect on orality 32
print wars, Evangelical 23
Promised Land 46, 232, 237
Prometheus 150
propaganda 184–5
prosperity gospel 220
prostitution 62; *see also* Magdalen
    Society
Protestantism: and the home 74–5; and
    imagery 94; and imagination 155, 159,
    166; Nativist 64–7; and print 13–36
Protestant groups: conservative 13, 62;
    Evangelicals 11, 16–18, 23–4, 41–4;
    Fundamentalism 234, 252;

Pentecostalism 215–22; Puritans 11,
    120, 140, 151, 236; Unitarianism 32,
    242; *see also* revivalism
Providence Lithography Company
    94–102, 260
public opinion 184–5
public school 7, 18, 30, 65–8, 193–5
Puritan: *see* Protestant groups

Ramakrishna, Sri 235
Rau, William 138, 155–6, 281n55; Her
    Guardian Angel 139; Street scene in
    Nazareth 157
Republican Party 66
Reformation 11, 31, 47
Religious Education Association 178–9
republicanism 7–9, 11, 263n3
respectability 60, 74, 104, 106
revivalism: camp meetings 236; technique
    64; urban 206
Reynolds, Herbert 175
Roberts, Oral 223
Roberts, Oral, Jr. 223
Roberts, Sarah 136
Rockwell, Norman 260
Roman Catholicism: and beauty 47;
    colonization 45–8; education 65–8;
    and Hispanics 69–70; and images 87,
    92–4, 110–11; immigration 68; violence
    against 65; *see also* Virgin Mary,
    Orestes Brownson, *and* popes
Romanticism 83, 234, 245
Roosevelt, Theodore 206
Root, Marcus Aurelius 199
Rose, Wendy 248
Rosenthal, Michele 289n48
Rosh Hashanah 121, 129–30
Rothermel, Peter Frederich 9, 11, 191,
    263n10; *Patrick Henry Before the
    Virginia House of Burgesses* 10
Roy, Rammohun 235
Ruby, Jay 145
rural cemetery movement 85, 272n18
Rush, Benjamin 63, 269n71
Ruskay, Esther 122–23, 126–8; *Hearth
    and Home Essays* 124; against
    intermarriage and assimilation 126; on
    religious observance 126–7

Sallman, Warner 145, 209, 213, 260; *Head
    of Christ* 210
Salvation Army 216, 217, 288n38

Sankey, Ira D. 77, 79, 94, 204
Santeria 250
Satan 17, 219
Schechter, Soloman 121
Schlereth, Thomas 115–16
Schmidt, Leigh 92
Schoolcroft, Henry Rowe 239, 241
Scudder, John 32
science fiction 228
sentimentalism 84, 272nn 10, 17
Shibata, Onyumishi Kanjuro 236; Zen
   rock garden 237
shopping 73
Sinclair, Thomas 54; *Christian Union*
   54
slavery 50, 52–61
Smith, Bertha 123, 128–9, 131
Smith, Gerrit 44–5
Smith, H. Augustine 189–90
Smith, Joseph 151, 213, 238, 257
Smith, Ryan K. 269n76
Smokey the Bear 259, 261
Snyder, Gary 258–9, 293n61; Smokey the
   Bear Sutra 258–9
social control 177
Social Gospel 189
Socrates 185, 244
Sorin, Father Edwin 48
Sorrows of the Young Werther: see
   Johann Wolfgang Goethe
souvenirs, religious 158–9, 246–7
Spalding, Bishop John Lancaster 46–8, 68
Spaulding, Rev. Henry 188–9
spectacle 160, 163, 172
speech act theory 218–20, 288n40
Spence, Mark David 238
stereograph 148–50, 173; and Holy Land
   151; and illusion 172; and virtual
   tourism 151
stereoscope 148, 154, 172
stereotypes 184–5
Still, Mary 58
Storm, Hyemeyohsts 249
Stowe, Harriet Beecher 57, 84, 105; *House
   and Home Papers* 119–21; *Uncle Tom's
   Cabin* 55–6, 101, 136
sublime 9, 232, 290n4
Sunday, Billy 204–7, 213, 216; Billy
   Sunday preaching 205
Sunday school 20, 30, 43, 75, 77, 94–6;
   graded curriculum 97; movement
   274n35; uniform curriculum 95

Syllabus of Errors 47, 65
syncretism 249

tableau vivant 1, 85, 146–50, 154–5, 166,
   172, 280n23; at Oberammergau 167–8
Tappan, Arthur 26, 62–4
tarot 251–2
Teichert, Minerva K. 256–7; *Last Battle
   between Nephites and Lamanites* 258;
   Loading the Ship 257
telegraphy 140, 223
television 224; live 226; production
   225
television programs discussed: *Buffy the
   Vampire Slayer* 227–8; *Charmed* 227,
   229; *Kung Fu* 227; *Touched by an
   Angel* 227; *The X-Files* 252
textuality: and biblical authority 172, 187;
   iconicity 15, 222; image-text 220–2;
   and Protestant imagination 159;
   surpassed by image 164; visual
   narrative 173, 177
Thoreau, Henry David 160, 241–5;
   Walden 241–2
Tissot, James 175
tourism 151–3, 156, 160; virtual 151, 155
tracts 15, 23; authorship 29; and
   consumer desire 18; distribution
   17–18, 27–9, 31; illustration 18, 20; as
   philanthropy 23–4, 29; and the power
   of print 30; and women 24, 26–7
tract societies: African Female Auxiliary
   24–5; American Tract Society (ATS),
   New York 11, 13, 20, 23–4, 29, 41, 50;
   and slavery 55; Boston 18, 27, 39; and
   slavery 55; Methodist Episcopal
   Church Tract Society 30; New England
   Religious Tract Society 26–7, 31; New
   York Religious Tract Society 26, 31;
   Religious Tract Society of Baltimore
   14–15, 17, 24, 26–8; Religious Tract
   Society of London 15–16
transcendental meditation 238, 250
transcendentalism 233, 244–5, 249
Truth, Sojourner 45
Twain, Mark 151–3, 155, 157, 168; *The
   Innocents Abroad* 152–3
Tweed, Thomas A. 70, 270n95

Uncle Tom's Cabin: see Harriet Beecher
   Stowe
United States Supreme Court 195

VanDerZee, James 143, 145; Child with angels and Mary 144
vanishing Indian 241, 290n16; see also Native Americans
vaudeville 178, 181
Vincent, John 95–6, 153–5
Virgin Mary: apparitions 48; devotion to 47–8; Assumption and Immaculate Conception 143; Our Lady of Guadalupe 69, 80, 93; Our Lady of Lourdes 48, 80, 93
Virgin Mary, images of: Our Lady of Knock 77–8, 80, 93; Our Lady of Talpa 69; Statues of the Blessed Virgin 49; Child with angels and Mary 143
vision 1–2, 148; and hearing 164
visual representation, forms of: deception 91; immediacy or transparence 173, 225; simulacrum 159; spectacle 150–6, 160, 172, 187; stereographic illusion 173; virtual presence or being-there 149, 168, 171–2; see also gaze and imagery
Vivekananda, Swami 235–6, 290n6
Vodou 250
Voyage of Life: see Thomas Cole

Walden: see Henry David Thoreau
Walker, David 45
Wanamaker, John 87
wars: Civil 50, 95, 136, 150, 193, 238; of 1812 16–7; Mexican–American 238; Revolutionary 7, 9; World War One 181, 185, 204; World War Two 185
Washington, George 7, 58, 87, 191, 193
Weber, Max 44, 207
Webster, Noah 7, 8, 32
Wedgewood, Josiah 81, 83, 261
Wells, Samuel 199–200
Wesley, John 87, 94, 244
Westminster Catechism 242
Weems, Parson Mason Locke 7–8, 19–20; on republicanism and Christianity 263n3
Whig party 7, 15, 62
whiteshamans 248, 254
Whore of Babylon 163
wilderness 230, 232–4, 259; as idyll 260–1; and Mormonism 257
Wilson, Edward 155–6, 281n55
Wilson, Woodrow 192
Winkelmann, Johann 81
Winston, Diane 288n38
witchcraft 228–9
women 24, 26, 83–4, 121, 125–8, 216–18; see also feminization and heroines
Wright, Fanny 64, 238

Young, Brigham 77, 238

Zalesch, Saul 268n39
Zen 236